RACE, GENDER, AND WORK

RACE, GENDER, AND WORK

A Multicultural Economic History of Women in the United States

TERESA AMOTT and JULIE MATTHAEI

Montréal/New York

BLACK ROSE BOOKS No. U161
Paperback ISBN: 0-921689-90-X
Hardcover ISBN: 0-921689-91-8

Canadian Cataloguing in Publication Data

Amott, Teresa L.
  Race, gender, and work

Canadian ed.
Includes bibliographical references and index.
ISBN 0-921689-91-8 (bound). —
  ISBN 0-921689-90-X (pbk.).

  1. Minority women—United States—Economic conditions. 2. Minority women—United States—History. 3. Minority women—Employment—History. I. Matthaei, Julie A. II. Title.

HQ1410. A46 1991   305. 48'0973   C91-090085-X

Cover Design: Associés Libres

Editorial Offices	*U.S. Orders*
BLACK ROSE BOOKS	BLACK ROSE BOOKS
3981 St-Laurent Boulevard,	340 Nagel Drive
Suite 444	Cheektowaga, New York
Montréal, Québec	14225
H2W 1Y5 Canada	

Mailing Address
BLACK ROSE BOOKS
P.O. Box 1258
Succ. Place du Parc
Montréal, Québec
H2W 2R3 Canada

Printed and bound in Québec, Canada
on acid-free paper

To Ruth and John Amott,
Nancy Wechsler,
and Women for Economic Justice

CONTENTS

LIST OF TABLES

LIST OF FIGURES

PREFACE AND ACKNOWLEDGMENTS

In the final months of writing this book, we came to see the project as the "book factory," because the book, like any manufactured product, owes its shape to the many hands and minds who collaborated to bring it into being. Every product has its inventors, its engineers, its skilled craftspeople, and its inspectors, as well as those who manufactured the inputs that went into producing it. There are many who have worked on or otherwise contributed to this project whom we would like to thank.

The book had its origins in a collective writing project undertaken by the Economic Literacy Project of Women for Economic Justice, a Boston-based organization which seeks to empower low-income women and women of color through a variety of organizing, advocacy, and educational projects. The Economic Literacy Project, started in 1980, is made up of feminist social scientists who provide training workshops, public speaking, and consulting services to groups working for social change. Over six years ago, the group began writing a pamphlet to address the then-popular concept of the feminization of poverty in a way that also took into account race and class oppression. Many women worked on the pamphlet, and Caren Grown, Elaine McCrate, Gail Shields, Pamela Sparr, and Nan Wiegersma each wrote substantial portions. However, the subject proved too complex for large-group writing, and, in 1985, we took on the project, eventually expanding the pamphlet into this book-length work. Women for Economic Justice provided critical resources and inspiration at the pamphlet stage of the project, and the organization will receive some of the proceeds from the sale of the book.

Over the years, many of our thoughts on the interconnections of race, gender, sexual preference, class, and nationality have been formed in discussions and study with our sisters in the Marxist Feminist 1 group. The analysis and sisterhood we continue to find in that group have informed all of our intellectual and political work. We are also indebted to the countless researchers on women whose painstaking work has opened up women's myriad experiences to our view, particularly the women of color who have insisted that the method as well as the content of women's studies requires radical transformation. The work of the Memphis State University Center for Research on Women, especially their bibliography, *Women of Color and*

Southern Women: A Bibliography of Social Science Research, was particularly helpful and inspirational.[1]

At both the early and later stages of this project, we have drawn on the talents and perseverance of many research assistants. Betsy Wright, of Women for Economic Justice, urged us to incorporate the stories of struggle and resistance into our analysis of the political economy of women's work, as well as uncovered many such stories; her insight and efforts immeasurably enriched the final product. We are also indebted to Michelle Anglade, Trina Haque, Tricia Horn, Jennifer Johnston, Chris McGee, Christine McRae, Sarah Pryor, and Gwynne Wiatrowski for research assistance which often involved important new insights or suggestions. In the final stages of the "book factory," Kim Cuddy and Jenn Kapuscik took responsibility for the difficult and laborious tasks of checking sources for the footnotes and bibliography, and called our attention to gaps and errors in the text. Loren Eng and Diane Matukaitis navigated us through a century of Census data, compiling tables and figures which were essential to the project with great care and patience.

We are indebted to Wellesley College, the Women's Studies Research Associate Program of Harvard Divinity School, and Bucknell University for financial assistance which made possible most of the research for the project. Claire Loranz of the Wellesley College Library demonstrated time and again her uncanny ability to locate needles in haystacks, while the rest of the library staff—especially the Interlibrary Loan office—was very helpful. Helen Graham, Norma Wakely, and Regina Coughlin provided excellent secretarial support. And the students in our classes at Wellesley, Harvard, and Bucknell, especially those in Economics 243, Writing 125Q, HDS 2493, and Economics 333, provided excellent feedback on the work in progress.

Many colleagues and friends provided us with materials, read and commented on various drafts of the project, or helped with the general development of our ideas. We owe thanks to Randy Albelda, Pat Albers, Delia Aguilar, Marcellus Andrews, Gloria Anzaldúa, Chris Bose, Claudia Castenada, Connie Chan, Connie Chisolm, Judy Claude, Kim Cuddy, Loren Eng, Ernestine Enomoto, Yukiko Hanawa, bell hooks, Jacqueline Jones, Jenn Kapuscik, Louise Lamphere, Mari Matsuda, Fred Matthaei, John Miller, Hung Ng, Laurie Nisonoff, Bruce Norton, Margarita Ostolaza, Milagros Padilla, Tirsa Quiñones, Migdalia Reyes, Miriam Jimenez Roman, Abel Valenzuela, Nancy Wechsler, Nan Wiegersma, and Rhonda Williams.

Many friends besides those listed above supported us through the difficult times and relaxed with us in good times. Our heartfelt thanks go to Betsy Aron, Maureen Brodoff, Toni Byrd, Gene Chenoweth, the *Dollars & Sense* Collective, Pam and Jim Crotty, Karen Dugger, Jean Entine, Michael Hillard, Ernie Keen, the MacEwan-Davies family, Rosa McGill, Amy and

Malora and Maru and Mimi and Morgan Matthaei, Libby Meadow, Ted Murphy, Chris O'Sullivan, Carol Reichenthal, Nancy Ryan, Charles Sackrey, Brenda Steinberg, Paul Susman, Ellen Wade, Stewart Wecker, and Ann Witte. Our dogs Pepito and Noche sat patiently—and not so patiently—at our feet during countless hours when they would rather have been chasing squirrels, while our cats sat on whatever papers they could find. Kassy, Kimmy, Nick, Anthony, Jill, and Abby provided the exact combination of distraction and company needed during long hot summer days of work, and were very patient when the book made Julie unavailable. Nancy Wechsler provided Julie with special love and understanding.

We wish to thank the South End Press Collective for their excellent work on the book and for the important role they have played on the left since 1977. Ellen Herman, Cynthia Peters, and Todd Jailer helped focus the project. Our editor, Karin Aguilar-San Juan, tried to hold us to deadlines, untangled confused syntax, and breathed new life into our sometimes tired prose, as well as making very helpful suggestions for revisions.

Since we first met 12 years ago, we have collaborated in so much political work and so many writing projects that it is now nearly impossible to attribute any portion of this work to one or the other, and only alphabetical accident puts Teresa's name ahead of Julie's. We literally wrote most of the first draft while sitting in the same space, in almost continual conversation, and most of the second draft on the phone. In this process, our style of collaboration has been tested by disagreement and exhaustion, and strengthened by commitment and humor. This book is, above all, a product of our friendship, a friendship which remains its own best reward.

Part One: Race, Gender, and Women's Works

Chapter 1

INTRODUCTION

Domestic servants descended from African slaves, Chinese women sold into the U.S. prostitution market, middle-class European American homemakers, and Puerto Rican feminist union organizers in the early-1900s. It seems the work experiences of women in the United States are so varied and multi-dimensional that a common history is beyond our grasp. Yet, the work lives of women in the United States have always been interconnected: in a very real sense, the lives of any one group of women have been dependent upon the lives of others, just as they have been dependent upon those of men (and vice versa). Unfortunately, the ties which have joined us have rarely been mutual, equal, or cooperative; instead, our interdependence has been characterized by domination and exploitation. American Indian women's lost lands were the basis for European immigrant wealth. The domestic work of African American and poor European immigrant women, along with the labors of their husbands, sons, and daughters in factories, underwrote the lavish lifestyles of upper-class European American women. The riches enjoyed by the wives and children of Mexican American *hacienda* owners were created by the poverty of displaced and landless Indians and Chicanas. And U.S. political and economic domination of the Philippines and Puerto Rico allowed U.S. women to maintain higher standards of living, and encouraged the migration of impoverished Filipina and Puerto Rican women to U.S. shores.

In this book, we attempt the difficult task of tracing women's work lives through the dynamic and complicated process which economists have called capitalist development. In the last five centuries, Native Americans have been joined by millions of immigrant women and men of diverse racial-ethnic and economic backgrounds. These immigrants came—some voluntarily, others at gunpoint—into a variety of different economic niches, including slavery, indentured servitude, contract labor, self-employment, and wage work. The United States expanded across Mexico and incorporated Puerto Rico, the Philippines, and Hawaii. And a fledgling economic system of profit-motivated production for the market, based on wage labor, grew into the dominant economic and social force determining women's work lives, not only

3

in the United States, but in the world.

Our goal in this volume is three-fold. First, to show the multiplicity and diversity of women's work contributions, both paid and unpaid, to U.S. economic history. Second, to lay out the interconnections and inter-dependencies involved in this multiplicity of works, with special focus on processes of exploitation and oppression and on the struggles of women and men for survival and against economic injustice. Third, to highlight major transformations in the gender, racial-ethnic, and class hierarchies accompa-nying the historical process of capitalist economic expansion, as well as the diverse ways in which these transformations have affected women's works. This is a broad project indeed, and one which we can only very partially achieve in this volume; we hope that our effort will encourage further research along these lines as well as further activism.

The book is organized into three parts. We begin in Part I with an introduction to our methodology and to our conceptual framework. Then, in the six chapters of Part II, we present the economic histories of women, treating each major racial-ethnic group separately. In Part III, we examine the commonalities and differences in women's work experiences across racial-ethnic groups over the course of U.S. economic history.

Our Method: Political, Economic, Feminist, and Historical

Our perspective is radical, feminist, and anti-racist, and we hope that this book may inspire and aid others in their work for a more just economic system. The intellectual and political origins of this book lie in the past two decades of scholarship on race and ethnicity; on workers, class, and poverty; and on women, gender, and sexuality. This scholarship had its roots in more than a decade of social activism: the drive for civil and political rights by people of color, Third World national liberation struggles, anti-war and New Left socialist movements, and feminist and lesbian/gay rights organizing. Inspired by their participation as activists in these movements, many academ-ics, including ourselves, began to focus their research on the systems of oppression and exploitation which these movements were confronting, as well as on the history of organizing against these oppressive systems.

We were trained in mainstream or "neoclassical" economics, but have rejected this paradigm as inadequate to our purposes, and have adopted instead the theoretical framework of radical political economics. Mainstream economists view economic life as the result of rational choices made by self-interested, free individuals. They explain race and sex inequality, in our view inadequately, as the result of biological differences or of unexplained, extra-economic discriminatory preferences. In other words, for mainstream theorists, the economic system has little to do with the creation of race, gender, or class hierarchies among people; indeed, they view economic life as essentially a struggle of "man" against nature, rather than as a power struggle among people. Radical theory, in contrast, takes into account the important ways in which economic institutions and practices structure our lives, as well as the important role which the economy plays in creating and sustaining racial-ethnic, gender, and class conflicts.[1]

We also see ourselves as part of the feminist studies (or women's or gender studies) field—a new, vital, interdisciplinary community of researchers. Feminist analysis points to the ways in which social institutions and practices both differentiate the sexes and make them, in most cases, unequal. Recent feminist research and activism have taken up the necessary and overdue project of examining racial-ethnic differences among women, beginning to break down the problematic feminist view of womanhood as a universal category and of women's oppression as a common, shared experience.[2] As we will show in this volume, we do not believe that race-ethnicity, gender, or class can be correctly understood if isolated from one another, for they have been constructed and experienced simultaneously.

Since we believe that it is not nature but society which is responsible for gender, race, and class hierarchies, we look to society's past, not to biology, for an understanding of the forces for continuity and change. Social practices and institutions are reproduced and transformed over time by individual actions; the latter are situated and constrained by those very social practices and institutions. The gender, racial-ethnic, and class hierarchies in any period are inherited from the past, and hence cannot be adequately grasped without an historical perspective. Indeed, we see historical analysis as key to the project of theorizing the relationships between race-ethnicity, gender, and class, since these never exist in an historical vacuum, but rather are always (as is all social life) rooted in a particular socio-historical context.[3] In our view, ahistorical theories are not only incorrect, but also inherently conservative, for they enshrine the status quo and deny peoples' capacities to radically transform their societies over history.

Our Epistemology: Seeking Liberatory Knowledge

Simultaneous trends in areas as disparate as literary criticism, physics, and the philosophy of science have led many in the academy to challenge the idea of an objective natural or social science. We share this perspective, according to which all social science embodies subjective points of view, and hence the preconceptions, vantage points, and concerns of social scientists.[4] Mainstream economists view market capitalism as the best of all possible worlds, taking the standpoint of those who benefit most from this system— white, heterosexual, and upper-class men. In contrast, radical economists take up the political cause of eliminating injustice, oppression, and exploitation; in this view, "every theory is wrong which justifies, promotes, or tolerates human oppression."[5]

As feminist philosopher Sandra Harding has argued, radical knowledge is liberatory knowledge, crafted with the goal of human liberation. This requires radical scholars to write with an awareness of their positions in the complex hierarchy of domination and subordination in which we live. Those in the position of the oppressed, people "on the margin," have a special contribution to make in the understanding of these oppressive structures: thus, the special contribution of women to feminist scholarship, of people of color to anti-racist scholarship, and of lesbians and gay men to anti-heterosexist scholarship. At the same time, Harding argues, even those with race, gender, class, and/or sexual preference privilege can become creators of liberatory knowledge if they become aware of the sources and uses of their privilege. Hence men can, through contact with feminist women or their writings, not only understand women's oppression but also understand themselves as men, shaped and privileged by gender. Similarly, whites can, through contact with anti-racist people of color or their writings, understand racial oppression as well as the meaning of whiteness, and uncover their individual roles in perpetuating racism. In this way men can do feminist work, and whites, anti-racist work.[6]

Unfortunately, most of us still lack awareness of the privileges we enjoy. Indeed, whites, men, and heterosexuals are usually not even aware of their identities as such. Whites tend to see themselves as generic humans, and to see only people of color as having a racial-ethnic identity. Similarly, men see themselves as having no gender—practicing, for example, "sports," while women, the gendered beings, practice "women's sports." Research and activism coming from such a limited awareness cannot be truly liberatory, and, however well-intentioned, may well contribute to oppression.

Harding notes that whites, men, and heterosexuals become more aware of themselves as such when in the presence of people of color, women, lesbians and gays. She suggests that it is through understanding themselves as "other" to the oppressed group that those with privilege can develop liberatory theory and practice.[7] Writing this book has helped deepen our awareness of race, gender, and class as constitutive of all aspects of social life. Our accounts of the histories of women of different racial-ethnic groups build heavily on writings by women of the group in question, many of them part of a recent blossoming of needed research on women of color. To further highlight the omnipresence of race-ethnicity as well as gender and class, we will, whenever possible, identify the race-ethnicity of the researchers we cite (frequently, a writer's gender is evident from her or his name). Our racial-ethnic backgrounds are as follows: Teresa is half-European American—Norwegian, German, and English—and half-Brazilian, while Julie is European American—Irish, Scotch, English, French, and German.

A Note on Sources, Language, and Scope

While research and data on women and race are improving, they are still far from adequate, especially for early U.S. history. New research on women of color, much or most of it by women of color, has made major contributions to transforming economic history from a history of white men into a multicultural history of men and women. Nevertheless, this research is still very uneven, with more depth of coverage of some racial-ethnic groups than others. Statistical sources are also incomplete; most, including the U.S. Census, provide only limited information on racial-ethnic and gender subgroups. Little, if any, comprehensive data on race are available for the period before 1900; even today, much data are not available for detailed racial-ethnic groups. Since only the decennial Censuses provide national data by detailed racial-ethnic group, our last major year of comparison is 1980. In addition, hardly any information about economic class is available. Data on wealth and land ownership are rarely collected, and that information hardly ever identifies the racial distribution of ownership. These difficulties add to the perennial problem of comparing Census statistics across time periods within which occupations and other statistics are defined differently.[8]

Throughout the book, we have had to take care not to embody sexism and racism in our language. For instance, we have avoided using masculine terms (i.e., man, men, he) to represent generic categories (all people, men and women). However, in Spanish, all words are gendered; instead of using the masculine as the generic, as is the traditional practice (mestizos, Chicanos, Filipinos), we have chosen to use the admittedly awkward terms mestizas/os, Filipinas/os and Chicanas/os when we are referring to a group which includes both men and women. To refer to women who are not European Americans, we faced a choice among the following terms: non-white women (which defines them negatively), racial-ethnic women (which, theoretically, should also include white women, who have racial and ethnic identities), and women of color (which ignores ethnicity and implies incorrectly that all non-European American women are not white). We chose women of color as the least inaccurate.

Nationality is also difficult to describe, particularly in the midst of immigration. Our convention is to describe the first generation of immigrants, those individuals born outside the United States, by their nationality of birth, whether or not they become U.S. citizens. We then describe those born in the United States, who automatically acquire U.S. citizenship, by a dual term

Table 1-1

United States Population by Racial-Ethnic Group, 1980

Group	Group Population (as Percent of U.S. Total)	3 U.S. States w/ Largest Numbers of Group	Percent of Group in Those 3 States	Percent of Population in Those 3 States
American Indian	1,478,523 (0.65%)	California Oklahoma Arizona	37%	12%
African American	26,482,349 (12%)	New York California Texas	22%	24%
Chicana/o	8,678,632 (3.8%)	California Texas Arizona	77%	17%
Puerto Rican	2,004,961 (0.89%)	New York New Jersey Illinois	67%	16%
Chinese American	812,178 (0.36%)	California New York Hawaii	65%	19%
Japanese American	716,331 (0.32%)	California Hawaii Washington	74%	13%
Filipina/o American	781,894 (0.35%)	California Hawaii Illinois	68%	16%
European American (non-Latina/o)	180,602,838 (79.7%)	California New York Ohio	21%	24%

NOTES: The total U.S. population in 1980 was 226,545,805. These calculations do not include Puerto Ricans living in Puerto Rico, who numbered 3,196,520 in 1980.
SOURCES: *1980 Census of Population*, see Appendix A.

(such as African American or Chinese American). However, following current language practice, we do not use "American" when we discuss Puerto Ricans (who move in and out of the continental United States and whose homeland is a U.S. colony) or Chicanas/os. Finally, since European and African Americans are often described in racial terms, that is as white or Black, we use the ethnic and racial terms interchangeably in their cases.

Finally, the scope of our examination of racial-ethnic groups in the United States is circumscribed. We chose to focus on the largest racial-ethnic groups, in order of their incorporation into the United States: American Indians, Chicanas/os, European Americans, African Americans, Chinese Americans, Japanese Americans, Filipina/o Americans, and Puerto Ricans. Table 1-1 shows the numbers and shares of these racial-ethnic groups in the 1980 U.S. population, as well as their geographical concentration. As we can see, in 1980, non-Latina/o European Americans comprised about four-fifths of the total population, with African Americans making up the second largest group.

Since 1980, the population of people of color has grown more rapidly than the white population: while the white population grew by 6 percent, the Black population grew by 13 percent, and the Asian by 70 percent. Hence, between 1980 and 1988, the share of people of color in the total U.S. population increased to almost one-fourth of the total U.S. population.[9]

In giving each of these racial-ethnic groups more or less equal coverage, we hope to help compensate for the disproportionate focus on European Americans in economic history.[10] However, as a result of space and data limitations, we have left out many smaller racial-ethnic groups, including Cuban Americans, Korean Americans, Indian Americans, indigenous Hawaiians, and Arab Americans. Much work remains to be done to develop a truly multicultural history, and we look forward to that new research.

Chapter 2

RACE, CLASS, GENDER, AND WOMEN'S WORKS

A Conceptual Framework

What social and economic factors determine and differentiate women's work lives? Why is it, for instance, that the work experiences of African American women are so different from those of European American women? Why have some women worked outside the home for pay, while others have provided for their families through unpaid work in the home? Why are most of the wealthy women in the United States of European descent, and why are so many women of color poor? In this chapter, we lay out a basic conceptual framework for understanding differences in women's works and economic positions.

Throughout U.S. history, economic differences among women (and men) have been constructed and organized along a number of social categories. In our analysis, we focus on the three categories which we see as most central—gender, race-ethnicity, and class—with less discussion of others, such as age, sexual preference, and religion. We see these three social categories as interconnected, historical processes of domination and subordination. Thinking about gender, race-ethnicity, and class, then, necessitates thinking historically about power and economic exploitation.

There is a rich and controversial body of literature which examines the ways in which economic exploitation, ideology, and political power create and, in turn, are created by, gender, race-ethnicity, and class; we cannot do justice to the complexity of these issues here.[1] Rather, in this chapter, we develop a basic conceptual framework for thinking about the racial-ethnic histories of women's works which follow in Part II. Then, in the detailed examination of these histories and in the comparison of women across racial-ethnic groups in Part III, we unravel the precise ways in which race-ethnicity, class, and gender have interacted in women's economic lives.

Gender, Race-Ethnicity, and Class Processes: Historical and Interconnected

The concepts of gender, race-ethnicity, and class are neither trans-historical nor independent. Hence, it is artificial to discuss them outside of historical time and place, and separately from one another. At the same time, without such a set of concepts, it is impossible to make sense of women's disparate economic experiences.

Gender, race-ethnicity, and class are not natural or biological categories which are unchanging over time and across cultures. Rather, these categories are socially constructed: they arise and are transformed in history, and themselves transform history. Although societies rationalize them as natural or god-given, ideas of appropriate feminine and masculine behavior vary widely across history and culture. Concepts and practices of race-ethnicity, usually justified by religion or biology, also vary over time, reflecting the politics, economics, and ideology of a particular time and, in turn, reinforcing or transforming politics, economics, and ideology. For example, nineteenth-century European biologists Louis Agassiz and Count Arthur de Gobineau developed a taxonomy of race which divided humanity into separate and unequal racial species; this taxonomy was used to rationalize European colonization of Africa and Asia, and slavery in the United States.[2] Class is perhaps the most historically specific category of all, clearly dependent upon the particular economic and social constellation of a society at a point in time. Still, notions of class as inherited or genetic continue to haunt us, harkening back to earlier eras in which lowly birth was thought to cause low intelligence and a predisposition to criminal activity.

Central to the historical transformation of gender, race-ethnicity, and class processes have been the struggles of subordinated groups to redefine or transcend them. For example, throughout the development of capitalism, workers' consciousness of themselves as workers and their struggles against class oppression have transformed capitalist-worker relationships, expanding workers' rights and powers. In the nineteenth century, educated white women escaped from the prevailing, domestic view of womanhood by arguing that homemaking included caring for the sick and the needy through volunteer work, social homemaking careers, and political organizing. In the 1960s, the transformation of racial-ethnic identity into a source of solidarity and pride was essential to movements of people of color, such as the Black Power and American Indian movements.

Race-ethnicity, gender, and class are interconnected, interdetermining historical processes, rather than separate systems.[3] This is true in two senses, which we will explore in more detail below. First, it is often difficult to determine whether an economic practice constitutes class, race, or gender oppression: for example, slavery in the U.S. South was at the same time a system of class oppression (of slaves by owners) and of racial-ethnic oppression (of Africans by Europeans). Second, a person does not experience these different processes of domination and subordination independently of one another; in philosopher Elizabeth Spelman's metaphor, gender, race-ethnicity, and class are not separate "pop-beads" on a necklace of identity. Hence, there is no generic gender oppression which is experienced by all women regardless of their race-ethnicity or class. As Spelman puts it:

> ...in the case of much feminist thought we may get the impression that a woman's identity consists of a sum of parts neatly divisible from one another, parts defined in terms of her race, gender, class, and so on...On this view of personal identity (which might also be called pop-bead metaphysics), my being a woman means the same whether I am white or Black, rich or poor, French or Jamaican, Jewish or Muslim.[4]

The problems of "pop-bead metaphysics" also apply to historical analysis. In our reading of history, there is no common experience of gender across race-ethnicity and class, of race-ethnicity across class and gender lines, or of class across race-ethnicity and gender.

With these caveats in mind, let us examine the processes of gender, class, and race-ethnicity, their importance in the histories of women's works, and some of the ways in which these processes have been intertwined.

Gender

Over the past 20 years, feminist theorists have developed the concept of gender as central to understanding women's lives and oppression. As we will see, while the concept of gender is invaluable, the gender process cannot be understood independently of class and race-ethnicity. Further, there is no common experience of gender oppression among women.

Gender differences in the social lives of men and women are based on, but are not the same thing as, biological differences between the sexes. Gender is rooted in societies' beliefs that the sexes are naturally distinct and opposed social beings. These beliefs are turned into self-fulfilling prophecies through sex-role socialization: the biological sexes are assigned distinct and often unequal work and political positions, and turned into socially distinct genders.

Economists view the sexual division of labor as central to the gender differentiation of the sexes. By assigning the sexes to different and complementary tasks, the sexual division of labor turns them into different and complementary genders. This process is illustrated in Figure 2-1. The work of males is at least partially, if not wholly, different from that of females, making "men" and "women" different economic and social beings. Sexual divisions of labor, not sexual difference alone, create difference and complementarity between "opposite" sexes. These differences, in turn, have been the basis for marriage in most societies.

Anthropologists have found that most societies, across historical periods, have tended to assign females to infant care and to the duties associated with raising children because of their biological ability to bear children. In contrast, men usually concentrate on interfamilial activities, and gain political dominance; hence gender complementarity has usually led to political and economic dominance by men.[5]

The concept of gender certainly helps us understand women's economic histories. As we will see in Part II, each racial-ethnic group has had a sexual division of labor which has barred individuals from the activities of the opposite sex. Gender processes do differentiate women's lives in many ways from those of the men in their own racial-ethnic and class group. Further, gender relations in all groups tend to assign women to the intra-familial work of childrearing, as well as to place women in a subordinate position to the men of their class and racial-ethnic group.

But as soon as we have written these generalizations, exceptions pop into mind. Gender roles do not always correspond to sex. Some American Indian tribes allowed individuals to choose among gender roles: a female, for example, could choose a man's role, do men's work, and marry another female who lived out a woman's role. In the nineteenth century, some white females "passed" as men in order to escape the rigid mandates of gender roles. In many of these cases, women lived with and loved other women.

Even though childrearing is women's work in most societies, many women do not have children, and others do not perform their own child care or domestic work. Here, class is an especially important differentiating process. Upper-class women have been able to use their economic power to reassign some of the work of infant care—sometimes even breastfeeding—to lower-class women of their own or different racial-ethnic groups. These women, in turn, may have been forced to leave their infants alone or with relatives or friends. Finally, gender complementarity has not always led to social and economic inequality; for example, many American Indian women had real control over the home and benefited from a more egalitarian sharing of power between men and women.

Since the processes of sex-role socialization are historically distinct in

Figure 2-1: The Sexual Division of Labor

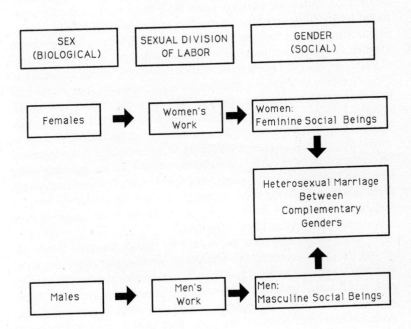

different times and different cultures, they result in different conceptions of appropriate gender behavior. Both African American and Chicana girls, for instance, learn how to be women—but both must learn the specific gender roles which have developed within their racial-ethnic and class group and historical period. For example, for white middle-class homemakers in the 1950s, adherence to the concept of womanhood discouraged paid employment, while for poor Black women it meant employment as domestic servants for white middle-class women. Since racial-ethnic and class domination have differentiated the experiences of women, one cannot assume, as do many feminist theorists and activists, that all women have the same experience of gender oppression—or even that they will be on the same side of a struggle, not even when some women define that struggle as "feminist."

Not only is gender differentiation and oppression not a universal experience which creates a common "women's oppression," the sexual divisions of labor and family systems of people of color have been systematically disrupted by racial-ethnic and class processes. In the process of invasion and conquest, Europeans imposed their notions of male superiority on cultures with more egalitarian forms of gender relations, including many American Indian and African tribes.[6] At the same time, European Americans were quick to abandon their notion of appropriate femininity when it conflicted with profits: for example, slave owners often assigned slave women to backbreaking labor in the fields.

Racial-ethnic and class oppression have also disrupted family life among people of color and the white working class. Europeans interfered with family relations within subordinated racial-ethnic communities through rape and forced cohabitation.[7] Sometimes whites encouraged or forced reproduction, as when slaveowners forced slave women into sexual relations. On the other hand, whites have often used their power to curtail reproduction among peoples of color, and aggressive sterilization programs were practiced against Puerto Ricans and American Indians as late as the 1970s. Beginning in the late nineteenth century, white administrators took American Indian children from their parents to "civilize" them in boarding schools where they were forbidden to speak their own languages or wear their native dress. Slaveowners commonly split up slave families through sale to different and distant new owners. Nevertheless, African Americans were able to maintain strong family ties, and even augmented these with "fictive" or chosen kin.[8] From the mid-nineteenth through the mid-twentieth centuries, many Asians were separated from their spouses or children by hiring policies and restrictions on immigration. Still, they maintained family life within these split households, and eventually succeeded in reuniting, sometimes after generations. Hence, for peoples of color, having children and maintaining families have been an essential part of the struggle against racist oppression. Not surprisingly, many women of color have rejected the white women's movement's view of the family as the center of "women's oppression."

These examples reveal the limitations of gender as a single lens through which to view women's economic lives. Indeed, any attempt to understand women's experiences using gender alone cannot only cause misunderstanding, but can also interfere with the construction of broad-based movements against the oppressions experienced by women.

Race-Ethnicity

Like gender, race-ethnicity is based on a perceived physical difference, and rationalized as "natural" or "god-given." But whereas gender creates difference and inequality according to biological sex, race-ethnicity differentiates individuals according to skin color or other physical features.

In all of human history, individuals have lived in societies with distinct languages, cultures, and economic institutions; these ethnic differences have been perpetuated by intermarriage within, but rarely between, societies. However, ethnic differences can exist independently of a conception of race, and without a practice of racial-ethnic domination such as the Europeans practiced over the last three centuries.

Early European racist thought developed in the seventeenth and eighteenth centuries, embedded in the Christian worldview. Racial theorists argued that people of color were not descended from Adam and Eve as were whites. Later, in the nineteenth century, with the growth of Western science and its secular worldview, racial-ethnic differences and inequality were attributed directly to biology. According to the emerging scientific worldview, human beings were divided into biologically distinct and unequal races. Whites were, by nature, on top of this racial hierarchy, with the right and duty to dominate the others ("white man's burden").[9] In this racist typology, some ethnic differences—differences in language, culture, and social practices—were interpreted as racial and hence natural in origin. The different social and economic practices of societies of color were viewed by whites in the nineteenth century as "savage," in need of the "civilizing" influence of white domination. We use the term "race-ethnicity" in this book to grasp the contradictory nature of racial theories and practices, in particular the fact that those people seen as belonging to a particular "race" often lack a shared set of distinct physical characteristics, but rather share a common ethnicity or culture.

European racial theories were used to justify a set of economic and social practices which, in fact, made the "races" socially unequal. In this way, racism and the practices which embody it became self-fulfilling prophecies, as shown in Figure 2-2. Claiming that people of color were inherently inferior, whites segregated and subordinated them socially, economically, and politically. Furthermore, by preventing intermarriage between people of color and whites, whites perpetuated physical and ethnic differences as well as social and economic inequality between themselves and people of color across the generations. Although few scientists today claim that there are biological factors which create unequal races of human beings, racist practices and institutions have continued to produce both difference and inequality.[10]

Does the concept of race-ethnicity help us understand the economic history of women in the United States? Certainly, for white racial-ethnic domination has been a central force in U.S. history. European colonization of North America entailed the displacement and murder of the continent's indigenous peoples, rationalized by the racist view that American Indians were savage heathens. The economy of the South was based on a racial-ethnic system, in which imported Africans were forced to work for white landowning families as slaves. U.S. military expansion in the nineteenth century brought more lands under U.S. control—the territories of northern Mexico (now the Southwest), the Philippines, and Puerto Rico—incorporating their peoples into the racial-ethnic hierarchy. And from the mid-nineteenth century onward, Asians were brought into Hawaii's plantation system to work for whites as semi-free laborers. In the twentieth century, racial-ethnic difference and inequality have been perpetuated by the segregation of people of color into different and inferior jobs, living conditions, schools, and political positions, and by the prohibition of intermarriage with whites in some states up until 1967.

Race-ethnicity is a key concept in understanding women's economic histories. But it is not without limitations. First, racial-ethnic processes have never operated independently of class and gender. In the previous section on gender, we saw how racial domination distorted gender and family relations among people of color. Racial domination has also been intricately linked to economic or class domination. As social scientists Michael Omi (Asian American) and Howard Winant (European American) explain, the early European arguments that people of color were without souls had direct economic meaning:

> At stake were not only the prospects for conversion, but the types of treatment to be accorded them. The expropriation of property, the denial of political rights, the introduction of slavery and other forms of coercive labor, as well as outright extermination, all presupposed a worldview which distinguished Europeans—children of

God, human beings, etc.—from "others." Such a worldview was
needed to explain why some should be "free" and others enslaved,
why some had rights to land and property while others did not.[11]

Indeed, many have argued that racial theories only developed after the
economic process of colonization had started, as a justification for white
domination of peoples of color.[12]

The essentially economic nature of early racial-ethnic oppression in
the United States makes it difficult to isolate whether peoples of color were
subordinated in the emerging U.S. economy because of their race-ethnicity
or their economic class. Whites displaced American Indians and Mexicans to
obtain their land. Whites imported Africans to work as slaves and Asians to
work as contract laborers. Puerto Ricans and Filipinas/os were victims of
further U.S. expansionism. Race-ethnicity and class intertwined in the patterns of displacement from land, genocide, forced labor, and recruitment
from the seventeenth through the twentieth centuries. While it is impossible,
in our minds, to determine which came first in these instances—race-ethnicity
or class—it is clear that they were intertwined and inseparable.

Privileging racial-ethnic analysis also leads one to deny the existence
of class differences, both among whites and among people of color, which
complicate and blur the racial-ethnic hierarchy. A racial-ethnic analysis
implies that all whites are placed above all peoples of color—as illustrated
in the top half of Figure 2-3. In this figure, the pyramid represents the unequal
economic structure of the United States, with a small minority of super-rich
on the top; the horizontal race line indicates that all whites are economically
superior to all peoples of color.

But, in fact, the race line, as European American economist Harold
Baron points out, is upward sloping as in the bottom half of Figure 2-3.[13] A
minority of the dominated race is allowed some upward mobility and ranks
economically above whites. At the same time, however, all whites have some
people of color below them. For example, there are upper-class Black,
Chicana, and Puerto Rican women who are more economically privileged
than poor white women; however, there are always people of color who are
less economically privileged than the poorest white woman. Finally, class
oppression operates among women of the same racial-ethnic group.

A third problem with the analysis of racial domination is that such
domination has not been a homogeneous process. Each subordinated
racial-ethnic group has been oppressed and exploited differently by whites:
for example, American Indians were killed and displaced, Africans were
enslaved, and Filipinas/os and Puerto Ricans were colonized. Whites have
also dominated whites; some European immigrant groups, particularly
Southern and Eastern Europeans, were subjected to segregation and vio-

Figure 2-2: The Social Construction of Race-Ethnicity

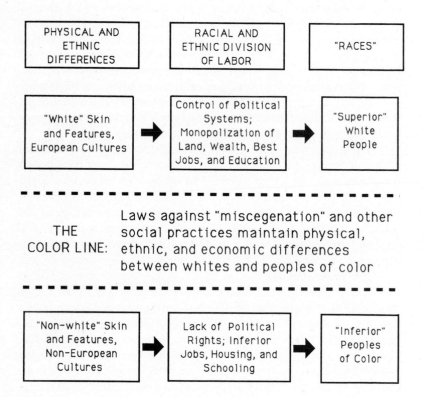

Figure 2-3: Racial Hierarchies

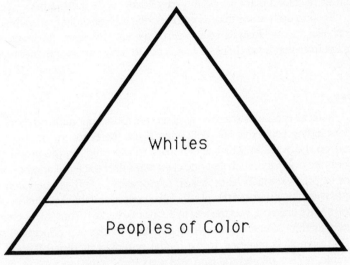

Racial-Ethnic Pyramid

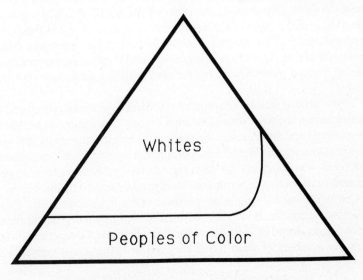

Racial-Ethnic-Class Pyramid

lence. In some cases, people of color have oppressed and exploited those in another group: some American Indian tribes had African slaves; some Mexicans and Puerto Ricans displaced and murdered Indians and had African slaves. Because of these differences, racial oppression does not automatically bring unity of peoples of color across their own racial-ethnic differences, and feminists of color are not necessarily in solidarity with one another.

To sum up, we see that, as with gender, the concept of race-ethnicity is essential to our analysis of women's works. However, divorcing this concept from gender and class, again, leads to problems in both theory and practice.

Class

Radical economists stress class as the most important category for understanding economic life. Following Marx, these economists have focused on the ways in which individuals' relationships to the production process are polarized, such that one class reaps the benefits of another class' labor (a process which Marx called "exploitation"). Struggle between the classes over the control of the production process and the distribution of its output, Marx claimed, was the key to economic history. Thus, Marx characterized different societies as involving different "modes of production," each with its own class relations. In the feudal system of medieval Europe, for example, nobles owned the land and serfs were forced to work it, giving over a portion of their product and labor to the leisured nobility. In slavery, slaveowners, by virtue of their property rights in slaves, owned the product of their slaves' labor, living and enriching themselves through their exploitation of the slaves. In capitalism, the owners of the machines and factories are able to live off the labor of the workers, who own nothing but their own labor and hence are forced to work for the owners. In the century since Marx wrote, radical economists have further developed Marx's conception of class, making it into a powerful concept for understanding economies past and present.

We believe that the concepts of class and exploitation are crucial to understanding the work lives of women in early U.S. history, as well as in the modern, capitalist economy. Up through the nineteenth century, different class relations organized production in different regions of the United States. The South was dominated by slave agriculture; the Northeast by emerging industrial capitalism; the Southwest (then part of Mexico) by the *hacienda* system which carried over many elements of the feudal manor into large-scale production for the market; the rural Midwest by independent family farms that produced on a small scale for the market; and the American Indian West by a variety of tribal forms centered in hunting and gathering or agriculture, many characterized by cooperative, egalitarian economic relations. Living within these different labor systems, and in different class positions within them, women led very different economic lives.

By the late nineteenth century, however, capitalism had become the dominant form of production, displacing artisans and other small producers along with slave plantations and tribal economies. Today, wage labor accounts for over 90 percent of employment; self employment, including family businesses, accounts for the remaining share.[14] With the rise of capitalism, women were brought into the same labor system, and polarized according to the capitalist-wage laborer hierarchy.

At the same time as the wage labor form specific to capitalism became more prevalent, capitalist class relations became more complex and less transparent. Owners of wealth (stocks and bonds) now rarely direct the production process; instead, salaried managers, who may or may not own stock in the company, take on this function. While the capitalist class may be less identifiable, it still remains a small and dominant elite. In 1986, the super-rich (the richest one-half of one percent of the households) owned 35 percent of the total wealth in our country, over 70 times the share they would have had if wealth were equally distributed. The richest tenth of all households owned 72 percent of all wealth, over seven times their fair share. This extreme concentration of wealth conveys a concentration of leisure and power over others into the hands of a small number of households, a concentration which is perpetuated through the generations by inheritance laws and customs.[15]

At the other end of the hierarchy, in 1986, the poorest 90 percent of households owned only 28 percent of total wealth, and had to send at least one household member out to work for the household's survival. Among these waged and salaried workers, a complicated hierarchy of segmented labor markets gives some workers greater earnings and power over the production process than others. Indeed, there are many disagreements over how to categorize managers, professionals, and government workers—to name only a few of the jobs which seem to fall outside the two-class model. In the chapters to follow, we examine the historical processes by which labor markets became and continue to be segmented.[16]

Class can be a powerful concept in understanding women's economic lives, but there are limits to class analysis if it is kept separate from race-ethnicity and gender. First, as we saw in the race section above, the class relations which characterized the early U.S. economy were also racial-ethnic and gender formations. Slave owners were white and mostly male, slaves were Black. The displaced tribal economies were the societies of indigenous peoples. Independent family farmers were whites who farmed American

Indian lands; they organized production in a patriarchal manner, with women and children's work defined by and subordinated to the male household head and property owner. After establishing their dominance in the pre-capitalist period, white men were able to perpetuate and institutionalize this dominance in the emerging capitalist system, particularly through the monopolization of managerial and other high-level jobs.

Second, the sexual division of labor within the family makes the determination of a woman's class complicated—determined not simply by her relationship to the production process, but also by that of her husband or father. For instance, if a woman is not in the labor force but her husband is a capitalist, then we might wish to categorize her as a member of the capitalist class. But what if that same woman worked as a personnel manager for a large corporation, or as a salesperson in an elegant boutique? Clearly, she derives upper-class status and access to income from her husband, but she is also, in her own right, a worker. Conversely, when women lose their husbands through divorce, widowhood, or desertion, they often change their class position in a downward direction. A second gender-related economic process overlooked by class analysis is the unpaid household labor performed by women for their fathers, husbands, and children—or by other women, for pay.[17]

Third, while all workers are exploited by capitalists, they are not equally exploited, and gender and race-ethnicity play important roles in this differentiation. Men and women of the same racial-ethnic group have rarely performed the same jobs—this sex-typing and segregation is the labor market form of the sexual division of labor we studied above. Further, women of different racial-ethnic groups have rarely been employed at the same job, at least not within the same workplace or region. This racial-ethnic-typing and segregation has both reflected and reinforced the racist economic practices upon which the U.S. economy was built.

Thus, jobs in the labor force hierarchy tend to be simultaneously race-typed and gender-typed. Picture in your mind a registered nurse. Most likely, you thought of a white woman. Picture a doctor. Again, you imagined a person of a particular gender (probably a man), and a race (probably a white person). If you think of a railroad porter, it is likely that a Black man comes to mind. Almost all jobs tend to be typed in such a way that stereotypes make it difficult for persons of the "wrong" race and/or gender to train for or obtain the job. Of course, there are regional and historical variations in the typing of jobs. On the West Coast, for example, Asian men performed much of the paid domestic work during the nineteenth century because women were in such short supply. In states where the African American population is very small, such as South Dakota or Vermont, domestic servants and hotel chambermaids are typically white. Nonetheless, the presence of variations in race-gender typing does not contradict the idea that jobs tend to take on racial-ethnic and gender characteristics with profound effects on the labor market opportunities of job-seekers.

The race-sex-typing of jobs makes the effects of class processes insep-arable from the effects of race-ethnicity and gender. Not only is the labor market an arena of struggle in which race-ethnicity and gender, as well as class, are reproduced. In addition, the race-sex typing of jobs has been central in determining the job structure itself. For example, secretarial work devel-oped in the late nineteenth century as a white woman's job; hence, in contrast to the white male job of clerk which it replaced, secretarial work cast white women in the role of "office wives" to white men, and involved no path of career advancement into management.

In the chapters of Part II which follow, the operation and maintenance of racism through the labor markets will be made abundantly clear—as will be the fact that white workers, not just white capitalists, helped impose this racial-ethnic hierarchy. White capitalists—wealthy landowners, railroad magnates, factory owners—imported Blacks, Asians, and, later, Puerto Ricans and Mexicans as a low-wage labor supply. The entrance of these workers of color into the labor force was met with hostility and violence by both white workers and small producers such as farmers and craftsmen. Since employers used immigrant workers of color as strikebreakers or low-wage competition, white workers trying to organize for higher wages resisted this immigration. The threat of competition from workers of color and an ideology of white supremacy kept most white workers from recruiting workers of color into their emerging trade unions on equal terms. European immigrants who spoke languages other than English also faced economic and political discrimination. Thus, in an environment of nativism and racial hostility, jobs came to be increasingly segmented along racial-ethnic lines as the result of combined capitalist and worker efforts.[18] Furthermore, as people of different racial-ethnic groups were drawn out of the many different labor systems from which they had come into wage labor, they were also segre-gated within the developing labor market hierarchy.

The processes which have perpetuated the sex-typing of jobs have, for the most part, been less overt and violent. White male unions, in the late nineteenth century, fought for the passage of "protective legislation" that, by excluding women from dangerous or unhealthy jobs and from overtime work, had the effect of denying them highly paid factory jobs and confining them in lower-paying (and also hazardous) sectors such as apparel and textile manufacture. Women were also confined to low-paid, servile, or care-taking jobs by the sexual division of labor in the home, particularly married women's assignment to the unpaid work of caring for children and serving their husbands. Many employers simply refused to hire married women, with the view that their place was in the home. Domestic responsibilities also limited women's ability to compete for jobs requiring overtime or lengthy training. Professional associations and schools, dominated by white men, restricted the entry of women of all racial-ethnic groups well into the twentieth century. When individual women gained the necessary qualifications and tried to break into jobs monopolized by men of their racial-ethnic group, or into elite, white men's jobs, they were rejected or, if hired, sabotaged, ridiculed, and racially and sexually harassed. These processes have been extremely costly to women in terms of lost wages and job opportunities. This combination of race- and sex-segregation in the labor market meant that, in general, only white men were able to earn a "family wage," adequate to support oneself and a family.

In these ways, the racial-ethnic and gender processes operating in the labor market have transposed white and male domination from pre-capitalist structures into the labor market's class hierarchy. This hierarchy can be described by grouping jobs into different labor market sectors or segments: "primary," "secondary," and "underground." The primary labor market—which has been monopolized by white men—offers high salaries, steady employment, and upward mobility. Its upper tier consists of white-collar salaried or self-employed workers with high status, autonomy, and, often, supervisory capacity. Wealth increases access to this sector, since it purchases elite education and provides helpful job connections. In Part II we investigate at greater length the racial-ethnic, gender, and class barriers erected in the primary sector which have confined most women to other sectors of the labor market and isolated the others in women's professions such as teaching and social work.

The lower tier of the primary sector, which still yields high earnings but involves less autonomy, contains many unionized blue-collar jobs. White working-class men have used union practices, mob violence, and intimidation to monopolize these jobs. By World War II, however, new ideologies of worker solidarity, embodied in the mass industrial unions, began to overcome the resistance of white male workers to the employment of people of color and white women in these jobs.

In contrast to both these primary tiers, the secondary sector offers low wages, few or no benefits, little opportunity for advancement, and unstable employment. People of color and most white women have been concentrated in these secondary sector jobs, where work is often part-time, temporary, or seasonal, and pay does not rise with increasing education or experience. Jobs in both tiers of the primary labor market have generally yielded family wages, earnings high enough to support a wife and children who are not in the labor force for pay. Men of color in the secondary sector have not been able to earn enough to support their families, and women of color have therefore participated in wage labor to a much higher degree than white women whose husbands held primary sector jobs.

Outside of the formal labor market is the underground sector, where the most marginalized labor force groups, including many people of color, earn their livings from illegal or quasi-legal work. This sector contains a great variety of jobs, including drug trafficking, crime, prostitution, work done by undocumented workers, and sweatshop work which violates labor standards such as minimum wages and job safety regulations.

We will explore these labor markets, and their role in reproducing racial-ethnic and gender inequality, in more detail in the chapters which follow. As they are one of the major mechanisms through which racial-ethnic, gender, and class differences are reproduced, they have been a major arena of struggle against oppression. White women and people of color have waged successful battles to gain admittance to occupations from which they once were barred. Union organizing has succeeded in raising jobs out of the secondary sector by providing higher wages, fringe benefits, a seniority system, and protection from arbitrary firing for workers. Similarly, the boundaries of the underground economy have been changed by struggles to legalize or make illegal acts such as drug use and prostitution—for example, by women's successful struggle to prohibit the sale of alcohol during the early twentieth century—as well as by immigration and labor laws.

Conclusion

Women throughout the United States have not experienced a common oppression as women. The processes of gender, race-ethnicity, and class—intrinsically interconnected—have been central forces determining and differentiating women's work lives in U.S. history. Thus, while the explanatory power of each concept—gender, race-ethnicity, and class—is, in itself, limited, together they form the basis of our analysis of women's works.

As we turn to the economic histories in Part II, a few words of introduction are necessary. These histories are selective and partial, as all histories must be. In these six chapters, we focus on the ways in which racial-ethnic, class, and gender relations have combined to structure women's work lives, and on the transformation of these relations over time with the development of the capitalist economy and the continuing process of struggle against oppression. Many historical events which are not specific to women alone have been central in shaping women's works. For example, Native American women's lives were irrevocably changed by the white takeover of their lands; Puerto Rican women's lives and works have been shaped by the colonial relationship between the United States and Puerto Rico; African American women were freed by the abolition of slavery; poor European immigrant women experienced ethnic and class oppression. Attention to the history of racial-ethnic and class, as well as gender processes is necessary if we are to truly understand women's work lives.

We have chosen to examine each racial-ethnic group of women separately. To avoid repetition, we have purposefully underemphasized the common processes affecting women's lives as a result of the development of U.S. capitalism. Women experienced this development in different ways, filtered through their race-ethnicity and class. In Part III, "Transforming Women's Works," we explore the differential effects of capitalist development on women's lives, and their implications for the future.

The histories we present can evoke strong emotions in the reader: anger that so much injustice has been done, guilt over the complicity of one's ancestors, fear that such injustice might occur again, and pride in the courageous efforts of women and men to survive and to resist. By treating each racial-ethnic group of women separately in Part II, we accentuate the differences and conflicts among women of different racial-ethnic groups. We do this purposefully, for we believe that recognizing these conflicts, and accepting and building on these differences, provides the only solid basis for radical social transformation. As African American lesbian feminist Audre Lorde has written:

> ...the strength of women lies in recognizing differences between us as creative, and in standing to those distortions which we inherited without blame but which are now ours to alter. The angers of women can transform differences through insight into power. For anger between peers births change, not destruction, and the discomfort and sense of loss it often causes is not fatal, but a sign of growth.[19]

Part II: Histories of Women's Works

Chapter 3

I AM THE FIRE OF TIME

American Indian Women[1]

i am the fire of time.

the endless pillar
that has withstood death.
the support of an invincible nation.
i am the stars that have guided
lost men.
i am the mother of ten thousand
dying children.
i am the fire of time
i am an indian woman!

—Niki Paulzine, Untitled poem[2]

As Niki Paulzine so eloquently writes, American Indian women have kept the fire of the Indian spirit alive through five centuries of European colonization. U.S. capitalism was built on the theft of the continent's abundant lands, minerals, lakes, and rivers from native peoples. Thus, U.S. economic development brought about the underdevelopment, indeed the annihilation, of thriving native economies. This process of combined development and destruction has been the essential force in the economic history of American Indian women. Although many individual Native Americans have found success within the developing white economy, others have struggled, as members and leaders of their nations, to maintain economic and cultural sovereignty and viability.

Our study of the economic history of American Indian women has two parts. First, we examine the economic organization of indigenous peoples before the European conquest, highlighting the egalitarianism which characterized many of them. Then, we examine the European invasion of the continent and the ensuing struggle by American Indians for survival and economic self-determination.

31

American Indian Ways of Life Before the Invasion

When the Europeans invaded the North American continent, they encountered a richly diverse indigenous population made up of different nations with distinct languages, cultures, and histories. The American Indian peoples migrated to the Americas from Asia by crossing the Bering Strait over 30,000 years ago. By 5000 B.C., civilizations marked by sophisticated social systems and complex religious, agricultural, and trading patterns were present throughout the continent. In 1500 A.D., there were between 10 and 20 million people, in over 300 nations, living in what we now know as the United States. Some of the most important language families were Algonquian, Shoshonean, Caddoan, Iroquoian, Muskogean, Siouan, Athabascan, and Sahaptin-Chinook. Within these families, different groups spoke variations, or dialects.[3]

This great diversity of languages extended to every other aspect of American Indian life, including the ways in which a society provided for its material needs, established a sexual division of labor, and organized its political and religious life. Much of this diversity can be traced to differences in geographical location—in climate, in topography, and in natural resources—differences which were especially important because tribal economies were based on either hunting and gathering or on agricultural production. Although there was significant variation among the groups living in a region, Native American peoples can be grouped into six cultural areas, according to the specific region in which they lived: Northwest Coast, Plains, Plateau, Eastern Woodlands, Northern, and Southwest.[4]

Societies along the Northwest Coast depended on salmon fishing, hunting, and gathering fruits and berries, and were noted for the artwork on their totem poles and dugout canoes. Northwest societies such as the Kwakiutl and the Haida practiced the potlatch, a ceremony in which the host bestowed gifts and food upon the guests. In the Plains, many of the native peoples were nomadic hunters. The Cheyenne, Blackfoot and Comanche hunted buffalo on foot, and later rode horses brought to the continent by Europeans, while other Plains peoples, such as the Mandan, farmed the fertile soil to support themselves. The Plateau peoples, who lived in California and the Northwest, were quite diverse. Some, such as the Paiute, hunted, fished, and dug roots to eat. The Nez Percé adopted the buffalo hunt of the Plains peoples after acquiring horses.

Many societies in the Eastern Woodlands were settled, living from a combination of agriculture, hunting, and trading. Those in the northern part of the Eastern Woodlands, such as the Delaware, the Huron, the Iroquois Confederacy, and the Mohegan, cultivated corn, squash, and beans and hunted deer, while the southern nations of the Woodlands—the Cherokee,

Choctaw, and Seminole—depended on farming and trading and produced beautiful pottery. Northern nations such as the Kutchin, Montagnais, and Naskapi survived in harsh, arctic regions by hunting caribou and following their seasonal migrations. In the Southwest, the Apache, Navajo, and Pueblo, descended from the Aztecs, developed basketry, weaving, pottery-making, and intensive agriculture.[5]

Recent women's studies and American Indian studies research shows that although some American Indian societies were hierarchical, others were in many ways more egalitarian and respectful of individual autonomy than modern U.S. society. According to Native American anthropologist Priscilla Buffalohead:

> Many tribal societies...stem from egalitarian cultural traditions. These traditions are concerned less with equality of the sexes and more with the dignity of individuals and with their inherent right— whether they be women, men, or children—to make their own choices and decisions.[6]

For instance, some of the Eastern Woodlands nations—the Mohawk, Seneca, Cayuga, Oneida, and Onondaga nations—formed an alliance known as the Iroquois Confederacy. Under the Iroquois Great Law of Peace, the Confederacy's 1390 constitution, decisions were made by representative democracy, and the whole tribe, including the women, voted on the war captains. The leaders held power through persuasion rather than coercion, and decisions were arrived at by consensus. In fact, it was the Iroquois example that inspired Benjamin Franklin with the idea of a democratic federation of states for the United States.[7]

The egalitarianism which characterized some native societies also described the Native American relationship to nature: American Indian peoples respected all forms of life, and their methods of economic production centered on preserving the balance and beauty of nature. Sioux Chief Standing Bear wrote:

> There was a great difference in the attitude taken by the Indian and the Caucasian toward nature, and this difference made of one a conservationist and of the other a non-conservationist of life. The Indian, as well as all other creatures that were given birth and grew, were sustained by the common mother—earth. He was therefore kin to all living things and he gave to all creatures equal rights with himself. Everything of earth was loved and reverenced.[8]

Today, activists seeking to arrest the ecological destruction wrought by advanced capitalism are looking to American Indian traditions for alternative ways of relating to nature.

Democracy and egalitarian relations did not, however, characterize all relationships among Native American peoples. Many nations lived in peace with one another, trading and intermarrying, but being "on the warpath" was equally common, and war was central to the lives of numerous native societies. Many American Indians were killed in warfare; captives were sometimes tortured and killed, sometimes enslaved, and sometimes (particularly women and children) adopted into the victorious nation.[9]

Women, Gender, and the Sexual Division of Labor

Much of what we know today about Native American ways of life from the seventeenth century through the early part of the twentieth comes from accounts by male European explorers and missionaries, and hence reflects these observers' class, racial-ethnic, gender, and cultural biases. For instance, in the early years of contact, Europeans described American Indian women as beasts of burden for their men. They were horrified by the hard work these women performed because, in upper-class European society, women were viewed as too fragile for such labor. Furthermore, American Indian men's work—hunting, fishing, and fighting—corresponded closely to the pastimes of upper-class European men, so European observers saw American Indian men as idle.[10]

A few white observers may have been able to provide a more accurate picture. Mary Jemison, a white colonist whose family was captured and killed by American Indians, was adopted by the Seneca Iroquois. She chose to spend her life among them, and married a Delaware Indian. In the late eighteenth century, Jemison wrote of her experiences among the Delaware:

> Our labor was not severe; and that of one year was exactly similar, in almost every respect, to that of the others…Notwithstanding the Indian women have all the fuel and bread to procure, and the cooking to perform, their task is probably not harder than that of white women, who have those articles provided for them; and their cares certainly are not half as numerous, nor as great. In the summer season, we planted, tended and harvested our corn, and generally had all our children with us; but had no master to oversee or drive us, so that we could work as leisurely as we pleased.[11]

New scholarship, much of it by American Indian women, has reinterpreted many of the old accounts of Native American life, stripping away the biases of the original observers and giving us new insights. This research has revealed that American Indian tribes practiced a degree of sexual freedom and equality unknown by and hence unrecognizable to European colonists.

Like all known societies, American Indian societies maintained sexual divisions of labor. For the Blackfoot, for example:

Camp was the domain of the women...the tipi, its furnishings, the food in it, clothing and other manufactures belonged to the woman; hers to give as she pleased. The marriage ceremony consisted of the woman inviting the intended to partake of food she had prepared...Women ridiculed men who attempted to perform sustenance activities.[12]

The particular division of labor varied greatly between nations. Among the Plains Indians, for example, wooden bowls were carved by Pawnee women and by Omaha men, while for the Blackfoot, Cheyenne, and Hidatsa, both men and women made bowls. Sometimes men and women shared different aspects of the same job: Cheyenne men crafted the foundations for saddles, while women covered them with hides.[13]

Nonetheless, these sexual divisions of labor did not always translate into sexual inequality. In many cases, specialization by sex conveyed power to both sexes, and the labor of one sex was not generally valued over that of the other. Each sex had control over its own work and over resources that were essential to the other sex. For instance, among the Ojibway, women were responsible for building the lodges, and they decided who could sleep there. Ojibway women's work also included processing furs for trading and negotiating directly with Europeans in the Great Lakes area. Among the Iroquois, women withheld corn and moccasins from warriors when they wanted to prevent them from forming a raiding party.[14] In the different Plains nations, women maintained a monopoly on the skills of quill-working (necessary to decorate buffalo robes, tents, and cradle-covers), tipi-making, and tipi-decorating by controlling access to the guild which taught the skills and by keeping the skills secret. The women generally received some form of payment for this work.[15]

The more agricultural, settled societies tended to be matrilineal (inheritance and name were passed through females) and/or matrilocal (upon marriage, the bride and groom resided in the household of the bride's mother). As Maryann Oshana, a Chippewa, explains:

Matrilineal tribes provided the greatest opportunities for women: women in these tribes owned houses, furnishings, fields, gardens, agricultural tools, art objects, livestock, and horses. Furthermore, these items were passed down through female lines. Regardless of marital status, women had the right to own and control property. The woman had control of her children and if marital problems developed the man would leave the home.[16]

For instance, among the matrilineal Iroquois, political power was held by the Council of Clan Mothers, composed of representative elder women. This council appointed and deposed tribal chiefs and subchiefs, chose the members (all of whom were male) of the Great Tribal Council, and decided whether or not to wage war.[17] According to the Iroquois Great Law of Peace:

> Women shall be considered the progenitors of the nation. They shall own the land and the soil. Men and women shall follow the status of their mothers. You are what your mother is: the ways in which you see the world and all things in it are through your mother's eyes. What you learn from the father comes later and is of a different sort…[the] Clan Mothers and their sisters select the chiefs and remove them from office when they fail the people…Clan Mothers! You gave us life—continue now to place our feet on the right path.[18]

Among the nomadic peoples of the Plains, the central activities of buffalo-hunting and war-making were dominated by men, leading most researchers to conclude that women in these societies were politically subordinate to men. However, feminist scholars point out that Plains women often had important responsibilities and powers. For instance, among the Blackfoot, women served as custodians for the medicine bundle necessary for the Sun Dance, an important religious ceremony. Small numbers of Piegan women, known as "manly-hearted women," took dominant roles in marriage, property ownership, and ceremonies. Some Blackfoot, Cheyenne, and eastern Dakota women also participated in warfare, either as a lifelong activity or for a particular reason, such as avenging the death of a husband or other relative. Women who excelled as warriors in these war-oriented nations achieved high status. Famous women warriors included Yellowhaired Woman of the Cheyenne, who fought against the Shoshone in 1869, the Other Magpie of the Crow, and Woman Chief, whose accomplishments in war elevated her to the rank of third person among the chiefs.[19]

Indeed, women of many nations participated actively in fighting wars, performing war ceremonies, and even killing prisoners. Cree, Natchez, Apache, and Menominee women celebrated war victories in scalp dances, rejoicing over the safe return of their loved ones and taking pride in avenging those who had died: "…the gory war trophies were usually suspended from the ends of poles or sticks, and the women waved the scalps about like flags as they danced…giving vent to rage, hostility, and fury."[20] Among the Creek, Caddo, and Apache, women participated in torturing both male and female captives, sometimes to death. At the same time, women often acted as peacemakers, a role formalized among the Shawnee in the "peace woman," who bore the responsibility of dissuading the war chief from waging unnecessary or unpopular wars by reminding him of the pain wars brought to Shawnee mothers and wives, and to the women and children of the enemy nation.[21]

The power of women was also evident in many American Indian religions, which accorded great value to women's fertility. In many societies, women and men had their own, equally important, religious rituals. Female deities were important in all American Indian societies, bearing names like Old Spider Woman, Serpent Woman, Corn Woman, and Earth Woman. In most American Indian creation myths, woman was created simultaneously with man, unlike women's derivative "Adam's Rib" status in the Bible. The Laguna Pueblo described their creator deity as the spirit of intelligence: "...In the beginning...Thought Woman finished everything, thoughts, and the names of all things. She finished all the languages."[22]

Another striking aspect of some American Indian societies was the separation of sex roles (or gender) from biological sex. Among certain Plains Indians, males who showed a clear desire to take up the work and lifestyle of women were able to do so, and were known as *berdaches*. Females could also take up men's roles. For example, a young female who felt strongly that she wanted to live as a man would go through a special tribal ritual. After this, the members of the nation would accept her/him as a man, and s/he would do men's work. Becoming a man also meant taking on a man's sexual practices—in other words, marrying women, and parenting children.[23] Woman Chief, whom we mentioned above, was one such female; not only did she excel in the manly activities of hunting and warring, and become a chief, she also had four wives.[24] Among the Mohave, lesbians, known as *hwame*, could undertake all masculine activities, including marriage, riding, and hunting. They were, however, denied roles as tribal heads or war leaders. The Navajo considered lesbians valuable assets to their family and community; since their mythology depicted homosexuals as wealthy, Navajos usually put lesbians in charge of the household and its property. Among the Canadian Kaska, parents with more daughters than sons would encourage one of the daughters to "become a man"; such women married other women, and were considered outstanding hunters. Many tribes accepted a range of sexual practices—heterosexual, homosexual, and bisexual—and allowed youths to experiment sexually before marriage.

The European invasion which began in the fifteenth century not only killed, displaced, and subordinated American Indians, but also undermined much of the equality and independence of American Indian women. For instance, U.S. government officials conferred the status of "treaty chief" only on males, ignoring women chiefs. (Nevertheless, many nations still have women chiefs today.) Missionaries played an important part in depriving American Indian women of their power. In the early nineteenth century, for example, Quaker missionaries were shocked by the Allegheny Seneca women's predominance in agriculture, which was considered men's work among whites. But the missionaries' attempts to replace women farmers with men by teaching only men to plow were unsuccessful. Seneca women continued to farm, taking the new skill for their own use, and were instrumental in resisting the Quakers' plan to divide land into individual plots.[25]

Early European Conquest of North America: Trade, Conversion, and Extermination

After Christopher Columbus's "discovery" of America for the King and Queen of Spain in 1492, Native American peoples were faced with an onslaught of European invaders. Lured by American gold, silver, furs, and fertile lands, the Spanish, the French, the Dutch, the British, and the Russians rushed to colonize the land and its indigenous peoples, often warring among themselves for this privilege and enlisting rival American Indian nations to help them. However, the continent was vast, and American Indian resistance fierce. By the American Revolution in 1776, almost 300 years after Europeans first arrived, less than half of the North American continent was under white control.

Early colonizers used a variety of methods to exploit and oppress the native peoples, ranging from trading and religious conversion to forced assimilation and violent extermination. Colonizers commonly took tribal lands through war, signed "peace treaties" recognizing the indigenous nation's right to remaining lands, and then broke these treaties and violently claimed more land. European armies also used existing conflicts between native peoples to extend their control over the continent, enlisting the aid of one nation in their subjugation of a rival nation. Historian James Axtell describes the ways in which colonizers made use of Native Americans, as well as their lands and resources:

> European merchants needed them to harvest the continent's furs as only they could and to consume trade goods. Missionaries sought to convert them to their various brands of Christianity and thereby to enlist them in the earthly warfare between the Catholic and the reformed [Protestant] churches. Similarly, the military leaders of the various colonies needed them as allies against hostile or recalcitrant neighbors, native and colonial, while empire builders at home sought to manipulate them on the giant chessboard of international competition for territory, wealth, and souls.[26]

European racial theories reduced the great variety of American Indian peoples to one biologically inferior and savage "red" race, which needed whites' "civilizing" influence. These theories helped whites justify their inhumane, and often genocidal, treatment of Native Americans.[27]

The American Indian peoples responded to the European invasion in a variety of ways: trading, economic cooperation, and intermarriage; fleeing and resettling further from the European frontier; taking on aspects of European religion and culture under pressures to assimilate; and fighting, often to the death, for their lands, cultures, and political sovereignty. Women chiefs played an important role in struggles against the invaders. For example, Quaipan, a Narragansett *sunksquaw* (woman chief), fought and was killed by the English in 1676; a Pocasset *sunksquaw*, Weetamoo, commanded over 300 warriors.[28]

The European invasion was multi-pronged and widespread. In the fifteenth and sixteenth centuries, Spanish raiding parties made slaving expeditions into Florida and New Mexico, killing and subduing the indigenous peoples, but were unable to establish any permanent colonies except for St. Augustine, Florida. In the seventeenth century, Britain laid claim to the Eastern Coast, confronting the powerful tribes of the Iroquois Confederacy and of the Powhatan confederacy of Virginia. French missionaries and traders established a lucrative fur trade with Northern nations such as the Algonquin, Montaignais, and the Ojibway. Meanwhile, the Spanish fought the Seminole and other nations in Florida and Georgia, and the Pueblo, Apache, and Navajo in the Southwest. When the English defeated the French in 1763, they took possession of "French" lands and ignored existing treaties with American Indian nations, accelerating their push westward.[29]

European attempts to destroy Native American resistance included not only military attacks, in which whites had the benefit of superior weaponry, but also germ warfare. As General Jeffrey Amherst (for whom the town of Amherst, Massachusetts was named) advised his colleagues in 1752, "You will be well advised to infect the Indians with sheets upon which small pox patients have been lying or by any other means which may serve to exterminate this accursed race."[30]

Religion served as another weapon in European colonization of Native Americans. Missionaries from France, England, and Spain traveled to the Americas with the intention of converting American Indians to Catholicism or to the different Protestant sects. In 1585, for instance, an ally of Sir Walter Raleigh, the English explorer and colonizer, described their goals as "...the gyninge [gaining] of the soules of millions of those wretched people, the reducinge of them...from the depe pitt of hell to the highest heavens."[31]

Missionaries sought to transform tribal gender relations, replacing their egalitarian, extended-family structure with more patriarchal forms. For example, in the early seventeenth century, Jesuit missionaries among the St. Lawrence Montagnais-Naskapi worked to eliminate the frequent divorce and extramarital sex. As one missionary commented, "The young people do not think that they can persevere in the state of matrimony with a bad wife or a bad husband. They wish to be free and to be able to divorce the consort if they do not love each other."[32] After several years of unsuccessful attempts, the same missionary complained:

> The inconstancy of marriages and the facility with which they divorce each other, are a great obstacle to the Faith of Jesus Christ. We do not dare baptize the young people because experience teaches us that the custom of abandoning a disagreeable wife or husband has a strong hold on them.[33]

Spanish colonizers established Catholic missions in New Mexico throughout the first half of the seventeenth century and in California in the latter eighteenth century. In 1680, the Great Pueblo Revolt drove the Spaniards from New Mexico for 13 years. Led by Popé, a medicine man accused by the Spaniards of witchcraft, Pueblos and Apaches killed friars, soldiers, and colonists, and resumed their native religion.[34]

Whether they cooperated or resisted, most eastern nations were gradually displaced or decimated by the European colonists. Many of the peoples who welcomed the Pilgrims to Plymouth—the Pequod, Natick, and Narraganset—had been virtually exterminated by 1700. However, the Mashpee—who, with the aid of a white farmer in the seventeenth century, acquired a "plantation" to farm communally—were able to maintain control of what whites called "Cape Cod's Indian Town" in Massachusetts up through the 1960s.[35]

Broken Promises: Early U.S. Policy Toward American Indians

The colonists' struggle to acquire American Indian lands intensified after the Revolutionary War against Great Britain, as settlers from the original colonies sought lands west of the Appalachian Mountains. Between 1795 and 1818, American Indians were forced to accept treaties ceding most of Ohio, Indiana, and Illinois to the United States. Although most of these treaties promised that no more territory would be lost, land-hungry white settlers continued to push further west and fought new wars against Native Americans. Meanwhile the Spaniards battled nations in the Southeast and Southwest, and the Russians advanced down the Alaska coast.[36]

Resistance was widespread. One of the greatest American Indian leaders against U.S. domination was Tecumseh, who with his brother and spiritual leader, Tenskwatawa the Prophet, worked to unite different nations against the white invaders in the first decade of the nineteenth century. Foreshadowing the American Indian Movement of the 1970s, Tecumseh urged Native Americans to reject the European customs they had begun to adopt, from drinking alcohol to acquiring trinkets, and called on them to return to their native ways. He argued against selling tribal lands, insisting that the land belonged to all Native American peoples, and no tribe could sell any of it: "Sell a country! Why not sell the air, the clouds and the great sea, as well as the earth? Did not the Great Spirit make them all for the use of his children?"[37] Unfortunately, his plans for a pan-Indian union were upset by the War of 1812 between the United States and the British, and Tecumseh was killed fighting in that war.

During this period, the four great southern nations—the Creek, the Cherokee, the Choctaw, and the Seminole—had remained relatively secure in their homelands, compared to other nations which had been exterminated or pushed west. Most of the Cherokee and Choctaw had adjusted to their reduced territories, formalized legal codes of their own, and allowed missionaries to establish schools. Sequoiyah, the great Cherokee scholar, had invented a written Cherokee language, allowing some Cherokees to become literate, and the nation prospered economically.[38]

However, a dramatic change in the fortunes of the southern nations came about with the 1828 election of President Andrew Jackson and the passage of the Indian Removal Act of 1830. Jackson had campaigned on a platform of forcible removal of the southern nations to a specified "Indian Territory" west of the Mississippi (the area known today as Oklahoma). Actually, by the time the Removal Act passed, many nations had already been forced to leave their homelands in Ohio, Michigan, Indiana, Illinois, Minnesota, and Wisconsin. Some tribes fought back, such as the Seminole, who engaged the U.S. army in a costly and lengthy war. Others, such as the Choctaw and the Creek, signed removal treaties in which they gave up their lands in exchange for new tribal lands in Indian Territory and some small payments. One woman taken up the Mississippi River in a steamboat sang sadly, "I have no more land. I am driven away from home, driven up the red waters, let us all go, let us all die together."[39]

The process of removal was physically and emotionally devastating. By the time removal from their beloved lands had been completed, many Choctaws and nearly half the Creek had either starved or succumbed to disease. Members of these nations who chose to stay behind (including a third of the Choctaw) were forced to abandon their tribal membership and received individual allotments of land. However, federal agents and land-hungry white settlers used legal manipulation (including forgery, bribery, and misrepresentation) to cheat Native Americans out of their allotments; most eventually joined their nations in the West.[40]

To prevent the same fate, and in the face of growing dispossession by white miners staking out claims to newly discovered gold in Georgia, the

Cherokee Nation appealed to the Supreme Court of the United States and won recognition in 1832 as a "distinct community, occupying its own territory, with boundaries accurately described, and which the citizens of Georgia have no right to enter, but with the assent of the Cherokee themselves." [41] However, the state government of Georgia ignored the ruling, and forced the Cherokee to leave their lands and homes for land west of the Mississippi. Four thousand Cherokees died on their "Trail of Tears." Several hundred escaped capture and hid in the North Carolina hills, used their relocation money to buy land through a trustworthy white man, and established a stable community. [42]

Displaced into Oklahoma, with treaties promising that they would never need to relocate again, the remaining Cherokees, Creeks, Choctaws, Chickasaws, and Seminoles eventually set up prospering republics with schools, courts, and businesses. Whites called them the "Five Civilized Tribes" because of their adoption of many aspects of European American culture. Some mixed-blooded American Indians even established large plantations worked by African American slaves. However, much had been lost in the move. For instance, Cherokee women had been skilled botanists, using over 800 plants found in the Southeast for food, medicine, and crafts; the completely different Oklahoma lands deprived them of their skills and their people of valuable products. [43]

As whites pushed westward they again began to encroach on tribal lands, defending their behavior with the philosophy of "Manifest Destiny," a doctrine which claimed that the United States had both the right and the duty to expand across the North American continent. The original Indian Territory shrank as settlers entered the territory, cutting down trees, stealing horses, and murdering American Indians. In 1854, Kansas and Nebraska became territories, and Native Americans were induced to take individual land allotments and cede tribal lands. By the beginning of the Civil War, the Delaware and other nations which had resettled in Kansas were once again displaced. The U.S. government eventually commandeered one-half of the lands of the "Five Civilized Tribes" to resettle other displaced peoples. Most of the northern Plains nations also moved west, to Arkansas, Wisconsin, or Kansas; after fighting a war in 1831, the Sauk and Fox were also removed from their lands. [44]

The pattern of white takeover intensified in the second half of the nineteenth century, accelerated by the Gold Rush of 1848. Between the 1850s and the 1880s, a period of fierce fighting known as the Indian Wars, western nations fought a losing battle to retain their lands. Some highlights of this struggle were General Custer's resounding defeat by the Sioux and Cheyenne in 1876; Nez Percé Chief Joseph's battle against a much larger U.S. army one year later; Geronimo's wars in the late 1870s; and the massacre at Wounded Knee Creek of 200 American Indian men, women, and children in 1890. The last stand was made by the Apache of the Southwest, who were not settled on reservations until the latter part of the nineteenth century. American Indian women were an important part of this resistance fighting. For example, Buffalo Calf Road (Cheyenne) distinguished herself in battles against General George Crook and General Custer and was given the honorary name "Brave Woman" by her people.[45]

War was not the only threat to Native Americans during the second half of the nineteenth century. After the Civil War, railroads built on tribal land (granted to the railroad barons by the U.S. government) cut across the country. Buffalo were hunted to supply meat to the railroad crews, but the real destruction of the buffalo came in the 1870s—in 1873 alone, over one-third of the Plains buffalo herds were slaughtered for their hides and for sport, destroying the way of life of the Plains Indians. Another blow to tribal cultures and sovereignty came with the Homestead Act of 1862, which promised free land to white settlers.[46]

Captive Nations: The Establishment of the Reservation System

One by one, nations were defeated and forced to give up territories. During the second half of the nineteenth century, they signed treaties with the U.S. government which recognized their tribal sovereignty over and ownership of certain restricted areas of land known as reservations. From 1851 to 1887, the official policy of the U.S. government was to confine American Indians on these reservations, some of which were located on part of their original tribal lands, and others on new lands to which they were forcibly relocated.

Under the reservation system some nations, like the Iroquois, Pueblo, and Papago, were able to retain enough of their tribal lands to preserve their economic and cultural ways of life. Others, like the Sioux and Cheyenne, lost their hunting lands and were forced by whites into unsuccessful agricultural efforts in the semi-arid Indian Territory. Sarah Winnemucca (Paiute) organized her people to resist relocation from Oregon to the Washington territory. A great orator, Winnemucca, who spoke five languages, used her skill to lecture against the forced exile of her people and collected thousands of names on a petition for Paiute land, which the U.S. Secretary of the Interior at first agreed to grant, but then never acted upon.[47]

Conditions were almost uniformly dismal on the reservations. Unable to farm the near-desert lands, Native Americans were often hungry; many starved since promised rations, to which they were entitled by treaty, rarely arrived. Disease, especially smallpox and cholera, decimated reservation populations; for example, the California Indian population fell from an estimated 150,000 before the Gold Rush to 17,000 in 1890. Those reservation lands which were not barren were the target of white greed. In one case, Apache reservation land was stripped from the nation and handed over to mining interests in the late 1870s, causing a decade of Apache wars.[48]

The U.S. government retained ultimate authority as "trustee" over reservation life, allowing nations only a very limited degree of self-government. Nations were made dependent upon the disbursements of federal monies for their food, schools, health services, and building materials. While, at first, the U.S. government administered reservation life through military and federal bureaucracies, missionary societies pleaded that their "Christian influence" was sorely needed. In the 1870s, 13 different religious denominations (from the Baptists to the Presbyterians to the Quakers) persuaded the U.S. government to give them shared control of reservation agencies, and divided the reservations up among themselves.[49]

Even though the reservation system appeared to acknowledge tribal sovereignty, in fact the system was bent on destroying the authority of tribal chiefs. As George Ellis, a well-known white clergyman and author, wrote in 1882:

> We have a full right, by our own best wisdom, and then even by compulsion, to dictate terms and conditions to them; to use constraint and force; to say what we intend to do, and what they must and shall do...This rightful power of ours will relieve us from conforming to, or even consulting to any troublesome extent, the views and inclinations of Indians whom we are to manage...The Indian must be made to feel he is in the grasp of a superior.[50]

A central part of whites' efforts to "domesticate" Native Americans was to deprive them of the right to parent and educate their own children. "In Indian civilization I am a Baptist," wrote Richard Henry Pratt, architect of the federal schooling program, "because I believe in immersing the Indians in our civilization and when we get them under, holding them there until they are thoroughly soaked."[51] Pratt, an army officer, developed a policy of off-reservation schooling beginning in the late 1870s. Native American children were forcibly taken from their parents and placed in boarding schools away from the reservations, where they were forced to speak English and wear European American clothing. To further acquaint them with white ways, children spent one-half of their time working for nearby white families—boys at farming and blacksmithing, girls at domestic work. When Native American parents resisted this practice by hiding their children from the authorities, the U.S. government used its financial and political power over their nations to force compliance. As later policies began to drive

American Indians off reservations, federal officials contracted with white public schools to take on their education. After 1890, one-half of the federal budget for "Indian Affairs" went to education.[52]

We have little information on how the devastation of tribal life by the reservation system affected sex roles. For instance, we know that, among the Plains tribes, men lost their warrior-hunter role. But as for women, we know little, as American Indian sociologist Beatrice Medicine points out:

> If a generalization may be made, it is that female roles of mother, sister, and wife were ongoing because of the continued care they were supposed to provide for the family. But what of the role of woman in relationship to agents, to soldiers guarding the "hostiles," and to their general physical deprivation in societies whose livelihood and way of life had been destroyed along with the bison? We are very nearly bereft of data and statements which would clarify the transitional status of Indian women during this period. The strategies adopted for cultural survival and the means of transmitting these to daughters and nieces are valuable adaptive mechanisms which cannot even partially be reconstructed.[53]

However, we can certainly assume that the practice of sending children to off-reservation boarding schools diminished women's responsibilities for childrearing, and interfered with the transmission of skills such as pottery-making, tepee decorating, and quillwork from women to girls.

In spite of American Indian protests, most U.S. government jobs on the reservations were held by whites. Chief Standing Bear noted that American Indians had been adept in learning and adapting the ways of the white man, adopting the horse, sports, and even beads (which women incorporated into their handiwork, along with and in place of the traditional quills). Still, whites had prevented them from entering high-paid professional jobs:

> Despite the fact that Indian schools have been established over several generations, there is a dearth of Indians in the professions. It is most noticeable on the reservations where the numerous positions of consequence are held by white employees instead of trained Indians. For instance, why are not the stores, post-offices, and Government office jobs on the Sioux Reservation held by trained Indians? Why cannot Sioux be reservation nurses and doctors; and road-builders too?...Were these numerous positions turned over to trained Indians, the white population would soon find reservation life less attractive and less lucrative.[54]

Divide and Conquer: The Allotment Policy

In the 1870s, U.S. government policy underwent another transformation, and steps were taken to destroy the reservation system in order to grant reservation lands to whites. The first step was the passage of an 1871 law undermining what little tribal sovereignty still existed. Congress stated that "here after no Indian nation or tribe" would be recognized "as an independent power with whom the United States may contract a treaty." Congress further increased its control over tribal life through the Bureau of Indian Affairs (which had been established in 1824).[55]

Whites in the West pressured the government to give Indian reservation lands to homesteaders, and corporations sought to exploit tribal lands for railroad, coal, cattle, and oil enterprises. Then, in 1887, Congress passed the Dawes Act, which forced nations to divide their lands into individual allotments and sell the surplus, as determined by the U.S. government, to the government. In essence, the nations and all their lands were to be liquidated, nation by nation, their governments dismantled, and their members "integrated" into U.S. society as individual citizens, on newly allotted plots often located away from their former village homes and interspersed with those of white settlers.[56]

Under the Dawes Act, each family head was to receive 160 acres; adults over 18 and orphaned children also received 80 acres. The land was to be held in "trust" for 25 years, during which time it could not be sold or taken by anyone else. At the end of the period, the individual would receive a title, or "patent," to the land. Those who refused to take their allotments were left with nothing.

The original Act provided that American Indian holders of allotment lands were to become U.S. citizens, although later amendments denied them citizenship until the 25-year trusteeship period had passed. Those who were not citizens were generally considered wards of the state, much as children in foster care; since they lacked legal rights, they were easily manipulated and exploited by money-hungry whites. But citizenship was a mixed blessing for Native Americans. On the one hand, it implied the termination of their tribal identity and allegiance, while on the other hand, it did convey some benefits, such as access to courts and the political process. American Indians who did not receive allotment lands could become citizens if they chose to leave their nations and take on the white way of life, but American Indians as a group were not granted citizenship until 1924.[57]

In spite of attempts to convince them that allotment was "for their own good" (many white philanthropists supported the policy), Native Americans were squarely against it. Within their nations, Native Americans could use their collective power to defend themselves against whites; as individuals within white society, they were powerless. Jacob Jackson (Choctaw) led a campaign to allow American Indians to sell their allotments, emigrate, and purchase tribal lands in Mexico or South America. "The white man came to this country to avoid conditions which to him were not as bad as the present conditions are to us...All we ask is that we may be permitted to exercise the same privilege," he argued in 1906 to the U.S. Senate, but Senators ridiculed and rejected his plan.[58]

Allotment proceeded over strenuous American Indian objections and resistance, extending even over the lands of the Five Civilized Tribes, whose treaties explicitly forbade it. Allotment was particularly damaging to cattle-ranching nations like the Cheyenne and the Sioux, for much allotment land was worthless for agriculture and, once subdivided, could not be used for cattle grazing. However, Native Americans were able to force an amendment to the original allotment plan. The plan had been to assign lands according to a "head-of-family" concept; this was an anathema to Native American cultures which accorded some rights to control property to married women and children. As a result of their opposition, the Act was amended to provide equal shares to each person.[59]

American Indians were allegedly protected from white takeover of their allotments by the 25-year trust provision (which also barred the land from taxation). However, since Native Americans had little experience with deeds, mortgages, leases, and powers of attorney, and faced a white-controlled legal system, it was easy for grafters to enrich themselves through leases, illegal purchases, incompetency hearings, and even murder. In an incompetency hearing, whites would declare American Indians, especially women and children, incompetent to own land, freeing their lands for purchase.[60]

Land, held and used collectively, had been the basis of tribal economic life. Through the allotment policy, however, tribal lands were reduced drastically and broken into individual parcels. American Indian lands had been reduced from the entire continent to 138 million acres by 1887, and to only 47 million acres by 1934. Moreover, even when land was legally under Native American ownership, whites often maintained control. When an American Indian died, his or her land was divided among all the heirs, and hence into small and often unusable parcels. The Bureau of Indian Affairs then managed these parcels as trusts, usually leasing them for virtually nothing to whites.[61]

Despite this catastrophic loss of land, Native Americans remained a predominantly agricultural, ranching, and fishing people. The 1900 Census reported that over two-thirds of employed Native American men and nearly one-half of the employed women worked in these areas (see Table 3-1). About one-fourth of Native American women workers were employed in manufacturing, mostly in wood-working and textiles, probably in their traditional crafts. About one-fourth of employed women worked in domestic or personal service, an occupation which was encouraged by off-reservation

Table 3-1

Occupational Distribution of American Indian Women Workers,
1900-1980 (in Percent)

	1900	1930	1960	1970	1980
Agriculture	47.2	26.1	10.5	2.1	1.2
Manufacturing	24.9	37.6	18.1	22.3	17.0
Private Household Service	13.4	22.5	16.8	6.6	1.4
Service (not Private Household)	12.1	2.9	25.8	25.9	23.9
Sales	0.2	1.7	3.6	4.3	8.0
Clerical	0.1	3.3	14.2	25.9	27.4
Professional & Technical	1.9	4.6	9.1	10.3	14.5
Managerial, Administrative, & Official	0.4	1.2	2.0	2.5	6.6

NOTES: Totals do not always sum to 100 because of rounding. Manufacturing includes craft and transportation workers; agriculture includes mining, fishing, and forestry; managerial, administrative & official includes some self-employment, and excludes farm managers. 1980 data include Eskimo and Aleut peoples. For a full listing of occupational categories included, see Appendix B. For a discussion of comparability problems betwee Census years, see Appendix D.
SOURCES: See Appendix A.

schooling. Two percent worked as professionals, most as teachers. These data describe only the 14 percent of American Indian women whom census takers considered gainfully employed, compared to 16 percent of white women and 41 percent of Black women. Native American women's low rate of participation in the formal labor force can be partially explained by their high rate of participation in subsistence production, which was often not counted as labor force participation.[62]

Limited Sovereignty: The Return of the Reservation System

Even when all seemed lost, Native Americans did not give up. By the 1920s, a combination of forces had begun to undermine allotment. A Pan-Indian movement fought to reverse federal policy. Zitkala-Sa, a Sioux also known as Gertrude Simmons Bonnin, was an important leader in this movement. She founded the National Council of American Indians, and was active in the Society of American Indians. Zitkala-Sa enlisted the support of the General Federation of Women's Clubs in her pro-Indian organizing. The Federation, made up of middle-class white women's clubs, followed her lead in creating an Indian Welfare Committee. Zitkala-Sa used the committee as a vehicle to conduct an influential investigation of federal treatment of various nations. This and other studies exposed the horrendous poverty and disease to which American Indians were subjected, and attacked the Indian Service (created to oversee Indian matters) and the off-reservation education system. In 1924, Congress responded to the federal investigation by granting citizenship to Native Americans (a mixed blessing, as we saw above). Then, in 1928, a private research agency in Washington, D.C. documented the shocking conditions of American Indian life under allotment, spurring the U.S. Senate to begin a many-year project of hearings across the country. Meanwhile, the Great Depression began to pull Native Americans even further into poverty. During the Depression, Congress passed a set of liberal social and economic policies, including New Deal legislation which established the Social Security System and guaranteed organizing rights to labor unions, but most of these laws had little impact on the economic and political status of American Indians.[63]

The allotment process was also losing force for economic reasons. According to European American historian Angie Debo, "Indian holdings had indeed melted away to the place where despoiling them was ceasing to be big business dominating the economic and political life of the states involved."[64] With the pressures of greed slaked, white reformers were able to recognize that the allotment policy they had promoted was having disastrous effects. Finally, the heightened public awareness brought about by American Indian political struggle and the many reports and hearings of the 1920s led to the passage of the watershed Indian Reorganization Act (IRA) in 1934. The new law halted the allotment process, returned unused surplus lands to the nations, decreased federal control, and both allowed and encouraged the development of tribal governments and constitutions. The IRA also allowed individual American Indians to exchange their lands voluntarily for shares in tribal corporations. Under John Collier, a reformist Commissioner of Indian Affairs, government funds were made available to the nations for buying back land and a loan fund was set up to help fund economic development projects.[65]

The IRA created splits among and within nations. Ninety-five nations adopted constitutions, and approximately 75 formed corporations for conducting tribal business. However, about half of all American Indians, including most of the Pueblo, rejected the plan. Opponents argued that the IRA did not allow true self-determination and economic independence. Under the Act, nations maintained their trustee status with the U.S. government and continued to be controlled and exploited by the government, and dependent upon it for services and funds, many of which were annual payments for previously "purchased" lands. Within the nations that accepted the IRA scheme, many Native Americans (called the "traditionalists," as opposed to the pro-IRA "progressives") boycotted their new tribal governments, claiming that the Bureau of Indian Affairs "set up puppet governments on the reservations and somehow mysteriously governs all aspects of tribal life by remote control."[66]

World War II created new economic opportunities for American Indians in military service and in defense industries. Many left the reservations in search of jobs: by 1951, for instance, over 17,000 Navajos lived off-reservation.[67] While the U.S. Census does not provide information on the occupations of American Indian women during the war years, we do know that the share employed in agriculture dropped from 26 percent to 11 percent between 1930 and 1960, while the shares in clerical, service, and professional jobs grew dramatically, as shown in Table 3-1. These data suggest that American Indian women did not benefit from the growth in direct wartime manufacturing jobs, but they did gain a greater share of the new jobs generated by wartime economic prosperity.

The Pendulum Swings Again: Termination and Urban Relocation

Under the Eisenhower presidency, whites advocating allotment and assimilation were able to reverse the pro-reservation policies of the New Deal era. In 1953 the House and Senate passed a resolution which called for termination of the special legal relationship between the U.S. government and tribal governments, and for the dissolution of tribal governments. American Indians were to be "freed" from their special status and treated like all other minority groups. A number of tribes were terminated between 1954 and 1959, including the Klamath and Menominee, who owned and controlled valuable timber lands in Oregon and Wisconsin, respectively. The disastrous allotment policy had returned, only this time it had another name. The federal economic development loan fund was frozen and, on many reservations, federal services were simply cut off, forcing Native Americans to leave or sell their land. (In the early 1960s, when the results of termination became clear—impoverishment and dislocation—federal programs were reinstated.)[68]

American Indians were pushed further from tribal life by the Urban Relocation Program (1950-1968), which established relocation centers in Chicago, Denver, and Los Angeles, purposefully far from Native Americans' homes in order to destroy their attachment to their tribes and their cultures. This relocation speeded the movement of American Indians to urban areas, a movement already under way because of economic pressures (many reservations simply could not support their growing populations). While some of the relocated were successful in their new lives, most were kept in low-level jobs by poor education and discrimination. In the words of Roxanne Dunbar Ortiz, urban American Indians, "...experienced grueling urban poverty and unemployment in place of the grinding rural poverty and unemployment, with the added inevitability of losing their homelands and their existence as peoples."[69] The stagnation of the reservation economy, coupled with the selective off-reservation migration of those with the highest education and skill levels, led to a growing economic gap between reservation and urban American Indians.[70]

Rapid economic growth in the 1960s and early 1970s provided some improvement in American Indian economic status. Between 1960 and 1970, Indian college enrollment more than doubled, and rapid population growth and greater ethnic pride brought a 50 percent increase in the number of American Indians counted by the Census Bureau. Infant mortality and death rates from tuberculosis dropped dramatically but still remained far higher than those for other racial groups. Despite this progress, in 1969 nearly 40 percent of American Indians lived below the poverty level (compared to 14 percent of the total U.S. population). Rural Native Americans, in particular, remained poorer.[71]

These changes had important effects on the work lives of American Indian women. With the movement off the reservations and out of traditional subsistence production, the share of American Indian women counted in the formal labor force more than doubled between 1950 and 1970, from 17 percent to 35 percent. The share of women working in agriculture fell from 11 percent in 1960 to only 2 percent in 1970. At the same time, as shown in Table 3-1, the share of Native American women workers in the professions rose slightly and the share in clerical jobs grew rapidly. These new job opportunities allowed American Indian women entering the labor force to avoid domestic service.[72]

Relocated urban women were in the lead of economic and cultural reorganization in the new, multination urban communities. They formed craft circles, building on their traditional arts of quilting, beading, and making ceremonial garb; held fairs to sell their work; and used the money earned to fund American Indian centers and to ship the bodies of their dead home for burial. According to Laura Waterman Wittstock (Seneca), "...these sisterhoods fueled the fires of urban Indian unity and made possible the debut of the urban-born 'warrior brotherhood' that sprang forth in Chicago, Minneapolis, and San Francisco."[73]

Red Power

The late 1960s and early 1970s were a time of militant American Indian nationalism. An urban "Red Power" movement—first organized against racism and police repression and in alliance with the Black Panthers and Chicano Brown Berets—soon began making alliances with "traditionalists" on the reservations. New and radical forms of American Indian resistance developed which challenged the tribal leadership for being too accommodating of the status quo. Activists focused on American Indian nationalism, especially on wresting control over reservation life away from the Bureau of Indian Affairs, its American Indian representatives, and corporations, and on winning back lost lands. Many Native American women were involved in establishing alternative schools which taught American Indian languages, traditions, and resistance to white domination, along with other subjects, often employing innovative techniques such as ungraded classrooms. During the 1960s, hundreds of these survival schools were founded, and many remain in operation today.[74]

The year 1968 was crucial to American Indian struggle. Native Americans occupied Alcatraz Island in the San Francisco Bay, a former prison site, to express their rage and their determination to survive as American Indian peoples. They unified in the American Indian Movement (AIM), and under AIM's leadership, thousands marched on the "Trail of Broken Treaties" to Washington, D.C. in October 1972. The following year, hundreds of Native Americans, organized by AIM, occupied Wounded Knee (the historic site of the 1890 massacre) for 71 days in an heroic and effective protest. Gladys Bissonette, a grandmother, participated in the negotiations, and 87 women were among the 275 arrested and charged. In other actions, American Indians occupied their white-controlled workplaces. In 1975, Navajo women electronics workers, fired for trying to form a union, called on AIM and with its help seized the plant. Later that year, Yankton Sioux meat-processing workers occupied their factory. In 1973, the Menominee were able to repeal their termination and restore themselves as a federally recognized tribal community; Ada Deer and Lucille Chapman, both Menominees, were leaders in this successful struggle. In 1974, several thousand Indians from different nations met in Wakpala, on the Standing Rock Reservation in South Dakota, to create the International Treaty Council to take Native American problems to the United Nations and other international forums.[75]

This heightened militancy encouraged the Kennedy administration to slow and eventually end the termination policy, in yet another reversal (Table 3-2 recapitulates the vicissitudes of federal policy). Federal loan funds for economic development projects were again made available, and Indian nations began to gain some control within the BIA. In 1974, the Morton v.

Table 3-2

U.S. Policy Toward American Indians	
1830	Indian Removal Act forces eastern nations to move west of the Mississippi into "Indian Territory" (area of today's Oklahoma)
1851-1887	Establishment of the reservation system
1887	Dawes Act mandates allotment, dividing up reservation and other tribal lands into individual plots; Native Americans lose 91 million acres in the process
1924	American Indians receive U.S. citizenship
1934	Indian Reorganization Act stops allotment process; allows and encourages tribal governments and corporations to form
1954-59	Termination policy disbands some nations
1950-1968	Urban Relocation Program
1968-1970s	Red Power Movement and repression
1974	Morton vs. Mancari decision recognizes tribal governments
1975	Indian Self-Determination and Educational Assistance Act

Mancari Supreme Court decision defended the reservation system, arguing that special Indian programs were not racist, but rather involved a unique political relationship between nations and the federal government. The Indian Self-Determination and Educational Assistance Act of 1975 formally replaced termination with Indian self-determination, reaffirmed the powers of tribal governments, and advised placing BIA programs under the tribal governments. American Indian tribes had won their right to exist as independent nations, and could thus maintain their own cultural and economic practices, and individuals were no longer forced to assimilate into white society.[76]

However, while most Native American leaders saw these reforms as a step in the right direction, the changes fell far short of establishing true tribal autonomy. Indeed, at the same time that the federal government was instituting the reforms, it was also engaging in the violent repression of the American Indian Movement. The police, the FBI, and reservation "goon squads" killed more than 60 American Indians in the period after Wounded Knee. One of those killed was Anna Mae Aquash, a Micmac who helped establish a Native American center in Boston in the 1960s and was active in AIM in the 1970s. The FBI followed and arrested Aquash, ransacked her house, and threatened to take away her children. She was found dead with a bullet in her skull in 1976.[77]

Native Americans struggling for tribal autonomy and for the recognition of broken treaties have also had to confront corporate greed, the modern-day successor to the individual claims of white settlers and farmers in earlier centuries. Government-recognized American Indian lands contain approximately 3 percent of U.S. oil and natural gas reserves, 15 percent of U.S. coal reserves, and 55 percent of U.S. uranium reserves. Often the U.S. government has colluded with business to deprive Indians of their rights to these resources. As Dunbar Ortiz points out:

> Throughout this century, the United States government has promoted the corporate exploitation of Indian lands and resources by making unequal agreements on behalf of Indian peoples and cooperating closely with transnational corporations in identifying strategic resources and land areas.[78]

The Reagan Administration opened up federal reserve lands and shores to manufacturing and mining, even though many of these lands were in treaty-guaranteed territories which American Indians are fighting to regain. Agreements have also involved outside use of American Indian non-renewable water supplies, increasing the desertification of these lands.

In their struggle against this corporate and government land grab, American Indian tribes have had some impressive victories. Ramona Bennett, chair of the Puyallup nation, led its successful struggle for fishing rights in the Pacific Northwest. Bennett was teargassed, threatened with assassination, and shot when seven months pregnant, before a 1974 court ruling awarded her people rights to half of the $200 million annual salmon catch. In a striking 1980 victory, the Passamaquoddy and Penobscot of Maine won 300,000 of the 12 million acres taken from them over 160 years, along with a $27 million trust fund for economic development. In the early 1980s, a coalition of American Indians, environmental groups, and fishers were successful in stopping the construction of a road for lumber-company use through sacred Yurok places; Abby Abinanti (Yurok) was one of the coalition's lawyers.[79] The Shoshone have resisted the construction of an MX-missile base on their lands, while the Sioux have fought a Honeywell plan to test munitions on sacred tribal lands. Norma Kassi, a Swich'in Nation spokesperson and elected member of the Yukon Legislative Assembly, has organized a network of American Indian and Inuit groups to fight proposed oil and gas development in Alaska which would threaten the caribou and hence the livelihood of her tribe.[80] Of course, many other battles have been lost. For instance, a Cherokee lawsuit which tried to stop the Tennessee Valley Authority from building the Tellico Dam (which would flood a Cherokee religious site and kill the rare snail-darter) was dismissed; the dam was approved and opened, without the promised economic and recreational benefits.[81]

American Indian women have led many of these struggles. Indeed, in 1981, about 70 chiefs or chairs of the 482 federally recognized Indian nations were women.[82] Women have also formed organizations of their own, such as Women of All Red Nations (WARN). As Madonna Gilbert, one of its founders, said of the role of women:

> Indian women have had to be strong because of what this colonial-
> ist system has done to our men…alcohol, suicides, car wrecks, the
> whole thing. And after Wounded Knee, while all that persecution
> of the men was going on, the women had to keep things going.[83]

WARN has been especially successful in publicizing reservation conditions such as poor health care, radiation sickness from uranium contamination, and forced sterilization.

Sterilization abuse has been a significant threat to American Indian women. A Government Accounting Office study covering the years 1973 to 1976 at four Indian Health Services hospitals found 3,406 sterilizations performed over three years, few with the federally required consent forms—proportionally, the equivalent of over half a million non-Indian women. In 1978, pressure by Native American groups led to new regulations requiring that women indicate their informed consent before the sterilization proce-dure can take place.[84]

American Indian women have also been active in the struggle to regain control of their children. In 1974, the Association of American Indian Affairs estimated that between 25 and 35 percent of Native American children were still taken away from their parents and put in non-Indian homes or institu-tions, with another 25 percent placed in boarding schools. As a result, less than half of all American Indian children lived with their parents. Sometimes the parents are accused of neglect when they leave their children in the care of extended family members such as grandparents, a common practice in American Indian homes.[85]

Much women's organizing takes place within the American Indian community, as we have seen above. Evelyn Lance Blanchard suggested that American Indian women were less visible in the women's liberation move-ments of the 1970s than were women from other racial-ethnic backgrounds because:

> [T]hey already hold some of the most important positions in their
> society. There are at least 25 tribal chairwomen in our country…the
> importance of their knowledge and strength is acknowledged not
> only by the men, but also by the Indian society.

American Indian women have a role in society that has been defined historically as more important than similar positions occupied by non-Indian women. Tribal identification for American Indian women enhances this definition and solidifies it.[86]

Nevertheless, in the 1980s, American Indian women continued to form pan-Indian women's organizations for self-determination and against sexism. In 1981, the Second Annual Alaska Native Women's Organization Conference hosted 180 women and urged them, among other things, to fight domestic violence, to struggle to regain subsistence fishing rights abrogated by recent laws, and to work for affirmative action in hiring American Indian women. In 1982, 300 women from 101 nations and bands met at the Ohoyo conference in Seattle. Their keynote speaker, Rosita Worl (Tlingit) called for renewed and united efforts against Reagan administration budget cuts, new threats of land loss and termination, and increasing social, economic, and sexual inequality.[87]

Today, many American Indian women community leaders are active in repudiating white-introduced male domination, and calling for a return to the egalitarian sexual relations of the past. Claudeen Bates Arthur, a Navajo attorney, argued at a 1982 conference:

> Our tribal government was developed by the federal people [reflecting] their view of what a tribal council should be. It doesn't take into consideration the clan system that the Navajo were used to; it doesn't take into consideration that Navajo women sat on the war council and made decisions about fighting the enemy....For the most part it leaves women out because that's how white men view you...they didn't let their women have a part...they developed governments that don't have women in them.[88]

The Native American Struggle for Economic Sovereignty

Since the 1950s, the American Indian community has been split; over half of all Native Americans live in urban areas, the rest mainly on tribal reservations. For most, urbanization has not brought integration into the white world or its riches. American Indians compete with other minority groups for the dead-end, low-paying jobs that characterize the secondary labor market, and are kept there by discrimination, poor education, and lack of wealth.

In addition, Native Americans face an insidious and structural form of discrimination in the clash between the white-defined corporate culture of hierarchy and competition, and the American Indian values of working together, sharing, cooperation, and autonomy. Although employment rates and incomes are higher in the cities than on reservations, urban American Indians often feel more impoverished because they are cut off from federal health and other programs and from the support of their extended families, their nations, and their cultures. Many eventually decide to return to their reservations. A BIA study for the years 1953 and 1957 found that a full 30 percent of migrants returned to the reservation in the same fiscal year in which they left; if they had studied how many returned over a more extended period, the figure would have been substantially higher. Those American Indians who return suffer large income losses, but most place a higher value on their cultural identity than on the economic advantages of urban life.[89]

On the other hand, reservation life is economically precarious. For example, 1980 unemployment among Indians was 65 percent in Wyoming and 64 percent in South Dakota, compared to 7 percent and 6 percent for whites. Reservation employment is concentrated in self-employment (subsistence farming, herding, and crafts), work for the BIA (which employs mostly women in clerical and social service work), and work for corporations located on or near the reservations. Consequently, communities vary greatly in their economic well-being. According to the 1980 Census, a few were very well off, such as the Saxman in Alaska, with only 3 percent of the population living below the federally defined poverty line, and the Camp Verde Reservation in Arizona, where poverty was negligible. Indeed, at Camp Verde, 1980 per capita income stood at $11,460, well above the white figure of $8,000. But more often, incomes and employment were much lower than the national average, and communities commonly had poverty rates of 40 percent or more. Among some, like the Winemucca Colony in Nevada, all members were poor.[90]

There are approximately 304 reservations left; about half contain only tribally owned land, while the other half also harbor non-Indian landowners. A BIA study of the labor force status of the 635,000 American Indians living on and adjacent to reservations in January 1989 showed that one-third were unemployed and over one-third of those with jobs earned less than $7,000. To address this situation, tribal governments have been making concerted efforts to promote economic development on the reservations and to develop their own resources, thereby providing economic opportunity for their children so they do not have to relocate to urban areas. Some nations have developed successful enterprises which produce traditional Native American crafts, such as the Zuni's silver and turquoise jewelry and artwork, sold to a growing, white market.[91] The Winyago of Nebraska stopped leasing their productive lands to whites and instead grow corn which they use for food, to feed livestock and for heating and automobile fuel. Others have purchased businesses; for example, the Spokane acquired a cabinet company and relocated it to their reservation.[92]

A central issue for nations has continued to be their relationship to white-owned and -run corporations. Some of the latter have set up plants on reservations to take advantage of their cheap and abundant labor forces. However, white corporations are often more interested in American Indian lands than labor; they lease large quantities of land for mining, oil drilling, cattle-raising, and military uses, but provide little employment for the residents on the lands. Recently, some nations have passed ordinances that force firms that do business on the reservations to hire American Indian labor. As Donna Wilson of the Nez Percé in Idaho explained:

> Initially there was a lot of resistance on the part of the contractors, because we were dealing with a lot of stereotypes. "Your people do not have the skills. They do not come to work after payday. They all drink too much." We spent a good 5 years in public relations efforts with employers and with construction contractors overcoming a lot of these stereotypes, and what really addressed it was the workers themselves.[93]

American Indian Women's Economic Status Today

Whether they live on or off the reservations, American Indian men and women live in difficult times, struggling daily against white control, the threat of cultural extinction, and the challenges posed by poverty. American Indian communities continue to suffer from higher-than-average infant mortality rates, extremely high death rates from preventable diseases such as tuberculosis and gastroenteritis, and devastatingly high alcoholism and suicide rates. In 1980, American Indians were almost twice as likely as whites to be unemployed.[94] Still, American Indians are growing in strength, cultural pride, unity, and militancy. American Indians have survived as a people; today, in the words of Wilcomb Washburn, they are "the only American minority that retains a separate legal status and (more persistently than others) remains aloof from the American melting pot."[95]

Native American women's labor force participation rates rose sharply between 1970 and 1980, from 35 percent to 48 percent. Those who held full-time, year-round jobs earned nearly 89 percent as much as white women—but these jobs were hard to come by. Almost two-thirds of American Indian women held part-time jobs—the highest rate for any racial-ethnic group of women except Chicanas—and American Indian women faced the highest unemployment rate (12 percent) of any racial-ethnic group except Puerto Rican women in 1980.[96]

Native American women have made substantial progress into the more highly paid, masculine jobs in the lower tier of the secondary sector. If we compare the share of a given job held by American Indian women to their share of the overall labor force, we can determine whether they are equitably represented in the job (this fraction, multiplied by 100, is called the relative concentration). For example, if American Indian women made up 1 percent of the labor force, they would need to make up 1 percent of physicians in order to have achieved their fair share of the profession. During the 1970s, American Indian women doubled their relative concentration in protective service and craft jobs and tripled it in transportation operative positions; however, by 1980, they still only held less than one-half of their labor market share of protective service and one-quarter of their labor market share of craft jobs. In the upper tier of the labor market, Indian women tripled their relative concentration in commodities and finance sales, and doubled it in managerial and administrative jobs; by 1980, they held just over one-third their share of commodities and finance and over three-fifths their share of managerial and administrative jobs.

Many American Indian women have attained professional and technical jobs in the public sector, a sector which, in 1980, employed three in every five American Indian women. Indeed, the percent of Native American women in the upper tier of the primary sector more than doubled between 1970 and 1980. However, nearly half of all those who held professional and technical jobs were teachers, librarians, or counselors, and cutbacks in federal, state, and local government spending in these areas during the 1980s no doubt slowed movement into the primary sector.[97]

Despite these gains, nearly three-quarters of American Indian women were employed in the secondary labor market in 1980, compared to two-thirds of European American women and one-third of European American men, as shown in Figure 3-1. Repressive, inaccessible, and inadequate education bears much of the blame for this low occupational status, along with discrimination by employers and fellow employees and the stagnation of the reservation economy. Almost one-quarter of all American Indian women had not completed high school in 1980, compared to 16 percent of white women.[98]

These educational and occupational disadvantages also make it very difficult for American Indian women to support families on their own. In 1980, nearly one in four American Indian families was maintained by a woman (over twice the rate for whites and Asians), and 47 percent of these single-mother families were considered poor by federal poverty guidelines. Among women with children under six, the poverty rate stood at a shocking 82 percent. In 1980, American Indian women were more likely to receive public assistance income than any other group of women except African Americans and Puerto Ricans, but on average, they received only $2,679.[99]

Women's access to income through American Indian men is also limited by discrimination and unemployment. Those men who managed to find full-time jobs earned slightly more than African American and Latino men in 1980, but only three-fourths as much as white men. Moreover, American Indian men have suffered high unemployment (17 percent in

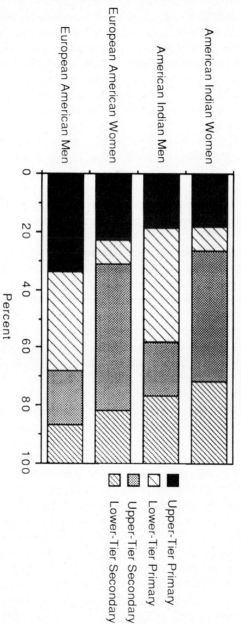

Figure 3-1: The Distribution of American Indian and European American Workers across Labor Market Segments, by Gender, 1980

NOTES: American Indian includes Eskimo and Aleut peoples. See Table 10-5 for a listing of the occupations in each labor market segment. See Table 10-6 for the actual percentages employed in each segment.

SOURCE: 1980 Census; see Appendix A.

1980), the highest rate of part-time work of any racial-ethnic group of men (58 percent), and a high rate of non-participation in the formal labor force (31 percent).[100]

Economic problems on and off the reservation will demand sustained organizing in the years to come. For that work, Native Americans can look to their rich cultural heritage for inspiration and guidance. In recent years, there has been an explosion of American Indian women's literature honoring that heritage and addressing the complex tensions of American Indian life in a white-dominated society. Paula Gunn Allen, Louise Erdrich, Leslie Marmon Silko, Chrystos and others have written eloquent novels and poems, often drawing on their peoples' storytelling traditions.[101] Their work, along with that of American Indian women scholars, continues to re-envision American Indian women's past and present. As Paula Gunn Allen, a Laguna Pueblo and Sioux poet, has said:

> The key is in remembering, in what is chosen for the dream.
> In the silence of recovery we hold
> the rituals of dawn
> now as then.[102]

CHAPTER 4

THE SOUL OF *TIERRA MADRE*

Chicana Women

Don't give in mi prietita
tighten your belt, endure.
Your lineage is ancient,
your roots like those of the mesquite
firmly planted, digging underground
towards that current, the soul of tierra madre—
your origin

—Gloria Anzaldúa, "Don't Give In, Chicanita" [1]

The *tierra madre*, mother earth, has a special place and meaning in the lives of Chicanas, extending back to the time when the U.S. Southwest was part of Mexico and even before, to their Native American ancestors. Chicanas/os were an agricultural and ranching people before they were dispossessed of their lands by Anglos as the aftermath of the Mexican-American War of 1846. Now, joined by Mexican immigrants, they are over-represented among low-paid migrant agricultural workers.

Much of the complex economic history of the Chicana/o people centers on struggles over land and national boundaries. The earliest ancestors of today's Chicanas were members of many different Indian nations who inhabited the lands now known as Mexico and the U.S. Southwest, including the Aztec, Pueblo, and Tlaxcalán. Beginning in the sixteenth century, these indigenous peoples were conquered by Spanish invaders. Sexual relations, many of them forced, between Spanish men and indigenous (and African slave) women soon produced a *mestiza/o* population.[2] Through colonization and settlement, the Spanish extended their territories north. The vast country of Mexico was formed after independence from Spain in 1821, stretching from what we know today as Guatemala up through Texas, California, Arizona, Colorado, New Mexico, and Nevada, and even into parts of Oregon, Utah, and Idaho.

In the early nineteenth century, Anglo settlers from the deep South migrated to Texas, sowing the seeds for a war between Mexico and the United States that eventually led to the annexation of almost half of Mexico's territories in 1848. From then up until the present, Mexican citizens have migrated to the United States in search of work, and many have become U.S. citizens. In 1980, almost two-thirds of the 18 million people of Latin American descent who lived in the United States (including the island of Puerto Rico) traced their origins to Mexico.

As a result of this history, the economics and politics of the U.S. Chicana population are inextricably linked to those of Mexico. The changing border between the two countries, the availability of work on either side of the border, the political currents of the two countries, and the relative difficulty of crossing the border—all have affected Chicanas. Hence, it is necessary to discuss events on both sides of the border in order to understand fully Chicana work experiences. But the history of shifting borders and migration creates many difficulties in terminology. We use the term Chicanas/os to refer to U.S. citizens of Mexican origin and the term Mexican, Mexicana, or Mexicano to refer to citizens of Mexico, including first-generation immigrants to the United States, as well as the first generation of people whose land was taken from Mexico by the United States. We do not use the term "Hispanic" because it reduces a complex, multi-racial and multi-cultural heritage to its European, or more precisely Spanish, component. Finally, we follow the practice of the Chicana/o community and use the word Anglo to refer to English-speaking whites.[3]

Women in Aztec Society

In 1519, when the Spanish conqueror Cortés landed in Mexico, the powerful Aztecs ruled over an empire of 25 million people, including the Tlaxcalán, Huastec, Mixtec, and Zapotec. Aztec society was highly sophisticated, utilizing complex irrigation, astronomy, medicine, and other sciences. It was characterized by a rigid class hierarchy, in which the elite—nobility, priests, and military leaders of both sexes—lived off the labor of the Aztec common people, slaves, and subjugated tribes. According to Chicana researcher Maria Apodaca, those at the bottom of the hierarchy "were required to produce corn, beans, and squash; to weave fine cloth; to mine precious stones for Aztec jewelry; and to build monuments to the Aztec ruling class."[4]

While there appears to have been a rigid sexual division of labor among the Aztecs, women played a number of important social and economic roles. The Aztecs worshipped female as well as male gods—about half of the Aztec calendar is devoted to female goddesses or cults—and women served as priests. Aztec women were also respected as *curanderas* (healers) and *parteras*(midwives), and served alongside warriors as cooks and courtesans. In addition, they worked as artists, seamstresses, textile workers, and marriage brokers. Among the common people, women were engaged in both agricultural and craft labor, as well as domestic work for their families and extended families.[5]

Aztec culture placed great importance on children and family. Women who died in childbirth were accorded the same place in heaven as that set apart for warriors. The *partera* recited a special prayer for these women:

> Awaken then, and arise, my daughter; for it is day, it has dawned…go to that good place that is the home of your father and your mother, the sun; for all who dwell there rejoice and are content and joyful; go to your father the sun, and may your sisters the celestial women carry you there.[6]

Parteras were revered as practitioners of medicinal skill and religious and ceremonial duties, such as a welcoming ceremony for newborn children.

Although some Aztec women held positions of high status, Aztec society also contained numerous practices oppressive to women. Virginity before marriage and fidelity afterwards were demanded of women. Women adulterers were stoned to death, while men were not punished so severely. Nonetheless, women could initiate divorce proceedings and hold property in their own names, and both boys and girls received compulsory education.[7]

The Spanish Conquest

Cortés was able to conquer the Aztec people through a combination of factors: superior Spanish weaponry, the cooperation of tribes who had been subjugated by the Aztecs and saw the Spaniards as liberators, and prophecies in Aztec religion which foretold the return of the god Quezalcoatl at the same time that Cortés arrived. Still, there were fierce battles until 1521, when Cortés finally took Tenochtitlan, ushering in three centuries of Spanish colonial rule.

After plundering Aztec riches, Spaniards used a variety of systems to extract more wealth from the native peoples. When Indians refused to pay tribute to the Spanish crown, the colonizers imposed *encomienda*, a system of forced labor in agriculture and in mines. In the 1540s, this system was replaced by *repartimiento,* a form of indentured servitude. Finally, about 1630, *repartimiento* gave way to the *hacienda* system, which lasted until the revolution of 1910. The *hacienda* was a large estate, similar to the feudal European manor, "given" to a Spanish settler by the crown; most *haciendas* specialized in cattle-raising. Indians living on the lands taken for the *hacien-*

das were displaced and turned into peons, poor and landless people who were allowed small subsistence plots on the *haciendas* in exchange for their labor for the *hacendado (hacienda* owner).[8]

The indigenous peoples were quickly decimated by the many diseases brought by the invaders, including typhus, smallpox, and measles, and by the harsh systems of work imposed upon them. By 1605, after fewer than 100 years of Spanish presence, the native population had declined from 25 million to 1 million. With the decline of the Indian population, Spanish colonizers imported Africans to work as slaves. As Apodaca notes, the thriving economy of Meso-America had come "to a virtual standstill by the middle of the seventeenth century." [9]

The Sexual Exploitation of Indian Women and the Creation of *La Raza*

A key aspect of Spanish domination was forced sexual liaisons between indigenous women and Spanish men. Although a few Spanish women migrated to New Spain, they were greatly outnumbered by Spanish men. Some Indian women were sold or given to the Spaniards as slaves by their tribes, while others were assigned to them by the colonial government to work as domestic servants or field hands. Under these circumstances, rape and sexual exploitation of Indian women by Spanish men were common. Spanish concern at this racial mixing prompted an edict from Cortés requiring that the men who served under him bring their wives from Spain, but this did little to halt the practice. The offspring of Spanish-Indian unions were called *mestizas/os,* mixed peoples. *Mestizas/os* occupied the middle of the racial hierarchy in New Spain, below the pure Spaniards (who were known as *peninsulares*) and above Indians, *castas* (persons of mixed Indian and African descent), and imported African slaves.[10] Although colonization, forced sexual relations, and conversion to Christianity under duress subordinated Indian peoples, these practices also brought about the integration of Indians and Indian practices into Spanish colonial society, creating the Mexican culture. This integration was far greater than in British colonies, as researchers S. Dale McLemore and Ricardo Romo point out:

> The place of the Indians in this society was at the very bottom; nevertheless, they were counted "in" rather than "out"...As a result, by the time Mexico achieved independence in 1821, the culture and population of Mexico was much more "indianized" than was the culture and population of the United States.[11]

The most famous relationship between a Spaniard and an Indian was that between Cortés and La Malinche. Sold into slavery by her own, relatively high-caste Indian people, La Malinche was given to Cortés at the age of 14. Gifted in languages, she served as Cortés's translator as well as his mistress, and bore him a son. While many other Indian women bore *mestiza/o* children during this period, legend points to La Malinche as the mother of the *mestiza* race, and *malinchismo* has come to mean betrayal, particularly selling out to foreigners, in Mexican slang. Chicana feminists have attempted a more positive reconstruction of La Malinche's role, stressing her skills as mediator and translator. They point out that she owed no loyalty to her own people since they had, after all, sold her into slavery—and that, in any event, Indian men as well as Indian women collaborated with the Spaniards.[12]

Women's Works During the Spanish Colonial Period

Women's experiences under Spanish rule were sharply differentiated by race and class. The wife of the *hacendado* had little in common with the subjugated Indian woman, although both were denied political rights. Spanish married women lived pampered lives, cared for by servants but restricted to their homes and subjected to the authority of their husbands. In contrast, the lives of Indian women and *mestizas* were filled with hard labor. In the *encomienda* and *repartimiento* systems of forced labor, the Spaniards relied on Indian men for mining. As a result, Indian women took on a larger share of subsistence agricultural and handicraft production. Chicana/o researchers Alfredo Mirandé and Evangelina Enríquez have written about the effects of these forced labor systems on Indian community and family life:

> The Indian male...suffered European labor demands so taxing that they curtailed and even eclipsed his responsibilities to his family and the Indian community. His former role in sharing in the upbringing of his children was transformed into a peripheral one, given the long work hours demanded of him. The outcome of this role displacement was that in the lower Indian classes the woman's domestic role became multifaceted and required more stoical endurance than ever. The woman's role was especially taxing in rural villages and urban barrios, where Indian populations were most concentrated and where the labor supply was most numerous.[13]

Indian women's work ranged from spinning yarn, weaving cloth, making soap, candles, and shoes, and planting and harvesting crops, to taking these products to market. Once the *hacienda* became the center of agricultural production, Indian women combined domestic work and subsistence production for their families with domestic service and other work for the *hacendado*.

Spanish colonization placed Indian women at the bottom of a hierarchy of race, gender, and class domination. Subordinated to the Spanish,

Indian culture became more patriarchal. Indian women lost their female deities and their roles as priestesses as the Spaniards imposed Christianity. Those who resisted conversion were punished harshly, even killed. The growing *mestiza/o* population also took on the Spanish practice of male domination. According to Apodaca, "The woman of the peasant class was completely subjected to the authority of men—the *hacendado,* the priest, the husband, and at times to the eldest son."[14]

There were few opportunities for women to obtain education in colonial Mexico. Upper-class women received instruction in music, French and embroidery. A few schools admitted *mestizas,* including the Colegio de San Juan Letrán, founded in the late 1530s, but there were no schools for Indian women. Catholic convents provided virtually the only outlet for women with a thirst for knowledge. The convents of New Spain were generally comfortable places rather than austere cloisters, and upper-class women even brought servants with them when they took the veil. Although most convents were reserved for Spanish women or *criollas* (women born in Mexico of Spanish parents), some were designated for Indian women, usually those of noble lineage.

The most famous nun of seventeenth-century Mexico was Sor Juana Inés de la Cruz, a *mestiza* child prodigy who learned to read at three, spoke Latin at 10, and was said to be proficient in theology, mathematics, and history by the age of 17. There was no place for a woman of her talents in Mexican society, so Sor Juana chose to enter the convent to continue her education. Soon, however, her fame spread beyond the convent, bringing her into conflict with the Catholic hierarchy. Perhaps her most famous writing came in the form of exchanges with the archbishop of Puebla, written in defense of women's rights to pursue knowledge and study science. Towards the end of her life, however, Sor Juana lost her battle with the hierarchy and gave up her learned pursuits, devoting herself to work with the poor until she died in an epidemic in 1695.[15]

Spanish Colonization of Northern Mexico

Soon after landing among the Aztecs, the Spaniards began extending their Mexican empire northward into what is now the southwestern United States. By the end of the sixteenth century, they had established many permanent settlements, including Catholic missions (which claimed land and attempted to convert Indians to Christianity and Spanish ways of life), *presidios* (military settlements), and civilian colonies. Spanish settlements in northern Mexico were spread out over a vast area, few and far between relative to the land area and indigenous Indian population. In 1848, native peoples still constituted three-fourths of the population of the region.[16]

The Spanish colonial government worked to attract settlers to these northern regions, drawing many poor *mestizas/os* and Indians from southern Mexico with promises of land, horses, clothing, and food. Colonizing expeditions employed Indians as guides, and Indians and *mestizos* as foot soldiers. Women were encouraged to migrate with their husbands. Although there were a variety of different colonial communities, two of the most important centers of Spanish colonization were New Mexico and California.[17]

The hub of Spanish society in the northern region was New Mexico, particularly Albuquerque and Santa Fe. Santa Fe had been settled in 1598 by Spaniards, *mestizas/os*, and Tlaxcalán Indians, to whom the Spanish had promised land grants in exchange for their help in overthrowing the Aztecs. The settlers faced fierce resistance when they tried to take this territory from the Pueblo Indians. As noted in Chapter 3, the Pueblo drove Spanish settlers out in 1680 with the help of other Indian nations and *mestizas/os*, but Spain reconquered New Mexico in 1693.[18]

Once Spain recaptured the territory, it was parceled out to the church, the military, and civilian settlers. By 1769, Spanish settlers had built 48 missions with forced indigenous labor. Land was granted to civilian settlers according to a racial hierarchy. Spanish settlers, who were known as *los ricos* (the rich ones), received huge land grants, on which they established *haciendas* worked by peons. *Mestizas/os* and Indian settlers, who had been enticed to join the expedition from Mexico with promises of land, mostly received small plots; known as *los pobres* (the poor ones), they eked out precarious existences in subsistence farming or worked as peons on the *haciendas*. The racial hierarchy thus coincided with a class hierarchy.[19]

The presence of greater numbers of women than in the original conquest of central Mexico did not prevent substantial sexual exploitation and formal and informal liaisons with the women of the Pueblo nation. The Pueblo were a matrilineal society in which women controlled land and had many ceremonial duties. Chicana researcher Marta Cotera speculates that "The high status and relative freedom of women which developed in the frontier settlements of New Mexico...may have...been the result of early intermarriage with the Pueblo women by some of the most prominent settlers."[20]

Women in small-landholder or peon families worked as unpaid family laborers in a variety of jobs. As Mirandé and Enríquez point out:

> Adherence to a rigid sexual division of labor, in which the man was responsible for economic production and the woman for bearing and rearing children, was a luxury that could not be maintained in a subsistence economy. Women were actively involved in activities outside the home such as tending grazing herds and butchering and

skinning animals, as well as planting, irrigation, and harvesting crops...Pioneer women performed multiple functions and were frequently knowledgeable about midwifery and plant medicine.[21]

Spanish colonization of California was slowed by the resistance of nomadic nations such as the Apache and Comanche, and the first missions were not established until 1769. All in all, the Spaniards established 21 missions, four presidial towns (San Diego, Santa Barbara, Monterey, and San Francisco), and two civilian settlements (San Jose and Los Angeles). As in New Mexico, settlers included both men and women and were descended from a variety of racial backgrounds. The wives of the founders of Los Angeles, for instance, included two Spaniards, one *mestiza,* two Africans, eight mulattos, and nine Indians.[22]

Although most lands were granted to male settlers, 66 women received land grants in California. Some were even able to maintain these lands after the United States annexed California in 1848. For instance, Juana Briones de Miranda, born in 1796, separated from her husband and procured a land grant in San Francisco on which she built a house and farmed until her death in 1889.[23]

Independence from Spain, the Texas Revolt, and the Mexican-American War

Mexico achieved independence from Spain in 1821 after an 11-year struggle that began with an armed rebellion led by Father Miguel Hidalgo. Many women participated in the Independence War and some died in combat or were executed by the Spaniards. One of the most famous *heroínas* (heroines) of the war was Doña Maria Josefa Ortiz de Domínguez, a wealthy Mexican-born woman of Spanish parentage who was imprisoned for her role in Hidalgo's revolt. When taken into custody, she shouted to the arresting troops, "It would be an honor to shed my blood and give my life before these young men, to teach them how a woman can die in defense for her ideals." (Nevertheless, her wealth and status protected her from execution.) Another *heroína,* Leona Vicario, ran a courier service which kept the lines of communication open among the revolutionaries. In 1813, Vicario sold her jewels and other belongings to build a cannon factory. She, too, was arrested for her rebellious activity.[24]

Twenty-three years after independence, Mexico dismantled the mission system, and the power of the large *hacendados* in northern Mexico increased. The period between 1834 and 1846 has been called the "Golden Age of the ranchos" because land became increasingly concentrated in the hands of a few wealthy ranchers, all of them of Spanish ancestry (or claiming to be). Next in the class hierarchy were *mestiza/o* small ranchers and farmers.

Following them were *mestiza/o* artisans, skilled workers, laborers, and seasonal workers in the cattle industry. Lowest of all were the Indians, the chief source of manual labor.[25]

The new country quickly became engaged in a bitter struggle with Anglo settlers in what we know now as Texas, culminating in the Mexican-American War of 1846. Anglo settlers began arriving in Mexico's northern territories in the early 1800s, granted land first by the Spanish government and later by Mexico, which encouraged migration to the sparsely settled area. Most Anglo settlers came to farm or raise cattle, but starting in 1829, an increasing number brought slaves from the deep South to work cotton plantations. Although there were some landed Mexicans in Texas, by the 1830s, Anglo Texans outnumbered Mexicans by five to one. To discourage slavery and stem further Anglo immigration, Mexico prohibited importation of slaves in 1830. In 1835, Anglo Texans, chafing under these restrictions, began the Texas Revolt to free themselves from Mexican rule. After losses at the Alamo and Goliad, they defeated Mexican forces in 1837 and set up the Lone Star Republic. In 1845, Texas became part of the United States. One researcher documented the transfer of land ownership from Mexicans to Anglos in Nueces County, Texas in the 1800s: "at the beginning of the Texas Revolt in 1835 every foot of land in Nueces County was held under Mexican land grants, two years prior to the Civil War all but one had passed out of Mexican hands, and by 1883 none was held by Mexicans." [26]

The United States had coveted Mexico's northern territories for decades. Both John Quincy Adams and Thomas Jefferson had attempted to purchase Texas from Mexico; gaining Texas in 1845 only whetted the U.S. government's appetite for more. In 1846, President Polk claimed that the Rio Grande was the U.S.-Mexico border and sent troops to protect the border. Mexico countered that the border lay 150 miles north of the Rio Grande, at the Nueces River. The Mexican government saw Polk's incursion as the invasion it was obviously intended to be, arrested some U.S. soldiers, and the Mexican-American War began. The war ended with the Treaty of Guadalupe-Hidalgo in 1848, in which Mexico was forced to give up more than half her territory—including California, New Mexico, Utah, Nevada, Colorado, and Arizona—in exchange for $15 million.[27] In the annexation, the United States acquired lands populated by over 80,000 Spanish-speaking people, most of them *mestiza/o* and *criolla/o*. The quarter of a million Indian peoples in these lands now faced U.S. rather than Mexican efforts to subordinate or exterminate them.[28]

While the language of the Treaty contained protections for Mexican land titles and water rights, the United States government made no attempt to safeguard these rights. Thus the annexation of Mexican territories placed annexed Mexicans in a vulnerable position. As Anglo settlers flooded into the Southwest, they took over the lands and wealth of its Mexican inhabitants, reducing most of the Mexican population in the Southwest to a landless, politically disempowered group.

Some of the *ricos* were able to protect their landholdings by intermarrying with Anglo newcomers. In San Antonio, for instance, marriage records between 1837 and 1860 show that one daughter from almost every *rico* family had married an Anglo. Such marriages were attractive to Anglo men since daughters as well as sons inherited property in Mexican families.[29]

But many other Mexicans, particularly those with smaller landholdings or subsistence plots, lost their lands through a variety of devices familiar to us from the history of American Indians. Anglo domination of the political and judicial systems, along with the use of force and violence, ensured Anglo economic domination. For instance, when floods, drought, or economic downturns made it difficult for Mexican ranchers to pay taxes imposed by the Anglo-controlled government, their lands were quickly sold to Anglos. California passed a law in 1851 that encouraged squatters to take over Mexican lands. Lynching was also a common tool employed by Anglos to terrorize Mexicans into leaving their lands. Some estimate that more Mexicans were lynched between 1850 and 1930 than African Americans during the same period.[30]

The speed of Anglo takeover varied according to the region. In northern California, Mexicans were quickly outnumbered by Anglo settlers during the Gold Rush. As a result, Mexican peons, small farmers, and skilled craftsworkers became wage workers and domestic servants for Anglos. In other parts of the Southwest, including New Mexico, Arizona, and Colorado, the Mexican elite was more firmly in control and far outnumbered Anglos, so the process by which Mexicans were reduced to a landless people took longer. In New Mexico, the *ricos* remained in power throughout the nineteenth century by allying themselves with Anglos. In southern California, in contrast, the arrival of the railroad in the 1870s accelerated the pace of Anglo domination; in Santa Barbara, Mexican ranchers lost their hold on the lands by 1873.[31]

Thus, the military and political process which transformed Mexicans into Chicanas/os, citizens of the United States, also transformed them from a landed to a largely landless people. Mirandé describes the land grab:

> By 1856, a massive change in landownership had been effected. As a result of force, armed conflict, legislative manipulation, and outright purchase much of the land was now in Yankee hands....by the 1870s, Chicanos found themselves at the bottom of the socio-economic order. They thus went from being an elite ranchero class

to being a source of cheap and dependent labor within the working class.[32]

In 1850, over 60 percent of Mexican households owned land valued in excess of $100; by 1860, the share had dropped to 29 percent. One Mexicano who lost his land spoke eloquently of their loss:

> On them [the lands] they have reared themselves homes—they have enclosed and cultivated fields—there they and their children were born—and they lived in peace and comparative plenty. But now— our inheritance is turned to strangers—our houses to aliens. We have drunken our water for money—our wood is sold unto us. Our necks are under persecution—we labor and have no rest.[33]

Mexicans did not endure this loss passively and there was armed resistance, particularly in California and Texas, where "social bandits" such as Joaquín Murieta robbed rich Anglos. Sometimes this social banditry turned into full-scale rebellion: Juan Cortina, a Texas Mexicano from a wealthy land-owning family, put out a pamphlet calling for resistance to the "oppressors of the Mexicans" and organized armed attacks on Anglo landowners in the 1860s.[34]

Even this armed resistance was unable to reverse the Anglo takeover. During the second half of the nineteenth century, the southwestern economy expanded rapidly. Subsistence farming began to give way to huge ranches and cash crops as railroads made it possible for southwestern products to reach eastern markets. Displaced Mexicans found jobs as seasonal agricultural workers, domestic workers, or miners in isolated, company-controlled towns.

This period also saw the birth of the *barrios*, ghettos where Mexicans clustered together, forced by discrimination into crowded, inferior housing. Although the residents of the *barrios* were materially impoverished—few, for instance, had any access to running water or proper sanitation—the *barrios* nonetheless enabled them to maintain their rich Mexican cultural heritage and language.

Mexico under Díaz

In Mexico, meanwhile, conditions were worsening under the brutal 34-year rule of dictator Porfirio Díaz, setting the stage for a revolution and a surge in migration to the United States. By the end of the Díaz regime in 1910, half of Mexico was controlled by 3,000 families and the purchasing power of peasants had fallen to one-fourth of its 1800 level. Díaz so encouraged U.S. capitalists to invest in Mexico that, by 1910, they owned three-fourths of Mexico's mines and half of her oil fields.

Opposition to Díaz was widespread. Indians rebelled in the late 1890s, inspired by a *curandera* named Teresa Urrea, the daughter of a Mexicano rancher and a Yaqui Indian. Although greatly outnumbered by Díaz's forces, Indians in many villages organized armed rebellions, sustained by their faith in Urrea, whom they called "La Santa." Urrea was considered so dangerous that Díaz ordered her deported to the United States in 1892. There she joined many other opponents of the Díaz regime who were publishing journals and organizing support for his overthrow.[35] Díaz was finally ousted by the Revolution of 1910, in which Mexicanas played a number of roles, from financiers to journalists. Two women, Carmen Serdán and Doña Filomena del Valle de Serdán, organized the first group of revolutionaries in the city of Puebla. These two and many others were imprisoned for years. Others fought in battle as *soldaderas* (soldiers) or worked as clerks, smugglers, or telegraphers.

One *soldadera* who fought against Díaz for decades was Juana Belén Gutiérrez de Mendoza, born in Mexico in 1875. Using money she earned by selling her goats, Mendoza founded a newspaper in 1901 that focused on the rights of miners. She was imprisoned in 1902 and 1903, but even in her jail cell she continued to write, along with other radical journalists. Mendoza was deported to Texas, but returned to serve under Emiliano Zapata, an Indian tenant farmer who led an army against Díaz with the goal of repossessing the land from foreigners and wealthy Mexicans. Mendoza rose to the rank of colonel during the Revolution. At the age of 60, she wrote:

> Thirty-five years of incessant struggle and sixty of life will place anyone outside the combat; or at least they serve to justify indifference or veil cowardice…I have that right, but I have no corner to retreat into. In all the corners of the world, an anguish lives…and I don't have the indifference to see, the cowardice to flee, or the meekness to accept it.[36]

In the United States, Chicanas supported the Mexican Revolution by raising funds or participating in political parties which supported the anti-Díaz forces, such as the Partido Liberal Mexicano (PLM). The PLM journal, known as *Regeneración,* often published articles on women's issues. These activists, along with the Mexicana *heroínas* of the Independence War and the many labor activists who fought to organize Mexican women in the twentieth century, were the true foremothers of later Chicana feminists, as Mirandé and Enríquez point out:

> Just as it is commonly assumed that Mexican feminism derived directly from the suffrage movements in the United States and Europe, it is assumed that Chicana feminism is a by-product of Anglo feminism. But a firm basis for the emergence of the contem-

porary Chicana feminist movement was laid during the early part
of the century by Chicanas themselves.[37]

Migration to the United States

Decades of impoverishment under Díaz and the chaos of revolution
uprooted many Mexicans, setting into motion a massive migration to the
United States. During the 1910s, labor shortages created by World War I
pulled between 11,000 and 22,000 migrants out of Mexico each year; by the
1920s, the number had risen to 50,000 every year. Although the U.S. Congress
had passed a number of laws restricting immigration between 1917 and 1924,
these generally exempted Mexicans. In fact, an informal U.S. government
program permitted Mexican workers to enter temporarily during the war
labor shortage. Migration reached its peak in 1930, by which time one-twelfth
of Mexico's population had immigrated to the United States.[38]

Migrants, along with Chicanas/os, found work in the huge "factory
farms" that spread over the fertile river valleys of the Southwest. In the
Imperial and San Joaquin valleys of California, the Salt River valley of Arizona,
and the Rio Grande valley of Texas, Mexican families harvested fruits,
vegetables, and cotton. Mexicans were also important in the sugar beet fields
of Minnesota, Michigan and Colorado. The new migrants faced terrible
hardships in the United States. The work was seasonal, backbreaking, and
so poorly paid that every member of the family had to lend a hand.
Agricultural and mine workers lived in company housing barely fit for human
habitation.[39]

Many Mexican and Chicana/o families worked as tenant farmers,
particularly in Texas. Under this system, landowners could count on a stable
labor force and cash rental income, but for tenants, the system created debt
peonage: unable to pay the rent, tenants were unable to leave the land and
remained virtually permanently indebted to their landlords. The unpaid labor
of women and children was particularly important to the Texas cotton
economy. Landowners preferred tenant families with, as one landowner told
a researcher in 1910, "at least eight children and a wife who worked in the
fields 'like a man.'" Another landowner told the same researcher, "A woman
who can't have a child a year isn't worth her salt." [40]

During the 1920s, as European immigration into the United States
slowed to a trickle, new jobs opened up for Mexicans and Chicanas/os, and
the population became more urban. Most urban workers, other than live-in
domestic servants, lived in *barrios* without electricity or running water. Both
men and women found jobs outside the agricultural and mining sectors of
the economy in manufacturing and services. By 1930, one-third of employed
Mexicanas and Chicanas worked as domestic servants; the share employed

Table 4-1

Occupational Distribution of Chicana Workers, 1930-1980
(in Percent)

	1930	1960	1970	1980
Agriculture	21.2	4.3	4.0	2.9
Manufacturing	24.7	29.1	29.9	26.0
Private Household Service	33.1	11.5	5.5	2.4
Service (not				
Private Household)	3.8	16.5	20.6	20.4
Sales	7.7	8.1	5.7	9.5
Clerical	2.8	21.8	25.9	26.2
Professional & Technical	2.7	5.9	6.4	8.4
Managerial, Administrative,				
& Official	4.1	2.7	1.9	4.2

NOTES: Totals do not always sum to 100 because of rounding. Manufacturing includes craft and transportation workers; agriculture includes mining, fishing, and forestry; managerial, administrative, & official includes some self-employment, and excludes farm managers. For a full listing of occupational categories included, see Appendix B. 1960 data are for "Whites of Spanish Surname in Five Southwestern States" only. For a discussion of comparability problems betwee Census years, see Appendix D.

SOURCES: See Appendix A.

in agriculture, forestry, and mining had fallen to 21 percent; and 25 percent worked in manufacturing, as shown in Table 4-1. Tiny numbers had found better jobs as clerical, professional, or sales workers, but the vast majority were barred from these white-collar occupations.[41]

Wherever Mexicans and Chicanas/os worked, they earned less than Anglos. In 1909, for instance, over 86 percent of Mexicanos and Chicanos working on western railroads earned less than $1.25 a day, compared to just over 10 percent of Anglos. In 1902, one study of a shirt and overalls factory found that Anglo women made $10-$14 per week, while Mexicanas and Chicanas averaged $9 or less. Mexicanas and Chicanas formed the backbone of the children's garment industry in Texas. According to Chicana researcher Rosalinda González, the women were highly skilled but shockingly underpaid. Their work consisted of:

> ...exquisite, delicate handwork on tiny infants' and children's clothing and on handkerchiefs, including embroidery...It took, for example, 12 hours of steady and concentrated work for a woman to finish one garment for which she received forty-two cents. These exquisite little dresses were then sold back east at eight dollars a piece.[42]

Mexicans and Chicanas/os worked in more arduous jobs than did Anglo women. For instance, the women were assigned the hard physical labor of chopping vegetables for canning, while Anglo women packed cans.

Depression, Deportation, and Resistance

In 1930, as the Great Depression began, approximately 640,000 Mexicans and 1.4 million Chicanas/os resided in the United States. The Depression was a terrible time for all people of Mexican origin, who faced stiff competition for scarce jobs. For instance, in 1930, only 28 percent of Mexican families were able to find employment for two or more gainful workers compared to 39 percent of all foreign-born white families.[43]

The Mexican and Chicana/o community faced a double challenge of joblessness and rising racism. Whites blamed growing unemployment on competition from foreign workers and organized to stop immigration from Mexico. In 1929, Congress passed a law making it a felony to enter the United States illegally and created the Border Patrol to enforce the new law. The effects of this legislation were as far-reaching as those of the Treaty of Guadalupe-Hidalgo 81 years earlier. As Mirandé notes, "During the decade Mexican migrants were transformed from being migratory workers who crossed an arbitrary demarcation with impunity to becoming criminal or illegal entrants into an area that was previously Mexican land."[44] While the law did not stop immigration, it created a new kind of entrepreneur, the "coyote," who transported undocumented workers across the border for a profit, further reducing the resources of poor migrants.[45]

But making immigration illegal was not enough to stem the tide of anti-Mexican hysteria which spread across the United States as unemployment continued to rise. White nativists organized to deport Mexicans living and working in the United States. Los Angeles county argued, for example, that it would be far cheaper to deport a trainload of Mexicans ($77,800) than keep them on welfare ($271,000). Social workers and caseworkers at relief agencies harassed and coerced both Chicanas/os and Mexicans to "return" to Mexico with their families. By the mid-1930s, the government had deported as many as one-third to one-half million persons of Mexican origin, including tens of thousands who were actually U.S. citizens, rounding them up like cattle and shipping them by trainload or truckload across the border. The deportations opened up jobs at the bottom of the hierarchy for Anglos. By the end of the decade, Anglo workers and their families had replaced many Mexican and Chicana/o field workers in California.[46]

Widespread unemployment, deportation, and anti-Mexican racism gave birth to a vibrant resistance movement, much of it based in organized labor. The militant Cannery and Agricultural Workers Industrial Union

(CAWIU) led the Great Strikes of California, involving thousands of Mexican and Chicana/o (as well as Filipina/o and Anglo) agricultural and cannery workers throughout the 1930s. The union's demands included wage increases, an eight-hour day, overtime pay, abolition of piecework and child labor, and equal pay for women workers.[47]

One of the most famous strikes took place in 1930 against the Southern Pecan Shelling Company, the largest employer in San Antonio, Texas. Most pecan companies had mechanized operations except Southern Pecan, which relied on:

> ...hand shelling, intense exploitation of Mexican family labor, and take-home work. The pecan-shelling families suffered the abuses of a contracting system whereby the company paid contractors who often pocketed the wages of the laborers they employed. The people worked under primitive and unhealthful conditions, with as many as 100 persons packed into a twenty-five-by-forty foot room, no toilets or running water, and wages that fell as low as $1.29 per week for a 34.8-hour week.[48]

Thousands of workers struck at over 130 plants to protest a wage reduction of one cent per pound. Mexicanas and Chicanas who picketed were gassed, arrested, and packed into jail cells—over 30 women were forced into a cell made for six. The workers won their demands, although in subsequent years the company mechanized operations, and employment fell from 10,000 workers in 1938 to 350 in 1950.[49]

Many in the leadership of this strike were experienced activists, including Luisa Moreno, a Central-American-born communist who had mobilized Latinas against police brutality in New York City in the early-1930s and organized the first National Congress of Spanish-Speaking People in 1938. Moreno worked for the United Cannery, Agricultural, Packing and Allied Workers of America (UCAPAWA), one of the few unions to welcome Mexican immigrant workers. Besides the pecan shellers, Moreno organized cotton workers in South Texas, beet workers in Colorado and Michigan, and 60,000 cannery workers in California before she was deported to Mexico during the anti-communist McCarthy era of the 1950s.[50]

Some inter-racial organizing survived the nativism and racism of the Depression era. In 1930, as unemployment began to rise, a national organization was formed to fight for the rights of unemployed people across the country. Local chapters, known as Unemployed Councils, marched and demonstrated for better relief benefits, equal unemployment benefits for men and women, free medical care for pregnant unemployed women, free housing for the homeless, and an end to evictions. Although most members of Unemployed Councils were white, people of color also participated, including Matilda Molina Tolly, who led the Chicana/o council in Los Angeles:

> We would move the furniture and people's belongings back into the houses emptied by the eviction notices. The landlords had a hard time, since it cost them $30 for a notice after the third time. After three attempts, the landlord had to stop. When relief was cut in the Chicano community, we had a big black casket, symbolic of what would eventually happen to these workers. This we displayed for several days until the relief was restored.[51]

Another instance of inter-racial organizing occurred in Texas, where Chicanas helped organize the International Ladies Garment Workers' Union in an industry that was one-third Chicana. The leadership of the union, however, remained predominantly Anglo.[52]

World War II and the Bracero Program

The labor shortages of World War II provided new opportunities for Mexican migrants, who were admitted into the United States under the Bracero Program (*bracero* means manual worker). The program, which lasted from 1942-1964, provided Mexicans with temporary work visas. In the early years, the majority of migrants were men who sought jobs as miners, railroad workers, and fieldworkers. However, most could only find work in California agribusiness or as fieldworkers in other states.[53]

The Bracero Program institutionalized the role of Mexican workers as a reserve army of labor. They were available to be drawn into the labor force at low wages whenever shortages threatened to cause wages to rise, but were always vulnerable to expulsion when the economy contracted or when other sources of cheap labor appeared. Even though the program was allegedly enacted to ease war-time labor shortages, growers and other employers obtained renewal of the program for decades thereafter. Although the Mexican government attempted to negotiate some protections for its workers, such as minimum wages, guaranteed round-trip transportation, and anti-discrimination provisions, employers often ignored these rules.[54] A U.S. Department of Labor employee who supervised the Bracero Program between 1959 and 1964 called it "legalized slavery, nothing but a way for big corporate farms to get a cheap labor supply from Mexico under government sponsorship....The braceros were hauled around like cattle in Mexico and treated like prisoners in the United States."[55] According to Rosalinda González, the program:

> ...created millions [of dollars] in profits for large growers and facilitated their corporate consolidation, and allowed the Mexican government to alleviate its chronic unemployment by shipping

thousands of poor braceros to be exploited at higher wages than they would have received in Mexico—if they could have found jobs—but much lower wages than American workers would be paid.[56]

Lured by the promise of better jobs, migrants—both legal and undocumented—streamed into the United States to take jobs in agribusiness, garment factories, and domestic work. Between 1942 and 1947 alone, over 200,000 temporary workers came in under the program. For every *bracero* entering under a legal work permit, at least four more came in without permits. Although these workers were referred to as "illegals," Chicana/o activists countered that it was Anglos who did not have legal status in the Southwest, since they had taken the land from Mexico through force and trickery. Anglo labor activist Frank Bardacke points out, "From World War II to 1965, labor unrest was controlled through the Bracero program; [those] causing trouble or expressing union sympathies had their contracts cancelled and were sent back to Mexico."[57]

Growers and other employers in search of cheap labor welcomed the migrants, but Anglo workers did not. In 1943, Anglo soldiers, sailors, and police rampaged through the *barrio* of East Los Angeles, attacking Mexicans, Chicanas/os, Filipinas/os and African Americans in what came to be known as the Zoot Suit Riots ("Zoot suit" was a term describing the style of dress adopted by Mexican and Chicano men).[58]

The war years produced several shifts in the Chicana/o and U.S. Mexican population.[59] Many left Texas for California, and the population became increasingly more urban. Women continued their move from the fields into garment factories throughout the Southwest. The Census did not provide detailed occupational data for Chicanas/os in 1940, but a comparison of the 1930 and 1950 data shows the magnitude of these shifts. For instance, the share of employed southwestern Chicanas working on farms dropped from 21 percent in 1930 to 6 percent in 1950, while the percentage in white-collar work doubled.[60]

Struggles and Setbacks in the 1950s

Although the Bracero Program continued to provide temporary jobs throughout the 1950s, the pace of illegal immigration picked up and new pressures arose to expel Mexicans. These pressures combined with anti-communist sentiment to produce another wave of mass deportations similar to those of the 1930s. During the so-called "Operation Wetback" of the 1950s, many Chicana activists were deported, along with millions of other Chicanas/os and Mexicans.[61]

Despite the deportation of many workers and activists, union organizing continued. Gregoria Montalbe and Sophia Gonzales led an important strike against the garment manufacturer Tex-Son, overcoming both company resistance and police brutality. Women's leadership was also crucial to the victories gained by workers in the 1951 Silver Zinc Mine strike outside Silver City, New Mexico. In their attempt to stop the strike, mine owners obtained a court injunction under the anti-union Taft Hartley Act, barring the miners from walking the picket line. In response, the strikers' wives and daughters maintained the line to prevent scab workers from entering the mines, and as a result, left their housework to be done by their husbands and fathers.

The Silver Zinc Mine strike was made famous by the movie, *Salt of the Earth*, which was produced and directed by members of the Hollywood Ten, a group of Anglo writers, actors, and directors who had been blacklisted and driven out of movie-making by anti-communist hysteria.[62] After its release, the film was banned as subversive. The director, Herbert Biberman, chose to film the story using as many actual strikers as possible, including the male lead, Juan Chacón. Rosaura Revueltas, who played the female lead, was a renowned Mexicana actress. She was arrested and deported in 1953 for her "subversive" activities, and Biberman was forced to finish the film without her. In the film, the character played by Revueltas expresses the feminist consciousness that developed among the women when she asks her husband:

> Have you learned nothing from this strike? Why are you afraid to have me at your side? Do you still think you can have dignity only if I have none? The Anglo bosses look down on you, and you hate them for it. "Stay in your place, you dirty Mexican"—that's what they tell you. But why must you say to me, "Stay in your place?" Do you feel better having someone lower than you?...Whose neck shall I stand on, to make me feel superior? And what will I get out of it? I don't want anything lower than I am. I'm low enough already. I want to rise. And push everything up with me as I go...And if you can't understand this, you're a fool—because you can't win this strike without me! You can't win anything without me![63]

Chicano historian Rodolfo Acuña notes that the 1950s also brought the menace of "urban removal" to Mexican communities across the country as developers displaced hundreds of thousands of people of color in order to build freeways, businesses, and public buildings. In Los Angeles, for example, the San Bernadino, Santa Ana, Long Beach, and Pomona freeways were all built through the *barrios*. The people of Chávez Ravine, a Mexican neighborhood in Los Angeles, had to be forcibly removed when their neighborhood was handed over to Walter O'Malley, the owner of the

Dodgers baseball team, for development. Mexican neighborhoods in Detroit, Chicago, and other cities suffered a similar fate.[64]

Migration to the cities intensified in the years following World War II, transforming the employment patterns of Chicanas/os. The share of Chicanas in the labor force rose from 22 percent in 1950 to 29 percent in 1960. As Table 4-1 shows, employment in domestic service dropped to one in eight Chicana workers. Chicanas began to break into clerical work, which employed more than one in six by 1960 (compared to one in three Anglo women). The share in manufacturing also rose to over one-third. However, few inroads were made into managerial and professional jobs.[65]

Brown Power in the 1960s

By 1960, the overwhelming majority of persons of Mexican origin residing in the United States were citizens by birth. Eighty-five percent of Mexicans and Chicanas/os were concentrated in the Southwest, and rural-urban migration continued so that, by 1960, the majority lived in cities.[66]

Mexicans continued to cross the border into the United States in search of work, even after the U.S. government terminated the Bracero Program in 1964. The program was terminated partly because the demand for farm labor had fallen and partly because growers feared militancy among Mexican workers. During the mid-1970s, growers increasingly turned to Asian workers, who were seen as less rebellious than Mexicans, seeking out Vietnamese, Koreans, and Cambodians.[67]

In the 1960s, Chicanas continued to increase their participation in the labor force and make some progress up the occupational distribution. As shown in Table 4-1, the share employed in private household service fell by half, continuing the decline in this occupation that had begun in 1930. The shares in manufacturing, other service, clerical, and professional and technical work all rose. Proportionately fewer Chicanas were employed in managerial, administrative, and official work by the end of the decade; although the 1960 Census provides very little detail on the work in these categories, it is likely that these categories declined as self-employment in small establishments such as boarding houses and retail shops gave way to work for others. Cotera points out that the federal government's Great Society programs helped to pry open the doors to professional and managerial work. She also observes:

> In this catalyst role, especially in the area of education, there were many Chicanas who played dual roles as government personnel developing new programs, and as community advocates who incorporated their sensitivity and knowledge into useful govern-

ment information and program efforts to benefit the Chicano community.[68]

For instance, Lupe Anguiano, a program officer with the Department of
Health, Education, and Welfare, had been involved for decades in community work and used her influence to procure funds and contacts for community groups throughout the United States. She also organized the Spanish
Speaking Women's National Consultation in 1972.[69]

By the late 1960s, Chicana/o activism—like African American and
American Indian activism—was at a peak. Between 1968 and 1970, Chi-
cana/o students organized school walkouts in Los Angeles and Crystal City,
Texas to protest the racist curriculum and teaching, as well as the absence of
Chicana/o teachers. They also objected to Anglo political control of Crystal
City, where 80 percent of the population was Chicana/o. The school boycott
mobilized Chicanas/os to found *El Partido de la Raza Unida* (the Party of
the United Race), a political party that achieved control in many local
elections in South Texas, including Crystal City.[70]

College students across the Southwest took up the banner of the
Chicana/o Student Movement. One slogan, "Of the Community, for the
Community," expressed the movement's concern with the entire range of
community issues. In addition, student pressure led to the establishment of
Chicana/o Studies Programs in several California and New Mexico universi-
ties.[71]

The Chicana/o movement was an important source of Chicana feminism. Chicanas found opportunities for activism and leadership in the
movement, but also encountered sexist behavior and assumptions there.
Chicana feminist Sylvia Gonzales describes some of the problems faced by
the Chicana activist:

> Along with her male counterpart, she attended meetings, organized
> boycotts, did everything asked of her for "El Movimiento." But if
> she [stepped beyond her traditional role and assumed leadership],
> she was met with the same questioning of her femininity which the
> culture dictates when a woman is not self-sacrificing and seeks to
> fulfill her own needs....The Chicano movement seemed to demand
> self-actualization for only the male members of the group.[72]

Chicana feminists were accused of splitting the movement and of repudiating
la raza. Chicanos argued that it was inappropriate and dangerous for
Chicanas to utilize concepts like women's liberation, sexism, and male
chauvinism, because these terms had originated in the Anglo women's
movement, were imbued with Anglo individualism, and were antithetical to
Chicana/o culture and traditions. And indeed, the Anglo women's movement
was insensitive to the concerns of women of color. Nevertheless, Chicanas

persisted in their own feminist organizing, both within Chicana/o organizations and within separate Chicana groups and conferences.[73]

At the same time as Chicanas were active in the student movement, electoral parties, and the Chicana feminist movement, organizing continued among poor Chicanas. Chicanas participated actively in the National Welfare Rights Movement of the late 1960s, which demanded higher benefits and an end to humiliating and restrictive requirements for women on welfare. In 1967, Alicia Escalante founded the East Los Angeles Welfare Rights Organization, as well as a separate organization, the Chicano National Welfare Rights Organization, to represent the interests of Chicana welfare recipients. Communities Organized for Public Service (COPS) was established in the early 1970s in San Antonio, Texas to represent poor Chicanas and Chicanos. A church-based organizing project, COPS began by demanding that the city enclose drainage ditches in the *barrios*, charging that frequent flooding and drownings there had gone unheeded by the city government for decades. Between 1973 and 1988, COPS elected five Chicana presidents (only one president was male during that time), and was responsible for passage of an alternative economic development plan for the city and the election of Henry Cisneros, San Antonio's first Chicano mayor.[74]

Chicana/o political activity during the 1960s and 1970s also drew attention to the plight of migrant farm workers. Jessie Lopez De La Cruz, a farm worker who became active in union organizing efforts, describes the work in the fields:

> ...we would pick grapes. The sun is very hot. It gets up to about a hundred-eight, a hundred-ten degrees during the summer out in the fields....The hardest work we did was thinning beets [with a] short-handled hoe....You walk down the rows stooped over. You have to work hard, fast, as fast as you can because you were paid by the row, not by the hour....Out in the fields there were never any restrooms. We had to go eight or ten hours without relief. If there wasn't brush or a little ditch, we were forced to wait until we got home! Just the women. The men didn't need to pull their clothes down.[75]

Together with Jessie Lopez, Dolores Huerta and César Chávez organized Mexican farm workers throughout the Southwest into the United Farm Workers (UFW), merging two unions that had represented only Filipina/o or Chicana/o workers. The UFW, an integral part of the rising tide of Chicana/o activism of the late 1960s and early 1970s, achieved extraordinary contract gains in pay and benefits. In addition, the UFW was instrumental in passing laws which had an enormous impact on working conditions for California farm workers, including regulations governing occupational safety and pesticide use. The UFW employed many innovative techniques, such as

hunger strikes and a national consumer grape boycott, to challenge successfully the firmly entrenched power of California's growers.

La familia chicana

In their feminist organizing and writing, Chicanas had the difficult task
of both supporting the Chicana/o family as vital to Chicana/o culture,
community, and economic survival, and criticizing it when it was oppressive
to women. To do this, they had to enter into an already ongoing and heated
debate. Indeed, more sociological and psychological studies have addressed
la familia than perhaps any other aspect of Chicana/o life.

Starting in the 1940s, social scientists had identified the Chicana/o
family as characterized by a macho father who dominated his wife, refusing
to share decision-making or household chores. These researchers—both
Anglo and Chicana/o—agreed that the roots of this "pathological" family
were to be found in Mexican culture. In response, Chicana/o social scientists
developed a literature which lauded *la familia* as the inspiration and strength
of the Chicana/o community, and criticized the racism inherent in the earlier
literature. These writers stressed the solidarity of extended families and the
importance of large families to Chicana/o culture.[76]

Chicana feminist scholars, such as Maxine Baca Zinn and Lea Ybarra,
have further developed an analysis of *la familia* from a Chicana/o perspective. Zinn argues that "the ideology of cultural differences has created an
image of the Mexican-American family as a deviant social form."[77] To get
beyond racist stereotypes, these researchers are studying the actual power
dynamics and decision-making processes within married-couple Chicana/o
families. They use their research to show that Chicana/o families are substantially more egalitarian than previously thought, sharing decision-making and
household chores much the same way as Anglo families of similar class and
educational backgrounds. Male dominance exists in both cultures and the
degree to which it influences family life depends on a variety of other social
factors, including wives' labor force participation and education. Lea Ybarra
concludes:

> Machismo, if defined as male domination, does exist in Mexican
> and Chicano societies, but as in all societies, it exists in varying
> degrees in some family structures and not at all in others. A problem
> in the previous study of Chicano families, however, is that ma-
> chismo has been seen as the basis for all familial relationships and
> has been utilized as a monocausal explanation for understanding
> family structure. For example, if familial structure was traditional
> and patriarchal, then it was considered to be only because of
> machismo; if it exhibited shared authority, then it was considered

to be only because of acculturation into Anglo American society and thus movement away from machismo.[78]

Today, Chicana feminists work on many family-related issues—such as domestic violence, housing, rape, and day care—where they fight against a complex interplay of racial-ethnic, class, and gender oppression. Forced sterilization has also been an important issue for Chicana activists, who point to the many cases in which Chicanas' rights have been abused by doctors and hospital administrators. In one instance, Los Angeles County Hospital performed numerous sterilizations in the early-1970s without appropriate consent, often on women with poor English-language skills who were not advised of the risks or the irreversibility of the operation.[79]

Chicanas in Today's Economy

In the 1970s and 1980s, Chicana labor force participation rates continued to grow. In 1985, over half were in the labor force. Relative to Anglo women and men, however, Chicanas still remained overconcentrated in low-paid, seasonal jobs, and suffered high poverty rates.[80]

In 1980, only 11 percent of employed Chicanas, and 12 percent of Chicanos, held professional and managerial jobs in the top tier of the primary labor market—the lowest shares of any racial-ethnic group. Figure 4-1 compares these shares to those for European American men and women. The relatively low representation of Chicanas and Chicanos in the primary sector is tied both to low educational attainment and to discrimination in the labor market. Nearly one-half of Mexicana and Chicana workers in the Southwest had eight or fewer years of schooling in 1980, compared to 10 percent and 19 percent of Anglo women and African American women, respectively; less than 4 percent held college degrees, compared to 17 percent and 10 percent for Anglo and African American women. Over 15 percent of Chicanas/os are illiterate by the standard measure (completion of less than five years of schooling), but studies of functional illiteracy in 1975 and 1982 suggested much higher rates—perhaps as high as 56 percent.[81]

This lack of formal schooling is partly the legacy of decades of child labor and disruption of schooling by migration. One woman from El Paso, Texas, describes working as a child:

> My mother used to have three jobs: at Neward Hospital, at night, and at Lev's. After school I worked at Newberry's, babysitting, and as a maid when I was nine. With three young children and myself, I had to help my mother. It was a hard childhood. I didn't have a father. My mother had to work day and night. I told her to let me work for her at the Neward Hospital—so I cleaned the beds and floors.[82]

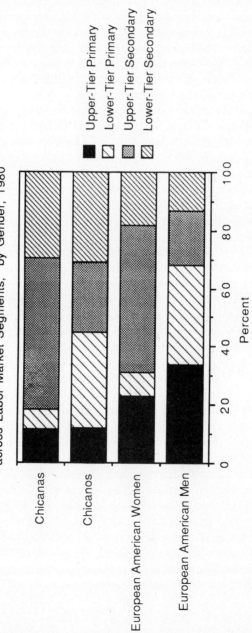

Figure 4-1: The Distribution of Chicana/o and European American Workers across Labor Market Segments, by Gender, 1980

- ■ Upper-Tier Primary
- ▨ Lower-Tier Primary
- ▨ Upper-Tier Secondary
- ▨ Lower-Tier Secondary

NOTES: See Table 10-5 for a listing of the occupations in each labor market segment. See Table 10-6 for the actual percentages employed in each segment.

SOURCE: 1980 Census; see Appendix A.

Racist instruction and discrimination in the schools also have driven many Chicana/o students away from higher education. Anglo teachers often ridiculed them for speaking Spanish and tracked them into vocational education rather than college-preparatory courses. In California, bilingual teachers reached less than 25 percent of the students requiring bilingual education in 1985, yet federal funding for bilingual education was a major target for Reagan administration budget cutters. Instead of appropriating the needed funding, many states have passed laws declaring English the official state language. Hence, the educational gap between Chicanas/os and the rest of the population may worsen in the future.[83]

Chicanas have made some progress into lower-tier, primary jobs that require less formal education, and their share of such jobs is close to that of Anglo women. The share of employed Chicanas in lower-tier, primary jobs grew from 4 percent in 1970 to 7 percent in 1980, compared to 8 percent of Anglo women in 1980. Chicanas were particularly well-represented in the crafts, and achieved one-third their labor market share, the highest relative concentration of any racial-ethnic group of women.[84]

Four-fifths of employed Chicanas held secondary labor market jobs in 1980. They remained overly concentrated in blue-collar, service, and farm work compared to Anglo women, and few held supervisory or skilled jobs in these areas. In 1980, over one-fourth held blue-collar jobs, compared to only 8 percent of Anglo women. Chicana social scientist Vicki Ruiz also points out that "23 percent of Chicano factory employees held skilled or supervisory jobs [compared to] only 4 percent of their Chicana co-workers." [85]

Over the years, fewer and fewer Chicanas, like Anglo and African American women, have been employed in domestic service. Domestic service was the most common form of employment outside the home for Chicanas and Mexicanas during the first half of the twentieth century, but by 1980, less than 3 percent were private household workers. However, one 1985 study of El Paso, Texas pointed out that only a very small share of domestic workers is counted by the Census, since the vast majority are Mexican women who cross over daily from Ciudad Juarez with work permits or as undocumented workers.[86]

The study estimated that more than 10 percent of El Paso's households used domestic workers, who earned an average of $15 a day for cleaning services—translating to an hourly wage of between $1.88 and $2.50. This was far below the minimum wage of $3.35, even though domestic servants are technically covered under minimum wage legislation. Very few employers made the required Social Security contributions on behalf of their servants. Working conditions varied widely, depending upon the mood and character of the employer, but some employers were abusive:

When Maria Christina Carlos left her job in a private home to work
in a tortilla factory, her employer refused to pay her for her final
two weeks' work. Adding insult to injury, the patrona then spread
the rumor that her maid had robbed her. With rising indignation,
Señora Carlos demanded, "But just who had robbed who?" [87]

Chicana and Mexican women face other serious problems in the labor
market, including high unemployment, overconcentration in seasonal jobs,
and a low rate of unionization. Since more than one-quarter held blue-collar
manufacturing jobs, they were especially hard-hit by the decline in U.S.
manufacturing employment in the 1980s. In 1980, 10 percent of Chicanas
were unemployed, compared to only 6 percent of Anglo women. Difficulty
finding any job at all pressures Chicanas to accept seasonal work. Ruiz points
out that this:

> ...limits their earning power, and equally importantly, prevents
> them from accumulating the seniority necessary for promotion to
> higher paying supervisory posts. The seniority situation for many
> Mexicana/Chicana workers is so poor that often they must compete
> with new applicants to retain their positions for the following
> season...employers can simply deny future jobs to activist
> women. [88]

Latinas are less likely to be represented by unions than African American women or Anglo, African American, or Latino men. (The Labor Department does not present union membership data by country of origin, so it is
impossible to obtain precise data on Chicana/o unionization.) The shares
represented by unions in 1988 were 14 percent for Latinas, compared to 20
percent for Latinos, 23 percent for African American women, 22 percent for
Anglo men, and 29 percent for African American men. Racism and sexism
within the unions themselves are partly to blame, as Ruiz argues:

> Although Mexican women [and Chicanas] have on occasion effec-
> tively controlled union locals, the degree of their rank and file
> participation has depended mostly on the attitudes of labor profes-
> sionals. Officials of conventional trade unions, purportedly acting
> on behalf of their constituencies, have many times reinforced ethnic
> and gender discrimination. They have often perceived Mexican
> women workers [and Chicanas] in one of two ways: as members to
> be ignored or as objects to be manipulated. [89]

Many union-hired business agents, such as those working in California
canneries, are male Anglos, even though the majority of workers are Chicanas
and Mexicanas. One exception to this rule is the United Farm Workers, under
Chicana/o and Filipina/o leadership, who have always relied on "involvement of family members in union affairs." In the UFW, Mexicanas and

Chicanas "run the service center, health clinic, *huelga* [strike] school, day nursery, and legal department."[90]

Although labor organizing during the 1970s and 1980s has been blocked by many obstacles, for Chicanas as well as for other racial-ethnic groups, the history of Mexicana and Chicana participation in labor struggles demonstrates that they will fight militantly for their right to unionize. For instance, in 1972, 4,000 garment workers in El Paso, Texas, 80 percent of them Chicanas, began a strike against Farah, a fiercely anti-union employer. After two years, the workers won the right to be represented by the Amalgamated Clothing Workers of America, triumphing over police dogs, strikebreakers, violence, and press silence. Along with their Chicano brothers, Chicanas have also participated actively in attempts to block plant closings and stop layoffs. Jessie Téllez led a ladies auxiliary which toured the Southwest in order to gather support for Chicano miners who struck the Phelps-Dodge company in 1983. However, these efforts and countless others were unable to prevent widespread joblessness among blue-collar Chicanas/os.[91]

One of the most important recent episodes in Chicana labor history took place in Watsonville, California, the "Frozen Food Capital of the World," where 1,000 workers, predominantly Chicanas, struck for 18 months between 1985 and 1987. In a nearly unprecedented show of unity, not one striker ever crossed the picket line, even though the strikers ran out of unemployment benefits and only a few collected welfare or food stamps. Families—40 percent of them maintained by a single mother—survived on weekly strike benefits of $55, food banks, and the generosity of relatives and friends. The entire Chicana/o community helped the strikers:

> Churches, school teachers, some small businesses and landlords provided food and material necessities, as well as an atmosphere of solidarity. Many people were allowed to delay rent payments, others bought on credit at small grocery stores, and many merchants refused to cash scab checks. So many turkeys were donated by the community in the 1985 Thanksgiving turkey drive that the food committee had enough…left over to serve turkey enchiladas at strike events months later.[92]

The workers defeated Watsonville Canning's attempt to break their union and even gained a concession from the company by defying their Teamster union bureaucrats and extending the strike for four more days.

The Watsonville strike illustrates the particular economic vulnerability of Chicana single mothers. Because of their low wages and high risk of unemployment and deportation, Chicana/o families have often sent more than one worker into the labor force. But Chicana single-mother families cannot rely on additional labor and thus are very likely to be poor. In 1960, less than 4 percent of Chicana/o families were maintained by a woman; by 1985, the figure had soared to nearly 19 percent. Over 50 percent of families with children under 18 that were headed by Chicanas fell below the official poverty line in 1980—approximately the same percentage as African American and American Indian families.[93]

High unemployment, low educational attainment, segregation in the secondary labor market, and obstacles to union organizing have combined to keep incomes low and poverty rates high for Chicanas and Chicanos. Comparisons of median incomes for full-time workers show that across the Southwest, Mexicanas and Chicanas had incomes equal to only 40 percent of Anglo men; for Mexicanos and Chicanos, the figure was 60 percent. In Texas and California, where most Mexicanas and Chicanas live, their incomes are even lower than those of American Indian or African American women, ranking at the very bottom of the racial-ethnic income scale. The situation appears to be worsening as blue-collar jobs disappear and the number of single-mother families rises: between 1978 and 1987, the poverty rate in the Chicana/o community rose from 21 percent to 28 percent.[94]

A Community in Flux: Undocumented Workers

Shifts in borders and in populations across borders have been major themes of Chicana economic history. The connection with Mexico continues to be active, maintained by a shared cultural tradition and lived out in migratory movements. Between 1971 and 1986, over a million Mexicans immigrated legally to the United States, more than from any other country.[95]

Along with these documented arrivals, many more undocumented workers have come without work permits. Although it is, of course, difficult to obtain information on undocumented workers, their number has been estimated at between 6 and 12 million. Studies in the late 1970s showed that most Mexican migrants were male (as many as 90 percent), over half were bachelors and between the ages of 18 and 25, and most stayed in the United States for only a few months, "sojourning" in order to earn wages substantially higher than they could earn in Mexico. In the 1970s, most worked in agriculture, but most recently, undocumented workers are finding jobs in services and manufacturing, and the share of women is rising.[96]

Echoing earlier exclusionary legislation, Congress reacted to the presence of these undocumented workers by passing the Immigration Reform and Control Act of 1986 (IRCA), which granted legal status ("amnesty") to over 3 million immigrants currently in the United States and imposed fines on employers who hire undocumented workers. The law was supposed to halt further immigration by dampening job prospects, but by all accounts, the absolute number of undocumented workers has grown in the 1980s, despite vigorous attempts by the Immigration and Naturalization Service (INS). The INS, known to Chicanas/os and Mexicans as *la migra*, apprehended nearly one million undocumented workers in 1988, over 90 percent of them from Mexico.[97]

In March 1990, the General Accounting Office released a report charging that employer sanctions under IRCA had led to widespread harassment of and discrimination against Latina/o workers, including Chicanas/os, who are routinely asked to prove their citizenship when applying for jobs or government benefits. Led by organizations such as the Mexican American Legal Defense Fund (MALDEF), the entire Latina/o community is protesting these discriminatory practices, which are expressly forbidden by IRCA but are nonetheless quite common. Jose Medina, an attorney with a Latino/a workers' rights group in San Francisco, argues that IRCA has become "a weapon [for] unscrupulous employers...to withhold paychecks, to deny vacations, to defend against discrimination charges and to refuse to pay the minimum wage and overtime salaries." [98]

Despite these repressive measures, immigration growth is likely to continue unchecked as long as Mexico remains in deep economic crisis. Between 1982 and 1988, Mexican real wages fell by half and unemployment increased by a factor of five as a result of a worldwide recession in the oil industry and the burden of Mexico's debt to First World banks. As Chicano political economist Abel Valenzuela points out:

> IRCA will not diminish the numbers or types of illegal immigrants because the bill does nothing to change either the political and economic reasons that make immigration to the United States so popular or the U.S. economy's structural need for immigrant workers.[99]

Research on the economic impact of undocumented workers has shown that immigration helps, rather than harms, the U.S. economy. Undocumented workers are not a burden to society; in 1985, for instance, the Rand Corporation, a conservative think-tank, found that only a tiny minority—5 percent—of Mexican immigrants received any public assistance, even though many employers withhold taxes from their pay. Furthermore, both the Rand Corporation and a 1984 Urban Institute study found that undocumented workers do not create unemployment. In fact, by taking the low-wage jobs spurned by U.S.-born workers who have better opportunities, undocumented workers keep businesses from leaving the United States or closing down.[100]

The Soul of *Tierra Madre*

Today's Chicanas and Mexicanas face great challenges in the years ahead. The desperate economic crisis in Mexico is generating greater pressures for immigration; if deportations such as those of the 1930s are to be avoided, Chicanas/os and Mexicans must organize and find allies in the struggle for more just immigration policies. The English-only movement threatens the future of bilingual education, and Chicanas must work even harder to maintain their rich cultural heritage. Poverty is growing among Chicanas maintaining their own families, and the basic economic rights of Chicana/o children must be defended. Declines in manufacturing jobs and an employer offensive against unions have worsened the bargaining power of Chicana/o workers; workers in the service sector must be organized, unions defended, and new job opportunities found for the Chicana/o community. The historical record makes it clear that Chicanas will rise to these challenges, following in the footsteps of their foremothers, the revolutionary *heroínas* and militant labor organizers who are the soul of *tierra madre*.

Chapter 5

WHATEVER YOUR FIGHT, DON'T BE LADYLIKE

European American Women[1]

As we come marching, marching, in the beauty of the day,
A million darkened kitchens, a thousand mill lofts grey,
Are touched with all the radiance that a sudden sun discloses,
For the people hear us singing: "Bread and roses! Bread and roses!"

As we come marching, marching, we battle too for men,
For they are women's children, and we mother them again.
Our lives shall not be sweated from birth until life closes:
Hearts starve as well as bodies; give us bread, but give us roses!

As we come marching, marching, unnumbered women dead
Go crying through our singing their ancient cry for bread.
Small art and love and beauty their drudging spirits knew.
Yes, it is bread we fight for—but we fight for roses, too!

As we come marching, marching, we bring the greater days.
The rising of the women means the rising of the race
No more the drudge and idler—ten that toil where one reposes,
But a sharing of life's glories: "Bread and roses! Bread and roses!"

—Poem by James Oppenheim, inspired by a banner carried by women
workers in the Lawrence, Massachusetts strike of 1912[2]

Since the early nineteenth century, European American women's work lives have been defined by and in contrast to an ideology of domesticity that proclaimed the home and childrearing "women's sphere" and the workplace "men's sphere." Over the past two centuries, the contradictions in this ideal of womanhood have been lived out by millions of European American women. Some lived like the pampered ladies of the European aristocracy, decked out in fine clothes, waited on by slaves or servants, and "protected" by their fathers and husbands. But many, especially the young and unmarried, were forced to leave "women's sphere" to toil in other women's kitchens, on farms, or in factories. Others labored in their dingy tenements to make ends meet. And many fought to break down the walls of domesticity: fighting for property rights and the vote, organizing in unions for "bread and roses," carving out careers for themselves, demanding help with their child-care responsibilities, or confronting sex discrimination. As Mary Harris "Mother" Jones, an Irish immigrant who was a famous socialist and United Mine Worker organizer, was fond of saying, "Whatever your fight, don't be ladylike."

The majority of whites in the early British colonies came from England. Upon independence from Britain, the fledgling United States established English as the dominant language and Protestantism as the dominant religion. European Americans shared with Europeans the conception of race that emerged in the eighteenth and nineteenth centuries, a conception that placed whites at the top of what Europeans saw as a naturally determined hierarchy. Therefore, when they established themselves in the "New World," European Americans set themselves, as a group, above people of color. For example, only white male property owners could vote in the newly established United States, and only white immigrants could become citizens.[3] At the same time, however, whites were far from a monolithic group, and became more diverse in the nineteenth century. Between 1820 and 1930, 28.5 million Europeans immigrated, most of them from non-English-speaking areas such as Germany, Scandinavia, Italy, and Eastern Europe, many of them Catholics or Jews.[4] These new immigrants encountered fierce economic, political, and social discrimination at the hands of the U.S.-born, mostly English-speaking and Protestant white majority. At the same time, the dominant white culture gradually incorporated many aspects of the more recent immigrants' cultures, from spaghetti and bagels to waltzes and polkas.

European American Women in the Colonial Economy

About 750,000 European men, women, and children journeyed to North America between 1600 and 1700, seeking religious freedom, land, and riches. The majority came from Britain, but the colonies also included settlers from Holland, France, and Germany. While some colonists arrived free of financial commitments, most landed in debt which they worked off in service to other colonists. Individuals or families who could afford part of the cost of passage came as "redemptioners," seeking work so that they could pay off the remainder of the cost. But the most common method of early European immigration was through the indenture system, under which one-half to two-thirds of colonial white immigrants came to North America.

In the indenture system, immigrants paid for the cost of their passage by allowing their creditors to "bind them out" as workers to other colonists for five to 10 years of hard labor. Indentured servants were far from free during their period of indenture; indeed, some indentured servants were convicted criminals, sent by the British penal system to the colonies. The Virginia Company used the indenture system to bring young single women to its colony, essentially selling them to interested men for the price of their passage—120 pounds of leaf tobacco or the sum of $80. Contemporary sources claim they were not forced to marry against their will. At the end of their indentures, most indentured servants married and worked in families of their own.[5]

Women colonists generally came over from Europe with their families, as daughters or wives under the control of their fathers or husbands. Others journeyed alone, hiring out to other families upon arrival and seeking to form families of their own. Some of the earliest colonies offered single women land. But this practice soon disappeared, perhaps because it allowed women to live independently and reduced their incentive to marry at a time when colonial men were experiencing a shortage of potential wives.[6]

Traveling to the colonies was a risky proposition, especially in the first half of the seventeenth century. The voyage took from seven to 12 weeks, and often as many as half of the passengers died. Children were the least likely to survive. Many of the early colonists were dismally unsuccessful, particularly in the Northeast, barely surviving famine, fire, cold, illness, drought, and Native American attempts to defend themselves against the European invasion. Conditions for indentured servants were even worse; in the early years of the Virginia colony, nearly two-thirds died before the end of their contracts. However, as the native peoples were increasingly displaced or exterminated, colonists were able to assert control over the land and begin producing timber and food for the market. Merchants and craftsmen took over the production of some goods and services from households, and colonial life became more settled and prosperous, attracting yet more immigrants. As European Americans extended their territory westward, this process repeated itself and the white population grew.[7]

Colonial society was extremely patriarchal: fathers and husbands controlled family life, economic, political, and religious institutions. In the area of land ownership, so central for a farming economy, principles of English common law prevailed. Only the heads of households, almost always male, had the right to own or exchange land. Wives had no separate legal identity or property rights: "In every lawful thing she submits her Will and Sense to his...she acts as if there were but one Mind in two Bodies," wrote Cotton Mather in his widely read eighteenth-century treatise on womanhood,

Ornaments to the Daughters of Zion.[8] Daughters fared no better, passing upon marriage from the control of their fathers to that of their husbands. Almost all daughters married since colonial society offered virtually no economic or social roles for single women. If there were male heirs, daughters inherited little (if any) of their fathers' property. Widows were the only group of colonial white women to own significant property, assured by colonial law of receiving at least one-third of their husbands' estates. However, a widow's estate reverted to her sons upon her remarriage or death. Although some colonial women were able to circumvent these laws, their combined effect was to concentrate the ownership and control of property in the hands of white men rather than white women, and the hands of older rather than younger men.[9]

Similarly, among free white families the colonial sexual division of labor concentrated the earning of income, and training for such work, in the hands of white men rather than white women. Most women focused on filling the immediate needs of their families while men, as the property owners and household heads, concentrated on earning money through cash-crop farming, craft production, or trade. The unpaid work of white women was essential to the success of these enterprises, but the nature and conditions of women's work in the family economy were usually defined by their husbands.

Childbearing was central to the lives and work of married white women in colonial times. The average woman bore eight children: children were needed as workers and heirs in family farms or businesses, but infant mortality was high (one of every three children did not reach a twentieth birthday). Childbearing was dangerous, ominously referred to as "a sentence," "a curse," and "the travail of woman." One in 30 mothers died in childbirth in colonial Plymouth; since a household could not survive without women's unpaid labor, their husbands generally remarried quickly. Beyond the bearing of children, however, a biological mother's responsibilities for her children varied according to her economic class. Wealthy women often put their infants in the care of wet nurses, servants, or slaves.[10]

Husbands as well as wives participated in disciplining and training children, who were seen as little more than miniature workers. Parents commonly apprenticed their children out to other families at the age of seven if they could not afford their keep or wanted them to learn a craft. Apprenticeships with other families and training within families were rigidly sex-typed: daughters worked at domestic service, spinning, sewing, and weaving, but not at the more lucrative, masculine trades of cobbler, silversmith, or cabinet maker.[11]

A wife's work varied according to the economic needs of her family, as determined by her husband's economic position. In cash-poor homes and among frontier families, women bore the burden of filling most of the family's basic needs. They worked to reduce cash expenditures by growing vegetables in the kitchen garden and making the family's clothes, candles, soap, and household furnishings; and raised chickens and cows for eggs, butter, and milk, often selling the excess to provide an important source of family income. Their unpaid labor allowed the farmer-husband to devote his energies to clearing the land, establishing a cash crop, and saving income for investment in tools or more land. If a husband were a craftsman or the proprietor of a shop or tavern, his wife and children might also work in the business in addition to all the other tasks described above. In contrast, the wife of a successful farmer, plantation owner, or merchant did little actual work; instead, she supervised household servants and slaves who purchased or made the goods the family needed, cooked the meals, and maintained the house.[12]

Although most white women's work was private and unpaid, when the father or husband was deceased or absent, women were forced to seek an income. However, since few white women had any income-earning skills, the majority of widows and their children lived in poverty, working as domestic servants or trying to survive as farmers or petty traders. Many widows who could not support themselves depended upon their communities for support. It was not uncommon in New England for town administrators to force poor women to give up their children to be servants, to expel widows and their children from their towns, or to sell indigent women into indentured service.[13]

From the late seventeenth century on, the numbers of single or widowed white women grew as a result of continued male migration west and the toll of the Revolutionary War. Desperate for an income, many women found employment in textile work. Merchants and entrepreneurs paid women pitifully low wages to work in their homes in the "putting-out" system, providing them with raw materials such as hemp, wool, and flax to be spun into thread.[14] An advertisement for one such enterprise in Philadelphia read:

> ...money will be given at the factory, up Market Street, for any parcel, either great or small, of hemp, flax, or woolen yarn. The managers return their thanks to all those industrious women who are now employed in spinning for the factory.[15]

Although some married women performed putting-out work, the vast majority of women who participated were single, and as a result, the word "spinster" came to mean an unmarried European American woman. Later, when the textile mills took over spinning and weaving, sewing clothing became spinsters' major home work and source of income.

Cracks in the system of colonial patriarchy allowed some white women to gain power and stature through their business ventures. A few widows managed to become successful entrepreneurs in their deceased husbands' stores, newspapers, farms, or plantations. Other widows established enterprises of their own, such as schools, inns, and cooking or sewing businesses in their homes. Despite the colonists' rigid sexual division of labor and concept of female inferiority (seventeenth- and eighteenth-century whites commonly believed that women had smaller brains than men), these widows and their successes were accepted and even applauded since entrepreneurship was, in their cases, consistent with the feminine role of serving their families.

Daughters were also called upon as family caretakers when their mothers fell ill and their brothers were unavailable. Their contributions were sometimes quite significant. Eliza Lucas, who ran her father's plantation when he was called away for military service, was responsible for the successful introduction of indigo into the southern plantation economy. When Eliza married, she gave up entrepreneurship for homemaking, but when her husband died, she again took over as family entrepreneur until her death.[16]

For the most part, even when white women stepped into white men's shoes in the economy, they were unable to win for themselves any political rights. In 1773, a group of widowed shopkeepers complained in a letter to a New York newspaper:

> We are House keepers, Pay our Taxes, carry on Trade, and most of us are she Merchants, and as we in some measure contribute to the Support of Government, we ought to be Intituled to some of the Sweets of it.[17]

The Mill Girls, The Working Girls

In the early nineteenth century, the putting-out system in which European American women spun fiber into thread and wove thread into cloth in their homes gave way to the factory system. The first factories established in the United States were textile mills set up in the Northeast in the 1820s. White fathers and sons were already engaged in farming, and mothers in homemaking, and there were few workers of color in the East. As a result, mill owners turned to young, white women as a source of labor. Recruiters for the mills drove around the countryside in long black wagons to collect their labor force and transport them to the mill towns. A daughter's mill employment offered less-than-successful families a source of needed cash income. At the same time, young women who worked in the mills gained a bit of independence and income before they married.[18]

Parents were reluctant to let their daughters leave the strict supervision of family life. As a result, factory owners in Waltham and Lowell, Massachusetts created the institution that came to be known as the Waltham system, promising parents that their daughters would lead tightly regulated lives in the mill towns. The mill girls worked 12 hours a day, six days a week. The hours they spent outside the factories were closely supervised by matrons in boarding houses. For most of these girls, mill employment was only temporary and they left the factories within a few years for marriage. Other mills, such as Samuel Slater's mill in Rhode Island, used a family labor system, hiring whole families, and paying the father for his wife and children's labors.[19]

Mill girls played an important role in early labor organizing. In the first half of the nineteenth century, workers all over the Northeast were organizing against the oppressive conditions of wage work. In the face of long hours, difficult working conditions, and factory owners' efforts to cut wages, mill girls "turned out" in a series of work stoppages in the 1830s, and formed the Factory Girls' Association with a membership of 2,500. Their protests sparked the first public speech by a woman in Lowell, an ardent appeal for women's rights.

These campaigns fizzled out during the depression which lasted from 1837 to 1842, but were reborn a few years later in response to the mill owners' attempts to speed up the pace and intensity of work. The mill girls organized the Lowell Female Labor Reform Association, helped to form a larger umbrella organization for workers, the New England Labor Reform League (formerly called the Workingmen's Association but renamed to reflect its female membership), and worked on the League's paper, *The Voice of Industry*. Besides organizing to prevent speed-up, the women (unable, as women, to vote) collected over 4,000 signatures petitioning the Massachusetts state legislature for a 10-hour working day.[20] The Lowell Female Labor Reform Association also argued for women's rights, to be won through the organizing efforts of women themselves, refusing to trust the supposed benevolence of their "male protectors," be they legislators or mill owners. One operative wrote her state legislator:

> Bad as is the condition of so many women, it would be much worse if they had nothing but your boasted protection to rely upon; but they have at last learnt the lesson which a bitter experience teaches, that not to those who style themselves their "natural protectors" are they to look for the needful help, but to the strong and resolute of their own sex.[21]

The mill girls' sense of sisterhood, however, did not appear to extend beyond U.S.-born white women. The Female Labor Reform Association wrote:

> We feel that if there is a place in the wide universe where true liberty and freedom should be enjoyed...and where woman should take her proper place and standing in society, as a rational intelligent being—a fit *companion* and *friend* of man, not a *slave*—it is in the United States of America! Too long has she been considered an inferior being....[22]

While their feminist rhetoric appropriated the horror of the slave experience to serve the mill girls' cause, the mill girls failed to develop a sense of solidarity with their enslaved sisters.[23] Neither did the Lowell U.S.-born mill girls feel much sisterhood for the mostly Irish immigrant women who poured into the mills in the 1840s. Immigrants were segregated into low-paid jobs and inferior housing, but there is no evidence that Yankee mill girls in this era either protested against the unfair treatment of immigrants or participated in work stoppages and other labor organizing alongside their immigrant sisters.[24]

The participation of unmarried U.S.-born white women in paid factory work, as well as in domestic service, continued through the nineteenth century. Families needed extra money and their daughters continued to respond to that need by moving to mill towns and urban areas to seek paid work. Indeed, the wage work of daughters helped to underwrite the emerging "cult of domesticity," which glorified white married women's domestic vocation. White mothers endeavored to stay out of the paid labor force, sending their daughters out for wages if funds were scarce; these working girls then quit the labor force when they married and started families. Thus, in 1900, among white women with U.S.-born parents, 22 percent of single women were gainfully employed, compared to only 3 percent of married women.[25]

The Cult of Domesticity: The Homemaker and the Domestic Servant

The ideal of the husband/breadwinner, wife/full-time-homemaker marriage emerged among U.S.-born whites in the 1820s. White upper-class women were the leaders in writing about, delineating, and in some cases, expanding women's new domestic vocation. Among the most prominent were Lydia Maria Childs (author of *The Mother's Book*), Catherine Beecher (author of *A Treatise on Domestic Economy*), and Sarah Joseph Hale (who edited the popular *Godey's Ladies Book*).[26]

The cult of domesticity fit neatly into the new landscape of a rapidly industrializing and growing U.S. economy. As family-based production declined and the factory system developed, white men increasingly earned their income by working for others for wages. The market took over production from the home, leaving the home as a private, personal sphere, men's shelter from the impersonal, competitive economy.

The theorists of the cult of domesticity argued that women were the natural keepers of this domestic sphere and of the children within it (who were increasingly banned from paid work). Having a home-bound wife was a sign of manhood, and white men competed and organized in the labor force to earn "family wages," wages which would support a wife and children. At the same time, the "cult of domesticity" elevated white women's work, homemaking and childrearing, as different from but equally important as white men's bread-winning:

> To render HOME happy, is woman's peculiar province; home is HER world...[She is] neither greater nor less than man, but different, as her natural vocation is different, and...each is superior to each other in their respective departments of thought and action.[27]

White women's homemaking "vocation," as it came to be seen, centered around mothering. Fathers, working outside the home, were no longer expected to spend much time parenting their children. It was no longer considered appropriate for a mother to hire a wet nurse for her baby, or to apprentice out her children. As whites gained more socioeconomic mobility, children's upbringing was recognized as having an important effect on their future economic and social success. The responsibility for children's successes was thus placed on the shoulders of their mothers, and women pored over books and formed mothering circles to study their vocation. A second aspect of the homemaking vocation was to create a home: a comfortable, secure, familial place in which husband and children alike were nurtured.[28]

While it advocated the domestic vocation as the natural role of all women, the cult of domesticity was distinctly white and middle or upper class. Electricity, telephone, running water, central heating, canned goods, refrigerators, washing machines, and automobiles were all unknown to the nineteenth-century homemaker, so the home was still a place where much hard, dirty, physical work had to be done. As European American historian Faye Dudden points out, "domesticity's new view of women's roles, while implicitly assigning the domestic to drudge work, called employers to 'higher' tasks and to supervision."[29] Working-class and poor families, and thus most families of color, could not afford servants, and hence could not realize the domestic ideal of womanhood. However, throughout the nineteenth century, female domestic servants were available and affordable to middle-income white families in most regions of the United States. Families in California, where women of all races were in shorter supply, employed

Chinese men as servants.[30] Several factors maintained the supply of servants, including the steady stream of European immigrants and the lack of better-paid, alternative jobs.

The population of domestic servants was diverse. During the nine-teenth century, the white servant labor force in rural areas (where most of the population still lived) was made up predominantly of U.S.-born girls, while immigrant girls predominated in the cities. For both U.S.-born and immigrant whites, however, domestic service usually was not a substitute for "cult-of-domesticity" womanhood, but rather a stage preceding it. Most white domestics were single, and were able to quit their jobs and become home-makers themselves upon marriage. Indeed, their employers—almost all U.S.-born whites who belonged to the middle and upper classes—saw themselves as providing their servants with education and training (an apprenticeship of sorts) for future homemaking careers. This European American view of supervision as edifying for servants was particularly pronounced when the servants were immigrants, unfamiliar with the English language and with North American ways.[31]

U.S.-born working-class and immigrant white homemakers could not afford servants to help them with their domestic vocation. Indeed, most had to take on extra work to supplement their husbands' meager earnings. While only 4 percent of married European immigrant women were listed as gainfully employed in 1900, these women's domesticity was far from the leisured life portrayed in the ladies' magazines. Engaged couples postponed marriage while both earned income and saved. Children, far from being educated and protected by their mothers, were sent into the labor force at early adolescence to help pay the bills—in 1900, 61 percent of single European immigrant women over the age of 10 were gainfully employed, compared to only 22 percent of single white women with U.S.-born parents. Homemakers worked to make ends meet by growing food, raising livestock, and making clothes to fill family needs; many homes, even in the cities, had gardens and a few animals. Home-based needlework was an important source of employment and income to poor white married women. Given the high rate of migration and immigration to the cities, urban women could often earn an income taking in paying boarders and lodgers. In rural areas, butter made by women and girls and sold to urban areas was an important source of farm income, and many wives and daughters helped with the field work.[32]

The cult of domesticity was inextricably bound up with the strict segregation into white men's and white women's jobs, paying family wages and supplementary wages, respectively. While white women's earnings were better than those of women of color, they were rarely sufficient to maintain a household, much less children. The temporary and supplementary nature of white women's wage earning helped employers justify their segregation into lower-paid, dead-end jobs, and dampened women's protests against these inferior working conditions. White men, on the other hand, were assigned by the domestic code to family-wage jobs, which paid enough to support a home-bound wife and sometimes involved upward mobility during a lifetime of wage work.

White women's bleak situation in the labor market relative to white men's reinforced the cult of domesticity's definitions of socially acceptable behavior. For their survival, and that of their children, white women had to focus their efforts on catching and keeping a hard-working, healthy, sober, and faithful white man. Thus, even though white women were among the first wage workers, they were not necessarily better off than during colonial times if they attempted to survive without the economic protection of a husband or father. Widows and their children crowded the cities, unable to support themselves on women's wages and falling upon the meager services of charities. Single white women fared little better.

The rigidity of sex roles and the economic and political subordination of white women led a few females to masquerade as males and live their lives as men. Some even married other women and raised families with them. One female, who called herself Charles Warner, explained her "passing" in the 1860s as follows:

> When I was about 20 I decided that I was almost at the end of my rope. I had no money and a woman's wages were not enough to keep me alive. I looked around and saw men getting more money and more work, and more money for the same kind of work. I decided to become a man. It was simple. I just put on men's clothing and applied for a man's job. I got it and got good money for those times, so I stuck to it.[33]

One of the more famous "passing women" was Murray Hall, who lived in the late nineteenth century. Hall not only voted at a time when women were denied suffrage, but also became a prominent New York politician.[34]

Whites Push West

While the cities and factories were to be the future of the U.S. economy, farming continued to employ the majority of the white population through 1900, and the farm population continued to grow rapidly during the nineteenth century. In order to assure the security of white settlers, the U.S. army fought and won numerous wars against different Native American tribes that lived on the land now sought by whites, pushing the indigenous peoples onto restricted reservation lands (see Chapter 3). At the same time, the U.S.

government took over vast territories from Mexico (see Chapter 4). A struggle then ensued about which whites would have access to these new lands. Much land was given as a subsidy to privately-owned railroad companies or sold cheaply in large tracts to wealthy speculators (individuals, banks, or land companies). Then speculators and railroad companies divided the land into small plots, selling it to would-be farmers at inflated prices. In 1860, speculators owned one-quarter of all the land in Illinois and Iowa, and half of the privately owned land in Minnesota.[35]

However, under pressure from reformers, the government developed homesteading policies through which it made lands directly available to propertyless individuals. Most homesteaders were third-generation European Americans, moving westward because family lands were exhausted or insufficient for a new generation or simply in search of greater wealth or adventure. Some new immigrants, especially Germans and Scandinavians, homesteaded land in the Midwest. When homesteads failed (as up to 43 percent did in Nebraska), families moved even further West.[36]

The specific provisions of homesteading laws varied over the years, but laws usually allowed the head of a white family to file a claim for 160 or so acres, making a nominal payment per acre; he would become owner of the land after clearing it, building a house, and living on it for a specified period of time.[37] The Homesteading Act of 1862 was the first to allow a woman to homestead, providing she was single and over 21, an immigrant who had filed citizenship papers, or the head of a household. This represented a major step forward for white women, who until then had been largely excluded from land ownership.[38] Elinore Rupert, a widow, left her job as a washerwoman in Denver to homestead successfully in Wyoming. She wrote her former employer:

> I am very enthusiastic about women homesteading. It really requires less strength and labor to raise plenty to satisfy a large family than it does to go out to wash, with the added satisfaction of knowing that their job will not be lost to them if they care to keep it...so much more pleasant than to work so hard in the city and then be on starvation rations in the winter... To me, homesteading is the solution of all poverty's problems...but I realize that temperament has much to do with success in any undertaking, and persons afraid of coyotes and work and loneliness had better let ranching alone.[39]

For all the frontier's promises, white married women who were financially secure often found moving to the western frontier far from attractive. Homesteads acted as outposts in the government's increasing occupation of Native American territories, and whites fought, even to the death, against American Indians who were defending their lands against this encroachment. Diaries of women moving westward expressed much discontent and dismay at the prospect of losing friends and extended family to begin again in an uncleared and dangerous place, sparsely populated by whites. Elizabeth Goltra wrote as she left Kansas for Oregon in 1853:

> Today we started across the dreary plains. Sad are the thoughts that steal over the reflecting mind. I am leaving my home, my early friends and associates never to see them again, exchanging the disinterested solicitude of fond friends for the cold and unsympathetic friendship of strangers. Shall we all reach the "El Dorado" of our hopes or shall one of our number be left and our graves be in the dreary wilderness, our bodies uncoffined and unknown remain there in solitude? Hard indeed that heart be that does not drop a tear as these thoughts roll across the mind.[40]

One can surmise that marital disagreements about such moves and about frontier life itself were common, given the opposite socialization of the sexes. Husbands sought their fortunes and adventure. Wives, however, desired a home and a secure community. The husband of one frontier woman so procrastinated on building her a much-needed oven that she finally built one out of bricks she made herself; an observer recounted that "[it] was such a success that people travelled out of their way to see it in action."[41] A work of fiction by European American author Mary Wilkins Freeman, "The Revolt of Mother," tells of a frontier woman's dismay when her husband, in spite of her pleas and protestations, builds a new barn for his livestock rather than a much-needed house to replace their shack. When he goes on a week's trip, she moves the family into the barn, claiming it as the home it should have been. When he returns, he is speechless, and submits.[42]

Farm life was often very hard. Rural poverty was prevalent, though less harsh than urban poverty in many ways—farm families at least had land, a home, and food. Farm families who had bought their land from speculators often carried heavy debts, while others worked as tenants for large landowners. Although manufactured goods from the cities were increasingly available, many farm families lacked the cash to buy them. The markets for agricultural products were unreliable and dominated by middlemen, who took a growing share of farmers' profits.[43] Farms were far apart, with only horse-and-buggy or train transportation. Women were isolated from other people, from basic medical services, and from schools for their children. Higher standards of living in the cities attracted the young, shrinking the supply of domestic servants and making it difficult for farm women to play out the domestic ideal.

Still, from 1865 to 1910, white families were able to maintain themselves in farming across the generations. Since white farm families had large numbers of children, there was rarely enough land for the children to farm. Sons and daughters worked as hired hands for other farmers (or for their parents) and saved their earnings. Later they became tenants, married other farm children, and eventually bought or homesteaded land to start farms of their own.

Given the continual availability of (formerly American Indian or Mexican) land through 1910, this ideal was within reach for whites of all ethnic groups. However, by the late nineteenth century, many southern white tenant farming families found themselves unable to make a living on the land. Southern planters, local bankers, and merchants set up textile mills in the 1880s to take advantage of this poor white rural population. Usually both parents and children worked in the mills at sex- and age-segregated jobs; African Americans were excluded.[44]

The difficulties of farm life led to a series of rural reform movements between 1870 and 1900, in which as many as half a million farm women participated, some as leaders. During this period, farmers across the country organized themselves into mutual-aid and social organizations, including Granges (centered in the Missouri River Valley) and Farmers' Alliances (further west and in the South). These groups were largely white, but unlike most white political organizations of the era, they allowed women to be members, officers, convention representatives, and public speakers. Many also championed white women's political rights and economic interests.[45]

Buying and selling cooperatives which circumvented the costly services of middlemen were central to farm organizing. Farmer-organized consumer cooperatives allowed farm women to afford time-saving consumer goods, such as sewing machines, while marketing cooperatives allowed farmers to get better prices for their crops. These organizations also campaigned against the manufacture of the new butter substitute, oleomargarine, which competed with farm women's homemade butter (still an important source of farm income).[46]

Mary Elizabeth Lease, an Irish Catholic from Pennsylvania, was one of the best known farm women activists. Lease helped found a third political party, the Populist Party, and became one of the party's major spokespersons. She was the first woman to take on this role for a political party. Lease and the Populists championed farmers' organizing and pro-farm legislation as well as women's rights, winning the vote for women in Colorado and Idaho in the 1890s. They also organized against the concentration of wealth and power, especially targeting mortgage foreclosures and farm losses at the hands of eastern bankers. In a speech to the Women's Christian Temperance Union (about which we will hear more later), Lease proclaimed:

> We are living in a grand and wonderful time...a time when the gray old world begins to dimly comprehend that there is no difference between the brain of an intelligent woman and the brain of an intelligent man.

She spoke of fighting for a world with:

> Exact justice to all, special privileges to none. No more millionaires, and no more paupers; no more gold kings, silver kings and oil kings, and no more little waifs of humanity starving for a crust of bread...We shall have the golden age...when we shall have not a government of the people by capitalists, but a government of the people, by the people.[47]

White Populists also fought to bring African American farmers into their party. They met severe opposition and setbacks in the South, where white politicians and vigilante groups terrorized Black and white Populists and forced many Black farmers to leave their communities. The southern power structure further set back the Populist movement by imposing poll taxes, which prevented poor white and Black males from voting, and by launching active anti-feminist campaigns.[48]

The 'Melting Pot': The White Immigrant Experience, 1850-1920

The growth of the U.S. economy in the nineteenth century created a high demand for labor, particularly for unskilled workers. As the industrial sector grew, it changed the character of jobs. Capitalists gradually replaced skilled craft workers with unskilled laborers who tended machines, in spite of the efforts of white male craft workers organized in the American Federation of Labor. Demand for domestic servants was also rising among middle- and upper-class white homemakers. Few U.S.-born whites (other than unmarried daughters) were willing to take such jobs, given their alternatives in farming or in the higher-paid craft and professional jobs; those U.S.-born whites who were working in factories were rapidly organizing to raise their wages. Factory owners might have used African American labor but, after the Civil War, southern landowners created a system of debt peonage that tied most former slaves to the land even though they were theoretically free.[49] Furthermore, white workers protested vehemently when African Americans were hired in their workplaces, fearing that their presence would drive wages down. Neither Asian nor Chicana/o workers were available on the East Coast in sufficient numbers to meet employers' needs.

The solution to this labor shortage came from Europe. The U.S. government encouraged European immigration, and, by a 1790 law, these immigrants were allowed to become U.S. citizens. Between 1850 and 1920, over 30 million new immigrants flooded into the United States from Southern and Eastern Europe, accounting for a major part of the population growth (from 23 to 106 million) during this period, and decreasing the African American proportion of the population from 16 percent to 10 percent.[50] (As we show in Chapter 7, Asian immigration was encouraged on the West Coast.) Germans, Irish, Scandinavians, Italians, Slavs, Russian and Eastern European Jews all came by the millions, fleeing poverty, famine, and persecution, and seeking economic opportunity. The flow of immigrants increased through the nineteenth and early twentieth centuries until it was cut off in the 1920s by racism and ethnic prejudice (Southern and Eastern Europeans were seen at this time as racially inferior peoples), resentment against the low-wage and strike-breaking competition of immigrant labor, and capitalist concern at the growing radicalization of the immigrant population.[51]

Lured by Opportunity

European immigrants were both pushed, by famine, poverty, and persecution, and pulled, by the lure of economic security and upward mobility, to the United States. Most settled in communities with others of their same national origin. Up through the 1880s, most immigrants came from Northern and Western Europe, primarily Great Britain, Ireland, Germany, and Scandinavia. A few Jews, mostly from Germany, arrived in the early nineteenth century. At the same time, large numbers of French Canadians took jobs in the mill towns of New England. Between 1846 and 1854, between 100,000 and 200,000 Irish immigrants arrived each year as a result of the great famines of the mid-1840s. Scandinavian and German immigration grew during the 1880s, surpassing the number of Irish immigrants in that decade.[52]

Southern and Eastern Europeans—mostly Italian peasants and Slavs—dominated the migration of the late nineteenth and early twentieth centuries, arriving by the millions. Between 1876 and 1926, almost nine million Italians came to the United States, although more than half eventually returned to Italy to buy land with their earnings. Starting in the 1870s, millions of Russian and Eastern European Jews fled to the United States from the devastating pogroms (massacres and persecutions that took place between 1881-83 and 1900-07) in Russia, Poland, and Rumania. After 1900, Polish, Italian, and Russian immigrants accounted for 40 percent of the immigrants to the United States.[53]

Between 1820 and 1860, two out of every five immigrants were women; this number declined to two out of seven between 1900 and 1910. Of the major immigrant groups, the Irish, the Russian and Eastern European Jews, the Danish, and the Swedish sent substantial numbers of women. The majority of Irish immigrants were women; 30 percent of Swedish immigrants were unmarried women. Immigrants from Italy, Scandinavia, and the Slavic countries were predominately male.[54]

'Greenies' and Work

Newly arrived European immigrants were called "greenhorns," and demand for their labor was so great that employment agents greeted their incoming vessels with offers of factory and domestic service work. But greenhorns found themselves restricted to dangerous, low-paid, and demeaning work. As one Slavic women put it, "Greenie not wanted in nice clean places." White jobs were assigned according to a worker's nativity, with third-generation European Americans on the top, second-generation immigrants below, and "greenies" on the bottom. For example, Irish immigrants in the eastern textile mills were introduced into the least desirable work of carding and spinning, paid less than U.S.-born workers of equal skills, and residentially segregated in inferior housing. A memo from the directors of the Salmon Falls Company, found in the papers of Amos A. Lawrence, read:

> If the Irish sh[oul]d predominate so as to disgust the American operatives, the character of the village must be very much changed *for the worse*. Every care must be taken to keep them in separate boarding houses, [and] to separate them in the mills.[55]

Sex and age also played a role in job assignments. For example, Bohemian immigrant women were segregated in the least desirable jobs in cigar factories. In their native Bohemia, women had rolled cigars by hand, but in the United States this skilled work was reserved for men. The next most skilled task, mechanized rolling, was reserved for U.S.-born men and women. As a result, immigrant women were consigned to the hardest part of cigar making: stripping tobacco in dank, unventilated, and unlit factory basements. In Pittsburgh at the turn of the century, women tobacco strippers made five dollars per week, half the amount earned by operators of rolling machines.[56]

Prejudice against immigrants was widespread, extending from the workplace to housing and all other areas of society. Ethnic stereotypes and racist attitudes were omnipresent, and persist to this day in slang and epithets which originated in the nineteenth century. Employment advertisements often specified "No Irish Need Apply." In 1891, a mob of U.S.-born European

Americans lynched 11 Italians in a New Orleans prison, despite the fact that they had been acquitted of murder charges.[57] Anti-semitism was strong, and persisted even against U.S.-born Jews. Christian employers often refused to employ Jews in any capacity. For example, the Levinson and Zenith Furniture Company told applicant Florence Cohen in 1912: "Jews are not ever permitted to work here. They are all troublemakers."[58] Jewish women were excluded from clerical work, which was cleaner and less strenuous than factory work.

Employers used inter-ethnic prejudice as a way to further depress wages and decrease worker solidarity and union organizing. According to European American historian Susan Kennedy:

> ...old and new hatreds kept working women apart. Eastern European Jewish girls resented the presence of Polish coworkers at their union meetings, when the Poles acted as spies for employers who would dismiss union members. And Russian Jewish women who made artificial flowers despised Italian women for accepting lower pay for their work, thereby depressing wage rates; most of the Jewish girls were self-supporting, while the Italian women worked within a family earning structure in which their wages only supplemented others' income. "If they were more civilized," said one Jewish woman, "they wouldn't take such low pay. But they go without hats and gloves and umbrellas." [59]

The combination of sex and ethnic discrimination kept immigrant women's wages pitifully low. Studies of immigrant women wage-earners found them barely able to survive; for instance, three-fifths of women working in Pittsburgh in 1906 made less than the seven dollars a week necessary to meet bare subsistence needs.[60] Most lived with their parents, as lodgers with other families, or in boarding houses in order to make ends meet.

Faced with these conditions, most immigrants looked to their children to achieve the "American dream" of financial success. Immigrant families saved and sacrificed so their children could go to school and learn English. By assimilating—speaking, dressing, and acting like the U.S.-born, English-cultured whites—white immigrants' children could blend in with the dominant white group, and many followed this strategy to escape prejudice. European American historian Barbara Wertheimer points out that ethnic working women:

> ...often went to great lengths to hide their parentage or place of birth from prospective employers, changing their names and lying about their addresses so that the area of the city in which they lived would not give them away.[61]

These assimilation strategies did provide some upward mobility. For instance, second-generation immigrant women were much less likely than the first generation to be employed in low-paid domestic work, and much more likely to be employed in clerical, teaching, and sales.[62] But mobility was not costless, and many language skills and cultural traditions were lost in the process of "Americanization." Still, many white ethnics maintained their languages and religions and developed strong ethnic organizations of mutual support. Immigrant communities had their own banks, newspapers, schools, churches, and synagogues. Gro Svendsen, a Norwegian immigrant to a frontier settlement in Iowa, sent her children to English schools during the week and Norwegian Sunday school. Explaining why she gave one of her sons an American name, she wrote:

> I thought I'd choose one that was a little more in conformity with American, so that he would not have to change it himself later in life if he should live to grow up.[63]

In spite of their difficult economic straits, immigrant families lived out a semblance of the cult of domesticity, often paralleling old-country conceptions of women's domestic place. Immigrant men, working as unskilled laborers in factories or mines, rarely earned the family wages essential to maintain the cult-of-domesticity ideal. White immigrant homemakers, however, rarely left their homes in search of income; rather, they performed a range of services for pay within their homes, from taking in boarders to industrial home work. In New York City in 1890, for instance, 19 out of 20 Italian wives and 49 out of 50 Jewish wives did not work outside the home. Families further supplemented husbands' earnings by sending their sons and daughters out to work or by assigning them to industrial home work. At the turn of the century, an investigation by the U.S. Senate found that 62 percent of immigrant families had more than one earner.[64]

Immigrant Life and Work in the Cities: Domestic Service and Factory Work

Most nineteenth-century immigrant women looked for work in the cities, where they lived in dirty, crowded tenements. By the turn of the century, poor immigrant families made up one-third to one-half of the population of major U.S. cities.[65]

Urban immigrant women found three main types of work: domestic service, work in their own homes (both paid and unpaid), and factory work. As we shall see below, nationality often dictated the particular form of work in which they were engaged. Irish and Scandinavian women entered domestic service, Italian women generally found ways to contribute to family income without going outside the home, Jewish women worked in garment factories, and Slavic women worked in laundries, canneries, and tobacco stripping.

A high percentage of single female immigrants worked in domestic service, although the vast majority left their jobs upon marriage. Living in as a servant solved the housing problem for a single immigrant just off the boat, and enabled her to begin earning wages almost immediately. First generation immigrants constituted about one-third of all domestic servants in 1890.[66]

Irish and Scandinavian women were most likely to enter domestic service. Almost every young Irish woman who came to the United States spent some time in domestic service. Beginning work around age 11, most left once they got married, at 18 or so—although a lifetime of single, domestic service was culturally acceptable. Most Irish servants sent part of their earnings home to assist their families' struggles for survival in famine-stricken Ireland. These payments, known as remittances, were enormous: by one estimate, remittances from the United States to Ireland totaled nearly two million pounds in 1845 alone. Nevertheless, damaging stereotypes of the "Irish biddy" abounded. An 1857 issue of *Harper's Weekly* characterized Irish domestic servants as disloyal, as well as "unwashed and totally ignorant of housewifery." Anti-Catholic sentiment was also a factor in the complaints against Irish servants. Some mid-nineteenth century writers charged that Catholic servants had been sent to the United States to spy for the Pope. In 1855 a rumor that Irish servants were poisoning the food of their Protestant employers resulted in the firing of many Irish servants.[67]

German and Scandinavian immigrants were also very likely to be domestic servants, although they were outnumbered by the Irish. In Scandinavia, it was common for rural women to migrate to cities and towns as domestic servants, so this pattern continued in the United States. In 1900, nearly two out of three Swedish immigrant women workers and half of Norwegian, Danish, and German women workers were employed as domestic servants. Most German and Scandinavian servants worked in midwestern cities or in ethnic ghettoes in the Northeast. On the other hand, at the turn of the century, only one-quarter of British immigrants performed household work. The newer immigrants from Russia, Poland, and Italy were also much less likely than Irish women to be in domestic service; only one in ten Italian women was a domestic servant or laundress.[68]

Daughters of European immigrants were not as constrained as their mothers and could choose among a slightly greater range of occupations. As a result, they were much less likely to perform household labor. For example, at the turn of the century, three in five Irish-born women workers were domestic servants or laundresses; but fewer than one in five of second-generation employed Irish women was a household worker.[69]

European immigrant women were found in all the growing manufacturing industries of the nineteenth and early twentieth century, including the steel industry, but women predominated in textile, garment, and tobacco- and cigar-making industries. Generally, immigrant women worked in factories while they were single, often going out to work when they were quite young. Rose Cohen, a 12-year-old Russian immigrant, worked alongside her father in a garment shop to earn money so that her mother and siblings could join them in the United States. Factory women's earnings, like those of domestic servants who sent their pay home, went directly to their families. In some communities, particularly those of Italians and Jews, the employer paid a young woman's wages directly to her father. Marriage usually meant retirement from the factory workforce. An 1887 study of female industrial workers in large cities found that three-fourths were under 25 and 96 percent were single.[70]

In the mid-1800s, Irish, French Canadian, and German immigrant women factory workers were most likely to be found in textile mills, where immigrants had displaced the U.S.-born mill girls of New England by the time of the Civil War. Northern European immigrants also entered the garment industry. In 1850, two-thirds of New York dressmakers, seamstresses, shirt and collar makers, embroiderers, and artificial-flower makers were foreign-born, and three-fifths of these were Irish or German.[71]

Beginning in the last half of the nineteenth century, large numbers of Italian and Jewish women entered the garment industry, with Russian and Eastern European Jews concentrated in ladies' garments and Italians in men's garments. Garment-industry work took place in factories (known as "outside" shops), sweatshops ("inside" shops), and workers' homes. Sweatshops were generally located in the tenement apartments of labor contractors. These middlemen, who usually came from the same ethnic group as the workers, paid workers to sew cut garments. The outside shops generally offered better working conditions than the sweatshops or industrial home work, but competition with the latter tended to drive wages down and hours up. Many Italian women worked with their husbands or brothers in small tailoring businesses.[72]

Bread and Roses: Labor Activism

Not surprisingly, these conditions met with considerable resistance from European immigrant working women, who made up the core of white women's unionization efforts in the late nineteenth and early twentieth centuries. Some of the greatest labor leaders of the era were European immigrant factory women. Socialist activist and union leader Rose Schneiderman fled the pogroms in Russian Poland in 1891, immigrating along with eight siblings. She worked in retail sales and then in the garment industry, organized her first union at the age of 21, and was the first woman vice-president of the United Cloth Hat and Cap Makers Union. Schneiderman was known for her speaking and organizing ability. At the time of her death, a *New York Times* editorial described her as "a tiny red-haired bundle of social dynamite [who] did more to upgrade the dignity and living standards of working women than any other American." [73] Mary Anderson, who was born on a farm in Sweden, immigrated in 1889 at the age of 16, working first as a domestic and then as a stitcher in a shoe factory. She became president of her International Boot and Shoe Workers' local and later headed the federal government's Women's Bureau. Both Schneiderman and Anderson were leaders in the Women's Trade Union League, an alliance of immigrant women workers and upper-class white women. [74]

Two of the most famous chapters in the history of immigrant women's organizing are the Uprising of the Twenty Thousand and the Triangle Shirtwaist Fire. In November 1909, 20,000 New York City waistmakers (factory-employed seamstresses) walked out to protest falling wages, the 56- to 59-hour work week, and the strict discipline of the industry's subcontractor system, which charged workers for electricity and needles, and fined them for minor offenses. At a mass meeting of the Women's Trade Union League, 20-year-old Clara Lemlich, a militant immigrant worker, began the strike by calling out in Yiddish:

> I have listened to all the speakers, and I have no further patience for talk. I am one who feels and suffers from the things pictured. I move we go on a general strike! [75]

The vast majority of the strikers were Russian Jewish women, joined by Jewish men, Italian women, and U.S.-born women. After a mere four days, half of the original strikers had won union contracts and returned to work. Some of the other gains included an end to the practice of charging for materials, a 52-hour work week, and a promise that the manufacturers would employ only contractors who used union labor. [76]

In 1911, a fire killed over 140 garment workers, most of them European immigrant women, who were unable to escape the 10-story Triangle Shirtwaist building. The factory building was typical of garment factories of the time: flammable materials scattered everywhere, narrow staircases, doors which either opened inward or not at all, and no sprinklers. Over a quarter of a million people attended the victims' funeral. At a mass meeting after the fire, Rose Schneiderman denounced the company's neglectful attitude:

The life of men and women is so cheap and property is so sacred. There are so many of us for one job it matters little if one hundred forty three of us have been burned to death...every time the workers come out in the only way they know how to protest against conditions which are unbearable [in unions], the strong hand of the law is allowed to press down heavily upon us...[77]

Public outrage led to the formation of the New York Factory Investigation Commission, whose work paved the way for industrial regulations.[78]

Although these were among the most well-known episodes in immigrant women's labor history, thousands of less-publicized strikes took place with women's leadership during the eighteenth and nineteenth centuries. Cap makers, buttonhole makers, laundry workers, hat trimmers, paper box workers, corset workers, and glove workers struck for better pay and working conditions. Often these women had to face the entrenched opposition of the major labor organization of the time, the American Federation of Labor, which was largely hostile to women's organizing as well as to the organizing of unskilled laborers and workers of color. In San Francisco, for instance, laundry women lived in dormitories and worked from six in the morning until midnight. When they applied to the international laundry workers' union for a charter, the men tried to block their application. Eventually, however, the international union admitted the women, who struck and won an eight-hour day. By 1912, the Laundry Workers International Union had raised wages 30 percent, improved safety conditions, and organized all San Francisco's steam laundries.[79]

Work at Home, Paid and Unpaid

One survey of a New York City working-class neighborhood in 1855 found that nearly one-third of immigrant wives worked for pay, most of them at home. Many wives took in laundry or garment work, rolled cigars, or made artificial flowers or buttons. For example, it was common in "Little Italy"—tenements in northeastern cities—for *padrones* (Italian labor contractors) to distribute piecework among women to be performed in the home. Taking in boarders or lodgers was another way in which immigrant wives added to family income, and was especially prevalent when men far outnumbered women within an immigrant ethnic group. One study in Lawrence, Massachusetts found that 90 percent of families where the husband was the sole wage earner took in boarders to supplement family income. In Homestead, Pennsylvania, most Slavic families took in boarders, adding on average more than 25 percent to the family's income. A typical Slavic household consisted of a husband, wife, three children, and anywhere from one to four lodgers—all in a four-room house.[80]

Regardless of the nature of the work they performed for pay, all immigrant women also performed unpaid work in their own homes. As we have seen, housekeeping in nineteenth-century cities was backbreaking work, made all the more difficult by the conditions in the tenements where immigrants lived. In the New York City tenement district in the 1890s, for instance, only 300 of the 225,000 residents had access to bathtubs. Women hauled water and coal up and down multiple flights of stairs, cooked and cleaned for their families and the boarders who crowded into every available space, and cared for the sick—infant mortality was high—and the aged. Many also gardened or kept chickens on tiny plots of land.[81]

Sometimes women gathered together to protest the conditions in which they were forced to perform their homemaking work. In 1902, thousands of Jewish women in Brooklyn, Newark, and Boston stormed butcher shops and poured kerosene on the meat to protest increases in kosher meat prices. In 1914, Italian women in Providence, Rhode Island, took to the streets to bring the price of pasta down.[82]

Immigrants in the Mines and on Farms

A small number of European immigrants settled in rural areas. In the late nineteenth century, some immigrant families went to farm in the northern Plains states. The Homestead Law of 1862 attracted Germans, Slavs, and Scandinavians, particularly Norwegians. Like U.S.-born women, immigrant women homesteaders endured the isolation and hardships of frontier life, writing in their diaries of their fears and their sorrows. Guri Olsdatter, a Norwegian woman in Minnesota, lost her husband and sons in the fighting between homesteaders and Sioux Indians defending their lands. Nevertheless, she chose to remain on the farm with her daughters. Writing to one daughter who remained behind in Norway, she said:

> Of the six cattle that I now have three are milk cows and of these I have sold butter, the summer's product, a little over two hundred and thirty pounds...one or another has advised me to sell my land, but I would rather keep it for a time yet, in the hope that some of my people might come and use it...if you would come here, you could buy it and use it and then it would not be necessary to let it fall into the hands of strangers....And may the Lord by his grace bend, direct, and govern our hearts so that we sometime with gladness may assemble with God in the eternal mansions where there will be no more partings, no sorrows, no more trials, but everlasting joy and gladness.[83]

Other immigrants, mostly men, went to mining communities in West Virginia, Pennsylvania, and the Northwest. Early white immigrant miners were English, Welsh, and Irish; in the late nineteenth century, Poles, Czechs, Slovaks, Serbs, and Croatians predominated.[84]

Immigrant male miners usually sent for their wives after establishing themselves in the United States. A miner's wife typically took care of as many as six to 12 boarders in a shanty house with no running water. Women worked through the day to prepare food, do laundry, mend clothing, and clean house, all the time fearing the sound of the siren or bell announcing a mine accident. The late nineteenth century saw bitter struggles to unionize mining, and many immigrant women actively supported the unions. One famous and effective activist was Mother Jones:

> Until she was nearly one hundred years old, Mother Jones was where the danger was greatest—crossing militia lines, spending weeks in damp prisons, incurring the wrath of governors, presidents, and coal operators—as she helped organize the United Mine Workers with the only tools she felt she needed: "convictions and a voice."...She organized women to shame scabbing men into joining the union...The wives [in Arnot, Pennsylvania] rose before the men, with babes in their arms, and pledged themselves to see that no one went to work. The company tried to bring in scabs, but Mother Jones persuaded the men to stay at home with the children while the women attended to the scabs, [conducting] a "round-the-clock" patrol of the mines...Her work was described as..."raising hell up in the mountains with a bunch of wild women." [85]

Mother Jones advised women of the time, "Whatever your fight, don't be ladylike."[86]

Social Homemaking

In the late nineteenth and early twentieth centuries, literally millions of middle- and upper-class, mostly U.S.-born, white women were involved in a series of clubs, organizations, and activist groups. (African American women, for the most part excluded from these groups, were involved in similar organizations, as discussed in Chapter 6.) Feminist historians have called this movement "Social Homemaking," for these women acted, for the most part, out of their interpretations of the homemaking vocation. Far from passively accepting a fixed set of housewifely duties and confinement to the home, white homemakers extended homemaking to include both paid and unpaid professions outside of the home.[87]

Catherine Beecher, Emma Willard, and Mary Lyons led the movement of white women into education, founding the Hartford Seminary, the Troy Seminary, and Mount Holyoke, respectively. As Willard argued, women's higher education was necessary because:

Unprovided with the means of acquiring that knowledge which flows liberally to the other sex...how should we be able to form enlarged and correct views, either of the character to which we ought to mould them [our children], or of the means most proper to form them aright?[88]

Higher education was also needed to prepare white women for teaching, which social homemakers argued was a natural extension of women's mothering role. According to Beecher: "Our Creator designed woman to be the chief educator of our race and the prime minister of our family state, and our aim [in female seminaries] is to train her to this holy calling." [89]

During the Civil War, young white women replaced white men in their teaching jobs, and the job remained mostly female after the War's end. For many women, teaching in isolated areas such as the Northwest Territory had a missionary-like quality; indeed, for some, teaching meant imposing Christianity and white ways on Native American children. Thousands of white women went South after the Civil War to teach freed slaves. According to European American historian Jacqueline Jones, the typical teacher was in her late twenties, single, and the well-educated daughter of a clergyman or a farmer from New England. She was Protestant and middle class, abhorred slavery and endured great difficulty and harassment to teach in the South. The teachers typically taught primary classes for three hours in the morning, intermediate classes for three hours in the afternoon, and adult classes for two hours in the evening. Esther Douglas painted the following picture of her Georgia classroom: "My room is 16 x 17 feet; in this I have often *packed* ninety five pupils of various sizes; for lack of seats about a score stand *huddled* up in one-quarter of the room." [90]

As public schooling became increasingly available in the latter part of the nineteenth century, the demand for teachers everywhere grew rapidly. Now U.S.-born, white, middle-class women had an alternative to domestic and factory work, although an equally low-paid one, and a respectable way to survive the shortage of eligible husbands. By 1900, 9 percent of European American women were employed as teachers.[91]

After the Civil War, social homemakers claimed and developed a second profession, nursing. Through the American Women's Education Association and the Sanitary Commission, among other organizations, social homemakers worked to elevate the status of nursing, which had been viewed as unskilled domestic work. In 1870, there were over 10,000 nurses in the United States, most of them older white women who sewed or did domestic work to supplement their low earnings from nursing. Formal training for nurses began in 1873 in nursing schools that generally were affiliated with hospitals. The student nurses were given an allowance for expenses of 12 dollars a month and received room and board. In exchange, they worked a 13-hour day, six days a week, 50 weeks a year. According to European American historian Susan Reverby, "The woman entering nursing school may have expected to *train*; what she did primarily, however, was to *work*."[92] Trained nurses were overwhelmingly single, young, and U.S.-born white women. As late as 1920, 97 percent of the trained nurses in the United States were white.[93] Upon graduation, most trained nurses worked in their patients' homes, although larger hospitals did hire some of the graduates. Despite their skills, hospital nurses in the late nineteenth century continued to make and roll bandages, wash dressings and laundry, and clean both their own quarters and hospital rooms.

The development of the nursing profession coincided with the take-over of medicine by white men, who forced midwives and other women healers out of health care. Instead, women were funnelled into the auxiliary role of nurse. Thus the masculine/feminine doctor/nurse team of modern medicine was born, and this new sexual division of labor was institutionalized in U.S. hospitals and doctors' offices.[94]

One group of social homemakers construed their task as "home protection." As Carry Nation, a nineteenth-century social reformer, wrote:

> We hear "A woman's place is at home." That is true but what and where is home? Not the walls of a house…If my son is in a drinking place, my place is there. If my daughter, or the daughter of anyone else, my family or any other family, is in trouble, my place is there. [A woman would be either selfish or cowardly if she] would refuse to leave her home to relieve suffering or trouble. Jesus said, "Go out into the highways and hedges." He said this to women, as well as men.[95]

White women home protectors were the main force behind the Temperance Movement, an anti-alcohol movement aimed at protecting families from the irresponsibility, impoverishment, and family violence attributable to men's drinking. The Women's Christian Temperance Union, an organization which boasted 800,000 members by 1920, was instrumental in winning the fight for the prohibition of alcohol consumption. Female Reform Societies fought against prostitution, which they saw as both tempting their husbands into sin and ruining the lives of young women. Consumer Leagues organized homemakers to protect their homes from shoddy and unsafe consumer goods, publishing lists of products which should be purchased or boycotted. When socialist Florence Kelley was elected president of the national Consumer League in 1899, their efforts were extended to solidarity with the women workers who produced consumer goods, and the League began pressuring employers for a shorter work week. Gaining more control over reproduction was the goal of social homemakers involved in the Voluntary Motherhood movement; as legal and effective birth control was unavailable, women argued for sexual abstinence or a rhythm method.[96]

Other social homemaking campaigns focused more directly on the needs of the less fortunate, and brought upper- and middle-class, U.S.-born, white women into direct contact and sometimes alliance with poor, immigrant, and enslaved women. Large numbers of white women were active in the Abolitionist Movement, which gained strength among whites and freed African Americans in the 1830s; female anti-slavery societies were formed throughout New England and had their first convention in 1837. Sarah and Angelina Grimke, daughters of a southern slave-holder family, became famous for their anti-slavery speaking, which drew fire both for its content and its form.[97] Writing in the *Anti-Slavery Examiner* in 1836, Angelina argued, "Slavery always has, and always will, produce insurrections wherever it exists, because it is a violation of the natural order of things, and no human power can much longer perpetuate it."[98]

Speaking and other public reform activities (such as gathering and signing the anti-slavery petition) were not considered acceptable for women, and so began white women's battle to obtain political rights so that they could more effectively perform their social housekeeping duties. For instance, Mary Livermore, a leader of the Civil War era's Sanitary Commission, was rebuffed by the builder to whom she attempted to address a check in payment for the construction of a hospital. In her astonishment, she said:

> Here was a revelation. We two women were able to enlist the whole Northwest in a great philanthropic money-making enterprise…We had money of our own in hand, twice as much as was necessary to pay the builder. But by the laws of the State in which we lived our individual names were not worth the paper they were written on.[99]

One important aspect of the fight came between 1839 and 1850, when state after state passed laws recognizing married women's rights to hold property in their own names (however, laws restricting property ownership by Asian immigrants and African American slaves excluded women of color from enjoying these rights). Many men supported this reform, including Judge Hurlbut of New York, who found himself unpersuaded by his own arguments against women's rights and joined the women's cause.[100]

The late nineteenth and early twentieth centuries saw new kinds of social housekeeping activities emerge. In the 1880s, women (and men) college graduates began the Settlement House movement; by 1910, there were 400 settlement houses, most in slums of the Northeast and Midwest.[101] Settlement house workers saw their mission as "civilizing" poor immigrants through classes, kindergartens, and literary events. When one worker asked an immigrant woman about her concern, as a mother, for the souls of her children, the contrast between the domestic ideal of mothering and the reality of slum life were revealed in the answer:

> Who's got time to think about souls grinding away here 14 hours a day to turn out contract goods? Tain't souls that count. It's bodies, that can be driven an' half-starved an' driven still, till they drop in their tracks, I'm driving now to pay a doctor's bill for my three that went with the fever. Before that I was driving to put food into their mouths.[102]

As a result of experiences such as these, settlement house workers increasingly realized that economics, especially long hours and low wages, was at the root of the immigrants' problems. Many settlement residents saw union organizing as the answer. In 1903, U.S.-born, white social housekeepers allied with white immigrant women workers to form the National Women's Trade Union League (WTUL), which encouraged and supported labor organizing among immigrant women. At the time, one-third of European immigrant women were employed in manufacturing, working long hours for low pay. The League trained and hired organizers from different immigrant populations and worked to attract women into the labor movement by offering them concrete, short-term benefits, such as instruction in English. New York WTUL member Violet Pike wrote a text, *New World Lessons for Old World Peoples*, which taught English vocabulary at the same time as it highlighted the advantages of unionism through stories of immigrant women's organizing successes. The WTUL published the book in Lithuanian, Italian, Yiddish, Bohemian, and English. The League also used the class privilege of its prominent members against employers: their picket in support of the "Uprising of the Twenty Thousand" was termed "The Mink Brigade," and included the sister of financial magnate J.P. Morgan. The League had much less success in its fight against the sexism of the white, male-dominated, craft-based American Federation of Labor.[103]

By the early twentieth century, white women reformers had "built a national organization network that was nearly as sophisticated in its own way as the corporate business world." This network, which involved literally millions of white women, consisted of national organizations with overlapping leadership, connected into the more social, less political white women's club movement. Led by the National Women's Suffrage Association (NAWSA), 2 million women (Black and white) participated in the struggle which won the vote for women in 1920. These social homemakers had turned the cult of domesticity on its head, from an ideal which limited and restricted women to the domestic sphere, to a rationale for women's rights.[104]

While white social housekeepers shared a common motivation to better the condition of the needy and oppressed, they had a wide range of political convictions. Some leaders, such as Florence Kelley (Consumers' League), Frances Willard (Women's Christian Temperance Union), and Vida Scudder were avowed socialists, critical of capitalism's system of class inequality. But most saw their work as reforming and humanizing industrial capitalism, not replacing it.

This range of views and practices was also present with regard to women of color. Some white social homemakers, especially in the Abolition Movement and the Women's Trade Union League, extended solidarity across class and race lines. For example, Florence Kelley was a founding member of the National Association for the Advancement of Colored People (NAACP).[105] However, the privileged white women in these movements were usually condescending and exclusionary of the women they were trying to help. For example, the white anti-slavery societies commonly excluded Black women from membership. Even worse, other social homemakers worked to expand or defend their class and race privilege. As African American scholar Bell Hooks has pointed out, many white women's rights advocates stepped up their organizing efforts when it appeared that African American men might win the vote before them. Famous suffragist Elizabeth Cady Stanton argued in the late nineteenth century:

> If Saxon men have legislated thus for their own mothers, wives and daughters, what can we hope for at the hands of Chinese, Indians, and Africans?...I protest against the enfranchisement of another man of any race or clime until the daughters of Jefferson, Hancock, and Adams are crowned with their rights.[106]

Other white leaders in the suffrage movement argued for educational restrictions on the vote, or for women's vote as a means to "insure immediate and durable white supremacy." [107] Still others sold out their poor and African American "sisters" in an attempt to win the backing of the white men in power. For example, the white leaders of the NAWSA defended the southern states' right to exclude poor whites and African Americans from voting through poll taxes, grandfather clauses, and educational restrictions. Margaret Sanger, the famous advocate of birth control, focused her efforts on poor women and women of color. Sanger allied herself with the racist and classist eugenics movement, writing in 1919, "More children from the fit, less from the unfit—that is the chief issue of birth control."[108]

Ironically, an indirect result of social homemakers' diverse efforts to live out the cult of domesticity was the carving out of socially acceptable, non-domestic careers for educated white women. Teaching, social work, nursing, and government service were now permissible jobs for white

Table 5-1

Occupational Distribution of European American Women, 1900-1980
(in Percent)

	1900	1930	1960	1970	1980
Agriculture	9.8	4.1	1.5	0.7	1.0
Manufacturing	32.6	21.2	18.5	16.8	12.6
Private Household Service	29.8	12.0	4.4	2.1	0.8
Service (not Private Household)	3.8	8.1	13.2	15.3	15.3
Sales	4.1	9.3	9.2	8.0	12.1
Clerical	6.9	25.3	34.5	36.8	32. 3
Professional & Technical	10.2	16.2	14.6	16.3	18.0
Managerial, Administrative, & Official	2.9	3.6	4.3	3.9	7.9

NOTES: Totals do not always sum to 100 because of rounding. Manufacturing includes craft and transportation workers; agriculture includes mining, fishing, and forestry; managerial, administrative, & official includes some self-employment, and excludes farm managers. European American includes Latinas classified as white, except in 1980. For a full listing of occupational categories included, see Appendix B. For a discussion of comparability problems between Census years, see Appendix D. SOURCES: See Appendix A.

women, although only a tiny minority of women of color were admitted. Table 5-1 shows the occupational distribution of employed white women from 1900 to 1980. By 1900, over 10 percent of white women workers held professional and technical jobs. Many of these jobs were directly linked to social homemaking, such as Rose Schneiderman's work as a WTUL activist, Mary Anderson's employment in the Women's Bureau, and Florence Kelley's employment as an Illinois factory inspector. The new sociologists and social scientists who studied women, including Edith Abbott, Sophinistra Breckenridge, Helen Sumner, and Mary Beard, among others, also found professional jobs as a result of social homemaking.

Further, white women had made these new vocations acceptable not just as a stage before marriage, but as lifetime career alternatives to marriage and homemaking. Many of the leaders of this movement, including Jane Addams, Vida Scudder, and Frances Willard, not only rejected marriage, but lived with women in intense emotional (and probably sexual) love relationships. As Willard wrote, "In these days when any capable and careful woman can honorably earn her own support, there is no village that has not its example of 'two hearts in consort' both of which are feminine."[109]

Boom to Bust: White Women's Employment from World War I to the Depression

The U.S. economy expanded dramatically during World War I and through the 1920s. The war created a serious labor shortage, not only because so many male workers had been drafted, but also as a result of the 1924 Immigration Act, which sharply curtailed the number of European immigrants. Nearly 10 million women entered the workforce during the war, over 1 million of them producing war supplies. Referring to World War I, one homemaker from a typical middle-class, white community told an interviewer: "I began to work during the war when every one else did; we had to meet payments on our house and everything else was getting so high."[110]

Not surprisingly, women generally earned less than men performing the same job—an investigation by the Women's Bureau of the Department of Labor found that six government contractors paid women between 10 and 33 percent less than men—and women rarely were employed in highly skilled jobs; most white women were confined to clerical, personal service, or unskilled factory work.[111]

The decade of the 1920s saw a surge in labor militancy, and white women played important roles. In Willimantic, Connecticut, a women's committee led a strike by 2,600 textile workers at American Thread; 80 percent of the workers were women. An even larger strike took place in Passaic, New Jersey. A Women's Bureau report found that of the 16,000 millworkers in Passaic, nearly 10,000 were women. The Consumer's League found terrible working conditions in Passaic:

> The noise and shriek of machinery, the oil-soaked floors, the close, humid air, and the strain of night work seem past belief...Most women...answered, "one, two hours, maybe" [to a question about how much sleep they got].[112]

Over 80 percent of the workers made less than $1,300 a year, although the National Industrial Conference Board judged that at least $1,400 was needed to attain a minimum standard of living. The women, most of them first- or second-generation European immigrants, brought their babies to the picket line, served as picket captains, and served on all strike committees. The strikers won recognition of their union, and other demands.[113]

Coal miners' wives also maintained their militancy through the 1920s, setting up important auxiliaries to picket and provide other support during the many strikes called by the United Mine Workers of America. Janet Guynn, the daughter, mother, sister, and niece of miners, described her participation in a women's auxiliary set up to aid in a 1928 strike in Lansing, Ohio:

I used to always stick in the house and sew patch-work quilts. And my lands, I was sick all the time! But now that I've got out fightin' and organizin' like this, I don't know a sick day. And I don't spend time cleanin' my house either, the way I used to. I used to think if I don't mop up that kitchen every day, something terrible would happen. But now I just leave everything and go out and fight.[114]

For white women, one of the most important aspects of the post-World War I expansion of the economy was the growth of white-collar employment, both in professional jobs (mainly teaching and social work) and in non-professional jobs (especially office work and retail sales). In 1900, 13 percent of employed white women worked in managerial and professional jobs, and another 11 percent in clerical and sales work. By 1930, these proportions had climbed to 20 and 35 percent, respectively (see Table 5-1), and the majority of white women workers held white-collar jobs.

Key to the growth of white women's white-collar work was the explosion of the clerical sector. Growing corporations, with their branch offices and multiple departments specializing in different aspects of business, required vast quantities of information and communication. In the late nineteenth century, offices had been white male enclaves, and a clerk was an apprentice for management positions. However, with the introduction of the typewriter, clerical work was transformed into a dead-end, white women's job. Women's movement into offices met some resistance. In 1900, the *Ladies Home Journal* warned:

> [I]t is a plain, simple fact that women have shown themselves naturally incompetent to fill a great many of the business positions which they have sought to occupy...The fact is that no one woman in a hundred can stand the physical strain of the keen pace which competition has forced upon every line of business today.[115]

These predictions notwithstanding, clerical work was feminized; by 1930, clerical jobs employed over one-fourth of white women workers. Most were single women, second-generation U.S. residents.[116]

Drawn by new opportunities in offices and stores, especially in urban areas, white women left domestic service in large numbers. This decline was also facilitated by new commodities which permitted homemakers to clean and cook without the aid of servants. By 1930, as shown in Table 5-1, only one in eight white women was employed in domestic service, less than half the proportion in 1900. The share in manufacturing work also declined, from 33 percent to 21 percent.

White Women During the Great Depression

The economic growth of the Roaring Twenties came to a halt in 1929, with the crash of the stock market. Over the next 12 years, the U.S. economy remained mired in the Great Depression, with unemployment soaring to historically high levels. As husbands, fathers, sweethearts, and brothers lost their jobs, women entered the workforce to support their families. Unable to afford families, couples postponed marriage and birth rates fell, particularly among second- and higher-generation (indicating the number of generations since the family immigrated to the United States) whites. Through most of the Depression years, white women's unemployment rates were actually lower than men's—partly because they worked for less, and partly because many women's jobs, such as domestic service, clerical work, and some factory jobs, were sex-stereotyped and men would not take them. Still, during the Depression, married working women faced substantial public disapproval: a Gallup poll in 1936 found that 82 percent of Americans opposed the employment of married women. Efforts to prevent the employment of married women occurred at the state and federal level. Although most of these laws did not pass or were repealed, they did have a chilling effect on women's search for employment. For instance, in 1930-1931, a survey of 1,500 cities found that three-quarters of cities did not employ married women.[117]

During the long Depression, working women's wages were low and falling, and job security was elusive. One study of working women found that most women changed jobs frequently—as often as nine jobs in eight years. Schoolteachers, predominantly white women, suffered a 30 percent cut in pay between 1932 and 1934 alone.[118] As a result of rising unemployment, white women's movement into professional and technical work slowed. One study of unemployment and employment in New York City pointed out that:

> ...these are the women who by their age and training and marital status largely belong to the women who have sought major satisfactions in their jobs, renouncing marriage and working years to reach their vocational achievements.[119]

For farm women, the Depression accelerated the movement off the land which industrialization and the declining availability of frontier land had begun. Before the Depression, there were over 7 million cotton sharecroppers in the South. The New Deal attempted to solve the farm crisis through the Agricultural Allotment Act, which paid farmers not to produce crops; however, many landlords used their checks to mechanize and to evict both African American and white sharecroppers from the land. Between 1935 and

1937 alone, over 300,000 white sharecroppers left Arkansas, Missouri, Oklahoma, and Texas. Most whites headed west to California, where they worked as migrant farmworkers until the wartime boom provided industry jobs. Other former sharecroppers and tenant farmers moved to the cities.[120]

This movement off the land into the cities was of profound social significance, transforming the experience of the average white woman from that of a farmer's wife to an urban housewife. Between 1929 and 1965, 30 million people of all races moved to the cities from the farms—more than foreign immigration brought to U.S. shores between 1840 and 1960.[121]

White women's housework—like that of women of other racial-ethnic groups—expanded during the Depression. As European American historian Lois Helmbold points out:

> Women couldn't be consumers when there was no money for purchases. Instead, women became producers once again. Women returned to subsistence work, producing the things people needed instead of consuming them…Any work that would involve an investment of a woman's time and energy, but not an expenditure of money, was a survival strategy.[122]

Women gardened, canned, remade clothing, scavenged for wood and other materials. The most popular quilt patterns of the Depression era were those which utilized tiny scraps of cloth. To cut corners, middle-class white families fired their domestic servants. However, wealth did insulate a small share of white women from the economic effects of the Depression. Society debutantes, for instance, continued to make their debuts at lavish cotillions.[123]

The New Deal brought some relief with the establishment of a number of federal government welfare programs such as Aid to Families with Dependent Children and Social Security in 1938. Most of these welfare programs aided white women more than women of color. For instance, Social Security excluded domestic and agricultural workers from coverage, and AFDC was administered by local relief workers who could deny women benefits if they considered them employable (and who generally considered women of color more employable than white women). However, the relief programs were barely adequate, even for whites.[124]

The New Deal also attempted some reforms of working conditions through the 1932 National Industrial Recovery Act, which developed minimum-wage and -hour standards. These industry codes raised wages in the New York garment industry by between 30 percent and 60 percent by 1934. The codes applied to factory and white-collar work, but not to domestic work or agriculture. Therefore, they afforded more protection to white women than to women of color, since the latter were concentrated in domestic work and agriculture in 1930. Even though the codes did establish minimum-wage standards, roughly one-quarter of the codes condoned lower wage rates for women by allowing employers to pay less for light, repetitive work or to employees who had earned less before 1929.[125]

New Deal legislation had a dramatic effect on unionization among white workers as well as workers of color. In 1935, a new labor organization had arisen in response to the American Federation of Labor's inability to respond to the rise of mass production. The new group, known as the Congress of Industrial Organizations, argued for industrial unionism, organizing all the workers in a particular industry (e.g., all workers employed in the automobile industry) rather than all the workers in a particular trade (e.g., all electricians). Although it was white-male-dominated, the union was one of the first to attempt cross-racial organizing. In the same year, the Wagner Act was passed, guaranteeing workers the right to organize. The Act gave the green light to new CIO organizers. Within weeks of its passage, for instance, the New York dressmakers' union grew seven-fold.[126]

Unionization expanded in industries such as automobile, electrical, and textile. However, most of the new industrial unions of the CIO, like the trade-dominated AFL before it, failed to target women workers in their mass organizing drives, continuing to view women as secondary workers who could not develop true labor militancy. Nonetheless, during the 1930s and throughout the 1940s, white women participated in CIO organizing as members of women's auxiliaries who supported strikes, set up communal kitchens to feed strikers and their families, leafletted, and sometimes fought police or company thugs.

One important exception to the CIO's failure to target women workers was the United Office and Professional Workers of America (UOPWA), established in 1937. The Depression had brought about a serious deterioration in wages and job prospects for clerical workers, partly because so many people were seeking office jobs, including middle-class women (and men) who were unable to find professional jobs and middle-class women who might otherwise have gone to college. This increasing supply of workers meant that wages dropped dramatically, paid vacations were abolished, clerical unemployment rose sharply, piecework and production quotas were established, and work sped up. The UOPWA fought back with a series of successful strikes by office workers. In the late 1930s, for instance, 33 office workers at the Maidenform Brassiere Company went on strike and 1,000 factory workers honored their picket line. Office workers at another brassiere factory struck in 1940, demanding "an uplift in wages because the company kept them flat-busted." [127] After the war, the union was expelled from the CIO because of its left-wing leadership, and office-worker organizing was not to revive until the late 1970s.[128]

White women also struck in southern mill towns, as wages fell, work hours increased, and whole families joined the workforce in order to make ends meet. The Gastonia strike was one of the largest of these strikes, which began in 1929 in North Carolina. Ella Mae Wiggins, a mill worker and strike leader wrote this song about working mothers for the Gastonia struggle:

> We leave our home in the morning,
> We kiss our children goodbye,
> While we slave for the Bosses
>
> Our children scream and cry.
>
> How it grieves the heart of a mother
> You everyone must know.
> But we can't buy for our children,
> Our wages are too low.[129]

Rosie the Riveter: White Women During World War II

World War II created job opportunities for the white women who had been unemployed during the Depression, drew new white women workers into the labor force, and allowed many to earn higher wages than had been possible before the war. Although the conventional wisdom holds that millions of women joined the labor force in response to appeals to their patriotism, three-quarters of the 19 million women who earned wages during the war had been employed before. What was different was that many of the white women who worked during the war were married and had previously withdrawn from paid work. Responding to appeals based on patriotism, these white married women returned to work alongside single women.[130]

Even though women's work was deemed of critical importance to the war effort, few special arrangements were made for mothers in the workforce. A paltry $400,000 in federal money was made available to build child-care centers, so child care remained scarce and expensive. A few manufacturing plants provided hot lunches. One model employer was Kaiser Industries, which provided working women with hot meals to take home to their children.[131]

Still, women of all races found better work now than before the war, and women of different racial-ethnic groups moved up a rung on the job ladder. When white women in the South moved from laundries to factories, African American women left domestic service to fill the laundry jobs. White professional women took white men's places in banking, insurance, civil service, education, and health. Seizing the opportunities created by the war, organizations representing white professional women (such as the American Association of University Women and the National Federation of Business and Professional Women) lobbied for access to positions of power in government agencies. However, these groups remained class- and race-biased. For instance, both groups focused their efforts on opening the Medical Reserve Corps to women physicians, ignoring military discrimination against African American women; they also failed to support the campaign mounted by a Black sorority, Alpha Kappa Alpha, to appoint African American staff to the Department of Labor's Women's Bureau.[132]

When the war ended, so did white women's opportunity to hold white men's jobs. White women in high-paying industries—such as chemical, rubber, and petroleum—were laid off at double the rate of men. One best-selling book, *Modern Woman: The Lost Sex,* warned women to stay out of "fields belonging to the male area of exploit or authority." Many of the white women who had not worked for pay before the war returned to the home and began childbearing. Nevertheless, the overall effect of the war on white women's labor-force participation rates was positive.[133]

The Feminine Mystique

While the Depression and World War II had lowered birth rates and marriage rates, the 1950s saw an increase in domesticity manifested by the "baby boom." During the decade, white women married and had children earlier than during the previous two decades. The proportion of women attending college fell sharply between 1940 and 1960, and only one-third of those who attended college received a degree.[134]

Wartime prosperity and the GI Bill made home ownership a possibility for many white families, and suburbs grew up around urban centers. By 1960, one-third of the U.S. population resided in the suburbs, which were almost exclusively white enclaves. (Not until the fair-housing struggles of the 1960s did African Americans and other people of color begin to gain entry to suburban housing developments.) White women in the suburbs spent substantial amounts of time in housework and child care. One study found that women actually spent more time on housework in 1960 than in the 1920s. The study also found that the amount of time spent on child care had doubled, even though the average number of children in a family had fallen. Some of this increase reflected a decline in the prevalence of domestic servants for white families, but an increase in standards for childrearing and cleanliness also boosted the amount of time suburban women spent in homemaking. For instance, washing machines replaced laundresses, but as a result, white women who could afford the machines now did their own laundry and spotlessness became the ideal. Childrearing became the focal point of a woman's life, even for upper-class women. Dr. Spock's instructions on childrearing were aimed entirely at the mother: "Some fathers get gooseflesh at the very idea of helping to take care of a baby and there is no good to be gained by trying to force them."[135]

But in spite of the pressures toward domesticity in the 1950s, white married women continued to enter paid work: their share in the labor force rose from 21 percent in 1950 to 28 percent in 1960. Much of this employment growth came among women in their late 30s and 40s. Since women's childbearing years were shorter and their life expectancies were longer than their foremothers', it became common for white mothers to re-enter the labor force after their children were in school or grown.[136]

A further impulse behind white married women's movement into the labor force was consumerism, which impelled them to seek income to raise their families' standards of living. As industrialization progressed through the twentieth century, there had been an increasing tendency for families to measure their social standing by the goods and services they consumed. By the 1950s, families found themselves in a consumption race to "keep up with the Joneses" or, if possible, to surpass them. But consumerism proved to be an endless treadmill—by the time one new commodity had been acquired, other new ones had been invented. White homemakers worked to buy a house, a second car, and a college education for their children. In this way, white married women left their domestic enclave in order to fulfill their domestic vocation—they could no longer fill expanding family needs without earning an income themselves. Once they had experienced paid work, many found personal satisfaction on the job, and stayed.[137]

A final impetus pushing white married women into the labor force was actual frustration with their domestic profession. White, college-educated women who were full-time homemakers found themselves unfulfilled by suburban domesticity, especially when their children left home for school. In 1966, Betty Friedan's book, *The Feminine Mystique*, called attention to their discontent. The book sold millions of copies, and within a year a new organization, the National Organization of Women, was formed with a mostly white, affluent membership with Friedan at its head.[138]

Social Activism and the Second Wave of Feminism

The growth of white married women's labor force participation has been called a "subtle revolution." In the 1950s and 1960s, another revolution was taking place—the civil rights struggle led by African Americans. Many white women participated in the struggle as members of organizations like the Student Nonviolent Coordinating Committee (SNCC) and the Congress for Racial Equality (CORE). For example, Viola Liuzzo, a Detroit housewife (as she was described in the media), was killed by Ku Klux Klansmen in 1965 after participating in the historic march of civil rights supporters in Selma,

Alabama. Radicalized by the civil rights movement, many of these women went on to participate in the protest movement against the Vietnam War and the growing New Left student movement.[139]

In the 1970s, many of these radical white women, most of them educated and middle- or upper-income in background, became involved in the plethora of grassroots activities that came to be known as the "women's liberation movement." White women gathered to explore their oppression in consciousness-raising groups, worked to win abortion rights, established shelters for battered women, and set up rape crisis centers. Lesbians took the leadership in many of these activities; many were also involved in the burgeoning lesbian and gay rights movement.

An attack on gender roles and the domestic ideal was central to the white women's liberation movement. In 1969, the Seattle Women's Majority Union criticized the sexual division of labor as "the mutilation of individual whole human beings to fit the half-size Procrustes' beds society assigns selectively to 'men' and to 'women.'"[140] Feminists rejected the prevailing view that full-time homemakers were privileged and pampered by exposing the difficulties and demands of housework, the prevalence of wife-beating, and the financial devastation that accompanies divorce. In consciousness-raising groups they expressed their frustration with the ways that the domestic ideal had oppressed them: as full-time homemakers financially dependent upon and often abused by their husbands; as women working a "double day," exposed to sexism and low wages in the workplace and then expected to wait on their husbands and children at night; or as women living in poverty without men, derided for being spinsters, and abused by the welfare system. They recognized that the idealization of white women's beauty converted them into sex objects, brought them disdain and divorce as they aged, and caused employers to ignore their abilities on the job.

White women also protested against being stereotyped as too fragile, emotional, and domestic to succeed in white men's jobs. NOW and other groups, such as the Women's Equity Action League, became involved in the fight for equal pay and access to men's jobs. These groups built on the landmark victories of the civil rights struggle by seeking enforcement of the sex provisions of the Equal Pay Act of 1963 and the Civil Rights Act of 1964.

Although the women's liberation movement and many of its early participants had their roots in the civil rights movement, the movement was dominated by white women, and reflected their perspective with all its racism. Feminists of color who participated in the movement criticized its insistence on lumping all men together as the oppressors of all women and its unwillingness to take up issues of racial oppression. Eventually, many women of color split off to form their own womanist or feminist groups.[141]

Even in their vision of women's liberation, white feminists were divided. Radical feminists envisioned feminism as a revolutionary transformation of all of society's institutions, which, although centered in struggle against sexual inequality, would eliminate all hierarchy. More conservative feminists saw it as a movement to end the discriminatory barriers which had prevented women with race, class, and educational privilege from receiving their share of elite economic and political power. White feminists also struggled over the issue of lesbian rights: while many insisted that women's right to love other women was central to a feminist agenda, others disagreed. For example, while Friedan was president of NOW, she denounced lesbian feminists as "the lavender menace" and tried to distance feminism from lesbianism so as to gain greater social acceptance for her branch of the women's movement.[142]

White Women in the Labor Force, 1960-1990

The three decades from 1960 to 1990 were a period of increasing labor force participation for white women, and of many struggles, both individual and collective, for labor market advancement. The share of European American women in the labor force rose from one-third in 1960 to over one-half in 1986; most striking were the rising rates for married women, which nearly doubled. The number of employed white women almost doubled between 1960 and 1980. Expanding job opportunities, particularly in the service-producing sector, helped fuel this labor force growth in the 1960s and early-1970s. In the mid-1970s, the U.S. economy entered a decade of economic crisis; the effect of this stagnation, the most severe since the Great Depression, was to further encourage labor force participation among white married women as white male real wages fell and unemployment rose. Unlike the 1930s, no one suggested that married women be kept out of jobs. That aspect of the cult of domesticity ideal was all but dead. White married women's employment was widely accepted.

Growing numbers of educated white women, armed with race and class privilege, were able to take advantage of affirmative action legislation and economic growth to break into primary sector jobs, even those which had been dominated by white men. By 1970, the share of white women in the upper tier of the primary sector had reached 13 percent. By 1980, nearly one-quarter of white women held jobs in this tier, as shown in Figure 5-1. (However, their share was still substantially lower than that of white men, over one-third of whom were found in this tier.) Another 8 percent of white women were employed in the bottom tier of the primary sector, mostly in nursing and other health assessment jobs. (This was roughly one-fourth the share of European American men.) In the 1980s, plagued by "nurse burnout" and in the midst of a nursing shortage, registered nurses successfully organized across the country to win higher wages and better working conditions.

Between 1970 and 1980, white women made progress into many of the upper-tier primary jobs which had been monopolized by white men, such as engineers, managers and administrators, and commodities and finance sales representatives. In fact, in 1980, the relative concentration of white women in the managerial and administrative category had reached three-quarters of their share in the labor force. Media images of the new, white executive woman abounded. In the words of one popular perfume commercial, she can "bring home the bacon, fry it up in the pan, and never let you forget you're a man." However, the new woman's salary was far from equal to that of her white male counterpart. Even as late as 1987, white women managers and administrators earned only 57 percent as much as white men. White women also increased their share of highly paid lower-tier primary jobs.[143]

But only a minority of white women achieved this economic success. More than two-thirds continued to be employed in the secondary labor market in 1980, including 18 percent in the lower tier's low-wage and dead-end jobs. For these women, economic reality was a far cry from the slick magazine images of the new managerial woman. Secondary labor market workers were particularly affected by the stagnation of economic growth that began in the mid-1970s. As their husbands, fathers, and brothers lost relatively high-paying blue-collar jobs, the women of the secondary labor market found themselves increasingly responsible for bringing home the family's income.

Jobs in the service sector grew from 58 percent of U.S. employment in 1948 to 74 percent in 1984. Much of this growth occurred in the suburbs, still disproportionately white, coinciding with white women's growing labor force participation. Almost two-thirds of white women's employment growth between 1960 and 1980 was in the service sector: the number employed in clerical jobs grew by 5 million; in sales jobs, by 2.5 million; and in service jobs, by 2.8 million.[144]

Some argue that the move to the suburbs was a conscious strategy on the part of some employers to escape the unions and militancy of urban women workers, disproportionately women of color heading their own households. Suburban shopping malls, insurance companies, direct mail, and credit card operations have all relocated in the suburbs and rural areas where they can employ married white women with no history of unionization. However, employers have found that white women are not as docile as they had anticipated. Much new organizing has brought unionism to the service sector, and feminist issues have served as a rallying point in many of

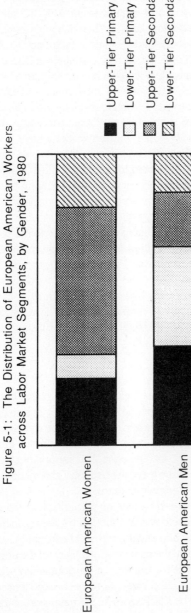

Figure 5-1: The Distribution of European American Workers across Labor Market Segments, by Gender, 1980

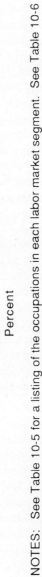

NOTES: See Table 10-5 for a listing of the occupations in each labor market segment. See Table 10-6 for the actual percentages employed in each segment.
SOURCE: 1980 Census; see Appendix A.

these struggles. One of the first to gain national attention was the 1977 strike by 11 bank employees in Willmar, Minnesota. Charging sex discrimination, these 11 women sued the Citizens' National Bank through the Equal Employment Opportunity Commission and organized an AFL-CIO affiliate, the Willmar Bank Employees Association Local 1. Their demands included equal pay for equal work, a promotional ladder, and an affirmative action plan. This was the longest bank strike in U.S. history, lasting from December 1977 to January 1979. The women walked a picket line in 60-degree-below-zero temperatures, sought and gained women's movement and trade union support from across the country, and won nearly all their demands as bank deposits were withdrawn by sympathizers. Other successful organizing drives involving predominantly white women workers have occurred in university settings, such as Yale, Columbia, and Harvard, where women support staff had traditionally accepted lower wages in exchange for Ivy-League status. Yale women printed bumper stickers charging "Beep Beep, Yale's Cheap," while Harvard women wore buttons that declared "You can't eat prestige."[145]

As women of color have increasingly gained entry to the same occupations as white women, new, multi-racial unions have made enormous gains in wages and working conditions. For instance, District 65, a division of the United Auto Workers, has organized clerical workers at private universities, publishing houses, and child-care centers. In 1979, its membership was one-third people of color. The American Federation of State, County and Municipal Employees (AFSCME) has also organized substantial numbers of women of color along with whites.[146]

Work and Family

European American economist Heidi Hartmann points out that one effect of the "deindustrialization" of the United States has been greater equality within marriage for white women. By 1985, white wives contributed on average 42 percent of married-couple income.[147] While the average woman's earnings are generally not high enough to support her family at the same standard of living should she leave the marriage, this income still gives women greater bargaining power within marriage.

Unfortunately, this increased bargaining power has not yet translated into equality in unpaid household work. Although white men increased the amount of time they spent in housework and child care during the 1970s, white women continued to bear the major responsibility for the unpaid work of maintaining a family.[148] While the burdens of the double day—paid work coupled with housework and child care—have been experienced by millions of women, particularly by Black women, the extension of this experience to middle- and upper-class white women brought it to public attention. White career women, struggling with the conflicts between demanding, time-consuming jobs and homemaking, have pushed for high-quality and affordable child care, better parental leave policies, and more husband participation in housework and parenting.

As the domestic ideal declined for white women, so did the importance of the nuclear family—husband, wife, and children. Although this has been true for all racial-ethnic groups, the decline was most pronounced for whites. In 1957, over 82 percent of white women between the ages of 20 and 54 were married; by 1984, this figure had dropped to 56 percent. Most of the decline has been the result of divorce—the percentage of white women who are divorced more than doubled between 1970 and 1986—but greater numbers of white women are also choosing not to marry at all. Certainly white women's increasing economic independence (as a result of greater labor force participation and smaller family size) is a factor in the increasing numbers of women who are living outside marriage. European American feminist and writer Barbara Ehrenreich has pointed to white men's growing flight from family responsibilities as another factor. European American economist Elaine McCrate suggests that a combination of the two may be at work, as men become increasingly threatened by women's greater power within marriage.[149]

Whatever its cause, the rising divorce rate has placed an increasing proportion of white mothers at least temporarily on their own, and often in poverty. Divorce can catapult a white women from the upper middle class into poverty. Research by European American policy analyst Mary Jo Bane has shown that three out of four poor white families headed by a woman fell into poverty because of a family transition (divorce, separation, death of the husband, or birth of an out-of-wedlock baby). In 1988, 18 percent of white families with children were maintained by a single mother, and over 38 percent of those lived below the official poverty line. On average, white women received only $2,294 per year in child support; for the 16 percent of white women who received alimony, the average payment was $3,858 in 1985. Nor is working for pay an automatic ticket out of poverty, although working full time is twice as likely to lift a white single mother out of poverty as a Black single mother. In 1987, over 7 percent of full-time, year-round working white women who maintained families with children were poor.[150]

European American women have been kept from economic and political power by the chains of domesticity, shackled by its promise of security and comfort. Few have lived lives of leisure; indeed, white women's labor, both paid and unpaid, has made a central contribution to U.S. economic development and growth. Furthermore, their intensifying struggles against these bonds have expanded the boundaries of womanhood and challenged white male domination.

Chapter 6

WE SPECIALIZE IN THE WHOLLY IMPOSSIBLE

African American Women[1]

It is from this past that I come
surrounded by sisters in blood
and in spirit
it is this past
that I bequeath
a history of work and struggle

Each generation improves the world
for the next.
My grandparents willed me strength.
My parents will me pride.
I will to you rage.
I give you a world incomplete
a world
where
women still
are property and chattel
where
color still
shuts doors
where sexual choice still
threatens
but I give you
a legacy
of doers
of people who take risks
to chisel the crack wider.

Take the strength that you may
wage a long battle.
Take the pride that you can
never stand small.
Take the rage that you can
never settle for less

—Pat Parker, "legacy, III"[2]

From slavery through the present, African American women's labor
has been crucial to U.S. economic wealth. Forced into slave labor before
emancipation, then trapped by Jim Crow legislation in racially segregated
housing, employment, and schooling, African American women's resistance
and courage have been essential to their people's struggle for survival,
freedom, and self-determination. For centuries, Black women have stood at
the intersection of race, class, and gender oppression, but they were rarely
cowed by the burden of these injustices. Instead, they created, as Black
lesbian poet Pat Parker so eloquently wrote, a legacy of hard work, fierce
dedication to family and community, and militant struggle against exploitation. The motto of the Nannie Helen Burroughs National Training School for
Girls in the early 1900s, "We specialize in the wholly impossible," describes
the special strength which all African American women have been forced to
develop since their arrival on this continent.

The Business of Slavery

Although many European Americans would prefer to see slavery as a
brutal aberration in U.S. history, slave labor was essential to the economic
growth of the colonial and nineteenth-century United States. Cotton and
tobacco exports provided needed foreign exchange for the colonies and
profits for investment, as well as high standards of living and wealth for slave
owners and their descendants. Furthermore, the companies which brought
Africans in chains to this continent to sell to the colonists earned very high
profit rates. The U.S. slave economy was an integral part, then, of a transcontinental economic system of wealth creation and trade: goods manufactured
in Britain, such as cloth and guns, were traded for slaves in Africa (when the
latter were not simply captured); slaves were sold to planters in the colonies,
and forced to produce agricultural products; and planters exported these
products and imported manufactured and luxury goods from Britain.[3]

The first Africans arrived in North America in the early 1600s as
indentured servants who had been obtained by colonists from an English
pirate ship. Colonists contracted for African (as well as European) indentured
servants for a specified period of time, obtaining some in exchange for

payment of their passage to the "New World," and others from traders and pirates. Some early African Americans worked as indentured servants side by side with white servants, and were freed after serving their time. Recent studies show there was at least one servant of African descent present during the first decade of the Pilgrims' Plymouth Colony. Mary Johnson and her husband were servants to a Virginia planter around 1620; by 1651, they were free, had imported and paid for five servants of their own, Black and white, and were cultivating 250 acres of land granted to them by the colonial government. Later generations of Johnsons expanded this African American community and its landholdings.[4]

By the 1640s, however, a racial caste system began to develop as Black indentured servants, unlike whites, were forced into lifetime servitude as slaves. Central to this process was the passage, in 1662, of a Virginia law dictating that the child of an enslaved Black woman was a slave, regardless of the status of the father. As African American historian Paula Giddings writes:

> ...the circle of denigration was virtually complete with this law, which managed to combine racism, sexism, greed, and piety within its tenets...Such legislation laid women open to the most vicious exploitation. For a master could save the cost of buying new slaves by impregnating his own slave, or for that matter having anyone impregnate her.[5]

Creating separate and unequal white and Black castes through changes in laws and social practices took time. Some changes addressed the employment status of whites and Blacks. Masters were heavily taxed for using white women for agricultural work, although they were free to employ Black women in the fields, and field work became the norm for Black women. Other changes addressed intermarriage. In the late 1600s, white women commonly lived with Black men and had children with them; in seventeenth-century Virginia, between one-fourth and one-third of children born to unmarried white women were of mixed race. Although these children were not white, they were not legally classified as slaves, even if their father was a slave. To discourage these interracial relationships, Virginia passed a law forcing any free Englishwoman who had a "bastard child by a Negro" to pay a fine of fifteen pounds, or be indentured to the church wardens for five years. Marriages between white servant women and Black men met with banishment and some states actually tried to enslave white women who married Black men.[6]

In these ways, property-owning colonists separated African Americans from white servants to form a separate, economically subordinate group. The resulting racial bifurcation and accompanying racist ideology prevented poor

Southerners from uniting against the white southern elite throughout the period of slavery. Upper-class whites used the subordination of Blacks to coopt poor whites—no matter how poor they were, they would always have higher status than Blacks. The inevitable and violent struggles of Blacks against their enslavement further fueled hostility against Blacks among lower-class whites.[7]

European Americans developed theories of racial superiority to justify this separation of whites from Blacks, even though the ideology of race was increasingly at odds with their developing ethics of liberty and equality. With these theories, whites claimed for themselves rationality and self-control, while viewing Blacks as threatening forces needing to be controlled. European American enslavement of African Americans for profit was thus intertwined with a complex ideology that portrayed Blacks as both inferior and dangerous. Furthermore, as Giddings points out, whites viewed white women as chaste and pure, charged with the task of ensuring that white men remained "civilized," while whites saw Black women as natural whores who enticed white men into sexual relationships. Whites viewed Black men, in turn, as hyper-sexual beings who threatened to violate white women. Laws prescribed castration of Black men as punishment not only for sexual offenses but also for non-sexual offenses such as striking a white person or running away.[8]

Most enslaved African Americans were taken from West Africa. Half came from what is now Angola and Nigeria. While the societies from which they came varied widely, there were some common features. Family systems included both matrilocal and patrilocal forms (living with the mother's and father's families, respectively). Group parenting and polygyny (marriage to more than one wife) were common, and the marriage tie was only one of a number of important extended-family relationships among adults. Tribal elders, not a woman's husband, assigned land to women to work. A woman's role in the sexual division of labor was to feed her husband and children by farming—indeed, in some areas, farming was exclusively women's work. In addition, women often controlled and traded whatever surplus they produced. An eighteenth-century missionary's description of women in Bakongo, north of the Zaire River, read: "each woman has her own hut, fields, gardens, and slaves over which the husband has no rights after she takes care of his needs."[9] Many of these societies practiced a form of slavery, in which one kin group bought or acquired control over a member of another, usually through wars and raids.[10]

European slave traders purchased slaves from African kin slaveholders or simply took them by force or trickery. During the voyage to the colonies, referred to as the "middle passage," one-half to two-thirds of the slaves died.

In this wrenching manner, about 400,000 Africans arrived in what is now the United States between 1741 and 1810. By 1790, African Americans made up about one-fifth of the U.S. population, and 92 percent were slaves.[11]

In 1790, almost one-fourth of all white families owned slaves, averaging about seven per family. Slavery was concentrated in the South, where 94 percent of all enslaved African Americans lived and made up one-third of the population. Almost three-quarters of the white families in the South Atlantic region owned slaves, averaging eight per family. Slaveholdings, like landholdings, were very unequally distributed, with a small elite owning a disproportionate share of both; in 1860, three-quarters of slaves worked for owners who had over 20 slaves, and one-quarter for owners with over 50.[12]

Exploitation in the slave system was clear and brutal. African Americans worked in the fields like beasts of burden to produce crops such as cotton and tobacco which were then sold for profit. Slaves were also used in tobacco, hemp, and textile-processing factories, as well as in sugar refineries and rice mills. Most slaves—adults and children—toiled in the fields, enduring backbreaking conditions and the vicious abuse of white overseers. On large plantations, a small proportion of the slaves, both adults and children, worked exclusively in the master's house as cooks and servants.[13]

Slavery was built on coercion and violence. Slave owners continually resorted to physical intimidation and punishment to keep slaves from rebelling and slaves continually resisted enslavement. Submission did not guarantee safety, as masters often took out their hostility against less rebellious slaves. In the words of former slave and prominent abolitionist Frederick Douglass, "...the doctrine that submission to violence is the best cure for violence did not hold good as between slaves and overseers. He was whipped oftener who was whipped easiest."[14] Slave resistance was both overt and covert. Slaves refused to work or slowed the pace of work, fought back, escaped, and organized armed rebellions. Women's special forms of resistance included arson, poisoning owners, faking illness in order to be reunited with their families, eavesdropping to obtain news, verbally confronting and physically striking masters and mistresses, and developing allies among discontented white women. As one slave woman advised, "Fight, and if you can't fight, kick; if you can't kick, then bite." [15] One of the most famous slave revolts was led by Nancy Prossner and her husband, Gabriel, who marched on Richmond in 1800 with 1,000 slaves; they were stopped by the all-white state militia. Successful escapees and their descendants formed what were known as "maroon communities" throughout the South, attacking plantations and fighting off attacks by slave-catching posses.[16]

The Sexual Division of Labor and Family Life Among Slaves

Planters set up a sexual division of labor in certain tasks. They usually trained only men for such crafts as carpentry, stonemasonry, milling, and shoemaking and they employed only men in chopping wood, clearing land, and plowing. Slave women were often trained for spinning and sewing. In addition, slave women's work involved midwifery, nursing and caring for white children, spinning, sewing, washing, and performing personal services for white "ladyfolk." [17]

However, slave owners abandoned notions of female difference and fragility when these conflicted with the profit motive. Much field and industrial work was not sex-typed, but rather assigned according to the availability and strength of slaves. Both women and men were forced to toil in the fields "from 'fore daylight to almost plumb dark." One white observer in Georgia was surprised to see men and women "...promiscuously run their ploughs side by side, and day after day...and as far as I was able to learn, the part the women sustained in this masculine employment, was quite as efficient as that of the more athletic sex." [18] While traveling in the Mississippi Valley, northern white Frederick Law Olmsted saw 40 of the "largest and strongest" women he had ever seen, who "carried themselves loftily, each having a hoe over the shoulder, and walking with a free, powerful swing, like *chasseurs* [hunters] on the march." [19] Mary Frances Webb remembered that her slave grandmother "sawed and cut cord wood just like a man. She said it didn't hurt her as she was strong as an ox." [20]

While slave women participated in tasks normally seen as men's work when needed, there is little evidence that slave men performed slave women's work of nursing and caring for white children. When asked to milk a cow because his mistress was ill, one male slave refused, arguing that "everybody knew that to be 'woman's work' and therefore [a job] impossible for him to undertake." [21] The same applied to homemaking work for the slave household. One former slave explained, "When slaves come in from de fields de womans cleant up deir houses atter dey et, and den washed and got up early next mornin' to put de clothes out to dry. Mens would eat, set 'round talkin' to other mens and den go to bed." [22] It appears that slave men did not help their wives or mothers with spinning, a task which engaged many women in the evenings. Husbands whose wives lived on other plantations did not do their own laundry, but instead brought it to their wives on weekend visits. African American writer and activist Angela Davis has pointed out that a woman's responsibilities in the household gave her special power in the slave community, since the household was a freer arena than the more public arena of slave labor. Christie Farnham disagrees, arguing, "Although women took pride in their strength and competence, their labor in the public sphere meant double duty, not power parity," with African American men.[23]

Women's ability to bear children, as well as their attractiveness as sex objects to white men, singled them out for special exploitation and abuse under slavery. When a slave woman bore children, the children were automatically slaves and the owner's wealth expanded. With this in mind, many owners pressured their female slaves into marriages or sexual relations with other slaves. The profit motive also combined with notions of sexuality as the violent domination of women to make the rape of slave women by their owners or overseers a commonplace occurrence. In the words of one slave woman:

> Ma mama said that a nigger 'oman couldn't help herself, fo' she had to do what de marster say. Ef he come to de field whar de women workin' an' tell gal to come on, she had to go. He would take one down in de woods an' use her all de time he wanted to, den send her on back to work. Times nigger 'omen had chillun for de marster an' his sons and some times it was fo' de ovah seer.[24]

Another profitable use of slave women, especially those who were light-skinned, was as concubines for wealthy planters, gamblers, or businessmen; these "fancy girls" sold for $5,000, compared to $1,600 for a prime field hand.[25]

Slave owners and drivers (overseers) used the threat of rape to demoralize, dehumanize, and control slave women. Although they had no legal rights, many slave women fought back against rape and terrorism by white men. Cherry Logue swung a club at a man who made "insulting advances." When Suki's master ordered her to take off her dress, she protested; when he then tried to rip her dress off of her and force her down onto the floor:

> Den dat Black gal got mad....She took an' punch ole Marsa...den she gave him a shove an' push his hindparts down in de hot pot o' soap. It burnt him near to death. He ran from de kitchen, not darin' to yell, 'cause he didn't want Miss Sarah Ann to know 'bout it.[26]

Suki was sold within a few days.

Some owners tormented their wives by flaunting their relationships with slaves. One slave owner slept on a pallet with his slave concubine in his wife's room. When his wife complained, he told her to leave if she liked, but pointed out that if she did, she would lose her substantial dowry to him by law. Jealousy led many white wives to torment the slaves whom they knew to be their husbands' concubines or children. Some male slave owners formed stable live-in relationships with their slaves even though other whites ridiculed them and laws prevented them from marrying. Sometimes these men freed their concubines, and many left substantial property to them or their children in their wills (although families often neglected to enforce such wills).[27]

In spite of and amidst this sexual abuse of slave women, owners encouraged female slaves to form conjugal relationships with male slaves—sometimes by promises of clothing, food, or other incentives, and other times by ordering them to marry. Even though slaves had to obtain their owners' permission to marry, slave marriages were not legally recognized. Slaves created their own ritual, "jumping the broomstick," to seal their vows, but marriage provided no guarantee that one spouse would not be sold away from the other. Studies of slave marriages find that over one-third were terminated by the master, roughly one-half by death of a spouse, and only about one-tenth by mutual consent or desertion.[28]

Just as slave marriages were not respected by slave owners, pregnancy and childbirth brought no respite from work in the fields or in the master's house. Consequently, infant mortality rates among slaves were twice those of whites. Between 1850 and 1860, fewer than two of three African American children lived to be ten years of age.[29]

Slave parents lived in continual fear of losing their children to sickness or the selling block. One child recalled how her mother had saved her:

> My mother often hid us all in the woods, to prevent master selling us. When we wanted water, she sought for it in any hole or puddle formed by falling trees or otherwise. It was often full of tadpoles and insects. She strained it, and gave it round to each of us in the hollow of her hand. For food, she gathered berries in the woods, got potatoes, raw corn [etc.] After a time, the master would send word to her to come in, promising he would not sell us.[30]

Another mother kept her children from being sold to her master and the slave trader by threatening, "the first man that comes into my house, I will split his head open." [31]

A majority of adult slave women married, but a substantial minority lived as single women and mothers, sometimes in a series of relationships with men. Single mothers were not penalized economically or socially relative to married couples. Out-of-wedlock children, like all slave children, were welcomed by owners as increased wealth, and they were accepted by slaves, as they had been in Africa. The mother-child bond was seen as central to family life, rather than the husband-wife bond, and children did not require legitimation by the presence of a father. Slave communities continued African extended-family systems, even augmenting them with "fictive" or chosen kin. These extended-family relations provided a community of parents for the children of single mothers. Relations among slave women, forged while doing laundry, spinning, or sewing together, were particularly supportive.

Hence it was more acceptable for enslaved Black women to live and parent without husbands than it was for white women.[32]

Free African American Women Before Abolition

The first U.S. Census in 1790 showed that 60,000, or 8 percent, of all African Americans were free. Over half of these lived in the South. Some were descended from ancestors who had never been enslaved. Others had been given their freedom by state law, by their former masters, or by other African Americans who had purchased and freed them; still others had purchased or escaped to freedom. Athelia Browning saved money to buy her freedom, and then, over the next 18 years, saved enough money to free 15 of her family members. Harriet Tubman, called the Moses of her people, helped over 300 African Americans escape enslavement through the clandestine system called the "Underground Railroad."[33]

The War of Independence against Britain brought with it heightened public support for the ideals of liberty and equality, and northern states began to abolish slavery and free their slaves. Massachusetts ended slavery as a result of court decisions, which included a legal battle between slave Elizabeth Freeman and her master. Freeman left her master after being struck by her mistress. In 1781, she defended herself in a Massachusetts court on the basis of the new Bill of Rights which said that all men were born free and equal under the law. Freeman was declared free by the court and her former master was ordered to pay her 30 shillings in damages. By 1810, more than two-thirds of the African Americans outside the South were free.[34]

Free African Americans did not, however, enjoy the same rights as whites. While they generally could own property, make contracts, earn wages, and choose their spouses and housing, local laws limited their rights in other areas. In South Carolina, for example, laws prevented them from starting schools or working as clerks or salesmen, restricted their ability to travel, and forced them to have a white guardian. Miscegenation, marriage between Blacks and whites, was illegal in most states, as was marriage between enslaved and free Blacks. Tried in special all-white "slave courts," free African Americans were denied the right to self-defense against whites and could not testify against whites. Free Blacks were also forced to pay special taxes.[35]

Neither did freedom exempt Blacks from strict segregation both in housing and in the labor market. African Americans were excluded from most white schools and faced many barriers to setting up their own. White workers jealously guarded their monopoly on the better jobs, excluding Blacks from white-dominated unions and from apprenticeship programs for skilled trades. Often this exclusion was achieved through violence or its threat. For instance, mobs of Irish immigrants drove African Americans out of service work and canal and railroad construction in the 1840s and 1850s. At the same time, however, laws in many areas specified that if a free Black, "fit to work, shall neglect to do so and loiter and misspend his or her time," magistrates were required to bind him or her out to indentured service.[36]

Faced with these restrictions, most free Blacks earned miserable wages in domestic service or as unskilled laborers. Free Black women were generally confined to work as servants, laundresses, or seamstresses. One observer of Pennsylvania free Blacks in 1795 wrote, "The Women generally, both married and single, wash clothes for livelihood."[37] A study of Charleston, South Carolina, in the 1850s found that over half of free Black working women were employed in "bench work" (as seamstresses and dressmakers), and one-third were house servants or washerwomen. As historians Lorenzo Greene and Carter Woodson point out:

> [T]he Negro washerwoman rose to prominence. She became in many instances the sole breadwinner of the family...Without any doubt many a Negro family would have been reduced to utter destruction had it not been for the labor of the mother as a washerwoman.[38]

The occupations of seamstress, dressmaker, laundress, and hairdresser offered Black married women the opportunity to work at home, care for their own children, and be free from direct white supervision. As a result, these jobs, particularly that of laundress, were to constitute the mainstay of Black women's employment through the early twentieth century. In the South, free African American women also earned their living as prostitutes. In 1804, the Grand Jury of Petersburg, Virginia complained of free Black women who came to the city "only for the purpose of Prostitution." [39]

Free African American women protected themselves against destitution by pooling their resources in mutual-aid and benevolent associations. In Philadelphia in 1838, for example, two-thirds of the free Black benevolent societies were exclusively female, including the Sisterly Union and the Daughters of Absalom. Each member would pay dues; if she fell ill, she would be given aid, and if she died, she would receive a decent burial and her children would be cared for. Such mutual-aid societies were so successful, the first African American newspaper, *Freedom's Journal,* noted, that there were only 43 African American women paupers in New York City in 1829, compared to 462 white women paupers.[40]

While most free Blacks lived in ghettos plagued by substandard housing and high rates of malnutrition and disease, their communities generally contained both a wealthy elite and an emerging middle class—and the economic inequality that accompanies such class divisions. Upper-class

Blacks tended to be lighter skinned and thus faced less racism from whites. Those in the upper class also had greater access to education, since poor Blacks could not afford to let their children leave work to attend school. Some free Blacks had large landholdings, and some even owned slaves. In Charleston, South Carolina, in the 1850s, the richest tenth of free Blacks owned over half of free Black wealth. In Philadelphia, wealthy society Blacks lived, according to one white observer writing in 1841, with "a strict observance of all the nicer etiquettes, proprieties and observances of the well-bred"; a foreign visitor noted that "the most extravagant funeral [he observed] was that of a black; the coaches were very numerous, as well as the pedestrians, who were all well dressed, and behaving with utmost decorum." [41] Whites' refusal to serve Blacks provided opportunities for a growing number of Black doctors, lawyers, shopkeepers, ministers, barbers, and undertakers. If they wanted to gain white clientele, however, Black businesses such as restaurants and barber shops had to bar Blacks—and some did, much to the disgust of their communities.[42]

A few elite African American women enjoyed leisure and luxury supported by the work of servant women, as did women of the white elite. Others worked in the professions. In Charleston, South Carolina, in the 1850s, over 3 percent of employed free Black women held professional or managerial jobs, most of them nurses or storekeepers. Elite Black women also held property in their own right. One study of free Black women in Petersburg, Virginia, in the early 1800s, found quite a few property owners; many of the women had acquired their property upon the deaths of their African American husbands or white fathers or lovers. Their holdings included a bathhouse, a livery stable, two stores, real estate, and slaves (lovers, family members, or laborers, many purchased at low prices during the financial panic of 1819). In fact, compared to white women, free Black women in Petersburg made up a much greater proportion of Black property owners—women were 40 percent of Black taxpayers, but only 13 percent of white taxpayers (only property owners paid taxes).[43]

Single-mother families were common among free Blacks, as among slaves. In some cities, they made up the majority of free Black families. In 1820, 58 percent of all free Black households in Petersburg were maintained by a single woman, and these households contained over half of the free Black population and 57 percent of the children under 14. In Charleston in the 1850s, 61 percent of all free Black family units were maintained by a single woman. One reason for the predominance of female-headed households was the sex imbalance among free Blacks in these cities: in Petersburg in 1820, there were 65 men to every 100 women, and in Charleston, that ratio was 73 to 100. The sex imbalance was compounded by laws prohibiting

Black women from marrying slaves or free whites and by the willingness of free single Black women to have children on their own. Some researchers also suggest that the prevalence of single mothers represented a refusal by many women to give up their independence and property by marrying their lovers.[44]

Political Activism Among Free Black Women

In the nineteenth century, when privileged white women were developing the cult of domesticity and its associated movements for white women's education and social homemaking, free Black women of means were leading a parallel movement for what they termed the "uplift" of their race. Part of their motivation appears to have come, as with white women, from their mothering and caretaking roles. Maria Stewart, a free Black and possibly the first U.S.-born woman to give public speeches, lectured in 1831, "O ye mothers, what a responsibility rests on you! It is you that must create in the minds of your little girls and boys a thirst for knowledge, the love of virtue, the abhorrence of vice, and the cultivation of the pure heart." [45]

On the other hand, the African American women's movement to uplift themselves had a much broader class base than the more upper-class white women's movement. Activists ranged from the daughters of very wealthy free Blacks, such as Charlotte Forten; to Milla Granson, a slave who learned to read and write from her owner's children and shared her knowledge with hundreds of slaves in her secret midnight school; to ex-slaves like Sojourner Truth, the renowned abolitionist and women's rights activist.[46]

In addition, the African American women's movement fought equally for men's and women's rights. Since Black men's rights were so limited, little was to be gained by struggling for rights equal to those of Black men. African American historian Linda Perkins argues that in this period, "race and not sex solidarity was the priority among African Americans." [47] But this solidarity went both ways: for the most part, Black men embraced the causes of women's education and women's rights, just as Black women fought in women's and gender-mixed groups for African American freedom and uplift. Some African American men, however, saw abolition as providing them with an opportunity to exert control over their wives: "As a people, we have been denied the ownership of our bodies, our wives, home, children and the product of our own labor," complained male leaders at an 1855 convention.[48]

African American women were usually rebuffed when they sought to participate in the white-dominated women's movement. In 1852, Sojourner Truth attended, uninvited, an all-white women's rights convention in Akron, Ohio. Her entry caused a furor among white feminists who feared the association of women's rights "with abolition and niggers." But Truth won the audience over with her famous lines:

> Look at my arm! I have ploughed and planted and gathered into barns, and no man could head me—and aren't I a woman? I could work as much and eat as much as any man—when I could get it—and bear the lash as well! And aren't I a woman? I have born thirteen children and seen most of 'em sold in slavery, and when I cried out with my mother's grief, none but Jesus heard me—and aren't I a woman?[49]

Truth's confrontation with white women's rights activists was to be followed by more than a century of exclusions and betrayals of Black women by white women seeking what they called "women's" rights.[50]

The abolition of slavery was a central goal of free Black women's activism. The Colored Female Religious and Moral Society of Salem, Massachusetts was formed in 1818 to "write and converse upon the sufferings of our enslaved sisters." The group welcomed "any plan that may be suggested for [a]melioration." The Female Anti-Slavery Society of Salem was formed in 1832 by African American women "to promote the welfare of our color." Black women were involved and prominent in two integrated female abolitionist groups, the Philadelphia Female Anti-Slavery Society and the Boston Female Anti-Slavery Society (both established in 1833), and attended the First Anti-Slavery Convention of American Women in 1837. But African American women in the abolition movement had to contend with the racism of many white abolitionist women who refused to allow Black women to become members of their organizations since such membership would make them appear, in the words of the white members of the Fall River, Massachusetts Female Anti-Slavery Society, "on an equality with ourselves."[51]

African American women also led the Free Produce Movement, which urged consumers to boycott the products of slave labor. Begun by the Colored Female Produce Society in 1831, the movement was also important in New York City, where Black women organized a display of free labor products at the Broadway Tabernacle. Free African American women—including Harriet Tubman, Ellen Craft, and Anna Murray Douglass—were also active in the struggle to help individual slaves gain their freedom, as well as on the vigilance committees that provided runaway slaves with clothing, food, money, and help in finding employment.[52]

During the Civil War, Black women as well as Black men served and lost their lives. Over a quarter of a million African Americans joined the effort as soldiers, laborers, and servants. Black women were especially active as teachers and nurses, and in aiding the Union Army in the South.[53]

A second major area of activism was education. Before the Civil War, even elementary education in segregated schools was often closed to free

African American girls; secondary schooling was even more rare; and almost all colleges and female seminaries refused to admit African American women. Denying African Americans access to education, and then arguing that their illiteracy proved their inferiority, was a central tool in whites' subordination of Blacks; proving whites wrong in theory and practice was a main concern of the free Black community. African American parents viewed their daughters' education as crucial, as shown by an article in the 1837 *Weekly Advocate,* an African American newspaper:

> In any enterprise for the improvement of our people, either moral or mental, our hands would be palsied without woman's influ-ence…let our beloved female friends, then, rouse up, and exert all their power, in encouraging, and sustaining this effort (education) which we have made to disabuse the public mind of the misrepre-sentations made of our character; and to show to the world, that there is virtue among us, though concealed; talent, though buried; intelligence, though overlooked.[54]

Unlike their white counterparts, African American men did not oppose women's education as too taxing to their "inferior brain power." Sometimes entire families moved to areas where their daughters could attend college or seminary.[55]

Free African American women's struggles for education began in the late 1700s, when women such as Caterine Ferguson began to establish schools. Large numbers of African American women, from ex-slaves to the daughters of wealthy free Blacks, dedicated their lives to teaching their people and expanding their educational opportunities. From the 1830s through the Civil War, African American women participated in mixed-gen-der Black literary societies or formed their own, such as the Female Literary Association of Philadelphia and the Afri-American Female Intelligence Soci-ety. The literary societies provided needed educational services such as day and night schools, lectures, libraries, and reading rooms. Membership in these groups was broad-based: in 1849, one-half of the free Black population of Philadelphia belonged to a literary society.[56]

Reconstruction and Reaction

While it was a great victory, the abolition of slavery in 1865 did not end white supremacy over African Americans. However, the Reconstruction period from 1865 through 1898 brought significant improvements in the lives of southern African Americans. The Freedmen's Relief Bureau, staffed by men and women such as Sojourner Truth, helped Blacks find employment. Some former slaves received plots of land on which to earn their livelihoods; by the mid-1870s, 4 to 8 percent of the freed families in the South owned their own farms. The number of Black-owned and -operated farms doubled between 1890 and 1910, and by 1910, African Americans made up 14 percent of southern farm owner-operators. In 1870, Blacks and progressive whites won the vote for Black men. Using the ballot box, Blacks gained numerical control in a number of southern legislatures, and soon elected 13 African American Representatives and two Senators to Congress. By the 1880s, African American banks, stores, and churches had developed. Many African Americans achieved literacy, and in the 1890s, Black agricultural colleges were formed, the most prominent being the Tuskegee Institute.[57]

Frances Ellen Harper, who had been a forceful abolitionist speaker, went south after the war to teach and support her newly freed people. Harper noted their progress: "As far as the colored people are concerned, they are beginning to get homes for themselves and depositing money in the bank. They have hundreds of homes in Kentucky...In Augusta, colored persons are in the Revenue Office and the Post Office."[58] Harper also observed that even African American women without husbands were having some economic success. She noted that many were running plantations as big as 100 acres with their children, and described one couple, Mrs. Jane Brown and Mrs. Halsey, who, "...leased nine acres and a horse and cultivated the land all that time, just the same as the men would have done. They have saved considerable money from year to year, and are living independently."[59]

Reconstruction was tragically short-lived. Southern whites organized and fought back against its reforms from the beginning, and they quickly reimposed racial segregation and white supremacy when the Union Army left the South in 1877. In 1883, the Supreme Court overturned the Civil Rights Statutes of 1875, which had given African Americans the right to equal access to public accommodation. By 1890, Mississippi (soon followed by other states) effectively had denied the vote to Black men through poll taxes, literacy and property ownership tests, and "grandfather clauses" (requiring proof that a male relative had voted in the 1860 election). The U.S. Supreme Court's 1898 *Plessy v. Ferguson* decision enshrined the principle of "separate but equal," making racial segregation of all kinds legal. With the Court's blessing, states passed Jim Crow laws which imposed extreme racial segregation of public and private facilities, including schools.

During this period of reaction, white workers and farmers actively organized to prevent Blacks from moving into positions of economic equality and competition. As African American sociologist and intellectual leader W.E.B. Du Bois wrote of the period:

> White labor saw in every advance of Negroes a threat to their racial prerogatives, so that in many districts Negroes were afraid to build decent homes or dress well, or own carriages, bicycles or automobiles, because of possible retaliation on the part of whites.[60]

The white movement against African Americans was made up predominantly of workers, small farmers, and small businessmen who wanted to prevent Black competition. Planters and other large employers, in contrast, sought to take advantage of the lower cost of Black labor, and played poor Blacks and whites off against one another. Rural whites drove Blacks out of areas in which the latter were trying to settle as tenant farmers or homesteaders, and threatened whites who rented to them. Freed men, an estimated 12 percent of whom were trained craftsmen, were prevented from practicing their crafts by hostile white competitors; as a result, they rapidly lost ground in occupations such as barbering, bricklaying, blacksmithing, carpentry, and the building trades. Freed Black women were barred from work in southern textile mills—while they made up about one-third of southern women workers in 1890, they held only 3 percent of the jobs in textiles. This exclusion was costly, as the daily wages for Black women in textiles were twice what they could earn for urban domestic work.[61]

With few exceptions, the white labor movement's strategy in the nineteenth and early twentieth centuries was to exclude African American labor whenever possible rather than bring Blacks into the unions as allies against employers. By refusing to organize Blacks, unions perpetuated the wage difference between Blacks and whites; ironically, this ensured that employers could undermine white wages by threatening to hire Blacks. In response, African American workers formed their own unions. In 1869, for instance, Black workers formed the National Colored Labor Union (NCLU) to improve their dismal labor force situation. The NCLU, under pressure from their Committee on Women's Labor, voted to support equal rights for women in industry and in unions, "profiting by the mistakes heretofore made by our white fellow citizens in omitting women." [62]

An integral part of the white struggle to protect their superior economic position was violence, especially as practiced by mobs and terrorist groups such as the Regulators and the Ku Klux Klan. White mobs attacked Blacks who crossed the color line (or were simply successful) with waves of lynchings; estimates of the number killed range from 3,500 to 10,000 between the Civil War and the early 1900s. In 1867, Regulators informed freed Blacks in southern Kentucky that they had to leave the area before February 20th—or else lose their lives. They also threatened white landlords that all buildings they rented to Blacks would be burned.[63]

One result of this violence was a mass exodus of African Americans from remote areas of the rural South to the North, to southern cities, and to large plantations in the South. African American historian Gerald Jaynes explains,

Throughout the South freedpeople were beaten and driven out of employment that was sought by whites. Black renters or purchasers of preferential properties were often burned out or forced to abandon their homes by some other means.

But Blacks found violent exclusion from employment and housing even in the North. For instance, in 1863 northern dockworkers prevented the use of African American strikebreakers from the South with a series of race riots, in which they forced Blacks off the docks and out of their homes.[64]

Thus, after the brief hiatus of Reconstruction, whites found new ways to segregate African Americans, confining them to low-paid service jobs and tenements in the cities, and to Black enclaves, especially plantations, in rural areas. In 1890, 96 percent of employed Black women and 85 percent of employed Black men worked either in agriculture or in domestic service.[65]

African American Women's Works After Abolition

Freedom from slavery allowed African American families to withdraw many married women and children from the labor force. By 1900, the share of Black women gainfully employed was 41 percent. Nevertheless, Black married women were much more likely to be gainfully employed than were white married women. About one-quarter of African American married women were in the labor force at any one time, eight times the share of U.S.-born white married women. Among married women over the age of 65, one-quarter of African American women were in the labor force as well, five times the share for white women.[66]

After the Civil War, some freedmen and freedwomen were able to join free-born Blacks in a small but influential Black middle class. About 4 percent of employed urban women worked as skilled laborers or in professions, mostly as seamstresses and teachers. In 1880, the first African American woman became a lawyer; the first female doctors to practice in the South were Black. By 1900, there were "160 Black female physicians, seven dentists, ten lawyers, 164 ministers, assorted journalists, writers, artists, 1,185 musicians and teachers of music, and 13,525 school instructors."[67]

However, the vast majority of Black women continued to be barred from nearly all jobs other than agriculture and private domestic service, as shown in Table 6-1. In 1900, 44 percent of African American women workers were concentrated in private household service, mostly as servants or laundresses, while another 44 percent worked in agriculture. Only 5 percent held jobs in higher-paid occupations: approximately 3 percent in manufacturing, 1 percent in professions (mostly as teachers), and a negligible number in sales, managerial, and clerical work. In contrast, less than one-third of employed white women worked in domestic service, and 10 percent in

Table 6-1

Occupational Distribution of African American Women Workers,
1900-1980 (in Percent)

	1900	1930	1960	1970	1980
Agriculture	44.2	24.7	3.7	1.3	0.5
Manufacturing	2.6	8.4	15.5	19.3	18.4
Private Household Service	43.5	53.5	39.3	17.9	5.0
Service (not Private Household)	7.9	7.5	23.0	25.5	24.2
Sales	0.1	0.6	1.6	2.6	6.1
Clerical	0.1	0.6	8.0	20.7	25.8
Professional & Technical	1.2	3.4	7.8	11.4	15.2
Managerial, Administrative, & Official	0.5	1.2	1.1	1.4	4.7

NOTES: Totals do not always sum to 100 because of rounding. Manufacturing includes craft and transportation workers; agriculture includes mining, fishing, and forestry; managerial, administrative, & official includes some self-employment, and excludes farm managers. African American includes Latinas classified as Black except in 1980. For a full listing of occupational categories included, see Appendix B. For a discussion of comparability problems between Census years, see Appendix D.
SOURCES: See Appendix A.

agriculture; almost one-third worked in manufacturing, 10 percent in professions, 7 percent in clerical, and 4 percent in sales.[68]

Because agriculture and domestic service were so important for Black women, we devote additional attention to these two occupations below, concentrating on the period between the Civil War and World War I. Our focus is on the South, for although some 450,000 African Americans fled north to escape southern racism between 1870 and 1910, 89 percent of all Blacks still remained in the South in 1910.[69]

Rural African American Women and Farm Work

In 1910, about three-quarters of all African Americans still lived in rural areas, and almost two-thirds of those living in the South were employed in agriculture. Although the federal government did not institute any comprehensive program to provide ex-slaves with land, and southern whites generally refused to sell land or extend credit to Blacks, some Blacks managed to acquire land. Approximately one-quarter of African American farm operators in 1910 owned their own land, but few could achieve economic success in farming. Compared to white farm owners, their farms were smaller, they had less available capital, and fewer could afford to fertilize or leave their fields fallow to maintain the soil over time. Usually, everyone in the family worked, and often, family members had to take on additional work for whites to make ends meet.[70]

Through 1910, more than two-thirds of freed rural African Americans remained landless and had to continue in dependent, impoverishing relationships to rich white landowners (the top 5 percent of white landowners owned 40 percent of the land). Still, the abolition of slavery brought a change in the manner in which white landowners employed African Americans. Early post-abolition work relationships were organized as wage-like "contracts" of food, clothing, and some money in exchange for labor. African Americans lived in old slave quarters and were put to work in labor gangs at low wages. If the owner did not make a profit, which was common during the bad harvests of 1866-67, Black workers simply were not paid.[71]

African Americans resisted this new system by slowing down the pace of work and by withdrawing women and children from the labor force, thus creating a labor shortage. Upon emancipation, anywhere from one-third to one-half of African American women refused to work for the planters. Black women and men saw withdrawal from wage labor as a way to escape economic and sexual exploitation by whites. In addition, wives' labor was needed in the production of food and clothing for their family's own consumption. As freedman Andy McAdams noted, this labor was central to the family's survival:

> If we did other work we did not get fair wages for it, they were so low that we could not feed ourself and so we farmed. We would make more that way because when we farmed we growed near about all that we ate and made our own clothes with [a] spinning wheel.[72]

Faced with a growing labor shortage, landowners conceded to Black demands and abandoned the early wage labor system in the late 1870s. Landowners replaced the system with sharecropping, under which Blacks labored on land owned by whites, paying half of their crops as rent.[73]

Black sharecroppers worked as families, often in extended-kin groups which had been reunited after slavery and were committed to mutual support. As one wealthy white Sea Island woman commented in 1866, "it is a well-known fact that you can't starve a negro" because they always helped one another.[74] Most farm households included a married couple—in 1870, married couples made up 80 percent of farm households in the Cotton Belt. A typical division of labor assigned the husband to work in the fields, the wife to domestic work, except when she was needed in the fields, and children to do schoolwork, unless they too were needed in the fields. Housework was performed within each individual household, rather than in the communal style of the large slave plantations. To save scarce cash, women grew most their of families' food and produced their clothing and medicines. As Black activist and writer Frances Harper observed in 1878, Black farm women did double duty, "a man's share in the field and a woman's part at home."[75] When women were widowed, however, survival on the farm became very difficult, and many migrated to the cities, where they supported themselves through domestic work.[76]

While sharecropping established some degree of independence for African Americans, it at the same time entrapped them in a cycle of subordination, impoverishment, and indebtedness to white landowners and merchants. Whites with large landholdings employed "riders" to supervise workers, often with physical violence and intimidation. It was not uncommon for a landlord to close a school if a tenant's children were needed in his fields. Since few sharecroppers owned their own equipment or had savings to buy needed food or supplies in advance of the crop's sale, they borrowed from the landlord, at interest rates up to 25 percent per year. By the time the crop was harvested and the accounts reckoned, plenty of opportunity had arisen for unscrupulous landlords to cheat those tenants who were illiterate (or even those who were not, given Blacks' lack of legal rights). Not surprisingly, many tenant families remained perpetually in debt. Supported by peonage laws, landlords used this indebtedness to force sharecroppers to remain against their will. Work mobility was further limited by vagrancy laws, under which Blacks looking for new work could be arrested and hired out to the highest bidder, with their previous owner given first preference. These oppressive practices backfired to some extent; anxious to escape their near-slave bondage, up to one-third of sharecroppers moved each year, after the December reckoning of accounts, to another town or county and, increasingly, to the North.[77]

African American Women in Domestic Service

Excluded from other jobs, 52 percent of employed African American women and 31 percent of African American men worked in domestic and personal service in 1890. Black women fought to obtain some degree of independence and control over the conditions of this work. Increasing numbers of servants refused to "live in," even though "day work" spelled a 12- to 14-hour day. Married women offered their services as laundresses in their own homes.[78]

In rural areas, the type of domestic service Black women performed varied according to their marital status. Over half of single employed women in rural areas worked as servants in the homes of whites, another quarter took in washing or did other such tasks, and a fifth worked on farms. Naomi

Yates described her rural, southern upbringing:

> By four you'd do field work; by six you'd be doing small pieces in
> a tub every washday and bring all the clear water for rinsing the
> clothes. By eight, you'd be able to mind children, do cooking, and
> wash. By ten you'd be trained up. Really, every girl I know was
> working-out [in domestic work for white families] by ten. No play,
> 'cause they told you: life was to be hardest on you—always.[79]

Live-in domestic work was rare among employed married rural women.
Fewer than 5 percent worked as servants, 40 percent did laundry or other
odd jobs that did not involve living in, and 56 percent farmed.[80]

In urban areas, an even larger proportion of Black women performed
domestic work for whites. In southern cities at the turn of the century, Black
women made up 90 percent of servants. Their wages were so low that all
but the poorest white families could afford some sort of help. As we saw
earlier, rural widows usually moved to the cities to work as domestic servants
or laundresses. Many urban Black married women were also employed in
domestic work; like their rural counterparts, few lived in. One African
American educator described his childhood experience of waiting until far
past mealtime for his mother, a cook, to be allowed to return home: "[W]e
would often cry for food, until, falling here and there on the floor, we would
sob ourselves off to sleep." [81] Black women greatly preferred the higher pay
and independence of factory work, in spite of its difficult working conditions,
but white employers excluded African American men and women from
almost all factory jobs, with the exception of tobacco stemming and oyster
shucking.[82]

As domestic workers for whites, African American women and children continued to be sexually exploited by white men. One Black woman
wrote:

> I believe nearly all white men take, and expect to take undue
> liberties with their colored female servants—not only the father, but
> in many cases the sons also. Those servants who rebel against such
> familiarity must either leave or expect a mighty hard time, if they
> stay. By comparison those who tamely admit to these improper
> relations live in clover. They always have a little 'spending change,'
> wear better clothes, and are able to get off from work at least once
> a week—sometimes oftener. This moral debasement is not at all
> times unknown to the white women in these homes. I know of
> more than one colored woman who was openly importuned by
> white women to become the mistresses of their white husbands,
> on the grounds that they, the white wives, were afraid that, if their
> husbands did not associate with colored women, they would
> certainly do so with outside white women.[83]

Many African American families sent their daughters north in hopes of escaping the widespread sexual exploitation of servants.

Rather than punish or ostracize white men for such behavior, whites perpetuated a stereotype of Black women as sexually promiscuous and barred them from working alongside white women. Black women faced continual sexual harassment on and off the job. Black feminist writer bell hooks writes:

> Everywhere Black women went, on public streets, in shops, or at their places of work, they were accosted and subjected to obscene comments and even physical abuse at the hands of white men and women...A Black woman dressed tidy and clean, carrying herself in a dignified manner, was usually the object of mud-slinging by white men who ridiculed and mocked her self-improvement efforts.[84]

Hooks also argues that the promiscuity stereotype channeled Black women into urban prostitution.[85] The hypocritical nature of southern life was revealed in the actions of white men, who put on Klan robes to lynch Black men on trumped-up charges of raping white women—and then themselves sexually harassed and raped Black women.

In the late nineteenth century, African American domestic workers began to organize for better wages and working conditions. In 1881, Atlanta laundresses, organized through and supported by Black churches, formed the Washerwomen's Association of Atlanta; under its auspices, 3,000 women struck to obtain $1 per 12 pounds of wash. Black women also formed locals of laundresses, chambermaids, housekeepers, and agricultural workers within the Knights of Labor, the largest workers' organization in the nineteenth century United States, and the only one to organize white women and people of color.[86]

Lifting as We Climb

After the Civil War, African American women continued to take on the struggle to defend their peoples, seeing themselves as "the fundamental agency under God in the regeneration...of the race, as well as the groundwork and starting point of its progress upward," as Black writer Anna Julie Cooper wrote in 1892.[87]

African Americans did not relent in their efforts to secure education, which they saw as central to their empowerment in the post-slavery era. During Reconstruction, the federal government helped Blacks to establish freedmen's schools and to integrate white schools. However, when southern whites regained power, they re-segregated the schools and refused to provide Blacks with more than a bare minimum of education. In 1910, the average Black school only operated four months a year, and no Black school in the South offered courses above the seventh-grade level.[88]

Women made up the majority of African American teachers. For Black women in those times, teaching was a form of social activism, and many of the late nineteenth-century national Black women leaders—such as Fannie Jackson Coppin, Lucy Laney, Charlotte Hawkins Brown, and Fannie Barrier Williams—began their careers as southern elementary school teachers. Some Black teachers struggled in segregated public schools at below-subsistence salaries. Others founded separate private schools on the elementary, secondary, and college level; by 1912, there were 14 Black women's colleges. The Nannie Helen Burroughs National Training School for Girls trained over 2,500 girls under the motto, "We specialize in the wholly impossible." Since sharecropping families could not afford to pay for schooling, those who established schools in the South raised funds from northern African Americans and white philanthropists. A 1904 article noted that African American women had raised $14 million for the education of Black children, and educated over 25,000 Black teachers.[89]

In the 1890s, a dynamic Black women's club movement was sparked by the anti-lynching campaign of Ida B. Wells, a columnist and co-owner of the Memphis newspaper, *Free Speech*. Wells began her campaign after her friend, Thomas Moss, was lynched for owning a grocery store that competed successfully with a white-owned store in the neighborhood. Wells specifically countered the myth of the Black rapist which was used to justify so many lynchings. Wells wrote:

> Nobody in this section of the country believes the old threadbare lie that Negro men rape white women. If Southern white men are not careful they will over-reach themselves…a conclusion will then be reached which will be very damaging to the moral reputation of their women.[90]

When Memphis whites read that editorial in *Free Speech*, they ransacked and destroyed the paper's office, and threatened Wells with lynching in front of the courthouse if she returned. Wells relocated to New York and continued a campaign which drew national and even international attention to the terrible injustice of lynching. Inspired and drawn together at a testimonial to honor Wells, African American women organized clubs throughout the country not "for race work alone, but for work along the lines that make for women's progress," as leader Josephine Ruffin explained.[91]

In 1896, Black women's clubs federated into the National Association of Colored Women (NACW) under the leadership of Mary Church Terrell, daughter of a millionaire former slave. Claiming as their motto, "Lifting as We Climb," club women dedicated themselves to educating and aiding poor

African American girls and women, as well as to politically mobilizing Black women of all classes. By 1915, 50,000 women in over 1,000 clubs participated in the NACW.[92]

Much of African American women's activism addressed the abuse of working women. Affluent Black women in New York City organized the White Rose Industrial Association in 1897, a settlement house which provided academic and vocational education, lodging, and other services aimed at protecting young migrants from exploitative employment agencies and employers. Phillis Wheatley Associations (named after the slave who was the first African American, and the second woman, to publish a book of poetry in the colonies) supported young Black female workers in cities in the South and Midwest. The Associations provided lodging for young Black women, acted as job placement agencies, and advocated for higher pay.[93]

When they tried to join white-dominated groups such as the powerful Women's Christian Temperance Union or the General Federation of Women's Clubs, Black women confronted, in African American historian Rosalyn Terborg-Penn's words, "the pervasiveness of white female prejudice and discrimination against Black females in woman's groups."[94] This discrimination, along with Black women's much greater commitment to fighting racism, meant that women's clubs developed as racially separate organizations, even though Black and white women worked on many similar issues—temperance, suffrage, and settlement.[95]

World War I and the Migration North

World War I was a watershed for African Americans. In the Northeast and Midwest, war production created a need for labor so great that white employers were forced to hire Black workers over white workers' protests. New jobs at higher wages attracted African Americans to northern cities, where per capita incomes were between four and seven times higher than in southern states. As they were pulled into the North, Blacks were also being pushed out of the South. As African American historian William Harris notes, "the migration was a strike against economic and social exploitation in the South…"[96] One study of Black migrants found they were motivated to leave the South by "injustice in the courts, lynching, denial of suffrage, discrimination in public conveyances, and inequalities in educational advantages"[97]— and, we would add, sexual exploitation of Black girls and women by white men.

As a result of these push and pull factors, 1.2 million Blacks uprooted themselves and migrated North between 1910 and 1930, both in families and as individuals. Often whole communities migrated: as one rural Mississippi woman told an interviewer in the 1920s, "If I stay here any longer, I'll go wild...There ain't enough people here I know now to give me a decent burial."[98] (Still, in 1940, over three-quarters of Blacks remained in the South. As late as 1975, a majority of Blacks were Southerners.[99])

But in the North, employers still placed immigrant Europeans above African Americans on the job hierarchy. Black men employed in industry were kept in the most menial positions, and were subject to frequent lay-offs. Common men's jobs were in Chicago's meatpacking plants and slaughterhouses, in Detroit's auto industry, in Pittsburgh's steel industry, and in New York City's apartment buildings as janitors. Nevertheless, mobs of white male workers resisted what they saw as Black encroachment on their jobs, by starting race riots. Forty Blacks were killed and thousands left homeless by a race riot in East St. Louis, Illinois in 1917. The year 1919 brought 25 major race riots; the largest was in Chicago, where 23 Blacks and 15 whites were killed and more than 500 people were seriously wounded.[100]

Because so few Black men earned a wage sufficient to support a wife who did not participate in paid labor, African American women continued their tradition of paid work. From 1900 to 1930, African American women were more likely than women of any other racial-ethnic group to be gainfully employed. (See Figure 6-1 for a comparison of Black and white women's labor force participation rates.) Nearly 40 percent of Black women were listed as gainfully employed in 1920, and Black married women were five times more likely than white married women to be in the labor force.[101]

During World War I, a few Black women were hired in war industry jobs, which offered higher pay and better conditions than agriculture and domestic service. Still, their jobs were the worst paid in the war industry, and they were the first fired. A woman railroad worker who worked nine hours a day, six days a week pulling trucks that weighed 186 pounds per load told an investigator in 1918:

> All of the colored women like this work and want to keep it. We are making more money at this than at any work we can get. And we do not have to work as hard as at housework which requires us to be on duty from 6:00 o'clock in the morning until nine or ten at night, with mighty little time off and at very poor wages...What the colored women need is an opportunity to make money. As it is, they have to take what employment they can get, live in old tumbled down houses or resort to street walking. And I think a woman ought to think more of her blood than to do that. What occupation is open to us where we can make really good wages? We are not employed as clerks. We cannot all be school teachers. So we cannot see any use in working our parents to death to get educated.[102]

During and after the war, Black women continued to be barred from most good jobs. *Monthly Labor Review*, an official publication of the U.S.

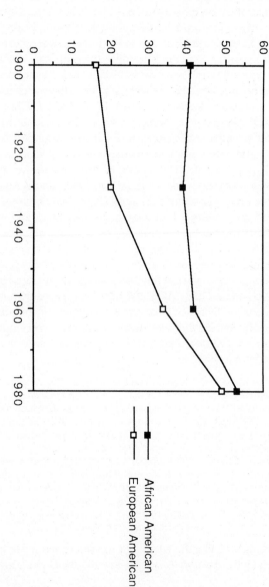

Figure 6-1: Labor Force Participation Rates of African American and European American Women, 1900-1980

NOTES: For detail on the definitions of the variables for the different years, and for the labor force participation rates themselves, see Appendix C.
SOURCES: See Appendix A.

Department of Labor, noted "strong prejudice against admitting [Black women] to more skilled and better paid kinds of work, which was reserved for white women."[103] White women refused to work side by side with Black women and demanded separate eating and sanitary facilities, which many small employers could not afford; in response to this demand, small businesses hired only white women. White customers refused to interact with Black saleswomen, secretaries, or receptionists. Restaurants in white business areas protested if Black workers tried to gain entrance, claiming they would lose their white clientele. Even in Black ghettos, most stores belonged to whites who refused to hire Blacks for anything but menial jobs. African American women were forced to compensate for their confinement to the lowest tiers of the labor market by working longer hours than white women and by remaining on the job after childbearing.[104]

Even though the clerical and sales sectors were growing rapidly after World War I, these sectors accounted for only 1 percent of Black women's employment in 1930, compared to over one-third of white women's. In fact, more Black men found employment in these jobs than Black women, in sharp contrast to the pattern among whites. Exclusion from clerical and sales work meant that Black female high school graduates were usually forced into jobs for which they were overqualified. Addie Hunter, a graduate of the Cambridge Latin High School in Massachusetts, could only find work in a factory. She unsuccessfully sued for a white-collar position for which she was qualified, concluding, "...the way things stand at present, it is useless to have the requirements. Color—the reason nobody will give, the reason nobody is required to give, will always be in the way."[105]

For most Black women, jobs in manufacturing were equally unattainable. The percentage of Black women workers employed in manufacturing was only 3 percent in 1910 and 8 percent in 1930, compared to 18 percent and 25 percent respectively for African American men. Of those African American women involved in manufacturing in 1930, 20 percent were dressmakers employed at home, 16 percent worked in garment factories, 16 percent in southern cigar and tobacco factories, and 11 percent in food processing. Black women were usually admitted to jobs rejected by white women, such as dangerous jobs in glass factories, hog killing or beef casing under disgusting conditions, or work in hot, steamy, and ill-ventilated commercial laundries where they made up one-quarter of the workers in 1930. Many of the Black women who worked in factories were not operatives, but service workers who cleaned the factory buildings and equipment.[106] During this period, growth in commercial laundries and the growing affordability of home washing machines undercut Black women's self-employment as laundresses. Between 1910 and 1920, the number of Black women laundresses fell from over 356,000 to roughly 280,000.[107]

In spite of the decline in laundressing, overall Black female employment in private domestic service grew: between 1900 and 1930, the share of Black women employed in domestic service increased from 44 to 54 percent. The growth is not surprising, since Black women were excluded from most manufacturing, sales, and clerical jobs, but continued to pour out of southern agriculture. As large numbers of white women left domestic service for better jobs, Black women replaced them.[108]

Thousands of young Black women migrated North to work as domestic servants. Many were recruited by employment agencies, such as the Dixie Maid Service, which promised a bus ticket and a job for a fee, but often failed to deliver on the promise. Many women were left stranded at northern bus stations with nowhere to turn. Those whose migration was arranged through family ties were more successful; many came to help their urban kin, who paid their travel and helped them get oriented. Most African American female migrants were young and had little formal schooling. They provided child care for their sisters and aunts, who were working as live-in servants, until they could find jobs of their own and begin sending wages home to their parents. At first, most new migrants were forced to accept live-in employment that isolated them from the African American community. Long work weeks prevented them from attending Sunday church service, a central part of Black community life. African American historian Elizabeth Clark-Lewis found that servants were determined to shift to day work, against the resistance of their employers, so that they could have social lives and eventually families of their own. To do this, they formed "penny savers clubs," and saved for an average of six years to obtain enough money to rent rooms in boarding houses.[109]

The vast majority of Blacks remained in the South during the first decades of the twentieth century. For them, conditions only worsened as time passed. World War I dealt a major blow to the cotton industry when Europe cut its purchases of southern cotton, and a boll weevil infestation in the late 1910s exacerbated the crisis. Many Black sharecroppers and farmers were unable to pay their loans, and all Black banks failed except for one. Black farmers lacked the capital to shift into cattle as many whites were able to do. When Black sharecroppers tried to organize a union in Arkansas in 1919, they were attacked by armed whites who had travelled from as far as Tennessee and Mississippi. After hundreds of African American men and women were arrested, and 12 men condemned to death, Ida Wells Barnett publicized the facts, helping to convince the Supreme Court to free the men.[110]

Black Entrepreneurship, Black Urban Communities

The 1920s saw some growth of African American entrepreneurship, spurred by the Great Migration. Black migrants were segregated into crowded ghettos, where they were served by at least a few Black businesses. Some African American women became successful businesswomen, like Madame C.J. Walker, distributor of hair-straightening products, and Mrs. Annie M. Turnbo Malone, manufacturer of "The Wonderful Hair Grower." More common examples were seamstresses and hairdressers, who ran their businesses from their homes.[111]

The ranks of the Black middle class were also swelled, in the early twentieth century, by immigrants from the British West Indies, where slavery had been abolished in 1838. Most migrants were literate and skilled, from urban and industrial or commercial backgrounds. Thirty thousand immigrated between 1900 and 1910, and 100,000 between 1910 and 1924, after which further immigration was cut off by Congress. West Indians settled in the cities; by 1920, they made up one-quarter of the Blacks in Harlem, where they owned a disproportionate share of African American businesses, most serving the Black community. Some West Indian women were able to find jobs in the needlework industry in New York—which had barred African American women—because their lighter skin and accents caused them to be mistaken by employers for "Spanish" (i.e. Puerto Ricans) or whites. Culturally distinct West Indians mixed little with U.S. Blacks, although they were subject to the same racist practices of white society unless they could pass as white.[112]

Harlem was the most flourishing African American community in the 1920s, home to the explosion of African American writing and music now termed the Harlem Renaissance. The Roaring Twenties also saw the mobilization of two million working-class Blacks in the Universal Negro Improvement Association led by West Indian Marcus Garvey, whose Black Nationalist agenda included a planned return to Africa. Amy Jacques Garvey, his wife, led the women's division, with "feminist views [that] embraced the class struggle as well as the problems of Third World women."[113]

Homemaking was difficult in the North. Housing discrimination and the pressures of continued migration caused extreme overcrowding in Black ghettos. Fires, rats, and inadequate plumbing characterized the housing conditions to which African Americans were restricted by zoning laws and racial covenants (agreements not to sell property to African Americans, Jews, and other groups). Although wages were higher than in the rural South, so was the cost of living. Children were exposed daily to gambling and crime on the streets as white communities drove commercial entertainment and vice districts out of their communities to locations in or near Black communities. Both white and Black men were clients for a flourishing prostitution industry, whose workers were young Black women unable to find other employment. As one Black woman commented about Washington, D.C. in the 1920s: "I have lived here long enough to know that you can't grow a good potato out of bad ground. Dis sho is bad ground."[114] Although many Black mothers did work in their homes, taking in laundry and sewing, many others worked outside the home, forced to leave their children with family, friends, or unattended. In response, middle-class African American clubwomen and National Urban League members established day-care, housing, training, and recreation programs to aid these working women.

African American Women During the Great Depression

The Great Depression of the 1930s was disastrous for Blacks. While overall unemployment was high, Black rates were even higher than those for whites. In urban areas, large numbers of industrial workers were fired and jobs in domestic service disappeared as white incomes fell. Unemployed white men sought jobs held by Black men: Blacks lost restaurant and other service jobs to whites, and white male railroad workers beat and even murdered Black firemen to get them off the railroads.[115]

Black women, already on the bottom rung of the labor market hierarchy, had a hard time finding any employment at all. European American historian Jacqueline Jones describes their job search:

> [M]ost of these women could find only seasonal or part-time employment; racial and sexual discrimination deprived them of a living wage no matter how hard they labored; and they endured a degree and type of workplace exploitation for which the mere fact of having a job could not compensate.[116]

In New York, a "slave market" for domestic workers developed in which Black women stood on street corners in the Bronx and Brooklyn while white women auctioned for their services. Though the New Deal administration passed a series of laws to protect workers from hazardous working conditions and to raise their wages, the legislation did little for the four out of five Black women who still worked in agricultural and domestic work—two sectors specifically exempted from the laws. In this way, New Deal policies officially marginalized Black women workers.[117]

By January 1935, 4 million African Americans, or about 30 percent of the African American population, were dependent on government relief. Even in relief, Blacks received less, especially from programs staffed by southern whites. One Black man complained in a 1935 letter to the head of the Labor Department's Division of Negro Labor, "The job is JIM CROWED, the commodities are JIM CROWED, the very air you breathe under the Adams

County Mississippi [Emergency Relief Administration] is contaminated with the parasite of JIM CROWISM."[118] At the same time, the New Deal brought a significant and permanent growth in government, particularly in social welfare programs, and Black men and women were later able to claim a significant share of the clerical and professional jobs in these programs.

The Depression years saw many uprisings of African American workers in unions and organizations of unemployed workers in the North and the South, and the first mass white-Black organizing. The Wagner Act guaranteed the right to collective bargaining, although Blacks were unsuccessful in adding a clause which would have denied federal protection to racist unions. The newly formed Congress of Industrial Organizations (CIO), which targeted unskilled and semi-skilled workers, undertook the first major campaign to organize Black and white workers; it had 210,000 Black members by 1941. With the help of the CIO, Black women working in commercial laundries joined with whites in the formation of the United Laundry Workers in the mid-1930s. One of the last straws that led African American laundry workers onto the picket line was a boss' insistence that they stop singing spirituals while they worked because "that was too much pleasure to have while working for his money."[119] Black women also formed the majority of workers in the Food Workers Industrial Union, and joined with whites in the International Ladies' Garment Workers Union. When a Black male tobacco worker died on the job after being refused sick leave, his Black women co-workers spontaneously started a sit-down strike. They won recognition of the Food and Tobacco Workers Union, affiliated with the CIO, over $1 million in back pay, and pay increases that more than doubled their wages. Ruby Jones, one of the strikers, described the impact of the union:

> You worked just like a dog and was talked to just like a dog. We didn't get no recognition or be treated like human beings until that union came in there. Even in the newspaper nobody had a Mrs. on their name until that union came. There were stores that you couldn't go into. When the union came, it was just like being reconstructed.[120]

Even domestic workers had many organizing successes in the militant labor movement of the 1930s. To protest low wages and disrespectful treatment by employers, they began an informal campaign, "Stand Up a Lady for Work." Dora Lee Jones led the formation of the Domestic Workers' Union in New York City in 1934; two years later, domestic workers in Washington, D.C. formed another union, eventually tripling wages. Black women activists also worked to open up sales positions to Blacks: Lillie Mae Jackson organized a campaign for African Americans to "Buy Where You Can Work," and Black boycotts of Blumstein's, a major Harlem department store, forced the store to hire Blacks for sales jobs. But these victories could not overcome the unemployment that spread through the African American community as the Depression deepened.[121]

During the 1930s, many young African Americans returned to the South to live with their tenant-farming parents, but found no refuge there, as agricultural prices fell rapidly. Recalling the massacre they had suffered 15 years earlier when they organized alone, Arkansas Blacks joined with white tenant farmers to form the Southern Tenant Farmers Union (STFU) in 1934. In 1935, 5,000 cotton pickers participated in their first strike, which resulted in higher wages, and membership subsequently swelled to 25,000. The STFU was able to draw national attention to the sharecroppers' plight, forcing the formation of a presidential commission to study their situation. At first, STFU locals were racially segregated, but when they got together on the district level, white and Black sharecroppers "decided we were all in the same boat," and began to attend one another's meetings. According to one African American male leader:

> [Black] women were very active and made a lot of the decisions.
> Women decided to do things that men felt like they couldn't do.
> We had several locals around Cotton Plant and I believe in one of
> the locals all the officers were women. This was because men were
> afraid. Owners never bothered women. They never beat up any
> women. Oh yes, I think they did in Mississippi and maybe one place
> in Arkansas. But usually they would pick on men. They was a little
> bit slow about bothering women.[122]

Unfortunately, the STFU was fighting a losing battle, and their higher wages were short-lived. The entire tenant-farming system, based on credit, collapsed as bank failures rocked the economy. These failures, combined with New Deal programs which paid landowners not to plant cotton, led to widespread evictions of Black tenants, and the number of Black sharecroppers fell by one-quarter between 1930 and 1940. This sped up rural-urban migration, and by 1940, half of the nation's African American population lived in urban areas.[123]

New Opportunities: World War II

The economic stimulation provided by weapons production for World War II brought some relief to the widespread economic hardship of the Great Depression. Still, African American workers fought their own battles stateside for their fair share of war-time jobs and for equal pay. Black socialist leader A. Philip Randolph, president of the Brotherhood of Sleeping Car Porters, organized a huge march on Washington, D.C. to protest race discrimination in war industry plants. As a result of this pressure, President Roosevelt signed

Executive Order 8802 in 1941, prohibiting discrimination in the federal government and defense industries, and establishing the Fair Employment Practices Committee. Despite the executive order, Blacks still faced discrimination from defense contractors. African American women demonstrated from 1942 to 1944 and stormed Ford plants to demand jobs.[124]

This Black militancy combined with the war-time labor shortage to open up new places for 1 million African American industrial workers, 60 percent of whom were women. Once again, migration out of the South accelerated and Black agricultural employment declined; 1.6 million Blacks left the South between 1940 and 1950. Four hundred thousand Black women left domestic employment, and the number of Black women in factory work doubled. Approximately 4,000 African American women served in the Women's Army Corps, although most of them were restricted to kitchen jobs and few were sent overseas. The majority of Black women workers, although still employed as domestic and institutional servants, found that they had more bargaining power than ever before.[125]

White workers protested violently against Black employment in war industry jobs: "in one three-month period in 1943, over 100,000 man-days of war production employment were lost to 'hate' strikes."[126] At the same time, militant Black male workers were able to force the CIO-affiliated United Automobile Workers to support the hiring of Black men and women; the UAW also formed its own Women's Bureau in 1944, headed by Lillian Hatcher, a Black autoworker. Black union membership increased six-fold from 1940 to 1945.[127]

But the end of the war threatened these gains as African Americans of both genders were pushed out of their newly won jobs. African American author Maya Angelou wrote in 1945, "We lived through a major war. The question in the ghettos [is], Can we make it through a minor peace?"[128] African American women were especially reluctant to return to the kitchens and laundries of white women. They continued to organize to keep wages high in domestic work and to improve working conditions, establishing training centers, placement bureaus, and support groups for domestic workers.

In spite of post-war setbacks, World War II was a watershed for Black women's employment, opening up jobs in factories and offices. During the 1950s, Black women were able to expand on these gains. As shown in Table 6-1, between 1930 and 1960 the share of Black women employed in manufacturing jobs almost doubled, while the share in clerical and sales jobs grew eight-fold. These changes finally allowed Black women to move out of private household service, which employed 42 percent of Black women workers in 1950, 39 percent in 1960, and 18 percent in 1970.

We Shall Overcome: Organizing for Freedom

Improvements in the economic status of African Americans between World War II and the mid-1950s came about primarily as a result of movement out of agriculture and into cities, and out of the South into the North, Midwest, and West. Tenant farming continued to decline in the South as larger farms increased their use of hired hands. Between 1940 and 1959, the total number of southern farm operators fell by 60 percent. The number of farms operated by African Americans fell even faster, reducing Black's share of farms by almost 30 percent. The share of southern Black workers employed on farms fell from 40 to 14 percent in this period, and most of those remaining in farming were men. Racial inequality continued to be much more extreme in the South than in the North: in 1959, southern Black family income was only 39 percent of white income, compared to 70 percent in the North.[129]

African Americans found jobs in emerging southern industries, but always in the lowest-paid and most dangerous jobs. Union organizing brought some gains. For instance, in the early 1950s, the National Negro Labor Council joined with the progressive United Electrical Workers to train Blacks for a new General Electric factory in Louisville, Kentucky. Said the Director of the NNLC, "The most significant and satisfying aspect of the programs was that it resulted in the hiring of Negro women as production workers, not merely maids."[130] But southern industries could not absorb all the workers displaced from agriculture, and the exodus from the South continued, as another 1.5 million African Americans left to seek better lives elsewhere.[131]

By the mid-1950s, African American resistance to racism led to growing waves of collective action, using the tools of voter registration drives, Supreme Court decisions, boycotts, freedom rides, and other nonviolent actions. Racists across the South quickly organized themselves in White Citizens Councils. White bankers, businessmen, and politicians used their economic leverage against all those individuals, white or Black, who supported integration, by refusing loans to farmers, foreclosing on mortgages, and firing workers. Civil rights activists risked physical intimidation, beatings, and even murder.[132]

But activists kept on "keeping on," gaining momentum as the decade progressed. Although the growing southern civil rights movement relied on participation from men and women of all races, African American women were its backbone. According to Jones, their emergence as leaders was the natural outgrowth of African American women's roles as "grannies, healers, and conjurers under slavery."[133] For example, the Montgomery bus boycott of 1955 was sparked by Rosa Parks. Portrayed in the white media as a worker who was just too tired to move to the back of the bus, Parks was actually a longtime activist in the National Association for the Advancement of Colored

People (NAACP). Along with other women founders of the Montgomery Improvement Association, Parks served as a catalyst and planner of the boycott. Women domestic and service workers were the mainstay of the bus boycott: they walked to their jobs in white households rather than be subjected to segregated buses.[134]

Again and again—at Monday-night church services, in southern jails, by feeding and housing civil rights activists—Black women showed their determination to achieve dignity and self-determination for their people. Older Black women mainly worked through the churches, although many long-time activists such as Fanny Lou Hamer of Mississippi, Septima Clark and Daisy Bates of Arkansas, and Ella Baker of New York rose to leadership in organizations such as the National Association for the Advancement of Colored People (NAACP), the Southern Nonviolent Coordinating Committee (SNCC), and the Southern Christian Leadership Conference (SCLC). Younger women such as Diane Nash and Cynthia Washington were also prominent in SNCC. Even very young Black girls joined the movement, enduring the abuse and violence of white mobs as they desegregated schools and joined in marches and demonstrations for civil rights. The movement continued to gain ground in the 1960s as southern activists united with supporters in the North. Hundreds of thousands of people of all races marched on Washington in 1963 to demand jobs and freedom and hear Dr. Martin Luther King, Jr.'s inspirational "I Have a Dream" speech.[135]

But Dr. King's goals and methods were soon challenged by Black Power activists whose experience was urban and northern rather than rural and southern. Black Power activists in groups such as the Black Panther Party for Self-Defense and Malcolm X's Nation of Islam rejected Dr. King's goal of peaceful integration into white society in favor of Black nationalism and separatism. They spurned the strategy of nonviolence in favor of militant and, sometimes, armed self-defense. These new groups reached back to Africa to revive their cultural roots, asserting defiantly that "Black is Beautiful." They emphasized family values, the right and duty of Black men to protect Black women from white man's oppression, and the need for Black women to concentrate their efforts in the home for the good of the community.[136]

Other forms of innovative Black urban organizing emerged in the 1960s. Reverend Leon Sullivan's community economic development programs in Philadelphia in the early-1960s, funded by contributions by church members, financed Black businesses and provided needed social services. Reverend Jesse Jackson formed Operation PUSH in Chicago, using the threat of Black consumer boycotts to pressure white businesses to hire Blacks and buy from Black suppliers. African American women played a crucial role in the development of alternative schools from Harlem to Alabama during the

1960s and 1970s. Designed, managed, and staffed by the community, these schools instilled African American children with pride in their culture and their history.[137]

The development of the Black Power movement was fed by, and in turn contributed to, a wave of urban rioting. Between 1964 and 1968, urban African Americans took their frustrations to the streets in a wave of rioting. After disturbances in 35 cities in July 1967, President Johnson established a commission to study the riots. After seven months of study, the Kerner Commission called for "a massive and sustained commitment to action to end poverty and racial discrimination."[138] Soon after, Dr. King was murdered, and that summer urban Blacks across the country exploded with rage. City after city came close to race war as white police forces tried to repress militant Black rioters.

Black activism also found expression in the labor movement. For instance, Local 1199, a predominantly Black and Puerto Rican union of New York City hospital workers founded in 1958, became a national union in 1969 after a long and bitter campaign in Charleston, South Carolina. The campaign was a model of community-labor coalition work, involving the support of the African American community and the Southern Christian Leadership Conference (SCLC); its slogan was "1199 Union Power Plus SCLC Soul Power Equals Victory." In 1968, Dorothy Bolden, a domestic worker in Atlanta, Georgia founded the National Domestic Workers Union of America. Meeting in churches, the union trained domestic workers to negotiate with their employers for higher wages and vacation pay.[139]

The Black Power and civil rights movements raised white consciousness about racial inequality and poverty, establishing a consensus that such conditions were neither acceptable nor safe. In 1964, the federal government had launched the War on Poverty, a series of government programs in education, health and nutrition, and community development aimed at poverty-stricken communities. After the riots increased the pressure, President Lyndon B. Johnson pumped additional sums of money into community-based employment, training, education, and health programs in poor urban and rural communities. The African American community organized to gain control over these funds, and a decade of anti-poverty activism was launched out of the smoldering ruins of urban riots.[140]

The movement also brought extraordinary changes in U.S. law and upset the Jim Crow legislation of the South. Voting rights cleared the way for African Americans to acquire political power, particularly in areas where they constituted the majority of the population. Civil rights legislation such as the 1964 Civil Rights Act brought down some employment and educational barriers.

From Margin to Center: Black Feminists Organize

In the late-1960s and early-1970s, Black women in the civil rights and Black Power movements began to respond to sexism in these movements and racism within the white feminist movement by striking out on their own. Led by a powerful and diverse group of writers, artists, and activists, Black feminism (or "womanism," in the words of Alice Walker) soon became a vibrant, multi-faceted movement, and a National Black Feminist Organization was founded in 1973. One important early document in Black feminism was the Combahee River Collective Statement, written in Boston in the early-1970s. The Collective was named after, "[the] guerrilla action conceptualized and led by Harriet Tubman on June 2, 1863, in the Port Royal region of South Carolina [which] freed more than 750 and is the only military campaign in American history planned and led by a woman." In the statement, the Collective describes itself as:

> ...actively committed to struggling against racial, sexual, heterosexual, and class oppression...our particular task [is] the development of integrated analysis and practice based upon the fact that the major systems of oppression are interlocking.[141]

Black feminism generated an abundance of powerful social criticism and political analysis. Michelle Wallace's forceful critique of sexism in the Black Power movement, *Black Macho and the Myth of the Superwoman*, initiated a heated dialogue between Black men and women. Ntozake Shange's *For Colored Girls who Have Considered Suicide When the Rainbow is Enuf* took Black women's stories to Broadway; Alice Walker's prize-winning novel *The Color Purple* brought them to the best-seller list. Barbara Smith, Gloria Joseph, and bell hooks took the white feminist movement to task for its unintentional as well as intentional racism with their respective books, *Home Girls, Common Differences*, and *Feminist Theory: From Margin to Center*.[142]

An important opportunity for Black womanist activism came even earlier, with the 1967 formation of the National Welfare Rights Organization (NWRO) by George Wiley, an African American anti-poverty activist. Wiley observed that Black women received unequal treatment under the Aid to Families with Dependent Children (AFDC) program, which was the major U.S. welfare program for poor families. Benefits were low and especially difficult for Black women to obtain, since they were administered by state governments which, particularly in the South, sought to ensure a large supply of Black women to menial jobs. Local NWRO chapters, many of which were headed by Black women, organized to empower poor women of all races to gain the benefits to which they were legally entitled. In response to

President Nixon's proposed welfare reform of 1969, the Family Assistance Plan (FAP), the NWRO organized demonstrations and rallies, culminating in a national campaign to "Zap Fap"—and the plan was shelved. Welfare rights activists were able to strike down restrictive eligibility rules and raise the level of welfare benefits significantly; as a result, the number of single mothers receiving Aid to Families with Dependent Children (AFDC) increased by 50 percent between 1970 and 1973. By 1974, the NWRO, which also included white and Puerto Rican women, had 800 affiliate chapters in 50 states.[143]

The NWRO struggle was implicitly feminist, seeking to legitimate and seek economic compensation for women's unpaid work of childrearing. The first chairwoman of the NWRO, Johnnie Tillmon, pointed out the ways in which the oppression of welfare mothers expresses the broader social devaluation of all women:

> I'm a woman. I'm a black woman. I'm a poor woman. I'm a fat woman. I'm a middle-aged woman. And I'm on welfare.
>
> In this country, if you're any one of those things—poor, black, fat, female, middle-aged, on welfare—you count less as a human being...
>
> For a lot of middle-class women in this country, Women's Liberation is a matter of concern. For women on welfare it's a matter of survival...
>
> The truth is that AFDC is like a supersexist marriage. You trade in *a* man for *the* man...
>
> *The* man runs everything. In ordinary marriage, sex is supposed to be for your husband. On AFDC, you're not supposed to have any sex at all. You give up control of your own body. It's a condition of aid...
>
> *The* man, the welfare system, controls your money...
>
> There are a lot of other lies that male society tells about welfare mothers; that AFDC mothers are immoral, that AFDC mothers are lazy, misuse their welfare checks, spend it all on booze and are stupid and incompetent.
>
> If people are willing to believe these lies, it's partly because they're just special versions of the lies that society tells about *all* women.[144]

African American Economic Advancement, 1950-1973

The multi-pronged push of African American activism, combined with continuous economic growth in the nation overall, brought important improvements in the economic status of African Americans through the mid-1970s. Educational levels and incomes rose, poverty rates fell, Blacks achieved greater access to white-collar jobs, and the Black middle class grew. In 1950, only 13 percent of African Americans 25 years of age and older had graduated from high school; by 1970, the figure had jumped to 31 percent, and by 1980, over half of all African Americans in this age group had completed high school. In 1959, more than half of African Americans lived below the poverty level; by 1974, the Black poverty rate had fallen to less than one-third. Median Black family income rose from 54 percent of white family income in 1950 to 64 percent in 1970. More African American men escaped their restriction to the bottom of the job market: in 1950, roughly one-half of employed Black men worked as unskilled laborers or in agriculture, but by 1970, only one in five Black men were so employed.[145]

Perhaps the most dramatic improvements came for African American women. Rapid job growth and anti-discrimination legislation allowed large numbers of Black women to enter white-collar jobs, as shown in Table 6-1. Between 1950 and 1970, Black female clerical employment grew by over half a million, increasing the share of Black women workers in these jobs from 5 percent to 21 percent. Professional employment almost doubled, to comprise over 11 percent of Black women's jobs in 1970. The lowering of racial barriers in the government sector under affirmative action accounted for a large number of these new jobs, and by 1979, almost one-third of employed Black women worked for the federal, state, or local government, compared to less than one-fifth of white women. Jobs also continued to open up in factories, which by 1970 employed 19 percent of African American women workers. With these new opportunities, African American women finally were able to leave the homes and kitchens of white women, and the share of Black women in private household work fell to 18 percent in 1970 and 5 percent in 1980. Median incomes of Black women who were year-round, full-time workers rose from 55 percent of white women's in 1956 to 91 percent in 1974. Nevertheless, both Black and white women still earned on average half of white men's incomes since most were excluded from white men's jobs.[146]

Black Economic Progress Stalls

In the mid-1970s Black economic progress slowed as the U.S. economy entered another period of crisis. Facing growing international competition, U.S. firms tried to restore profitability by transferring production overseas to countries where labor costs were lower and corporations faced lower taxes and fewer environmental and worker-safety regulations. U.S.-based firms also began to seek an alternative to Black workers, as European American economist Michael Reich points out:

> By the late-1960s employers began to recognize that blacks were no longer a source of docile and cheap labor. This shift in the character of the black labor supply should be understood primarily in terms of the heightened consciousness of blacks developed by

the civil rights movement...employers began actively to recruit and to switch to new labor supplies, mainly Latinos already in the United States and new immigrants from Latin American, the Caribbean, Asia, the Pacific Islands and elsewhere...These groups became a major source of new labor supplies for the private sector...Employers succeeded in reestablishing low-wage employment, which grew rapidly, but a remarkably small percentage of these jobs were filled by blacks.[147]

Plant closings in Detroit, Chicago, and other cities with large African American populations hit Blacks hard. Job losses in the steel and automobile industries, which had provided good wages to Black men with little formal education, were especially devastating. Between 1981 and 1985, 5 percent of Black men and 6 percent of Black women lost their jobs as a result of plant closings alone. On average, Black women took almost two years to find new jobs, compared to about one year for Black men (whites took approximately half as long to obtain new work).[148]

African Americans lost more jobs as retail and office jobs were transferred out of central cities to mostly white suburban and rural areas. The most visible transfer took place as large, center-city retail stores moved to suburban shopping centers, 15,000 of which sprouted up between 1953 and 1978. As work moved out of the center cities, overt and covert racial discrimination in housing, made visible by cross-burnings and arson, kept most Blacks from following the jobs into the suburbs. By 1980, 58 percent of Blacks lived in central cities, where they made up almost one-quarter of the population. In contrast, more than half of whites lived in the suburbs, compared to only 23 percent of Blacks.[149]

Black unemployment rose and remained high—usually at least twice the white rate, as shown in Table 6-2. Between 1975 and 1986, Black unemployment averaged 15.2 percent, compared to less than 7 percent for whites. Unemployment was particularly high in the early-1980s, when the economy sank into the deepest recession since the Great Depression. In 1983, the height of Black unemployment, almost one-third of all Blacks and half of Black teens were unemployed. Teenage African American women faced the highest unemployment rate—47 percent—of any racial-ethnic group.[150]

Even though the economy as a whole had recovered from the recession by the mid-1980s, roughly one-tenth of all Blacks and one-third of Black teens remained out of work. The ratio of Black to white unemployment increased from 2.0 to 2.5 between 1972 and 1988. Because most of the jobs lost in the early-1980s involved unskilled or semi-skilled workers, Blacks without high school degrees have been hardest hit by these trends; the unemployment rate for Blacks with one to three years of high school in 1988

Table 6-2

Unemployment Rates by Race-Ethnicity, Gender, and Age, 1972-1988

	WOMEN			MEN		
	Black	White	B/W	Black	White	B/W
1972						
16 and Over	11.8	5.9	2.0	9.3	4.5	2.1
16-19	40.5	14.2	2.9	31.7	14.2	2.2
1975						
16 and Over	14.8	8.6	1.7	14.8	7.2	2.0
16-19	41.0	17.4	2.4	39.5	18.3	2.2
1982						
16 and Over	17.6	8.3	2.1	20.1	8.8	2.3
16-19	47.1	19.0	2.5	48.9	21.7	2.3
1988						
16 and Over	11.7	4.7	2.5	11.7	4.7	2.5
16-19	32.0	12.3	2.6	32.8	13.9	2.4

SOURCES: U.S. Department of Labor, *Handbook of Labor Statistics*, Bulletin 2217, June 1985, Table 27; U.S. Department of Labor, *Employment and Earnings*, January 1983, Table 51, and *Statistical Abstract of the United States 1990*, Table 638.

was 16 percent, compared to 3 percent among Black college graduates.[151]

Black men and women responded to skyrocketing unemployment somewhat differently. During this period, an increasing share of Black women entered the labor force; their labor force participation rate rose from 42 percent in 1960 and 53 percent in 1980 to 58 percent in 1988. However, high teen unemployment rates may have begun to dampen Black girls' efforts to find jobs. In 1988, only 38 percent of Black girls aged 16 to 19 were employed or looking for work (a quarter were unsuccessful in finding jobs), compared with 57 percent of white teen girls. This stands in sharp contrast to Black women over 20 years of age, who are more likely to be in the labor force than their white counterparts.[152]

Declining employment opportunities have clearly discouraged labor force participation for African American men: rates have been falling since 1960 in all age groups. African American sociologist William Julius Wilson notes that between 1965 and 1984, the percentage of Black men aged 25 to 34 who were employed in civilian jobs—excluding those in the armed forces or institutionalized—fell from 90 percent to 76 percent. During the same period, rates for white men of this age group fell less than 2 percent. As a result, in 1988, there were more African American women in the labor force than African American men.[153]

For Blacks who had migrated to northern and midwestern cities in search of work, this evaporation of jobs represented a cruel twist of fate. Crowded into inner cities by housing discrimination, northern Blacks have been increasingly forced to seek their livelihood in the growing underground economy of unreported or illegal activity. In the South, Blacks had often struggled for survival by living outside the cash economy, foraging, fishing, and producing goods for themselves outside of the control of white people. In the North, such marginal economic activity has increasingly taken the form of illicit activity, particularly in the ghettos' only growth industry, drugs. At the same time, burgeoning drug trafficking and addiction, and the associated teen gangs and violent crimes, are tearing apart the fabric of ghetto communities, and making education and upward mobility through inner-city schools extremely difficult.

Already hindered by declining job opportunities and limited mobility, urban African Americans also faced cutbacks in public services and income in the 1970s and 1980s. As companies closed their doors, cities in the Northeast and Midwest lost their tax bases; tax revenues fell and public spending had to be trimmed. New York City's near bankruptcy in 1974-75 attracted the most attention, but Boston and Cleveland also faced the threat of bankruptcy. For the nearly 60 percent of African Americans, many of them low income, who were urban residents and utilized public schools, public housing, or other public services in cities, these budget crises resulted in devastating losses of crucial human services and well-being. Furthermore, since the public sector employs a disproportionate share of Blacks, layoffs in state and local governments hit Blacks especially hard. To add insult to injury, the Reagan administration directly attacked the poor, among whom African Americans were overrepresented, by slashing federal social service expenditures from 1980 to 1988. These cuts were especially deadly during the recession of the early 1980s, during which 36 percent of all Blacks and almost half of all Black children fell below the official poverty line (compared to 12 percent of whites and 17 percent of white children).[154]

Budget cutbacks and layoffs were accompanied by a shift of white public sentiment from the 1960s-inspired critiques of poverty and inequality as social problems and an associated commitment to government intervention, to a world view, coinciding with Reaganism, that blamed the poor and especially Blacks for their increasing poverty. Ignoring the structural failures of the economic system, conservatives—including some prominent Blacks such as Harvard economist Glenn Loury—branded poor Blacks as a pathological, marginal, and deviant "underclass," characterized by high rates of criminality and out-of-wedlock births.[155]

Some analysts, such as William Julius Wilson, have placed some of the blame for the persistence of Black poverty on the Black middle class. By moving out of ghetto communities, these analysts argue, the Black middle class has deprived inner-city youth of the role models and connections necessary for the climb out of poverty. However, a recent study found that the decline of the Black middle class in the inner cities was not caused by geographical movement out to the suburbs. In fact, declining property values (which make it difficult for families to sell their inner-city homes) and continuing racism in middle-class suburbs have made such relocation difficult. Indeed, there is less residential segregation by class among Blacks than among whites, Asians, or Latinas/os. Instead, the shrinking of the Black middle-class population in the inner cities, the study found, has been caused by their downward economic mobility, as more and more Blacks have lost their middle-class jobs in the midst of the economic decline of their neighborhoods.[156]

In a recent critique of conservative underclass theories, Black economist Julianne Malveaux appropriately asks, "Does the 'underclass' have a behavior problem or does capitalism?" Malveaux notes that the concern about underclass "behavior" may really be a concern about Black militancy:

> The poor no longer come to us as supplicant on one knee, willing to do anything for a little welfare change. Some stand before us as angry as the agitators of the sixties, speaking of the homeless unions, jobless unions and dignity. In response, many who write about public policy recoil and talk about "behavior." [157]

African American Impoverishment and the Single Mother

The growing proportion of families which are headed by single mothers has also eroded the economic position of the African American community. The share of African American families maintained by women virtually doubled in the course of 25 years, from 22 percent in 1960 to 43 percent in 1988. While this proportion also rose for other racial-ethnic groups, especially Puerto Ricans, Black families were over three times as likely as white families to be maintained by a woman in 1986.[158]

There are several reasons for this high proportion of single-mother families. First, as we have seen, African Americans have a tradition, traceable from Africa and to slavery, in which living without a man, even with children, is an acceptable option for women. Whether due to the lack of sex education, birth control and abortion, or to choice, Black women are still more likely than white women to bear children outside of marriage and to bear children at earlier ages; they also tend to marry at later ages, often after becoming mothers.[159]

Second, there is a shortage of men in the Black community. Racial oppression results in higher mortality for men of color. Black (and Latino) men face higher risks of occupational accidents and illnesses than whites, as a result of their relegation to the riskiest jobs in the occupational hierarchy. Ghetto and police violence also take a high toll: the death rate from homicide is nearly seven times higher for Black men than for white men. Men of color also constitute a disproportionate share of combat troops, and thus, combat fatalities, for the United States. Racism in the criminal justice system—expressed through higher arrest, conviction, and sentencing rates—also removes many Black men from their community: in 1986, Blacks made up 41 percent of jail inmates, 37 percent of juveniles in public custody, and 29 percent of persons arrested.[160]

A third reason for the high numbers of single-mother families in the Black community is high rates of divorce and separation. In 1982, for instance, 18 percent of African American women were divorced or separated compared to 10 percent of white women. Welfare policies prevent two-parent families from collecting AFDC benefits in 25 states; in some states, African American men have had to leave the household in order for women and children to have access to welfare and Medicaid. High unemployment rates, and the associated psychological stresses and pressures to relocate, also contribute to divorce and separation for Blacks. Like other racially subordinated groups who have played an important role as a labor force for capitalism, African Americans have had to migrate often to find work. Migration can play a de-stabilizing role in family life. Between 1940 and 1970, almost 4.5 million Blacks left the South. Not only are pressures for separation higher on Black couples, but the length of time between separation, divorce, and remarriage is usually longer for Black women than for white because of the shortage of Black men.[161]

The high share of single-mother families has combined with race and gender oppression to create a very high poverty rate for Black women and their children. Since most Black women are crowded into low-paid jobs and bear the burden of childrearing, it is very difficult for Black single mothers to keep their families out of poverty. In 1988, the poverty rate for persons living in Black single-mother families was a crippling 52 percent. Single-mother families raised half of all Black children, and they represented three-quarters of poor Black families.[162]

Nonetheless, we should not overestimate the importance of family structure in creating Black poverty. European American social scientist Mary Jo Bane has shown that two out of three African American families headed by women were poor *before* they experienced divorce, separation, death of the husband, or birth of an out-of-wedlock baby. Two-parent Black families' risk of being poor is twice that of white two-parent families.[163]

The poverty of Black single-mother families has been the subject of much academic analysis and social policy attention, much of it either misdirected or openly sexist and racist. From our point of view, single-mother poverty has its roots in the intersection of race, class, and gender oppressions that they experience. However, the mainstream media has focused attention on the families themselves rather than on the larger economic processes behind their poverty, and has attacked these family forms as inherently pathological.

This assault on the Black single-mother family was voiced by African American E. Franklin Frazier in his 1939 book, *The Negro Family*, and revived 25 years later by Democratic policy-maker Daniel Moynihan in the so-called "Moynihan Report." Moynihan put forward the thesis that slavery and continued discrimination had created an alarming proportion of "matriarchal" families among African Americans, and claimed that this family form produced instability and disorganization in the African American community.[164]

In the 1980s, the Frazier-Moynihan position was bolstered by a new conservative charge that government support for poor single mothers in the form of welfare benefits was directly responsible for creating more single-mother families. This argument was developed most fully by European American neoconservative Charles Murray in an influential 1984 book entitled *Losing Ground*. Murray argued that welfare programs have encouraged Black women to leave the labor force and to raise children without husbands. By the early 1980s, conservative policy-makers in the Reagan administration had applied these ideas to national social policy, restricting eligibility for welfare, cutting the level of payments, and developing "welfare reform" programs to force poor single mothers into the labor force.[165]

Welfare rights activists have responded to this latest attack by linking up their struggles with those of the homeless and the unemployed. Meanwhile, progressive researchers are working to debunk the prevailing view that single-mother families are to blame for their own plight. As they point out, even when they are in the labor force, most Black women continue to be confined to low-paying jobs which cannot lift their families out of poverty. Nearly half of all Black women work in unskilled manufacturing, service, and private household jobs, and Black women are overrepresented in jobs such as chambermaids, cleaners, child-care aides, and fast-food counter workers. In addition, joblessness among younger Black women is very high as a result of capital flight out of the cities, the suburbanization of white-collar work, and the continued residential segregation that separates African Americans from better-paying jobs in the suburbs. The only solution to the poverty of single mothers, white as well as Black, is to reverse the processes which place them at the bottom of the economic hierarchy. Needed changes include raising welfare benefits above the poverty line, developing a full-employment economy, eliminating institutionalized race and sex segregation in the labor force, and cultivating male responsibility for childrearing and child support. Until these changes come about, a majority of Black single-mother families are likely to live in poverty, with a median income only 35 percent that of a Black married-couple families, and under 30 percent that of white married-couple families.[166]

While the economic oppression of single-mother families makes survival a daily struggle, and poverty and deprivation a way of life, the bravery, independence, and determination of these women deserve recognition. As African American historian and activist Barbara Omolade points out:

> ...Black single mothers and their families have something to offer us all. By daily demonstrating that they can survive and succeed without marriage, that they may even be better off without it, they challenge the basic patriarchal ideal. My children and other children of Black single mothers are better people because they do not have to live in families where violence, sexual abuse, and emotional estrangement are the daily, hidden reality. They are not burdened by violent sexist nightmares that block their strength and sensibilities at the core of where they live. They know that fathers and mothers are only men and women, not infallible tyrants or gods. They have choices and a voice. In a society where men are taught to dominate and women to follow, we all have a lot to overcome in learning to build relationships, with each other and with our children, based on love and justice. For many Black single mothers, this is what the struggle is about.[167]

An innovative community organization that builds on Black sisterhood and seeks to create a better world for Black people is the Brooklyn-based Sisterhood of Black Single Mothers. In the words of its founder, Daphne Busby, "Black families are not 'fatherless,' they are 'motherful.' " The organization puts younger and older mothers in teams for mutual support, runs a variety of training and educational sessions, and designs and operates its own housing, built specifically to meet the needs of Black single mothers.[168]

African American Women Today

The present economic situation of African American women is mixed. They have certainly made progress: for example, Black women now work in almost every job category. However, these gains have been unevenly distributed. While an increasing share of Black women hold managerial and professional jobs, in 1980, 12 percent were unemployed, 32 percent worked at the bottom of the labor market hierarchy, and almost one-third of all Blacks continued to live in poverty.

As shown in Figure 6-2, by 1980, 15 percent of Black women workers were employed in elite jobs as managers and professionals, up from 9 percent in 1970. Surprisingly, the top-tier primary jobs employed a higher share of Black women than of Black men in 1980—not because Black women's share was high, but because Black men's share was low. A high proportion of African American managerial and professional women continue to be employed in the public sector, where discrimination is less. Sixty percent of Black managerial and professional women in the 15 cities with the highest Black populations worked for national, state, or local government, compared with only 31 percent of white women managers and professionals. Many of African American women's professions, such as teaching and social service work, are largely in the public sector. Inside and outside the public sector, most Black women professionals are found in jobs that serve Black, mostly poor and working-class, clients. Hence their progress is both partial and tenuous: partial, because their employment opportunities are still limited, and tenuous, because their jobs are dependent upon the size of the government sector in an era of budget austerity and lessening commitment to affirmative action.[169]

Still, African American women did make some progress between 1970 and 1980 in entering high-paid jobs which have been dominated by white men. Table 6-3 shows the relative concentrations of Black women in selected jobs in 1970 and 1980. A relative concentration of 100 means that Black women have their fair share of these jobs (equal to their share of all jobs); a lower number means less than their share, a higher number, more. Black women's relative concentrations increased in all of the white masculine top-tier primary-sector jobs except farm owner and manager, and more than doubled in engineering, sales representatives in commodities and finance, and executives, administrators, and managers. We can expect these trends to continue as long as the share of Black females who complete college continues to rise. Between 1970 and 1988, the share rose from 4.6 percent to 11.3 percent. However, current cutbacks in financial aid and affirmative action legislation may well threaten this progress.[170]

As we can see in Figure 6-2, another 7 percent of employed Black women were employed in the lower tier of the primary sector, mostly as nurses; the share of Black men in such jobs is four times larger. However, Black women also made progress into masculine jobs in this lower tier. As shown in Table 6-3, Black women substantially increased their relative share of protective service and transportation jobs during the 1970s. Nevertheless, this progress, and their entry into white men's managerial and professional jobs, was only relative: in 1980, Black women held less than half of their share of all the jobs shown in Table 6-3.

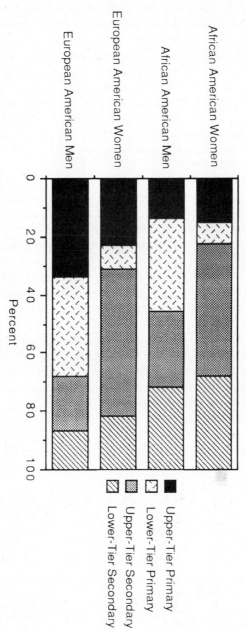

Figure 6-2: The Distribution of African American and European American Workers across Labor Market Segments, by Gender, 1980

NOTES: See Table 10-5 for a listing of the occupations in each labor market segment. See Table 10-6 for the actual percentages employed in each segment.
SOURCE: 1980 Census; see Appendix A.

Table 6-3

Relative Concentrations of African American Women in Selected
White-Male-Dominated Occupations, 1970 and 1980

	1970	1980
UPPER-TIER PRIMARY JOBS		
Engineering	1	7
Health Diagnosing	7	13
Farm Owners & Managers	8	5
Sales Representatives (Commodities & Finance)	7	22
Executives, Managers, & Administrators	17	45
LOWER-TIER PRIMARY JOBS		
Protective Service	19	44
Craft	10	18
Transportation	10	22

SOURCES: Calculated from the 1970 and 1980 Censuses. See Appendix A.

Economists have pointed to the closing wage gap between African American and European American women workers as a measure of the growing economic security for Black women. Between 1950 and 1978, the mean income for full-time, full-year Black women workers rose from 53 percent to 96 percent of their white counterparts. However, this trend to convergence halted in the 1980s, and actually reversed itself. By 1986, the figure had fallen to 88 percent. Furthermore, the relatively high income of Black women full-time workers relative to that of white women masks other inequalities, as African American economist Rhonda Williams points out. Relative to white women, Black women suffer from higher unemployment rates (twice white women's), experience greater difficulty finding full-time work, and are much more likely to support families alone (heading the majority of Black families during the mid-1980s while white women headed fewer than 20 percent). Finally, when we compare Black women with white men—who are, Williams argues, the appropriate comparison group—severe inequality is evident: Black women's full-time, year-round median income was less than 60 percent of white men's in 1988. Black women are also hurt by Black men's higher unemployment rates (twice those of white men) and low earnings (73 percent of white men's).[171]

The continuing economic oppression of Black women is also evident if we look at the distribution of Black women workers across labor market segments. As Figure 6-2 shows, over three-fourths of Black women's paid jobs are in the secondary labor market. Almost one-third—the highest share of any racial-ethnic group of women—are in the low-paid, low-status jobs at the bottom tier of the secondary labor market, most of them in service jobs. This is almost three times the share of white men working in the lowest tier.[172]

By the late-1980s, the share of Blacks who lived in poverty had increased; in 1988, nearly one-third of all Blacks lived in poverty. The share of Blacks who were very poor—living on less than half of poverty-line income—increased by 69 percent between 1978 and 1987. Blacks are far less likely to escape poverty than whites: a Black person's chances of being persistently poor in the late-1980s were eight times higher than those of a white person. Black poverty tends to be concentrated among female heads of household, particularly those with children, and in inner-city ghettos. Blacks are still segregated in inferior public schools, where drop-out rates are high; in 1988, only 63 percent of Black females over the age of 25 had graduated from high school, compared to 78 percent of white females. (It is interesting to note that poor whites have a slightly higher drop-out rate than poor Blacks; higher drop-out rates for Blacks are thus the result of their greater concentration in poverty rather than a lesser commitment to education.) In this way, a significant share (about one-fifth) of all Blacks is caught in the long-term cycle of poverty, segregated into inferior housing, schools, and jobs.[173]

African American women persist in their struggles for economic justice, organizing on issues affecting the survival of the their community, including reproductive rights and sterilization abuse, health issues, welfare reform, union organizing, housing, education, and police brutality. Black women's health has constituted one area of creative and successful organizing. African American women's location at the center of class, race, and gender oppression has exposed them to greater health problems because of dangerous working conditions and lack of access to health care. In response, Byllye Avery founded the National Black Women's Health Network in 1983, holding a national conference attended by 1,500 women. Today, the Network continues to grow, building on the principle of Black women's self help, and adding local chapters around the country. Black women continue to be active in community development and political organizing, much of it through churches. As committed professionals or as volunteers, they continue to form the backbone of the movement for Black liberation.

And since the abolition of slavery over 120 years ago, African American women have made incredible economic progress. They have gradually freed themselves from servile work relationships to whites, first as slaves, and then as domestic servants, gaining entry into the factory and then the office. They have held their families together, often alone; worked to support their men as well as themselves and their children; and organized with one another, within their communities, and in multi-racial groups to win rights and extract justice from a hostile society. We can all find inspiration and direction in the strength, resilience, and bravery of African American women. More than any other group of women, they have refused to allow themselves to be bifurcated into false categories of "women" or "Blacks," demanding that Black men confront their sexism and forcing feminists of all races to confront the racism which divides women.

CHAPTER 7

CLIMBING GOLD MOUNTAIN

Asian American Women

born into the
skin of yellow women
we are born
into the armor of warriors

—Kitty Tsui, "Chinatown Talking Story"[1]

As Chinese American lesbian Kitty Tsui writes, Asian American women have needed "the armor of warriors" to survive. For 150 years, Asian women have worked and raised families in the United States, overcoming racism and exploitation from their earliest days as farmworkers, prostitutes, and domestic servants. Today, Asian American women are represented in the most prestigious managerial and professional jobs, and Asians are viewed as a "model minority" whose upward mobility stands as an example for other racial-ethnic groups. This climb up "Gold Mountain," as Chinese workers called San Francisco, has been arduous and dangerous, calling on the courage and endurance of men and women alike.

Asian American women's economic history displays many common themes across ethnic groups, yet each group has had unique experiences. We begin by bringing out the similarities which derive from their common history as low-wage workers who were imported into a U.S. economy dominated by whites. Then we look in depth at the economic histories of Chinese, Japanese, and Filipinas/os in the United States. We conclude the chapter by drawing out commonalities in the contemporary experiences of Asian American women.

The Asian population in the United States numbered over 6.5 million in 1988, or about 3 percent of the total U.S. population. It includes people whose cultural roots are in China, Japan, the Philippines, Vietnam, Cambodia, Korea, Thailand, India, Pakistan, Bangladesh, Laos, Malaysia, Burma,

Indonesia, and other countries. Here, because of space limitations, we focus on the three largest Asian groups in the United States in 1985: the Chinese (1,079,000), the Japanese (766,000), and the Filipinas/os (1,052,000), who together accounted for 56 percent of Asians in the United States. During the 1970s and 1980s, these three main groups were joined by over one million immigrants from Korea, Vietnam, India, and Cambodia; the Indian, Korean, and Vietnamese populations each numbered about 500,000 in 1980.[2]

Asian populations in the United States are richly diverse. Since there has been a substantial amount of recent immigration from Asia, a count of Asians in the United States will include high proportions of people born in Asia as well as many whose ancestors have lived in the United States for five, six, or even seven generations.[3] The different Asian countries represented are themselves culturally varied, with distinct languages and many religions, including Buddhism, Confucianism, Islam, and Christianity. Furthermore, from the sixteenth century, Asian countries were differentiated by their subjection to different European colonial regimes—French colonization of Vietnam, British reign over China and India, Spanish rule in the Philippines, and Dutch domination of Indonesia. Asian countries rarely united in their struggle against Europeans and were themselves often at war over territories and sovereignty. China, for example, dominated its neighbors under the Tsin and T'ang dynasties and Japan repeatedly invaded other Asian countries, including China and Korea, beginning in the late nineteenth century.

From 1840 through World War II, Asian immigrants—first Chinese, then Japanese, and finally Filipinas/os—were recruited as a low-wage, second-class labor force by employers in the western United States and Hawaii. The U.S. legal system denied Asian immigrants the legal rights which had been accorded their European counterparts, relying on the 1790 naturalization law that restricted the privilege of citizenship to "free white persons." When the law was revised after the Civil War to make African Americans eligible for citizenship, the phrase "persons of African descent" was added, and the law continued to bar Asian immigrants from naturalizing.[4] Unable to become citizens, Asian immigrants remained permanent "aliens" (non-citizens), and whites were able to pass numerous laws which restricted their rights simply by referring to their alien status. For example, in the early twentieth century California passed laws which prevented Asian immigrants from purchasing land. However, children of immigrant Asians were allowed to become citizens and escape these restrictions if they were born in the United States.

On the West Coast, where the vast majority of Asians lived, whites bolstered their own relative economic status at the expense of Asian immigrants. White employers achieved higher profits by using Asians as low-wage replacements for white workers and as strikebreakers. White workers resented the threat Asians appeared to pose to wages and unionizing efforts. Self-employed whites felt threatened by Asian successes in small business.[5]

To defend their economic positions, whites formed broad-based movements to restrict Asian immigration and even to send migrants back to Asia. Filipino historian Paul Valdez wrote of the anti-"Oriental" movement of the 1920s, "They used to pass out leaflets saying that the Japanese were taking the lands from the Americans, the Chinese were taking the businesses, and the Filipinos were taking the women."[6] Under these pressures, white-controlled federal and state governments passed close to 50 laws specifically aimed at restricting and subordinating Asian immigrants between 1850 and 1950. These sentiments culminated in laws excluding further immigration: Chinese immigration was cut off in 1882 and 1892; Japanese in 1907-08 and 1924; Indian in 1917; and Filipina/o in 1934.[7]

Whites also discriminated against second-generation Asians who, unlike white ethnics, could not disguise their ethnicity by speaking English and adopting European American ways. These barriers to upward mobility in the labor market compelled many Asian Americans to seek advancement through self-employment in family-based businesses—for the Chinese, laundries and restaurants; for the Japanese, truck farming; and for the Koreans, grocery stores.[8]

Another common element in early Asian American history, central to our study, is the small numbers of Asian women relative to Asian men. In the United States, the ratio of men to women among the Chinese in 1860 was 19 to 1; among the Japanese in 1900, it was 25 to 1; among the Filipinas/os in 1930, it was 14 to 1. The imbalance occurred because employers sought out single male workers, so most men came as "sojourners," planning to return home after they had made their fortunes. Although women's immigration experiences varied among groups, each group faced the difficulty of forming families across the ocean, especially when further immigration was cut off, since miscegenation laws prevented marriage between whites and Asians. Decades passed after the first immigrants arrived before a sizeable second generation of Asians was born in the United States.

CHINESE AMERICAN WOMEN

From China to Gold Mountain

In the mid-nineteenth century, the needs of U.S. capitalists for cheap labor coincided with economic crises and dislocation in China. During this period, many peasants lost their lands to large land-owners, but industry had not developed enough to provide new employment to the landless. Political strife was rampant, marked by the Taiping Rebellion against the Manchu dynasty (1848-65). In 1849, a major flood devastated southeastern China, transforming even wealthy families into beggars. The search for work forced hundreds of thousands of men to leave their villages for other parts of China and overseas.[9]

China's connection with the West had already been established by three centuries of European traders. Then, in 1842, China lost the Opium War, and was forced to give up territories, including the island of Hong Kong, to the British. Unable to resolve domestic upheavals and dislocations, pressed to accommodate foreign impositions and demands, and unaccustomed to western-style international agreements, China's government neither regulated emigration nor had any influence on policies under which China's immigrants might locate in other countries.[10]

In the midst of domestic confusion and European domination, European and U.S. firms set up a lucrative "coolie" trade ("coolie" means bitter labor in Chinese). While physical coercion was not unknown in the coolie trade, most Chinese came to the United States voluntarily in response to desperate economic straits at home, expecting to strike it rich on "Gold Mountain" and return to China. Employers were aided by well-paid Chinese middlemen who recruited workers and contracted them out to work for a specific period of time. In this fashion, Chinese workers were exported all over the world, to Australia, Peru, and Cuba in addition to the United States. To finance their passage and the necessary legal papers, some immigrants obtained loans from their kinsmen in the United States, but most had to borrow from middlemen.[11]

Chinese labor was favored by U.S. and Hawaiian employers who were able to contract able-bodied young men for work and to prevent the married workers' wives and children from joining them. By 1852, 11,787 Cantonese Chinese had come to the United States, only seven of whom were women. Although workers did send some wages home to their families, most of the costs of producing another generation of workers and caring for the infirm and aged were borne in China. This allowed employers to keep wages very low, especially by U.S. standards. As single men, Chinese workers were ideal for migrant farm work, mining, and railroad construction: employers could move them around easily and house them in cheap dormitory-like structures rather than family homes. In addition, Chinese men were desirable as workers because of their experience in excavation and sugar cultivation.[12]

Early Chinese Male Employment in the United States: Mines, Railroads, Fields, and Factories

Chinese workers first came to the United States in large numbers during the Gold Rush in the late 1840s. By 1860, they made up 10 percent of California's population and almost 25 percent of its labor force. Over the next 20 years, another 105,000 immigrated. Independent white miners had exhausted most lands, but mining companies used Chinese contract laborers to search for the dregs in California and other northwestern states. A second wave of Chinese workers came to work on the most dangerous segment of the transcontinental railroad, through the Rockies. Thousands lost their lives in this work.[13] Chinese men were employed in San Francisco's woolen mills as a cheap substitute for white workers: "Stop paying American workmen three dollars a day and substitute Chinamen at a dollar and a quarter, and then you will make money," advised businessman Louis McLane.[14] Chinese men also labored in citrus- and celery-harvesting and fisheries. Urban Chinese workers manufactured cigars, slippers, garments, and shoes. Also, since there was a severe shortage of white women workers in the West, Chinese men were recruited to perform the traditionally feminine work of domestic service, laundry, and food service.[15]

Chinese immigrants formed the lower tier of the workforce. They earned the lowest pay while white men monopolized skilled and supervisory jobs. For example, in the garment industry in 1870, Chinese men averaged $300-400 a year, compared to $600-900 for white women, and $900-1,200 for white men.[16] With few exceptions, the white labor movement refused to allow Asian workers into their unions.[17] However, Chinese garment workers organized labor guilds, patterned after traditional Chinese guilds, which won concessions from both Chinese and white employers: garment workers couldn't be fired without guild approval, and wages were almost doubled.[18]

A few Chinese immigrants worked for themselves. Some miners, especially the early migrants, labored independently, even if under debt. In response to the shortage of domestic servants, Chinese men set up hundreds of small laundries in San Francisco, and Chinese laundries became a California institution. Many Chinese were successful in truck gardening and large-scale tenant farming, and some even accumulated large amounts of land which they farmed and ranched. In southern California villages, Chinese fishermen successfully exported millions of dollars worth of abalone and shrimp yearly in the 1870s and 1880s. In one such village, Chinese women worked at baiting fish hooks (150 on each fishing net), and drying and processing the catch as well as seaweed.[19] Chinatowns hosted many small Chinese businesses: in 1878, San Francisco's boasted "over 150 wholesalers and retailers of fresh and preserved foods, 12 restaurants, 25 apothecaries,

35 fancy goods stores, 10 jewelry stores, 10 tinsmitheries, and over a dozen small craftsmen and artisans."[20] Although women were in short supply, their unpaid labor as wives was crucial for the success of many small businesses.[21]

Wealthy import-export merchants from the scholar-gentry class formed the elite of nineteenth-century Chinese communities in the United States. These merchants were different from other Chinese immigrants in class, culture, and language. Some merchants were also capitalist producers, hiring poor Chinese at meager wages to produce goods such as cigars and garments. Others enriched themselves by contracting out Chinese workers to white capitalists, or by profiting from prostitution. Merchants' wives enjoyed sheltered lives, cared for by servants and filling their time with decorative needlework and socializing with others of their class.[22]

Chinese merchant-capitalists also dominated the tight-knit organizations that were at the center of life and work for Chinese in the United States. In these organizations, poor immigrants and rich merchants unified under the latter's leadership to protect themselves against the hostility of white society. Chinese groups included patriarchal clan associations which united all individuals with the same family name, *tongs* (secret societies), and the Chinese Six Companies, also called the Chinese Consolidated Benevolent Association, which oversaw the San Francisco Chinese community and acted as Chinese America's representative and defender against white society.[23]

Chinese Workers on Hawaiian Plantations

The Hawaiian sugar industry developed as a plantation system similar to the slave South, in which white planters with large plots of land used unfree and racially subordinated groups. Native Hawaiians were the first labor force but, like other indigenous peoples, their numbers fell rapidly as a result of white takeover of their lands—from 300,000 at "discovery" in 1778 to 44,000 in 1878. As a result, the planters turned to Chinese laborers, and later to Japanese and Filipinas/os, for over 85 percent of their labor force (Puerto Ricans, Portuguese, and other whites made up the rest).[24]

Chinese men were the largest group of workers in the Hawaiian sugar plantations from the 1850s through the 1870s. By 1884, there were 18,000 Chinese in Hawaii, and almost half of the men in Hawaii between the ages of 15 and 50 were Chinese. Most Chinese immigrants to Hawaii came under contracts with government or private immigration companies, and an estimated 93 percent were men. A few immigration companies did encourage men to bring their wives, with an eye to using female labor in the fields and to encouraging stability among the workers. Faced with a shortage of Chinese women, many Chinese male laborers married Hawaiian women.[25]

The majority of women immigrants were Cantonese, many of whom had bound feet. "Lily feet," as they were called, were seen as desirable for brides, even though they made walking unassisted very difficult and painful. Women with bound feet performed relatively lighter work such as cane cutting and stripping. Some women who immigrated were Hakkas, southern Chinese who did not practice foot-binding. These women worked in the fields with their husbands. Chinese American historian Judy Yung notes, "while the men undertook the heavy tasks of watering, hoeing, ploughing, cultivating, and ditching, women helped with the planting, weeding, stripping, and cutting." [26] Even after Chinese immigration to the continental United States was terminated in 1882, Hawaiian employers still encouraged the wives and children of their Chinese residents to immigrate. In 1898, Hawaii was annexed by the United States and employers were forced to adopt the latter's exclusionary practices.[27]

Chinese labor in Hawaii was governed by the "Master and Servant Act" of 1850, which tied a worker to a particular plantation for a fixed number of years. Their freedom was further restricted by payment schemes that replaced wages with payment-in-kind and "scrip" which could be spent only at the plantation store.[28]

White planters purposefully divided work and segregated workers by race and ethnicity to discourage worker organizing. Immigrants were assigned to ethnically homogeneous labor camps, often with people from their own villages. The planters' strategy, as reported by the Hawaiian Labor Commissioner in 1895, was to, "Keep a variety of laborers, that is different nationalities, and thus prevent any concerted action in the case of strikes, for there are few, if any cases of Japanese, Chinese, and Portuguese entering into a strike as a unit."[29]

The Split-Household Family and the Gum-Shan-Poo

The migration of Chinese women into the United States from the mid-nineteenth century to the twentieth century was kept to a trickle by a combination of factors, both in the United States and in China. U.S. contractors and employers preferred single men. In China, the economic motives of family patriarchs (who wanted to insure that wages were sent back), the view that it was indecent for a woman to travel abroad, reports of sexual molestation by sailors and of anti-Chinese violence in the United States, and male emigrants' plans to return to China all discouraged women from emigrating. Between 1850 and 1882, only 8,848 Chinese women came to the United States, compared to over 100,000 men.[30]

Most Chinese men who migrated to Hawaii and the United States planned to return to China after making their fortunes. However, many of them maintained families through what Japanese American sociologist Evelyn Nakano Glenn has called the "split-household family system." [31] Many emigrants married before they left. Marriages were arranged between parents, according to Chinese tradition; the couple met on the day of their marriage, and the wife moved to the husband's village to live with his parents. Village leaders pressured the male emigrant to marry and conceive a male descendent before he left. The emigrant had to promise to send money for his family and village. Following Chinese custom, his parents kept his wife and children in their home in an effort to guarantee his cooperation with the arrangement. Others emigrated as single men, returned to China to marry, and then left their wives and growing families in China when they went back to "Gold Mountain." Thus, thousands of Chinese women led the life of a *Gum-Shan-Poo* (Golden Mountain Lady), married to a man who lived and worked in the United States and returned seldom, if ever, to China. [32]

Most immigrant men sent enough money home to China to keep their families alive—one observer estimated that remittances averaged $30 per year, enough to buy food for a family of one adult and two or three children. This supplemented whatever a wife and children could provide for themselves in China through subsistence farming or other means. While fewer than one-quarter of China's immigrant men were able to return home for good, the remainder maintained families in this way. Those who could afford it returned home to visit and to father children. Male children often joined their fathers in the United States when of age. When the flow of money stopped during times of war or natural disaster, however, families in China were left in dire straits, and, in the words of Chinese American researcher June Mei, "became refugees or were compelled to sell their belongings, homes, children, or even themselves to stay alive." [33]

The absence of her husband did not free the *Gum-Shan-Poo* from Chinese patriarchal practices. The Confucian "Three Obediences" decreed that a woman serve first her father, then her husband, and if widowed, her eldest son, with the "Four Virtues": chastity and obedience, shyness, a pleasing manner, and domestic skills. Chinese American sociologist Paul Siu described how the *Gum-Shan-Poo* remained under her husband's power:

> She has to consult him on every important matter…and he alone can make the decision. In case his wife or anyone of his family disobeys his wishes, he may punish them by cutting his financial support to the family…If his wife is proved to be unfaithful to him, he can even disown her…There need be no divorce nor any other legal action, for he has the moral support of the relatives and he is away from China. What he has to do is simply cut off his relation with her by putting an announcement in the local magazine or newspapers. [34]

By custom, the *Gum-Shan-Poo* was also subservient to her mother-in-law, in whose home she resided. These older women exercised strict control over their daughters-in-law, and it was not unusual for them to inflict harsh and even cruel treatment on the *Gum-Shan-Poo*. Chinese women who immigrated to the United States also faced economic hardship and abuse.

Chinese Prostitutes in the United States

As Chinese American historian Lucie Cheng has pointed out, prostitutes provided immigrant males with temporary liaisons compatible with their split-household marriages. Prostitution was also supported by white capitalists, who wanted to keep wives and children from immigrating and increasing labor costs, and by racists who wanted to keep the Chinese from reproducing in the United States. The unbalanced sex ratio among whites further fueled the demand for Chinese prostitutes—in the total California population in 1850, there were over 12 men for every woman.[35]

A few Chinese women came to the United States of their own initiative during the early years and worked independently as prostitutes. Ah Toy arrived in San Francisco in 1849 to "better her condition," worked as a prostitute, and then became the madam of a brothel of Chinese women.[36] Soon, however, the *tongs* took over and organized this lucrative trade, establishing a monopoly over prostitution in 1854. The major *tong,* Hip Yee Tong, earned an estimated $200,000 between 1852 and 1873 by importing an estimated 6,000 women, 87 percent of all Chinese women arrivals.[37]

Chinese purchasing agents for the *tongs* went to Canton and Hong Kong to recruit young Chinese girls into prostitution. Sometimes the exchange was conducted openly: men bought girls outright from poor families as slaves, or put them under contract for an average of four and one-half years. In other cases, agents kidnapped girls or lured them onto ships with promises of gold, marriage, jobs, or education. Sale of one's children, especially daughters, was common among destitute families in China. Daughters were seen as expendable since they left their parents' homes upon marriage and, as a Chinese proverb put it, "Eighteen gifted daughters are not equal to one lame son."[38] Many girls remained loyal to their parents, sending home up to $200 or $300 a year. Prostitutes under contract were theoretically free when their contracts expired, but rules which lengthened the years of contract if she fell ill or had a child made such freedom difficult to achieve.[39]

When girls arrived in California, they were sold either to wealthy Chinese men as concubines, to higher-class brothels reserved only for Chinese men, or to lower-class establishments serving whites as well as Asians. Some were shipped into mining camps, where treatment was especially harsh. The Hip Yee Tong charged each buyer an extra $40, of which

$10 went to pay off white policemen, and imposed a weekly tax of 25 cents on all Chinese prostitutes. One procurer cleared $1,700 when he sold his prostitute for $1,750; the brothel owner who bought her grossed about $7,000 on her work over two years, and then resold her for $2,100. Along with the police, a plethora of white lawyers and customs officials also enriched themselves from prostitution, especially as increasingly restrictive immigration codes were passed. Even the American Consul's office in Hong Kong made money, receiving $10 to $15 for each woman shipped during the late-1870s. Chinatown landlords, most of them white and many of them prominent San Franciscans, profited from the exorbitant rents they charged to brothel owners.[40]

In 1870 there were 159 brothels in San Francisco's Chinatown alone, and almost two-thirds of the Chinese women in the city worked as prostitutes. Chinese prostitutes worked under slave or semi-slave conditions, even more difficult and degrading than those faced by white prostitutes. None received regular wages, although they were allowed to keep gifts from customers. Women in low-grade brothels lived locked into rooms four feet by six feet square, often facing dim alleyways. In the daytime, when business was slack, employers forced prostitutes to perform sub-contracted sewing work.[41]

It is hard to know how many prostitutes were able to escape their bondage. Six Chinese prostitutes in Nevada committed suicide rather than continue their oppressed lives. A few served out their indentures, saved money, and started businesses or returned to China; many married Chinese working men. China Annie successfully escaped to Boise, Idaho to marry Ah Guan. When charged by her owner of grand larceny (for "stealing" herself), she convinced the judge to set her free. With the help of supportive Chinese, white social homemaker Donaldina Cameron of San Francisco was said to have rescued 3,000 Chinese women from prostitution over 40 years. Cameron demonstrated limited aspirations for her charges, however, since she often contracted them out as laborers to fruit growers. Polly Bemis, owned by a Chinese saloon keeper in an Idaho mining camp, was won in a poker game by Charlie Bemis, who later married her. She became a valued citizen and homesteader on the Salmon River, and a creek which ran through her property was named after her. While many Chinese prostitutes were never able to free themselves, almost all found ways to keep their daughters out of prostitution.[42]

White society saw prostitution as a natural avenue for Chinese women: "The Chinese are lustful and sensual in their dispositions; every female is a prostitute of the basest order," said the *New York Tribune* in a typically racist editorial in 1856.[43] Indeed, the immorality of Chinese prostitution was cited as one of the reasons to stop Chinese immigration in 1882, a hypocritical concern given the prevalence of white prostitution at the time.[44]

Organized Chinese prostitution began to decline in the 1870s as whites passed laws against it and then terminated Chinese immigration in 1882. More and more Chinese women married and worked as homemakers. In cities, they earned income at home by taking in laundry, sewing, rolling cigars, making slippers and brooms, or taking in boarders. In rural areas, homemakers brought in income by gardening, fishing, or raising livestock. Chinese women also earned wages as servants, cooks, and farm laborers. Some fished, mined, ran lodging houses, or worked on the railroads. Rural Chinese women were isolated from other Chinese, and often were called "China Mary" by whites who refused to learn how to pronounce their Chinese names.[45]

The Anti-Chinese Movement and the Chinese Exclusion Act

By the 1870s, U.S. whites, resentful of competition from low-paid Chinese laborers and independent producers, began a movement against the Chinese. In rural areas, town after town passed laws that pushed Chinese out of mining. White family farmers resented the employment of Chinese field workers by rich landowners. A Montana journalist wrote: "We don't mind hearing of a Chinaman being killed now and then...Don't kill them unless they deserve it, but when they do—why kill 'em lots."[46] All over the West, whites expelled Chinese from small towns and rural areas in what the Chinese called the "Great Driving Out."[47]

Sinophobia (anti-Chinese sentiment) was also strong among urban whites in California, stirred up by employers' use of Asian workers as strikebreakers or low-wage competition in manufacturing. The white Workingmen's Party of California led the assault, with "The Chinese Must Go" as its slogan. The party called the Chinese "the most debased order of humanity known to the civilized world." These racist epithets were combined with complaints about competition from Chinese labor:

> [I]t is to the influence which their competition with the intelligent and civilized labor of the State in all our industries will have upon the future, that the people are looking with the most concern, and from which unwholesome and unnatural competition the people are anxiously seeking for relief....[48]

Political and labor leaders incited violence. White mobs attacked Chinese in San Francisco, Los Angeles, Denver, Rock Springs, Tacoma, and Seattle. In one episode, a mob attacked the Los Angeles Chinatown in 1871, lynching 19 and stealing $40,000 in cash.[49]

Racist organizing resulted in numerous anti-Chinese laws in states, especially California, and localities. Some of these were struck down in the courts, including Article XIX of the California State Constitution, which prohibited the employment of Chinese in any California corporation. (Business pressure was probably responsible for this court decision, rather than any political power of the Chinese or a concern for their human rights.) Many other laws were not struck down. For instance, California levied special taxes on Asian immigrants, kept them from testifying against whites (absurdly enough, by declaring them American Indians), prevented them from buying land from 1913 to the 1950s, and legalized their exclusion from public schools.[50]

Ultimately, anti-Chinese agitation also succeeded in passing the Chinese Exclusion Act in 1882, a federal law terminating Chinese immigration. The act was renewed in 1892. In 1924, Congress passed an Immigration Act that denied Asian immigrants the right to be "immigrant aliens" (i.e., to stay in the U.S. permanently), justifying the law with Asians' ineligibility for citizenship. The Act allowed only temporary visitors from China into the United States, such as teachers, students, diplomats, and transients. As mentioned above, China did not intervene on behalf of Chinese people in the United States. Chinese in Hawaii did attempt to pressure the U.S. government to lift its immigration restrictions by organizing a boycott of U.S. goods by China.[51] As a result of these laws and anti-Chinese sentiment, many Chinese left the United States. The Chinese population actually contracted from 124,000 in 1890 to a low of 85,000 in 1920, and then expanded only very gradually to 106,000 in 1940. West Coast and Hawaiian employers turned to Japan for cheap labor.[52]

The Institutionalization of the Gum-Shan-Poo

The Chinese Exclusion Act of 1882 institutionalized the sex imbalance and the split-household family in the Chinese immigrant community. The Act prevented single Chinese women and the wives of U.S. residents other than merchants from immigrating. Those sojourners who now wished to send for their wives or to return to China, marry, and bring their brides to "Gold Mountain," could not do so. Furthermore, miscegenation laws prevented Chinese men from marrying white women. (These laws remained in effect until 1967, when they were struck down by the Supreme Court.)[53] Some Chinese men married Indian, African American, or Chicana women. However, most single Chinese men could begin a family only by going back to China, marrying, and leaving their wives and children behind. Thus, the split-household family system continued over generations. (Conditions for family formation in Hawaii were somewhat better. The Exclusion Act was not applied to Hawaii until it was annexed in 1898. Also, there were no laws against inter-racial marriage in Hawaii, and intermarriage with Hawaiians was common.)[54]

Some family reunification was possible after the San Francisco earthquake of 1906. The earthquake and the fire that followed destroyed the city's birth records and Chinese took advantage of a loophole in the Exclusion Act which permitted children (but not wives) of citizens to immigrate to the United States. Many Chinese claimed U.S. citizenship by birth, and these claims could not be disproved. If they did not have children of their own, they claimed fictitious children and sold the immigration rights of these "paper children" to non-citizens at high prices. Most children who tried to immigrate in this way were "paper" sons, not daughters. Immigrants were held in prison on Angel Island in the San Francisco Bay for between six months and two years (compared to one or two days for European immigrants on East Coast Ellis Island) while they were interrogated by immigration officials about their relationships to U.S. citizens. They were permitted no visitors other than missionaries. The Chinese community developed an intricate system of coaching books to cue would-be immigrants on the details of their "families," while Chinese cooks at the facility smuggled messages between prison inmates and their Chinatown contacts. Still, many failed the tests and were sent back to China, including legitimate relatives of U.S. citizens.[55]

Thus the institution of the *Gum-Shan-Poo* continued well into the twentieth century, modified somewhat by the migration of sons to the United States. Between 1938 and 1947, an estimated $7 million was sent annually by U.S. Chinese and Chinese Americans to their families in China. In one typical family history, a 21-year-old college student in the 1980s was the first in four generations of split-household families to be U.S.-born: his father, grandfather, and great-grandfather all worked in the United States, while his mother, grandmother, and great-grandmother all raised their families in China. The precarious existence of the *Gum-Shan-Poo* is illustrated in a letter written by Teh-oi to her husband, a laundryman, in 1939:

> ...I have written you previously and I think you must have received
> my letters. But you have never answered me; in fact, you have not
> written home for one whole year! Such an act of yours makes me
> most miserable and always worried...If you don't tell me clearly
> why you don't write for so long, my heart will never be sweet even
> after my death...As I tried so hard to help you get over to America,
> you have now gold and silver, but you have lost your sense of duty
> to the family...Please, Husband, send me a letter every month. You
> are worrying us to death...[56]

The Retreat to Chinatown: Between the Exclusion Act and World War II

During the Great Driving Out of the late nineteenth century, many Chinese lost their lands and businesses, and moved into the urban ghettos known as Chinatowns. Chinese fell as a proportion of farm laborers, as white farmers who employed them were often attacked, and those who remained in agriculture sought jobs with Chinese employers. The Alien Land laws, passed in 1913, made it illegal for Chinese to purchase land for farming on their own. In urban areas, participation in wage work dropped because white workers prevented white capitalists from hiring Chinese workers. Employment growth in Chinese-owned businesses was limited by the size of the Chinese market, since white consumers boycotted Chinese-made products.[57]

Many Chinese attempted to circumvent racism in the labor market by forming small businesses—laundries, restaurants, grocery stores, and small shops—although whites also tried to stop these developments. In 1937, the Chinese community in San Antonio, Texas organized to block a drive to push Chinese out of the grocery business, and Rose Don Wu served as their spokesperson before the state Senate. Most, but not all, Chinese businesses were in Chinatowns. Some Chinese set up small shops in the South to serve Blacks, whom white businesses often refused to serve.[58]

Small business ownership was also attractive to immigrant Chinese men because they were permitted to send for their wives and children once they were established as merchants. "Small-producer" families were formed in which all family members were put to work without wages, much like the European immigrants' family businesses in colonial times. In order to turn a profit, families drove themselves to the limits of endurance. One woman from Boston's Chinatown described her family's laundry business, which employed all four children and both parents in the 1930s and 1940s. The work day lasted from seven a.m. to midnight, six days a week. The children worked the same hours as the adults, except for school and a short nap, and did their homework from midnight to two in the morning. Labor was divided by age and sex. Still, women in family businesses saw some advantages to life in the United States. Helen Hong Wong, who worked peeling vegetables in the back of her husband's restaurant in Indiana, noted this about the United States: "At least you can work here and rule the family along with your husband. In China it's considered a disgrace for a woman to work and it's the mother-in-law who rules."[59] Family businesses were hard hit during the Depression. Judy Yung describes how Yee Shee Lee, the wife of a laundry-man, survived, "[she] made clothes out of old rice sacks for her six children, reinforced their shoes with tin cans to make them last longer, and made a lot of thin soup out of rice, oatmeal, and vegetables from the family garden."[60]

Table 7-1

Occupational Distribution of Chinese American Women Workers,
1900-1980 (in Percent)

	1900	1930	1960	1970	1980
Agriculture	7.3	2.5	0.7	0.4	0.3
Manufacturing	41.1	20.8	24.0	24.9	20.8
Private Household Service	35.6	12.1	1.7	1.6	0.8
Service (not Private Household)	8.7	8.8	9.2	13.0	13.0
Sales	1.0	12.0	8.3	4.7	9.7
Clerical	0.5	11.7	32.1	30.8	24.7
Professional & Technical	1.4	22.0	17.9	20.1	20.4
Managerial, Administrative, & Official	4.4	10.0	5.8	4.3	10.4

NOTES: Totals do not always sum to 100 because of rounding. Manufacturing includes craft and transportation workers; agriculture includes mining, fishing, and forestry; managerial, administrative, & official includes some self-employment, and excludes farm managers. Data for all years include Hawaii. For a full listing of occupational categories included, see Appendix B. For a discussion of comparability problems between Census years, see Appendix D.
SOURCES: See Appendix A.

Generational upward mobility for Chinese Americans was blocked through World War II by the racism of employers, customers, landlords, and schools. Shanghai-born Mary Tape took the San Francisco Board of Education to court in 1885 after they excluded her daughter from public school, proclaiming, "Will you please tell me...Is it a disgrace to be born a Chinese?" Tape won her case, but white educators evaded the ruling by creating separate Oriental Public Schools which continued through the 1920s. In some areas, school segregation persisted until the 1954 Supreme Court school desegregation ruling.[61]

Census-takers in 1900 found most Chinese women at work in unpaid labor in their homes. One in 10 was recorded as being in the paid labor force in that year, compared to 16 percent of white women and 41 percent of Black women. By 1920, this rate had risen to 13 percent, compared to 87 percent of Chinese men. As shown in Table 7-1, domestic service and manufac-turing employed the greatest shares of Chinese women in 1900. By 1930, the jobs of Chinese women wage workers had diversified, with substantial shares working in the professions (mostly in Hawaii), in non-household service, and in sales. Still, 21 percent of all Chinese women remained in manufacturing.

The most common manufacturing jobs held by Chinese women were garment work and canning. Some began work in garment factories as early as the age of seven. In 1938, in the middle of the Depression, Chinese women garment workers employed by the National Dollar Stores organized their own union chapter, went on strike for 13 weeks, and won a contract and better wages and working conditions. They were aided in their efforts by the International Ladies Garment Workers Union (ILGWU), with whom they affiliated. The Chinese Workers Mutual Aid Association, which organized Alaskan canneries in the 1930s, also made breakthroughs in working with the usually all-white and racist labor movement.[62]

Discrimination limited, but did not totally block, Chinese women's access to white-collar jobs. Clerical and sales jobs were available in Chinese-owned businesses. In Hawaii, where the Chinese population was large and well-established, many women could find office jobs in white-owned businesses outside Chinatowns. Also, in cities with small Chinese populations, whites were less threatened and discrimination less pronounced, making it easier for Chinese to obtain jobs in white firms. Furthermore, white-owned businesses that dealt with Chinese-speaking clientele were forced to hire Chinese. For example, in San Francisco, banks and the telephone company employed Chinese women as tellers and operators in their Chinatown offices. Operators had to be fully bilingual and know several Chinese dialects; at one time, they needed to memorize over 2,100 telephone numbers.[63]

However, especially on the continent, most white firms refused to hire Chinese women in their non-Chinatown offices or stores, even if they had completed high school and were fluent in English. As Lonnie Quan of San Jose, California reported of her job search in 1941, "...I went to look for a job with an insurance company in San Francisco and they came right out and told me, 'We do not hire Chinese.' Well, after a few times of THAT, you just give up and say, the heck with it."[64]

As a result of this pattern of discrimination, Chinese women were slower to move into clerical jobs than were white women, but had more opportunities than Black women. In 1930, 12 percent of employed Chinese women were in clerical work and 14 percent were in sales, compared to 25 and 9 percent of whites, and less than 1 percent of Blacks in either category. Since good job opportunities were limited, daughters whose labor was needed in family businesses rarely completed more than an elementary school education in the pre-World War II period.

A similar pattern of limited opportunity had emerged in professional employment by 1930. The share of employed Chinese women who held professional jobs grew from about one in 100 in 1900 to more than one in five in 1930. Three-quarters of professional Chinese women worked as teachers. Opportunities were greatest in Hawaii, where Chinese were allowed into the best public schools. Many Chinese women took advantage of this to gain entry into professional jobs and, by 1930, one-third of all Chinese women workers in Hawaii were teachers. A handful of Chinese American women also broke through racism and gender roles into white- and male-dominated professions. Among them were Effie Chew, who became the first Chinese American public school teacher in 1918, and Margaret Chung, the first Chinese American woman physician.[65]

World War II: A Watershed

World War II was a watershed for Chinese American workers. Since Japan had invaded China in 1931, Chinese Americans felt a common bond with the United States when war was declared on Japan in 1941. Many Chinese American women and men served in the armed forces. Meanwhile, in response to the wartime labor shortage, the U.S. government prohibited discrimination against Chinese workers in defense industries. White employers "discovered" Chinese abilities; as one shipyard publication noted:

> We have learned that these Chinese Americans are among the finest workmen. They are skillful, reliable—and inspired with a double allegiance. They know that every blow they strike in building these ships is a blow of freedom for the land of their fathers as well as for the land of their homes.[66]

Hence the need for workers began to turn the tide of anti-Chinese racism.[67]

As Chinese American women took advantage of these opportunities, their labor force participation rate rose rapidly from 16 percent in 1930 to 29 percent in 1950 and 34 percent in 1960. Chinese American women workers were allowed into office work outside Chinatowns at this time and a new stereotype of Chinese women as obedient "office wives" was formed. Jobs in the civil service, professional fields, and factories also opened up. By 1960, as shown in Table 7-1, the share of Chinese women employed in clerical work had tripled to almost one-third of all workers. At the same time, the share in private household work fell from 12 to 2 percent between 1930 and 1960.[68]

World War II also brought about the lowering of immigration restrictions. Political alliances between the United States and China and the visit of Madame Chiang Kai-shek to the United States further eased anti-Chinese American sentiment, and the Chinese Exclusion Act was repealed in 1943. This brought Chinese under the prevailing national-racial quota system for immigration, permitting only 105 Chinese immigrants a year compared to 65,721 for Britain. Chinese immigrants became eligible for citizenship if they could prove they had entered before 1924, or had come in as permanent residents under the new laws. Still, children under 18 years of age who were born before their parents' naturalization were not admitted to citizenship. However, further opportunities were provided by the 1945 War Brides Act, which allowed foreign wives of U.S. servicemen to immigrate. While the Act originally had racial restrictions, it was amended in 1947 to allow Chinese servicemen to bring their wives and children to the United States once the servicemen became citizens. Many men rushed to China to marry before the law expired in 1949.[69]

In the late-1940s and early-1950s almost all immigrants from China were women and children.[70] Upon arrival they were detained and interrogated on Angel Island to establish their right to immigrate. In 1948, Leong Bick Ha hung herself in an immigration detention center after being held there for three months. Leong had immigrated to the United States in order to join her husband after 15 years of separation, but had not performed well at her immigration interrogation. One hundred Chinese women detainees protested her death with a day-long hunger strike. Finally, in response to adverse publicity and public pressure, the Immigration and Naturalization Service ended its 100-year long policy of detaining Chinese immigrants.[71]

Further immigration was enabled by the McCarran-Walter Immigration and Nationality Act of 1952. The Act allowed 30,000 Chinese who wished to leave China after the socialist revolution in 1949 to enter the United States. This massive immigration quickly eased the sex imbalance in the Chinese American community. Nevertheless, the ratio was still almost two men to one woman in 1950. Among Chinese Americans in their thirties, the ratio was three to one, and for those above 65, six to one.[72]

The flow of Chinese immigration in the 1940s and 1950s was a trickle compared to that after the Immigration Act of 1965, which abolished racial-national quotas on immigration. The Chinese American population grew fourfold from 1960 to 1985, from 236,080 to 1,079,400. However, the specific provisions of the two immigration laws created two very different Chinese communities, in the words of Chinese American activist and writer Peter Kwong: the "Uptown" and the "Downtown" Chinese.[73]

The Uptown Chinese

Anti-communist refugees admitted under the McCarran-Walter Act of 1952 were, according to Kwong, an elite group of "former government officials, top financial managers, diplomats, and generals."[74] The Act also admitted 5,000 top Chinese students who had been studying at U.S. graduate schools or research institutes at the time of the Chinese revolution and did not wish to return home. The group included two Nobel Prize winners in physics; the late An Wang, the founder of Wang Laboratories, an extremely successful computer company; and Dr. Chien-Hsiung Wu, one of the world's top experimental physicists (and a woman).[75]

While most of the 20,000 slots allotted to the Chinese under the 1965 immigration law were reserved for relatives of Chinese Americans, the U.S. government has used the rest of the spaces to bring in Chinese with professional skills, particularly in the sciences and engineering. Taiwan has groomed its best students for U.S. needs, and many elite Taiwanese families encourage their children to move to the United States. Between 1965 and 1985, about 150,000 came to U.S. graduate schools, mostly in the sciences, and 97 percent successfully applied for immigrant status.[76]

Uptown Chinese, many of them women, come to the United States with excellent English, top-level educations, and often with considerable financial resources. Since these credentials allow them to find lucrative professional jobs, their presence raises the average income statistics for Chinese Americans and gives the false impression that Chinese are easily upwardly mobile in the United States. In reality, uptown Chinese were already educationally and socially advantaged in Taiwan and China, and simply transferred these achievements and status to the United States. Indeed, their experience in the United States is one of *downward* mobility. Discrimination exists even against such "model" immigrants, who earn less than whites with equal educations and have less access to managerial promotions than equally qualified whites.[77]

The Downtown Chinese

According to the family reunification provision of the 1965 Act, 74 percent of the 20,000 Chinese immigration spaces were reserved for relatives of Chinese American citizens. Chinese men who had been living in split-household families were finally able to send for their wives, children, and grandchildren. Most of these relatives were poor, rural Cantonese who had resettled in urban Hong Kong, and the majority were women. In 1979, the United States normalized diplomatic relations with the People's Republic of China, and increased the Chinese immigration quota to over 40,000 per year.[78] These new Chinese immigrants live and work in Chinatowns where they need not know English. Their numbers have revitalized Chinatowns, which had declined as second-generation Chinese moved out. New York's Chinatown, the first choice of new immigrants, grew seven times between 1965 and 1987, and over 80 percent of its population is now foreign-born. Chinatown rents have skyrocketed and businesses have proliferated.[79]

Most of the downtown Chinese immigrant families support themselves by the combined wages of husband and wife. A 1979 study of San Francisco's

Chinatown found that 68 percent of women between the ages of 18 and 65 worked for pay. Nearly half were employed as sewing machine operators, most in small sweatshops within Chinatown and some within their own homes. Many had worked in the garment industry in Hong Kong before immigrating. Dong Zem Ping, a war bride, was one of these women:

> I can still recall the times when I had one foot on the pedal and another one on an improvised rocker, rocking one son to sleep while the other was tied to my back. Many times I would accidentally sew my finger instead of the fabric because one child screamed or because I was falling asleep on the job.[80]

Other common jobs for women in San Francisco's Chinatown were clerical and sales positions, accounting for one-fifth of total employment, and restaurant work, one-sixth. The women interviewed for the study complained that their jobs were dead end, taught no new skills, and were meaningless and physically exhausting. Their lack of education and low proficiency in English, however, made it nearly impossible to find better jobs. Few of the women had any time to take English courses since their earnings were vital to family income. With husbands working mostly as waiters, cooks, janitors, or store helpers, upward mobility has been difficult and few families have achieved the Chinatown dream of success, a restaurant or garment factory of their own.[81]

The San Francisco study also found that relationships within the family made life even more difficult for Chinatown women. Three-fourths of working mothers had sole responsibility for household work and one-fourth reported that they received no emotional support from their husbands. More than one-fifth complained that their husbands did not respect them. When asked what she would do differently if she could live her life over again, one woman answered: "I don't want to be a woman...because it's too much responsibility to take care of the family and go out to work."[82]

Nevertheless, growing numbers of Chinatown immigrant women are breaking out of the cycle of resignation and low self-esteem caused by oppression on the job and at home, and are organizing for better pay and working conditions. Activism has been slowed by community and family pressures, since worker organizing can often require breaking racial-ethnic solidarity with Chinese bosses. Activists also risk deportation, firing, or blacklisting by other employers, and experience racism at the hands of both unions and government agencies.[83]

In spite of these many barriers, thousands of garment workers have organized and are dues-paying members of the ILGWU. However, union standards are rarely maintained by their employers since many garment sweatshops and other Chinatown employment in restaurants and laundries are part of the underground economy, and, as such, are unprotected by labor laws.[84] Garment workers have become increasingly militant. In the 1970s, students and garment workers organized the San Francisco Chinatown Coop, a worker-owned garment factory that provided workers not only with better wages and conditions, but also with a variety of services, such as English classes and trips to the beach. In New York in 1982, over 15,000 Chinese and Korean striking garment workers demonstrated in the streets, winning job security and medical and pension benefits with the acceptance of their union contract by their Chinatown employers. In Boston in the late 1980s, Chinese women garment workers laid off by a plant closing organized to obtain the same retraining and job counseling that a state agency had provided to white male workers who had been similarly dislocated.[85]

Chinese women have taken leadership in the struggles over community control and education in Chinatowns across the United States. In Los Angeles in the 1970s, the Chinatown Education Project organized and won improved education for Chinatown children. In Boston, Chinese women have led the fight for local input into "urban renewal" plans that were shrinking Chinatown. Chinese immigrant women organized and run "It's Time," a New York City group which serves a mostly Chinese community where tenants face evictions, harassment, and deteriorating buildings. The most organized and effective tenant association in San Francisco in the 1970s and 1980s, the Ping Yuen Residents Improvement Association, has been led by Mrs. Chang Jok Lee. Through rent strikes and other protests, they have successfully stopped many development projects that threatened to displace low-income and elderly tenants and small shops in Chinatown. Mrs. Lee, who faced a charge by police horses in 1977 during a nonviolent protest of evictions, said of her activism, "At first I was scared, or rather, kind of embarrassed. I didn't speak English and was not used to speaking in front of people. But after a while, I got used to it. As long as I am fighting for a just cause, then I am not scared."[86]

Through education, the children of Chinese immigrants have achieved impressive upward mobility. In traditional China, the elite Mandarin class was comprised of the top male academic achievers; now that jobs in white America are opening up, Chinese immigrant families place great emphasis on educational achievement as a road to success for both sons and daughters. In 1980, a larger percentage of Chinese American men and women had college degrees (44 percent and 30 percent, respectively) than white men and women (21 percent and 13 percent, respectively). Large numbers of Chinese American students concentrate in accounting and business, where the most job opportunities exist for them. Dong Zem Ping, mentioned above, sent her children to prestigious universities. These well-educated, second-generation Chinese men and women are moving out of Chinatowns into predominantly white suburbs and entering well-paid professional jobs.[87]

However, as time passes, this road to success may become more difficult. As in other urban areas, Chinatown social conditions are deteriorating as a result of youth gangs, drugs, and worsening schools. Admission rates for Asians at top universities are declining, and the privileged uptown Chinese Americans are getting more university places than downtowners.[88]

Chinese American Women Today

As a result of declining racial segregation after World War II and eroding sex discrimination in the labor market, growing numbers of Chinese American women have been moving into the labor force—and out of Asian women's traditional jobs. Chinese American women's labor force participation rates grew from 44 percent in 1960 to 58 percent in 1980; a full 61 percent of those living with husbands were in the labor force in 1980.[89]

Chinese American women have adopted and transformed the traditional Chinese emphasis on *male* education as a means to upward mobility. In 1980, almost one-third of Chinese American women held college degrees, and almost one-third of employed Chinese American women held a managerial, administrative, or professional position. Between 1960 and 1980, the share working in these jobs rose from 24 to 31 percent, while the share in clerical jobs fell from 32 to 25 percent. Unlike most other groups of women, Chinese women have a share of managerial, and administrative jobs equal to their share of all jobs and are actually overrepresented in health-diagnosing professions. They also have the highest relative concentration in engineering of any racial-ethnic group of women.[90]

Nevertheless, educated Chinese women suffer from race and sex discrimination in the labor market, and receive less monetary return to education than do whites. For example, in 1975, median earnings of college-educated Chinese American women who were employed stood at $6,421, compared to $8,106 among white women graduates. Still, this represented a major improvement over 1959, when their earnings were little more than 25 percent of white women's earnings ($487 compared to $1,739).[91]

Because of the large share of educated, managerial and professional women, the median earnings for full-time full-year Chinese women workers are relatively high: $11,891 in 1980, compared to $10,564 for non-Latina white women, $17,945 for Chinese men, and $18,157 for non-Latino white men. But medians can be misleading. Chinese American women (and men) are still characterized by a bipolar occupational distribution, with one group concentrated at the high end of the labor market hierarchy and another large group concentrated at the bottom, corresponding to the uptown and downtown populations, respectively. At the bottom of the spectrum, over one-third of Chinese American women workers were counted as employed in low-paid sales or service jobs, or as laborers and machine operators in 1980, and this is probably an underestimate, since the Census undercounts Chinatown residents. Figure 7-1 shows the distribution of Chinese women workers across labor market segments, compared to white women and Chinese men; 66 percent of Chinese women were in the secondary labor market, compared with 69 percent of non-Latina white women, 41 percent of Chinese men, and 32 percent of non-Latino white men. Higher shares of both men and women in the secondary labor market bring higher poverty rates, even though Chinese are more likely to be employed than whites: 18 percent of Chinese were living in poverty in 1980, twice the share of non-Latina/o whites.[92]

While Chinese American women are improving their position in the labor force, many traditional and patriarchal practices continue to play an important role in their lives. Traditional conceptions of feminine behavior, such as politeness, neatness, reserve, self-sacrifice, and respect for parental authority, continue to influence Chinese American women's behavior. As in other racial-ethnic groups, there is no evidence that Chinese American men take on a substantial share of unpaid work in the home. Chinese couples have the lowest divorce rate of any group. However, arranged marriages are no longer practiced, and growing numbers of Chinese American women (28 percent of those aged 20 to 24 in 1970) defy parental disapproval to marry non-Chinese men. Married Chinese women tend to have fewer children than whites or Blacks.[93]

Chinese American women have made the long ascent up "Gold Mountain" to achieve considerable economic success, but they still face racial injustice and poverty. Japanese American women, to whom we now turn, were the second major group of Asian women to travel to these shores, and, in many ways, their experiences have echoed those of their Chinese sisters.

JAPANESE AMERICAN WOMEN

Employers in the United States and Hawaii sought Japanese immigrants after Chinese immigration ended in 1882. Although there were similarities between Japanese and Chinese immigration, including the prevalence of contract work in Hawaii and on the West Coast, limitations on immigration as a result of U.S. racism, and unbalanced sex ratios, there were also profound differences. For one, Japanese women arrived in greater numbers than Chinese women and earlier in the immigration period. In addition, the Japanese government intervened to obtain better treatment for its citizens, unlike the governments of China or the Philippines.[94]

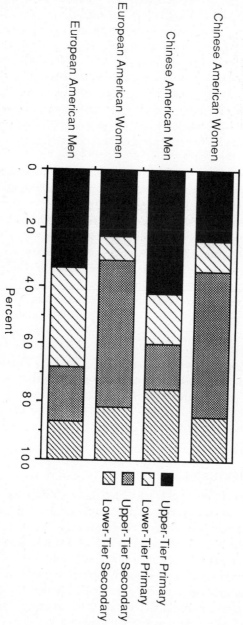

Figure 7-1: The Distribution of Chinese American and European American Workers across Labor Market Segments, by Gender, 1980

NOTES: See Table 10-5 for a listing of the occupations in each labor market segment. See Table 10-6 for the actual percentages employed in each segment.
SOURCE: 1980 Census; see Appendix A.

Japanese immigrants refer to themselves by generation. The "Issei" were the first generation of Japanese to arrive in the United States. The children of the Issei, U.S. citizens known as "Nisei" (second-generation Japanese Americans), lived and worked in Japanese communities in urban areas or on farms throughout the Northwest. The "Sansei" and "Yonsei," third- and fourth-generation Japanese Americans, are dispersed across a number of occupations and throughout the United States.

Japanese immigration to the United States and Hawaii began on a large scale after 1880, when the Japanese government first permitted emigration abroad. Until the middle of the nineteenth century, the Japanese government had taken an isolationist stance, but U.S. military forces opened Japanese ports to foreign trade in 1854. In 1868, the Tokugawa military rule was replaced by the Meiji oligarchy and Japan began an ambitious plan of modernization and industrialization. The plan was financed by heavy taxes on farmers, and that burden, combined with falling farm prices, left many small farmers destitute, particularly in southwestern Japan. Over 350,000 farmers lost their land between 1883 and 1890. Rising numbers of landless farmers turned to emigration and their remittances became an important source of income for the impoverished families they left behind in Japan.[95]

Immigration to Hawaii

Between 1885 and 1894, the Japanese government sponsored immigration to Hawaii, sending over 29,000 workers to labor on sugar plantations. Wages in Hawaii were four to six times greater than could be earned in Japan. Contract workers came to Hawaii as sojourners, intending to return to Japan after three years. The vast majority of plantation workers were men, but women also worked in the fields and as cooks and laundry workers for single men. The workers' contracts required them to labor 26 days a month, 10 hours a day in the field. Men were guaranteed $15 a month in compensation, women $10.[96]

Conditions worsened when government-sponsored emigration came to a close. Thereafter, private companies contracted for Japanese workers as a part of a "divide-and-conquer" strategy for blocking labor militancy. By 1896, there were more Japanese than Chinese in Hawaii, and by 1910, Japanese outnumbered Chinese by two to one. The divide-and-conquer strategy was not entirely successful, however. Over the years, Japanese sugar workers struck often over such issues as low wages, long hours, and mistreatment by the *lunas* (foremen). The two largest strikes took place in 1909 and 1920. In 1909, over 7,000 Japanese workers walked out under the auspices of their Higher Wages Association. The planters evicted strikers from company housing, and over 5,000 workers moved into strike headquarters and eventually won concessions from the companies. In 1920, Japanese and Filipina/o workers collaborated to demand wage increases, an eight-hour day, and paid leave for childbirth. According to Japanese American historian Alan Moriyama, this rank-and-file unity between Japanese and Filipina/o workers paved the way for "later multiracial industry-wide unions which brought about a social revolution in Hawaii."[97]

Immigration to the Continental United States

By 1910, there were over 72,000 Japanese in the continental United States. Most migrants were young, single males with an average of eight years of education. Those who came directly to the continent were generally less impoverished than those who went to Hawaii. Most worked as unskilled laborers in agriculture, railroading, and mining, or as gardeners, laundrymen, and "houseboys" in domestic service. In 1909, around 10,000 Japanese men were employed by railroad companies in the West; 3,600 worked in salmon canneries in Alaska, Oregon, and Washington; and 38,000 worked as field hands, most of them in California. According to the 1900 Census, 13 percent of Japanese men throughout the United States were employed as domestic servants.[98]

Conditions for field hands were harsh and many workers died from heat stroke, beriberi, and tuberculosis. One account from the 1890s described the conditions in the labor camps where the field hands lived:

> During those days around Fresno [California], laborers did not even carry blankets. They slept in the field with what they had on. They drank river water brought in by irrigation ditches....If they ate supper, it consisted of flour dumplings in a soup seasoned with salt.[99]

Nearly all of these agricultural workers were recruited by Japanese labor contractors who earned high incomes by charging the workers fees. The largest fee was the daily commission, withheld from the laborers' wages. In addition, labor contractors also charged their workers a "translation office fee," medical fees, service fees for sending money back to the workers' families in Japan, and high prices for food and clothing.[100]

Most Japanese men intended to return to Japan, but once in Hawaii or the United States many men established families and became permanent residents. Studies suggest that the relatively high wages Issei could earn in Hawaii and the United States were an important factor in decisions not to return to Japan. Some Issei set up small businesses or took up farming on their own. By 1900 there was a sizeable number of Japanese sharecroppers and tenant farmers. Japanese farmers tended toward high-yield, intensive cultivation, specializing in fruits and vegetables. Their small businesses included laundries, hotels, and stores that catered primarily to Japanese clients who faced discrimination from white-owned businesses.[101]

Issei Women: Farmers, Servants, and Prostitutes

Men dominated Japanese migration in the nineteenth century. By 1900, there was one woman for every 25 Japanese men. Most women immigrants came as part of families, and most were literate as a result of the Meiji Restoration's plan for universal education. Although women were educated under the plan, historian Yukiko Hanawa has pointed out that "the focus on women's education was not...designed to raise levels of culture or intellect, but simply to make wise mothers of young Japanese women."[102] In its emphasis on developing *ryosai kenbo* (good wives and wise mothers), Meiji education had much in common with the cult of domesticity, which spelled out appropriate roles for European American women in the nineteenth century.

Even though they possessed education, Japanese women were hampered in the U.S. labor market by their lack of English and by discrimination. Almost 90 percent of employed Japanese women in the United States and Hawaii in 1900 worked either in agriculture or as domestic servants, as shown in Table 7-2. The share of Japanese women listed as gainfully employed—30 percent—was higher than any racial-ethnic group other than Blacks, and about twice the rate for white women.[103]

Among Japanese immigrants, as with the Chinese, the unbalanced sex ratio contributed to a thriving prostitution business. The first reports of Japanese prostitutes in the United States date from the 1880s. Although little is known about the lives of these women, an observer in San Francisco described them as "exhibited in a kind of cage"; another from Fresno recounted that between 50 to 60 prostitutes lived in "crude hovels of two nine-by-nine-foot rooms in several filthy three- to four-feet-wide alleys wedged in a slum area."[104]

Many women who came as prostitutes were abducted or tricked into immigration. Others were sold into prostitution by their impoverished families. Most prostitutes were brought to the United States by Japanese men, particularly sailors. One woman from Amakusa, a desperately poor group of islands, described how she had been lured on board a U.S.-bound ship:

> Around 1889-90 a smooth-talking man appeared on my island...His stories were about foreign lands...Gold nuggets were waiting to be picked up on the riverbanks of America...He took me to a seamen's inn in Nagasaki and fed me a nice meal. On the next day I went with him to look at a foreign ship...[A] seaman on the ship jokingly

Table 7-2

Occupational Distribution of Japanese American Women Workers,
1900-1980 (in Percent)

	1900	1930	1960	1970	1980
Agriculture	58.1	22.9	6.7	2.2	1.3
Manufacturing	7.7	12.2	19.0	15.4	12.5
Private Household Service	28.6	29.9	8.2	3.7	1.4
Service (not					
Private Household)	3.8	10.1	12.9	17.5	15.8
Sales	0.2	7.6	6.7	6.8	11.3
Clerical	0.1	3.7	30.5	34.7	31.6
Professional & Technical	0.3	6.6	12.3	15.8	17.8
Managerial, Administrative,					
& Official	1.0	7.0	3.8	4.0	8.3

NOTES: Totals do not always sum to 100 because of rounding. Manufacturing includes craft and transportation workers; agriculture includes mining, fishing, and forestry; managerial, administrative, & official includes some self-employment, and excludes farm managers. Data for all years include Hawaii. For a full listing of occupational categories included, see Appendix B. For a discussion of comparability problems between Census years, see Appendix D.
SOURCES: See Appendix A.

said, "Why don't you go to America on the ship…many Japanese are in America, and they're all rich"…Just as I was half thinking about wanting to go and half worrying, the passengers quickened their pace…the ship had hoisted anchor and had left port. The seaman put me in a room to sleep. "I'll bring you meals so don't leave it," he said. "If by chance you're discovered, you'll be thrown into the sea."

Once they arrived in the United States, the women were often held in bondage by *amegoro* (pimps). Some prostitutes worked as *shakafu* (barmaids) but most worked in brothels. Prostitution was segregated by race: those called *hakujin-tori* catered to whites, *Shinajin-tori* to Chinese, and *Nihonjin-tori* to Japanese.

In the 1890s, San Francisco and Seattle newspapers began to publish a series of sensationalist articles about Japanese prostitutes, declaring that "Perhaps Japan has sent us her very worst, but the samples seen here have given our people anything but a good opinion of Japanese morals."[105] The Japanese government adopted a number of measures to stem the immigration of prostitutes to the United States, fearing that exclusionary measures such as had been applied to the Chinese would be brought to bear on Japanese immigrants. Japanese student leaders in San Francisco petitioned the Japanese Foreign Ministry for an end to the immigration of prostitutes, arguing:

> These women are a blot on our national image and national morality…The reasons for the ban on Chinese immigration and the call for the expulsion of the Chinese were many and varied, but the main one was that Chinese women were prostitutes…It is evident that, if this notorious vice spreads, America will adopt measures against us in the same manner as she did formerly against the Chinese.[106]

Having observed the virulent hostility that European Americans directed against the Chinese, Japanese leaders worked to disassociate themselves from Chinese immigrants. In 1908, a Japanese diplomatic official warned Japanese immigrants against living side-by-side with the Chinese, for fear that anti-Chinese sentiment would spill over to harm Japanese immigrants. Such measures proved ineffectual, however, and Japanese workers and farmers became targets of racist violence and agitation.[107]

The Gentlemen's Agreement and the Arrival of the Picture Brides

In 1906, the all-white San Francisco school board ruled that Japanese children should be segregated into all-Asian schools, like the Chinese before them. When the Japanese government protested, a foreign policy crisis ensued. President Theodore Roosevelt interceded and the school board reversed the decision; in exchange, the United States forced Japan to limit emigration. In 1907, the two governments signed the "Gentlemen's Agreement," barring entry of unskilled Japanese men to the United States. As a result, between 1910 and 1920, the number of Japanese men in the United States actually declined. Unlike the Chinese Exclusion Act, however, the Gentlemen's Agreement permitted the entry of wives and relatives.

With the entry of wives, the ratio of men to women began to fall. By 1920, 34 percent of the Japanese immigrant community was female. There were three means by which Japanese women immigrated to the United States as wives. Some were married to Japanese men who had migrated, and eventually followed their husbands to the United States. Other women married men who returned to Japan seeking wives. This was costly and carried the risk that the men might be conscripted into the army. Over half of Japanese women who arrived between 1909 and 1923 were "picture brides," women who never saw their husbands prior to immigrating. An estimated 23,000 picture brides came to the United States during that period.[108]

The picture-bride practice was a creative variation on the traditional Japanese marriage. In Japan, families selected marriage partners for their children using go-betweens, often family friends or relatives, who negotiated terms and plans. Heads of households considered prospective mates for their children on the basis of education, family background, economic status, health, and other criteria. The difference in the picture bride practice was that go-betweens had never met the prospective mates. Instead, they facilitated the exchange of photos and information. Picture brides, like the men they married, came from southern Japan and usually had completed eight years of formal education. Typically, a bride married a man 10 years her senior who had lived in the United States for some years.[109]

The Japanese government regulated photo marriages in a number of ways. It required men to show evidence of stable employment, it ruled out marriage for laborers until a change in the rule in 1915, and it demanded that prospective husbands have savings of anywhere from $800 to $1,000. The brides had to pass physical examinations and could not be more than 13 years younger than their husbands.

Picture brides did not necessarily choose freely to emigrate. Most simply obeyed their parents' wishes that they marry, since, according to Japanese American historian Yuji Ichioka, "to refuse would have been an act of filial disobedience, a grave moral offense."[110] Others married with the intent of providing financial assistance to their families by remitting money back to Japan.

The voyage to the United States from Japan lasted one month, and most women traveled in third-class steerage. One traveler described her trip:

[G]azing upon the rising majestic Mount Fuji in a cloudless sky aboard the ship, I made a resolve. For a woman who was going to a strange society and relying upon an unknown husband whom she had married through photographs, my heart had to be as beautiful as Mount Fuji. I resolved that the heart of a Japanese woman had to be sublime, like that soaring majestic figure, eternally constant through wind and rain, heat and cold. Thereafter, I never forgot that resolve on the ship, enabling me to overcome sadness and suffering.[111]

When they arrived in the United States, picture brides were subjected to degrading and intimidating inspections prior to seeing their husbands for the first time. Because the U.S. government did not recognize photo marriages as legal until 1917, group marriage ceremonies were conducted on arrival. Husbands outfitted their newly landed brides in U.S. clothing. Accustomed to open slippers and sandals, these Japanese women found Western shoes painful and were shocked by corsets and tight sleeves. Mrs. Okamura, a picture bride who arrived in 1917, described her new outfit, "It felt very tight. I couldn't even move my arms. That was the first time I had ever worn western clothes, so I thought they were supposed to be like that."[112]

Once "properly" attired, picture brides followed their husbands to their new homes. Although most Issei marriages were stable, some women deserted their husbands, typically to live with other men. Desertion, called *kakeochi*, was common enough to be featured in articles in the Japanese immigrant press and in notices in which husbands offered rewards for information about the deserting wife.

Issei Wives and Work

The new brides entered into lives of hard work. The 1920 Census reported that 26 percent of Japanese women participated in the labor force. Although lower than their 1900 rate, this was still the highest employment rate of any racial-ethnic group except for African American women. Even those who did not participate in the formal labor force nevertheless worked long hours cooking and cleaning for their husbands and for other single Japanese men. According to Japanese American sociologist Evelyn Nakano Glenn:

> Some went to remote labor camps that were built for railroad workers in the Mountain states, coal miners in Wyoming, sugar beet field hands in Utah and Idaho, laborers in lumbering camps and sawmills in Washington, and fish cannery workers in Alaska. Others, particularly those who stayed in California, went into the fields where their husbands tilled the soil as tenant farmers. In addition to working alongside their husbands, women in labor camps and farms often drew their own water, gathered wood to cook and heat the house, and fought to keep dirt out of houses that were little more than shacks…Women whose husbands resided in urban areas were more fortunate. They too worked long hours and kept house in crowded quarters, conditions were less primitive, and the presence of an ethnic community eased their adjustment.[113]

Taiko Tomita, a poet gifted in the traditional *tanka* style of poetry, came to Washington state to farm with her new husband. Farming in the desert land of the Yakima Valley was hot and arduous, as she described:

> As we busily pick beans
> Even the Breeze stirring
> The weeds at our feet
> Feels hot.

Like other Issei women, she looked to her children to fulfill her aspirations:

> Soon the heat will be gone
> While picking beans

I encourage my children
And myself.[114]

While agriculture continued to be an important occupation for Japanese women, between 1900 and 1930 Japanese women began to diversify into other occupations, as shown in Table 7-2. Their shares in domestic service, service, sales, manufacturing, clerical, professional, and managerial jobs all increased during this period. Domestic service was the largest occupation, employing nearly one-third of all Japanese women workers.[115]

Many Japanese women in domestic service specialized in laundry and ironing. One woman who started housework in 1921 recounted how difficult it had been:

> When we first started, people wanted you to boil the white clothes…When you did day work, you did the washing first. And if you were there eight hours, you dried and then brought them in and ironed them. In between you cleaned the house from top to bottom.[116]

Wages for domestic workers in the San Francisco area ranged from 15 to 25 cents an hour in 1915, slightly more than could be earned in other unskilled women's jobs. Japanese domestic workers faced a wide variety of working conditions. Some were insulted and paid low wages, while others received automatic raises and fair treatment.[117]

A Japanese Harvest

Through their work in the fields and orchards, women played key roles in shaping the economic status of Japanese Americans. As we have seen, Census enumerators counted over one-half of employed Japanese women as working in agriculture in 1900, and about one-fourth in 1930—and these numbers probably underestimate the true share involved, especially in family farming. According to Asian American sociologists Victor Nee and Herbert Wong, the unpaid labor of women and children "allowed Issei truck farmers to compete effectively with white farmers, enabling them to gain a dominant share of the produce market."[118]

Japanese agricultural success was impressive. In 1900, there were only 37 Japanese farms in California, covering less than 5,000 acres. Ten years later, over 1,800 farms, totaling nearly 100,000 acres, were run by Japanese. By 1920, they produced one-third of the truck crops in California. Japanese success was the result of a labor-intensive, high-yield style of farming. This style was very different from most of California agriculture, which used more machinery on larger plots of land and generated relatively low yields per acre. There were four types of Japanese family farms: contract farming, where landowners paid Japanese laborers a set wage; sharecropping; cash leasing, which offered more independence and higher profits; and land ownership, achieved by only a small minority of farmers.[119]

As we saw above, California and other western states passed a series of laws in 1913 that banned aliens "ineligible for citizenship" from purchasing land, from willing land to other non-citizens, and from leasing land for more than three years. Still, Japanese agriculture expanded between 1914 and 1920, and Japanese acreage grew from approximately 32,000 to 75,000. This was achieved largely because Issei farmers bought land in the names of Nisei or through land companies set up to circumvent the laws.[120]

In 1920, however, California passed another law aimed at plugging loopholes in the Alien Land Laws. The Japanese associations took up a fierce but unsuccessful two-year legal battle to overturn the law, arguing their case all the way up to the Supreme Court. A Los Angeles Japanese paper reported the mood of the Japanese upon learning of their defeat as:

> ...extremely dejected...Some people are thinking of returning to Japan...[or] planning to change occupations despite the lack of experience...Businessmen who handle agricultural produce and many merchants who have farmers as their main customers have also been affected greatly.[121]

After the Court's ruling, Japanese farmers found that they were denied bank loans and many could no longer meet payments on their land. Total Japanese acreage dropped by two-fifths between 1920 and 1925.[122]

During the next decade, Japanese farmers developed a variety of new strategies to keep their farms. In addition to forming land companies that would issue stock to Nisei or other U.S. citizens, some Japanese farmers arranged for Nisei middlemen to lease on their behalf. These middlemen then hired the Issei as managers or foremen. Other farmers entered into oral agreements with landowners who publicly hired them as employees, but privately permitted them to sharecrop or tenant farm. Whites entered these arrangements for economic reasons, since Japanese farmers were so skilled at intensive cultivation that they were able to pay higher rents and achieve higher yields. In the words of Japanese American historian Jerrold Takahashi, they paid a "racial rent premium."[123] Ichioka suggests that these strategies "helped to mitigate, but not eliminate, the negative impact of the law."[124]

Keeping Issei Culture Alive

Issei society depended heavily on institutions that kept Japanese language and culture alive. The most important of these were local associations, the immigrant press, language schools, and churches, which included both Buddhist temples and segregated Christian churches. The Japanese government subsidized the language schools and the Buddhist temples.[125]

These institutions exercised tight control over the community and maintained strong ties to the Japanese government. Local Japanese associations were often involved in apprehending fleeing spouses in cases of marital desertion. The associations reacted in order to uphold the moral tone of their community and out of a concern that such incidents reflected badly on Japanese immigrants in general.

Japanese associations also played a role in the termination of the picture-bride practice, which ended in 1920 in response to a new wave of anti-Japanese sentiment. This wave began when California Senator James D. Phelan built a re-election campaign on his stance against the picture bride. Phelan called the practice barbaric, and charged that the brides were breeding a new generation of Asians who were citizens and would take over agricultural land. In response, the Japanese associations and the Japanese government decided to stop issuing passports to picture brides on March 1, 1920. This stranded over 24,000 single male Issei in the United States with little possibility of marriage, given miscegenation laws and the fact that the vast majority of them could not afford to return to Japan to find a wife.[126]

Women were excluded from membership in Japanese associations, but they formed their own groups, including churchwomen's clubs, handicraft clubs, and rotating credit associations called *Ko*. Each month, every member contributed a fixed amount to the *Ko* and a lottery was held at the end of the month. Winners continued to pay into the pot, but could not draw again in the lottery. The *Ko* ended when every member had won. Women used their proceeds to purchase expensive items such as a trip to Japan or school clothing for their children.[127]

The Depression Years

Concentrated in the Pacific Northwest, an area whose agricultural base was not affected by drought, Japanese Americans did not suffer enormous setbacks during the 1930s.[128] In 1940, after nearly a decade of economic crisis, slightly more than one-half of Japanese men and one-third of Japanese women were still employed in agriculture, forestry, and fishing. More than 60 percent of the women in agriculture were listed by the Census as unpaid family workers. By 1941, Japanese farmers accounted for most of California's snap beans, celery, and strawberry production, and Japanese farms had an average value slightly higher than the overall average farm value in California, Oregon, and Washington.[129]

Immigration of picture brides also made possible the second generation of Japanese Americans, the Nisei. By the early 1930s, the bulk of the

Japanese population consisted of Issei between the ages of 40 and 50 and Nisei between the ages of 4 and 16. The generation gap between the Issei and the Nisei was a distinctive figure of Japanese communities, and could be seen in the conflict over the local associations. The Nisei had less incentive to support the associations since they had fewer ties to Japan. In a sense, the associations had undermined their own community base by insisting on the importance of assimilation and education for the Nisei. Following this advice, most Issei sent their children to predominantly white schools.[130]

During the late 1930s, the oldest Nisei entered the labor force. They were a well-educated group; in 1937, Nisei accounted for three of the nine Seattle valedictorians. Still, they were denied the occupational success that their education should have earned for them, especially on the continent. Many college-educated Nisei were forced to take jobs as gardeners or domestic servants. Professional or managerial jobs outside the ethnic enclaves of Little Tokyos were almost impossible to find. The first Japanese American law graduate from the University of Oregon found work in a Japanese consulate only after being rejected by many white-owned law firms. A few Nisei professionals did find jobs in government or white-owned firms, especially in Hawaii, but they were the exception.[131]

In 1940, on the eve of World War II, 38 percent of Japanese American women were employed in agriculture, 10 percent in domestic service, and 20 percent in other personal services such as laundry operatives. Their jobs shared certain common characteristics: they tended to be extensions of women's work in the home, they were labor intensive and paid low wages, they demanded long hours, and many of them were located in family-owned or other Japanese enterprises.[132]

By 1940, many Japanese Americans had achieved impressive economic gains over their beginnings as contract laborers, particularly in agriculture, but bitter times were ahead. European American historian Roger Daniels has suggested:

> Nothing more dramatically symbolizes the barriers that the United States placed between Japanese America and the rest of our society than the ironic fact that Japanese America flourished during the worst economic period in U.S. history, and that, when the tonic of global warfare was reviving the larger economy, Japanese America was being economically ravaged.[133]

World War II Concentration Camps

The bombing of Pearl Harbor in 1941 set into motion two wars: the war between Japan and the United States and a war against Japanese Americans in the United States. One day after the bombing, the U.S. government froze Issei assets and the FBI rounded up and detained hundreds of Issei community leaders. Japanese American historian Valerie Matsumoto described the conflict that erupted over the next few months:

> Rumors spread that the Japanese in Hawaii had aided the attack on Pearl Harbor, fueling fears of "fifth column" [espionage] activity on the West Coast. Politicians and the press clamored for restrictions against the Japanese Americans, and their economic competitors saw the chance to gain control of Japanese American farms and businesses.[134]

This anti-Japanese hysteria was completely unfounded: not one incident of sabotage or espionage by an Issei or a Nisei was reported throughout the duration of the war. Nevertheless, on February 19, 1942, President Roosevelt signed an executive order authorizing the evacuation of 110,000 Issei and Nisei—virtually all the ethnic Japanese in the United States—from the so-called Western Defense Command, the coastal areas of Washington, Oregon, and California, citing the danger of sabotage or espionage. There were no mass internments on Hawaii, in contrast to the continental United States, largely because racial attitudes were quite different on the island and the Japanese were crucial to the Hawaiian economy.[135]

Japanese American families in the "Western Defense Command" area were given one week to dispose of their possessions, close up their businesses and homes, and report to a temporary assembly center. Many farmers who had invested years of painstaking effort to raise orchards from seedlings were forced to liquidate them at low prices. Once they arrived at the assembly center, Japanese Americans were tagged like luggage and transported to 10 "permanent relocation camps" in Utah, Arizona, Colorado, California, Wyoming, Idaho, and Arkansas. Each camp held an average of 10,000 people. The camps, located in desert or swamp areas where temperatures fluctuated between freezing and broiling, were surrounded by barbed wire, searchlights which burned all night, and armed guards who patrolled the perimeters.

Camp life was extraordinarily difficult. Families lived in tar paper barracks divided into small rooms, each housing an average of eight people. There was no privacy: walls did not reach the ceiling, latrines and showers had few or no partitions, and all meals were eaten in large communal mess halls. Adult internees were expected to work for very low wages at such jobs as cooking, farming, teaching, and providing medical care. Professionals earned $19 per month while most workers earned $16.

As Matsumoto points out, camp life, in spite of all its horrors, transformed women's roles and relationships in some positive ways. While extremely low, wages were equal for men and women. Communal mess halls and small living quarters freed women from some of the burdens of housework and increased their leisure time. Many took classes in English, in handicrafts, and in traditional Japanese arts. Women who had previously endured isolated rural conditions now found themselves in the company of other women from both urban and rural backgrounds. Matsumoto observes, "Gone were the restrictions of distance, lack of transportation, interracial uneasiness, and the dawn-to-dusk exigencies of field work."[136] Since they were now able to meet young men on their own, Nisei women moved further away from traditional Japanese practice of arranged marriage.

Japanese Americans contested the constitutionality of their internment in the courts. One of the key plaintiffs was Mitsuye Endo, a Nisei woman who had worked for the state of California before being fired and interned at Topaz Camp. In 1942, Endo requested a writ of habeas corpus (a court order guaranteeing due process of law to persons held in custody). Supported by the American Civil Liberties Union, Endo pursued her case for 30 months up to the Supreme Court. On December 18, 1944, the Supreme Court found that the indefinite detention of loyal U.S. citizens against their will was unconstitutional. Although the Court failed to declare the entire process of internment unconstitutional, its ruling did begin to undermine the legal basis for the camps.[137]

Teiko Tomita was interned at Tule Lake in California and later at Heart Mountain in Wyoming. There, she continued writing poetry:

> Within the iron stockade
> Always composing poems
> From the sorrows of war
> A little consolation.[138]

In 1943, she wrote hopefully of freedom:

> In the war concentration camp
> The New Year's day's sun rises
> Look up at the light
> Which breaks up the darkness of night.[139]

Freedom was not to come until 1944, when the Tomita family received a work release.

The war generated a severe labor shortage, and in 1942 the War Relocation Authority allowed internees to leave the camps to do domestic, agricultural, or factory labor. Although most work release requests were for domestic servants, some Nisei women also found clerical and factory jobs for the first time.[140] As shown in Table 7-2, only 4 percent of Japanese women worked in clerical jobs in 1930. By 1960, that figure had risen to over 30 percent.

Many Nisei also left the camps as students. In 1942, a War Relocation Authority program placed over 4,000 Nisei students in schools outside the western zone. Of the first 400 students to leave, one-third were women. Said one women who eagerly sought to become a teacher, "Mother and father do not want me to go out. However, I want to go so very much that sometimes I feel that I'd go even if they disowned me. What shall I do? I realize the hard living conditions outside but I think I can take it."[141] Issei parents were reluctant to let their daughters leave for school or work outside the camp, but they recognized that their hopes for the future rested with the Nisei generation.

Some internees left to join the Armed Forces. Nearly 3,000 Nisei men from the camps joined other Nisei in the segregated 442nd Combat Team, which became the most highly decorated combat unit of the war. One hundred Nisei women joined the Women's Army Corps. Their bravery in battle went unrecognized by the white press, which commonly refused to print the names of the Nisei war dead.[142]

In 1945, the War Relocation Authority began closing the camps, allowing Japanese Americans to return to the areas previously barred to them under the West Coast exclusion policy. By that time, over one-third of adult internees had already left the camps, returning to a dramatically altered way of life. Whites in many of their former home towns greeted them with signs warning, "No Japanese Welcome." Much of their agricultural land had been lost, along with businesses and homes. The Federal Reserve Banks estimated in the 1940s that Japanese Americans had lost $400 million in property, but the true economic and psychological costs can never be calculated. Japanese Americans dispersed across the United States, even though many remained on the West Coast.[143]

Immediately after the war, the Japanese American community began a struggle for reparations which has continued to the present. The Evacuation Claims Act, passed in 1948, set in motion the payment of compensation to former internees for their losses. However, only $38 million was paid out, less than 10 percent of even conservative estimates of financial losses, and nearly two decades passed before this amount reached the victims.[144]

For many internees, the experience of the camps had been so degrading that they wanted nothing more than to get on with their lives, attempting to erase these memories from their minds. Pinning their hopes on the Sansei (third generation) and the Yonsei (fourth generation), ex-internees struggled to pick up the pieces of their shattered lives.

The Decline of the Japanese Enclave Economy

The end of internment coincided with the end of the highly segregated Japanese America of the prewar years, where Japanese had been concentrated in the Pacific Northwest and in Japanese-owned or -operated businesses. Some of those who had been relocated to the Midwest and the East remained there. Others found that their small farms had been displaced by competition from huge corporate farms. Still others left the Japanese ghetto in cities like San Francisco and Oakland to disperse throughout the city. Sometimes there was simply no more Japanese ghetto to which they could return; in San Francisco, for instance, the Little Tokyo area had been taken over by African American workers employed by the war industry.[145]

One measure of the extent of the destruction of the Issei family economy was the drop in the percentage of Japanese American women in California employed as unpaid family laborers, from 21 percent in 1940 to 7 percent in 1950. By 1950, the occupational distribution of Japanese American women had been completely transformed. From only 19 percent in 1930, the share of Japanese American women in the paid labor force had risen to 42 percent (compared to 28 percent of European American women). Relative to white women, however, they were still underrepresented in all areas except private household and factory work. The movement of Japanese workers out of family businesses became even more dramatic during the 1950s.[146]

Dispersion was not simply occupational or geographic. As the Issei died out and the Sansei grew to adulthood, Japanese Americans interacted more and more with whites. Intermarriage is quite common among the Sansei and the Yonsei; by one estimate, as many as 50 percent of the Sansei have married whites. Generally speaking, Japanese American women tend to marry whites more often than do Japanese American men. Some have speculated that these women are pursuing upward mobility, or that they are dissatisfied with male-dominated Japanese families and seek more equal marriages. As we shall see later in this chapter, some white men may prefer Japanese (and other Asian) women because they view them as exotic and submissive.[147]

The ban on Japanese immigration was lifted in 1952 with the McCarran-Walter Act. Nevertheless, the Japanese quota allowed only 100 persons to immigrate. This Act also struck down racial barriers to naturalization, making those born in Japan but living in the United States finally eligible for U.S. citizenship. The 1965 Immigration Act further opened up immigration to Asians by eliminating the quota system. Yet, in contrast to the Chinese American and Filipino/a American communities, the Japanese American community has not experienced a huge second wave of immigration in response to the 1965 Act. Only about 100,000 of the 770,000 people of Japanese origin who lived in the United States in 1980 immigrated after 1961. These relatively low numbers are probably due to the post-war economic boom in Japan. An estimated 45,000 Japanese women who married U.S. soldiers during the occupation of Japan immigrated between 1947 and 1975. Unlike earlier women immigrants, these war brides were more likely to come from urban areas in Japan than from rural areas.[148]

The 1960 Census revealed the extent of the occupational gains made by Japanese American women during the 1950s. Employment in household service and agriculture had dropped dramatically. By 1960, over 30 percent held clerical jobs, over 12 percent were professionals, and 19 percent were found in manufacturing (see Table 7-2). Gains continued to be made during the decade of the 1960s, as a result of economic growth, greater public awareness of the injustice of discrimination, and continued investments in education by Japanese Americans. At last, the educational attainments of the Issei and the Nisei had begun to translate into occupational achievement.

Today, the Japanese American community is dramatically different from that of the pre-war period. Most Japanese Americans do not live in ethnic ghettoes. Although they continue to experience discrimination and racist violence, most rank economically in the nation's upper-middle class. During the past two decades, Japanese Americans have sought to reclaim their ethnic identity. One important step in the assertion of that identity was an opening up of the long-suppressed memories of the camp experience. In the early-1970s, more than 25 years after their internment, former camp residents made the first of many "pilgrimages" to Manzanar and other camps, reviving the struggle for redress as an issue in the community. In 1976, as a result of such efforts, President Gerald Ford declared the Executive Order which had authorized the camps a mistake and rescinded it. Said Ford:

> We know now what we should have known then—not only was that evacuation wrong, but…on the battlefield and at home, Japanese Americans…have been and continue to be written into our history for the sacrifices and contributions they have made to the well-being and security of this, our common Nation.[149]

In 1988, as a result of intense pressure from the Japanese American community, President Reagan signed a bill which provided for the payment of $20,000 to each evacuee who was alive at the time of bill. Only half of those who had been interned were still alive at the time. The heirs and dependents of those who died will receive no payment. While the total amount to be paid out should reach over $1.2 billion, the Federal government has dragged its heels on payments, and every month another 200 survivors of the camps die.[150]

Japanese American Women Today

Japanese American women today continue their long traditions of labor force participation and educational attainment, and their present labor market status ranks high among U.S. women. By 1980, Japanese American women's labor force participation rate, at 59 percent, was surpassed only by Filipinas. Nearly 20 percent had college or advanced degrees, compared to 13 percent for European Americans. Over 26 percent of Japanese American women held managerial or professional jobs.[151] Their median income as full-time, full-year workers was 13 percent higher than that earned by European American women, and very close to that earned by Filipinas and Chinese American women. Japanese American women had the lowest unemployment rates of all racial-ethnic groups and the lowest poverty rates for female-maintained households.

Nonetheless, Japanese American women continue to feel the effects of discrimination, and are denied the full occupational status to which their education should entitle them. Japanese American women are over-represented in the female-dominated professions of nursing and teaching, and in lower-paid female jobs such as domestic service and clerical work. Like Chinese American women, they earn less than comparably educated white women. Finally, Chinese American researcher Deborah Woo has demonstrated that the high incomes of Japanese American women are partly the result of their concentration in parts of the country where the cost of living is high, and hence overrepresent their actual economic well-being.[152]

Figure 7-2 shows the distribution of Japanese American women across the labor market hierarchy in 1980. Twenty-three percent held jobs in the elite upper tier of the primary sector. Another 9 percent were employed in the bottom tier of the primary sector. Much of Japanese American women's progress into these two sectors occurred in the years between 1970 and 1980, when they increased their relative concentrations among engineers, managers and administrators, and commodities and finance sales representatives, upper-tier primary jobs traditionally dominated by white men. In 1980, the relative concentration of Japanese American women in the managerial and administrative category had reached 80, where 100 represents equality. Furthermore, Japanese American women more than doubled their relative share of highly paid craft jobs (lower-tier primary). In fact, Japanese American women raised their relative share of all the white masculine jobs we studied except transportation operative, farm owner and manager, and health diagnosing.

Despite these successes, two-thirds of Japanese American women held jobs in the secondary labor market in 1980, and one in five was trapped in the lowest tier, which consists of low-paid and low-status jobs, many of them

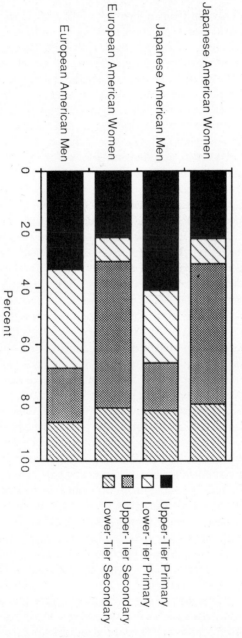

Figure 7-2: The Distribution of Japanese American and European American Workers across Labor Market Segments, by Gender, 1980

NOTES: See Table 10-5 for a listing of the occupations in each labor market segment. See Table 10-6 for the actual percentages employed in each segment.

SOURCE: 1980 Census; see Appendix A.

in the service sector. These numbers are very close to those of European American women, and show the extent of discrimination that Japanese American women continue to experience.

By 1980, 12 percent of Japanese American women were the sole support of their families. Only European American women had a lower share of female-maintained households. The poverty rate for single-mother Japanese American families was 15 percent—higher than the overall poverty rate, but the lowest poverty rate for single-mother families for any racial-ethnic group. It is likely that these relatively low poverty rates can be explained by Japanese American women's relatively high occupational and educational status, by the high incomes of Japanese American men (who may consequently pay larger alimony and child-support sums to their former wives), and by relatively low rates of teen pregnancy. Still, one in seven Japanese American women maintaining their own households fell below the official poverty line in 1980.

These numbers suggest that Japanese American women have made extraordinary economic progress since their beginnings as contract laborers and picture brides. However, like other women, their earnings are far less than those of the men of their racial-ethnic group: median incomes for Japanese women employed full-time, full-year were only 59 percent of Japanese men's. Also, like other Asian American women, they have fallen victim to the "model minority" myth and must also battle against racist and sexist stereotypes which depict them as exotic and docile; we discuss this problem at the end of the chapter.

FILIPINA AMERICAN WOMEN[153]

The Philippines is an archipelago made up of 7,000 islands in the South China Sea. Filipinas/os are racially and culturally varied, descendants of aborigines, as well as of Indonesians, Malays, Chinese, Japanese, and Spanish peoples who migrated to the islands and intermarried; they speak a total of 87 languages.[154]

Filipinas/os immigrated to the United States in several waves. The "old-timers" came between 1909 and 1934, a second wave immigrated after World War II, and a third wave arrived after the 1965 Immigration Act. There were few women in the first wave, but more in the second, which included newly naturalized citizens and brides of servicemen, and women comprised a majority of the third wave. U.S. colonization of the Philippines, lasting between 1898 and World War II, has played a major role in this migration to the United States.

Ferdinand Magellan "discovered" the islands in 1521 and claimed them for Spain, naming them after King Philip II. The Spaniards used Manila, the capital city, as a commercial port, and the islands as a source of needed agricultural products such as tobacco, sugar, hemp, and coffee. These crops were produced instead of subsistence foods on lands controlled by the colonial government, the Catholic church, and a growing Filipina/o upper class. The landless labored under a feudal system, characterized by excessive and unjust taxation, forced labor, and widespread poverty. As elsewhere, the Spaniards imposed Catholicism as a way to control the population, destroying indigenous cultures and religions, including more egalitarian sexual relations.[155]

Rebellions against the tyranny of Spanish rule were frequent, and in 1896, an outright revolutionary struggle began. Filipinas such as Gabriela Silang, Melchora Aquino, and Trinidad Tecson distinguished themselves as leaders in this fight for independence. However, in 1898, when Filipina/o forces controlled almost all of the territory and were about to claim their independence, Spain ceded the Philippines to the United States in the Treaty of Paris. Hence, another bloody war for independence was launched, this time against the United States. In what Filipino historian Renato Constantino has called "the original Vietnamization," U.S. troops devised excruciating tortures, massacred entire village populations, and burned and forcibly relocated others in their attempt to subjugate the islands. By 1902, the independence movement had been crushed, and a Sedition Law imposed the death penalty or long imprisonment on anyone advocating independence, even by peaceful means. The economy was in a shambles.[156]

As the Philippines' new colonizer, the United States used the islands as a source of agricultural crops and as a growing market for U.S. manufactured goods. Land ownership became even more concentrated, and poverty, landlessness, and tenancy grew in the rural areas. The United States also established English-language public schools. The stage was set for the first wave of Filipina/o migration to the United States.[157]

As we have seen in previous chapters, U.S. workers and small businessmen fought to restrict the immigration of Chinese and Japanese. Because the Philippines was a U.S. colony, however, Filipinas/os were U.S. nationals with the right to immigrate freely to the United States. Nevertheless, they remained non-citizens, for they were not allowed to naturalize unless they had served in the U.S. Navy.[158]

Recruitment by Hawaiian Sugar Planters

In 1907, when Japanese immigration to the United States was restricted, Hawaiian sugar planters turned to the new U.S. colony, the Philippines, for cheap labor. Over 113,000 Filipinas/os came to Hawaii between 1909 and 1931. By 1932, they comprised 70 percent of the plantation labor force. Like other Asian workers before them, Filipinas/os were desired exclusively for their labor. As the president of the Hawaiian Sugar Planters Association wrote in 1930, "From a strictly ethical standpoint, I can see little difference between the importation of foreign laborers and the importation of jute bags from India."[159]

As with the Chinese and Japanese, the plantation owners' policy was to recruit young, single men. In 1916, the Hawaiian Commissioner of Labor explained, "Plantations have to view laborers primarily as instruments of production. Their business interests require cheap, not too intelligent, docile unmarried men."[160] Recruiters offered free round-trip travel, and aimed their promises at illiterate, rural migrants. In Hawaii, almost half of Filipinas/os over 10 were illiterate in 1920. Planters kept the sex ratio among immigrants to about 10 men for every woman through the mid-1940s. This meant that most men either remained single or married very late, while women married young. There were no laws against interracial marriage in Hawaii, and many Filipinos married Anglo and Portuguese whites, Puerto Ricans, and Hawaiians. There was, however, little intermarriage with other Asians.[161]

Life was hard for the few women who lived and worked on the plantations. During the growing season, they worked at *hoe hana* (weeding the fields) and loaded sugar cane into box cars during the harvest. Whereas Filipinos earned $18 to $20 per month between 1915 and 1933, Filipinas earned only $12 to $14 per month. Like the Chinese and Japanese women in Hawaii, Filipinas performed paid domestic work on the side, and cooking and laundering for bachelor workers. They also grew produce and tended livestock. Apolinaria Gusman Oclaray did not work in the fields with her husband, a foreman. She described her work, "I sewed work shirts, aloha shirts, work pants, and underwear, and went to different camps and plantations to sell them...I sewed a lot and got so good at it that soon I was making more money than my husband."[162]

Like other Asian workers before them, Filipina/o workers soon organized in protest against low pay and long hours. According to sugar growers, Filipinas/os were "the most unsatisfactory of any unskilled laborers we ever hired. They were the very essence of independence, taking every advantage to cause the employer trouble."[163] Plantation owners tried to prevent labor organizing by firing active workers (which also meant eviction from company housing), by maintaining a surplus of labor, and by keeping workers racially and ethnically segregated.[164]

Nevertheless, Filipinas/os were active in nine strikes between 1909 and 1925. In the 1920s, Filipina/o workers organized the Filipino Labor Union, led by Pablo Manlapit. In 1920, Manlapit called a strike over wages which had remained frozen at 77 cents per day while wartime inflation had increased prices by over 40 percent. At that time, 2,600 Filipinas/os on five plantations went on strike. As we have seen, these workers won support from the Japanese labor union, whose members also joined the strike. Over 12,000 strikers were evicted from plantation housing. Although the 1920 strike won no wage increases, it forced planters to spend over $1 million to improve workers' living conditions and was followed by a series of worker actions over the next 20 years. Beginning in 1943, plantation workers organized the first multi-racial union, the International Longshoremen's and Warehousemen's Union. Approximately 28,000 sugar workers of all racial-ethnic groups from all over Hawaii went out on strike in September 1946, winning pay increases and other improvements.[165]

The goals of plantation workers were varied: to send money home, to move off the plantation onto their own farms, to secure better jobs in the cities, or to return home. Most Filipinas/os considered returning home highly desirable; many, however, could not afford to do so. By 1935, 58,000 (about one-half of all immigrants) had returned to the Philippines, having achieved some economic success abroad. In the Ilocano region of the Philippines, from which most workers had come and to which they returned, "Hawaiia-nos" and their relatives increased their land holdings noticeably.[166]

Upward mobility in Hawaii proved more difficult, however, partly because the Filipinas/os were latecomers, competing for jobs with the Chinese and Japanese, and partly because of discrimination. In 1930, 84 percent of employed Filipinos and about one-half of all employed Filipinas worked in agriculture, most as farm or plantation workers. It was difficult for Filipinas/os to enter independent farming, which the Japanese already dominated. When Filipinas/os did move to the cities (only 13 percent of Hawaiian Filipinas/os lived in cities in 1940), they worked at the bottom of the labor market in seasonal jobs. Fifteen percent of employed Filipinas worked in low-paid manufacturing jobs such as pineapple canning, where women earned 10 cents an hour, one-half of men's wages; about one-fourth worked in service jobs, both for private households and for restaurants and hotels. Filipinos were also segregated into service work. Young Filipino boys made up three-quarters of the waiters in Honolulu hotels, for example. In urban areas, single men changed jobs often and shared rented housing with as many as six to ten fellow workers.[167]

Wherever they went, Filipinas/os faced discrimination by whites. Whites harassed Filipinas/os on the streets, calling them "go-go" and "mon-key," and refused to serve them in their restaurants, barbershops, movies, swimming pools, and tennis courts.[168] This treatment came as a painful shock to new Filipina/o immigrants, who had believed their colonial school lessons promising a special American commitment to freedom and equality. One immigrant said:

> My school teachers at home were idealistic Americans who told me of America's promises of liberty and equality under the law, but forgot to mention the economic discrimination and racial complexes with which you interpret your rainbow-hued promises.[169]

Until World War II, the vast majority of Filipinas/os in Hawaii were low-paid farm or urban laborers. About 19,000 moved to the continental United States, where they faced equally virulent discrimination, and found themselves segregated in similar jobs. Nevertheless, a few Filipinas/os were able to find higher-paying jobs or to start businesses of their own. In Hawaii in 1930, 4 percent of employed Filipinas worked in professions, most as trained nurses; less than 1 percent did clerical work. Apolinaria Gusman moved to Oahu from a plantation and started a successful laundry and dry-cleaning business. When her husband joined her, they saved enough to buy another laundry and a barbershop. During World War II, business boomed for the Gusmans because their military clientele refused to do business with Japanese firms.[170]

Filipinas/os Come to the United States

Colonial connections also brought Filipinas/os to the continental United States. In the early-1900s, the U.S. colonial government in the Philippines provided scholarships to about 300 to 400 privileged students to train them for government service and teach them the political values of their colonizers. (Our sources imply, but do not explicitly establish, that these students were male.) When they returned to the Philippines, the graduates moved into high positions in the colonial government. Their success attracted other, less affluent Filipinos to pursue upward mobility through education in the United States. Families scrimped and saved, even mortgaging their land to pay their sons' fares. An estimated 14,000 young Filipinos came to the United States in this way.[171]

It was considered chic among whites at the time to employ Filipino "houseboys," so most Filipino students worked as domestic servants in the mornings and evenings to finance their studies. While many Filipinos earned high school or college degrees, most ended up in menial, low-paying jobs. In one typical example, an immigrant worked as a janitor to put himself through engineering school. Unable to find professional work as an engineer after graduation, he continued working as a janitor. Most students were too ashamed of their failures at upward mobility to return home and face their parents.[172]

In the 1920s, 16,000 other Filipinas/os from Hawaii, and another 9,000 from the Philippines, came to the United States. Most settled in California or other areas on the West Coast, but some moved to major cities in the Midwest and East. As in Hawaii, most Filipinas/os in the continental U.S. found jobs at the bottom of the economic hierarchy. In 1930, an estimated 20,000 were working in agriculture, 11,000 as servants or in hotels and restaurants, and 4,000 in Alaskan canneries.[173]

In agriculture, Filipinas/os performed backbreaking field work, called "stoop labor" because it required much bending for long periods. While most were males, 11 percent of employed Filipinas on the continent worked in agriculture in 1930.[174] White landowners hired Filipinas/os through Filipino labor contractors who shared the workers' cultural heritage and provided housing between seasons, but also skimmed off substantial profits in the process. Filipina/o farmworkers migrated to follow the crops through California, Oregon, Washington, and some Midwestern states. They were the main labor source for the asparagus industry in Stockton, California. The strenuous work of cutting and preparing the asparagus, which was grown in dusty peat moss, involved long hours and extreme heat. Immigrant Roberto Vallangça noted, "Many Filipinos passed out from the heat prostration and exhaustion while harvesting and could not be revived."[175] Nevertheless, racist stereotypes justified such working conditions by claiming that this work was easier for Filipino men because of their short stature.[176]

Abuses by both contractors and farm owners were common. Workers had to pay contractors whatever they charged for food; housing was substandard; and owners commonly held back a part of workers' pay until the end of the season to make certain the workers stayed on the job. Farmworker organizing was inhibited by the fact that Filipinas/os were working for Filipino contractors and by the hostility of the white labor movement. Employers, organized into the Associated Farmers of California, worked hard to prevent migrant organizing, keeping workers ethnically segregated and using one group as strikebreakers against another. White workers rioted against Filipina/o farm laborers in 1929 and 1930. In one raid on a Watsonville, California labor camp, whites shot and killed Fermin Tabera, who became a martyr to Filipina/o farmworkers.[177]

The AFL led the struggle to exclude Filipina/o immigrants, introducing exclusionary legislation in 1929 and 1930 that, however, did not pass. In 1934, Filipina/o immigration was halted by the Independence Act, which promised independence to the islands over a period of 10 years, declared that Filipinas/os were no longer U.S. nationals, and imposed a quota of only 50 immigrants per year. The AFL then won the passage of a repatriation act, which paid Filipinas/os' transportation back to the Philippines on the condition that they never return to the United States.[178]

Despite this treatment at the hands of the white labor movement, Filipinas/os remained loyal to union ideals, organizing the Filipino Labor Union in California and striking against lettuce growers in 1934. After World War II, the AFL-CIO created the predominantly Filipina/o Agricultural Workers Organizing Committee (AWOC), led by Larry Itliong. Meanwhile, César Chávez, a Chicano, founded the National Farm Workers Association (NFWA), discussed in Chapter 4. These unions joined together in a seven-month grape-pickers' strike in 1965. In the next year they merged to form the United Farm Workers Organizing Committee (UFWOC).[179]

As in Hawaii, urban Filipinas/os in the continental United States found work in service jobs: as domestic servants, as waiters/waitresses and busboys in restaurants, and as janitors. In 1930, one-half of employed Filipinas and nearly one-third of employed Filipinos on the continent worked in domestic or personal service. Housing discrimination forced workers to live in crowded rooming houses in "Little Manilas," as Filipina/o areas in large cities were called.[180]

In the 1920s and 1930s, a few Filipinas/os overcame poverty and discrimination to achieve economic success in the continental United States. There were relatively few Filipina/o small businesses, because few Filipino workers could call upon the labor of wives and children, and most Filipino savings were sent back to relatives in the Philippines. Success through farming was hindered by the Alien Land Laws. Nevertheless, about 7 percent of employed Filipinas were professionals, one-half of them trained nurses; 2 percent of Filipinos held professional jobs. Some Filipinas/os were able to set up barbershops and restaurants which catered to Filipinas/os, whom whites refused to serve. One enterprising Filipina, Francisca Domingo, first came to the United States as a domestic servant for a U.S. major who had been stationed in the Philippines. After 20 years of work as a domestic servant, she married and started a nursery, flower, and vegetable farm in Palo Alto, California. Domingo reported, "We sold our produce and flowers to everybody. People came to the farm and bought from me—that was how I made my business. We worked hard but could not buy property because we were not citizens."[181] Other Filipinas made Philippine finger-foods and sold them in the streets, took in laundry or sewing, or ran boarding or lodging houses. Less than 3 percent did clerical work.[182]

Another colonial connection to Filipina/o immigration was provided by the U.S. Navy. In World War I, the Navy recruited single Filipinos fluent in English and without dependents to serve as stewards for white naval officers. Stewards were essentially domestic servants who prepared and served officers' meals and cared for their quarters, on land and at sea. Granted U.S. citizenship if they had served more than three years, many stewards moved to West Coast ports where they worked in the Merchant Marine. A 1930 study estimated that 25,000 of the 60,000 Filipinos in the United States had served in the Navy.[183]

Women, Family, and Social Life Among the First Wave

There were very few Filipinas in the United States through World War II. Of the 24,000 Filipinas/os who entered California between 1925 and 1929, only 1,300 were women. In 1930, the male/female ratio was 14 to 1. In Hawaii, the sex ratio was only slightly less unbalanced: 10 to 1 in 1910, and 3.5 to 1 in 1940.[184] Employers' preferences for single men were the most important cause of the imbalance, as was true for the Chinese and Japanese. On the other hand, in response to worker unrest and strikes in 1920 and 1924, planters imported some 3,000 Filipinas, endeavoring to distract and calm the male strikers and with a view to dissuading Filipinos from returning home. The distinctive Philippine family structure also played a role in creating the sex imbalance. When a Filipina married, she did not give up ties to her blood family, which remained equal in importance to those with her husband's family. Hence many Filipinas may have been unwilling to migrate as part of a nuclear family. It also appears that parents rarely pressured their daughters to migrate.[185]

Thus, many Filipina wives waited in the Philippines for their immigrant husbands to return, as did the Chinese *Gum-Shan-Poo*. Most Filipinas/os were Catholic (a legacy of Spanish colonization) and divorce, even after 10 or 20 years of separation, was unacceptable to them. Men who were financially successful tended to return home, either to marry or to rejoin their wives and families. Less successful men were more inclined to stay in Hawaii or in the continental United States. In most instances, these remained single, but some formed split-household families. When Filipina/o immigration was halted in 1934, this sex imbalance was perpetuated.

As with earlier Asian groups, anti-miscegenation laws in California, Washington, and Oregon, where most continental Filipinas/os lived, prevented Filipinos from marrying white women. In 1933, Salvador Roldan successfully challenged the California statute which prohibited marriages between whites and Blacks, Mulattos, or Mongolians, with no mention of Filipinas/os. However, the law was later amended to prevent marriages between whites and Filipinas/os by including "Malays" in the list of prohibited groups (even though many Filipinas/os are not of Malay origin). Some Filipinos married white women in states where this was legal, even though mixed couples frequently faced harassment by whites when they were together in public. Intermarriage between non-Caucasians was not prohibited, however, and many Filipinos married American Indians, Blacks, other Asians, or Chicanas. In Hawaii, as we have observed, marriage to whites was not prohibited.[186]

In Filipina/o families, a sexual division of labor assigned most wives and daughters to unpaid household work and most husbands and sons to work for pay. In Hawaii in 1920, for example, 12 percent of Filipinas and 97 percent of Filipinos were gainfully employed. Because Filipina immigrants often had more education than their husbands (many who immigrated in the 1920s and 1930s had been school teachers), women often played the role of the family go-between with white society.[187]

For the most part, however, traditional families were absent from first-wave Filipina/o immigrant life. Some men lived with white women whom they were prevented by law from marrying, but most remained bachelors. Sometimes they formed stable households among themselves, and paid prostitutes or "taxi-dance girls" (many of them white) for female company. Filipino workers found other reprieves from weeks of backbreaking labor at dance halls, pool halls, Chinese-run gambling houses, Filipino social clubs, and the traditional Filipino cockfight.[188] As anti-Chinese racism had focused on the danger that allegedly immoral Chinese women posed to white men, so anti-Filipino racism flared up at the idea of Filipinos socializing with white women. At a 1930 House Committee on Immigration hearing, Fred Hart of Salinas exclaimed, "The Filipinos are poor labor and a social menace as they will not leave our white girls alone and frequently intermarry."[189]

Since there were so few marriages among Filipinas/os, a second generation was late in coming. Compared to the children of Chinese and Japanese immigrants, second-generation Filipinas/os appear to have enjoyed fewer opportunities for upward mobility, both in Hawaii and on the continent. Illiteracy remained widespread among the children of plantation workers. Those who were educated were effectively barred from most professions and from owning land or other property. In Hawaii in the 1940s, only six out of 1,000 Filipinas/os were professionals. Filipinas/os experienced the lowest proportion in white-collar work and the lowest average earnings of any other ethnic group.[190] Rapid elevation of Filipina/o economic status in the United States, when it came, resulted from the immigration of large numbers of highly educated Filipinas/os after 1965 rather than from upward mobility of the second generation.

The Second and Third Waves of Filipina/o Immigration

Some Filipino Americans were drafted to fight in World War II. Others found work in war-related industries. In Hawaii, planters contracted workers out to war industries, paid them their former wages, and pocketed the difference. Some Filipino Americans felt that their participation in the war diminished the prejudice against them and opened up job opportunities. Another tangible result of the war was 1946 legislation that finally permitted Filipinas/os who had entered the United States before 1934 to become naturalized citizens, giving them the right to vote for the first time and freeing them from the restrictions imposed by the Alien Land Laws.[191]

New immigration, especially by women, accompanied these changes. In 1942, an act of Congress gave foreign veterans the right to naturalize, and many Filipinos who served in the Navy during the two world wars became citizens. As a result, when the War Brides Act was amended in 1947 to eliminate racial restrictions, these naturalized Filipinos were able to bring their wives to the United States as citizens. Filipinos, often in their 50s and 60s, returned to the Philippines to find wives.[192]

By this time, many Filipinas were eager to marry and migrate to the United States. Colonial ideology had convinced them, as one war bride put it, that "all Americans were beautiful and rich and that America must be like heaven." War brides found employment in agriculture, West Coast canneries, family businesses, or as domestic servants in cities. In addition to those Filipinas who married Filipino veterans, a large number of Filipinas came to the United States after World War II as the wives of white servicemen. Filipinas migrating to join their husbands in the United States made up fully half of all immigrants from the Philippines by 1960.[193]

The 1965 Immigration Act was a watershed for many racial-ethnic groups since it eliminated racial quotas on immigration. The numbers of recent immigrants are so high that three-quarters of Filipinas/os in the United States are Philippine-born and Filipinas/os were one of the largest Asian American groups in the 1980s. New immigration has also eliminated the sex imbalance: in 1980, more than one-half of the 782,000 Filipina/o Americans were female.[194]

The 1965 Immigration Act provided for immigration of skilled professional workers and family members. The effect of these provisions has been bipolar income and job distributions among Filipinas/os, just as among the Chinese. Most immigrants who have come to join their families are poor (although many have basic education in English from Philippine schools) and most find low-wage, seasonal work. Among the new immigrants are the wives of former plantation workers. Economic necessity has pushed many of these women into the labor force, reversing patriarchal roles. Many husbands do the domestic chores as in their bachelor days, although some attempt to keep their wives out of the labor force.[195]

Most of these "third wave" immigrants, like their earlier counterparts, occupy jobs in the secondary labor market. In Hawaii, 44 percent of Filipino immigrants begin work as janitors, dishwashers, food service workers, cannery or pineapple field workers. Filipinas go into service work (especially as hotel maids) and into female-dominated manufacturing and food-processing jobs. Their jobs tend to be seasonal and low-paying, so families usually require multiple workers to make ends meet. It is difficult for immigrants to break into the primary labor market, not only because of discrimination, but also because their family and neighborhood contacts, which help unskilled immigrants find jobs, do not extend outside the restricted set of seasonal, secondary-labor-market jobs.[196]

The other highly visible group of Filipina/o immigrants is made up of well-trained scientific professionals. Their immigration, often referred to as a "brain drain," is caused by factors both in the Philippines and in the United States. Demand for such professionals increased dramatically in the United States during the 1960s. Meanwhile, in the Philippines, 40 percent of college graduates were trapped in menial jobs because low standards of living in the Philippines limited the market demand for their services. Thus, there were few jobs for doctors even though most Filipinas/os desperately needed health care, and many doctors migrated to the United States from the Philippines. In fact, by 1969, India and the Philippines supplied more scientists, engineers, and doctors to the United States than did Europe.[197]

Demand in the United States was greatest for medical personnel such as doctors, nurses, pharmacists, medical technologists, and nutritionists. Women are highly represented in these professions in the Philippines. Hospitals recruited Filipina nurses under a U.S. government program that allowed foreign nurses to practice without having to pass state licensing exams provided they returned to their homeland after two years. Many highly educated Filipinas emigrated to the United States in response to these opportunities. Then, in 1976, the Health Professions Educational Assistance Act severely limited the immigration of foreign medical graduates. Nevertheless, immigration continued as Filipinas/os fled the worsening economic and political situation created by the U.S.-supported dictatorship of Ferdinand Marcos.[198]

As a result of this influx of professionals, Filipinas have become the most highly educated group of women in the United States—41 percent have college or advanced degrees, more than three times the proportion of non-Latina white women. Filipinas have three times their labor force share of health-diagnosing jobs such as doctor and dentist, which are normally male-dominated, and eight times their labor force share of nursing jobs.[199]

However, the economic situation of these professional Filipina immigrants is not all favorable. In a study of San Francisco and Los Angeles, Amado Cabezas, Larry Hajime Shinagawa, and Gary Kawaguchi found that, had Filipinas received the same rewards for their education as white men, Filipinas would have earned much more; in fact, Filipinas earned only 59 percent as much as white men. Severe institutional discrimination at hospitals and in government licensing procedures is partly responsible for this wage gap. For instance, 9 of every 10 Filipina nurses who take state licensing exams fail, but Filipina advocates point to intentional and unintentional discrimination as the problem rather than a lack of qualifications. Norma Rupisan Watson has brought suits against the American Nurses Association and the Affiliated Hospitals of California for discrimination on the basis of race, color, and national origin. She charges:

> Even though I and other foreign-born and -trained nurses have previous experience and training, this is not credited when we are employed and we are therefore hired at substandard wages, are not put into positions commensurate with our backgrounds, are forced to work on undesirable shifts…are not able and are not permitted to work in supervisory positions…do not receive appropriate transfer credit from our universities to upgrade ourselves in American universities, if on H-1 visas when hospital sponsorship expires, are forced to become illegal aliens even though licensed, cannot claim Social Security benefits even though we pay them and cannot collect unemployment insurance.[200]

Difficulty obtaining licenses forces many professionally trained Filipinas/os to take clerical, sales, and even manual jobs.[201]

Most Filipina/o American professionals do well, nonetheless, and their successes have raised the average economic status of Filipinas above all other racial-ethnic groups of women. The median income for full-time, full-year Filipina American workers was the highest of any racial-ethnic group of women in 1980: $12,007, compared to $10,564 for non-Latina white women. Also, the share of Filipina/o Americans living in poverty is lower than that for non-Latina/o whites.[202]

The great influx of women immigrants, combined with transformations in the U.S. economy, dramatically altered the economic position of Filipinas. Filipina labor force participation rates have risen substantially, from only 12 percent in 1920 to 68 percent in 1980, when they were at least 9 percentage points higher than those of any other racial-ethnic group of women. As shown in Table 7-3, Filipinas moved rapidly out of domestic service after World War II. The share employed in clerical jobs rose from 2

Table 7-3

Occupational Distribution of Filipina American Workers, 1930-1980
(in Percent)

	1930	1960	1970	1980
Agriculture	27.5	4.3	2.3	1.2
Manufacturing	15.3	17.4	12.9	13.8
Private Household Service	34.4	3.7	2.2	0.9
Service (not Private Household)	4.1	16.6	17.1	15.8
Sales	2.3	5.7	3.5	6.6
Clerical	1.6	24.3	30.0	28.2
Professional & Technical	6.0	26.4	30.6	27.1
Managerial, Administrative, & Official	8.7	1.7	1.5	6.4

NOTES: Totals do not always sum to 100 because of rounding. Manufacturing includes craft and transportation workers; agriculture includes mining, fishing, and forestry; managerial, administrative, & official includes some self-employment, and excludes farm managers. Data for all years include Hawaii. For a full listing of occupational categories included, see Appendix B. For a discussion of comparability problems between Census years, see Appendix D.
SOURCES: See Appendix A.

to 28 percent between 1930 and 1980, while professional employment grew from 6 percent to over one-fourth of all employed Filipinas. Employment in managerial and administrative jobs fell between 1930 and 1970, with the decline of self-employment; however, between 1970 and 1980, the share in these jobs more than quadrupled as Filipinas gained a foothold in salaried management work.

Figure 7-3 shows the share of Filipina Americans in different labor market segments, compared to Filipino Americans, white men, and white women. Almost two-thirds of Filipina Americans are employed in the secondary labor market as clerical, manufacturing, or service workers. Filipina Americans are more than twice as likely as white women to hold lower-tier primary-sector jobs, most of them in nursing. Filipino Americans do better than their female counterparts in the primary labor market, but have a higher representation in the lowest labor market segment, which includes service, farm work, helpers, and laborers.

A Rosy Future?

Although the recent surge of professional migration has elevated the average income and occupational status of Filipinas/os, this trend may not

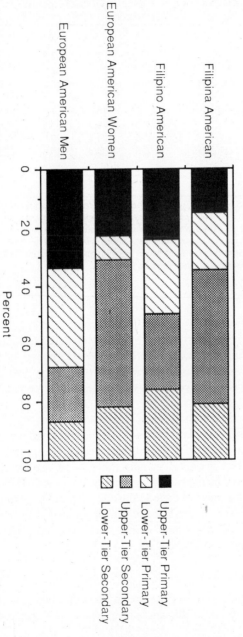

Figure 7-3: The Distribution of Filipina/o American and European American Workers across Labor Market Segments, by Gender, 1980

NOTES: See Table 10-5 for a listing of the occupations in each labor market segment. See Table 10-6 for the actual percentages employed in each segment.

SOURCE: 1980 Census; see Appendix A.

continue. In spite of the influx of professionals, Filipinas are still over-concentrated in low-paid service, clerical, and factory jobs. The migration of Filipina/o professionals declined sharply after 1973-74; the share entering on professional visas fell from 27 percent in the early 1970s to 2 percent in 1981. The large majority of immigrants now appears to be entering under the family reunification provisions of the Immigration Act. One study of immigrants from the Ilocos Norte province found that over three-quarters of those with occupational skills were blue-collar, fishing, or farming workers. In California, many immigrant Filipinas work for low wages in dangerous conditions in the Silicon Valley electronics industry, where 80 percent of production workers are women, mostly women of color. As on the Hawaiian plantations, electronics employers keep workers ethnically segregated to discourage organizing. Nonetheless, organizing efforts continue and workers have sued at least one major employer, the National Semiconductor Corporation, for discrimination. Many Silicon Valley manufacturing companies began moving production facilities abroad in the 1980s, and Filipinas have been hard hit by these plant closings.[203]

Finally, studies of second generation Filipinas/os in the U.S. educational system show that many have not attained the high educational levels of the professional immigrants. Filipina/o Americans' school enrollment rates are low, closer to those of Blacks and Latinas/os than to those of Chinese and Japanese Americans. In California high schools from 1980-81, for example, one-quarter of Filipina/o eleventh-graders failed to graduate from high school, compared to 11 percent for all other Asians and 31 percent and 35 percent of Blacks and Latinos/as, respectively. The proportion of Filipinas enrolled in higher education is significantly lower than that of other Asian groups: in 1970, only 23 percent of Filipinas aged 18 to 24 were in school, compared to 58 percent of Chinese women.[204]

Asian American Economic Success and Its Price: From Yellow Peril to Model Minority

In 1966, an article in the *New York Times Magazine* praised the economic success Japanese Americans had achieved despite their internment a mere 20 years earlier, and the notion of Japanese as a "model minority" was born. The praise was double-edged, however, since it was intended to prove that government affirmative action programs were unnecessary. Since then, the model minority stereotype has come to be applied to all Asians and maintains its double-edged quality. While the stereotype reflects real economic successes by some Asians, it also masks the persistence of poverty and self-exploitation among Asians as well as the presence of virulent anti-Asian sentiment.[205]

There are many signs of Asian American economic success. Slightly more than 2 percent of the population, Asians made up 23 percent of the undergraduates at the University of California at Berkeley, and 8 percent at Harvard University in the early 1980s. Much higher percentages of Chinese, Japanese, and Filipina women (30 percent, 20 percent, and 41 percent, respectively) have college or advanced degrees than do white women (13 percent). In 1980, median family incomes of Asians exceeded those of non-Latina/o whites. Poverty rates for Japanese and Filipinas/os were lower than for whites, although Chinese poverty rates were higher as a result of the immigrant poor. Asian women who worked full time and year round had 1980 median earnings of $11,519, more than the average for women of all races, $10,380. In many primary-sector jobs, the relative concentration of Asian women was higher than that of white women, as shown in Table 7-4.[206]

While the economic successes of a segment of Asian Americans appear to support the model-minority myth, the myth obscures the fact that many Asians are at the bottom of the economic hierarchy. Average measures of well-being, in particular, are misleading since they mask the bipolar distribution of income among Asians. A full 74 percent of Asian Americans are foreign born; of these, many speak little English and are segregated into low-paid, secondary labor market jobs. In 1980, 32 percent of Asian American women were in the lowest-wage, lowest-status occupations of machine operator, farmworker, or service worker, compared to only 26 percent of non-Latina/o whites. In that same year, the overall poverty rate for Asian Americans was 13 percent, compared to only 9 percent for whites. Asian political refugees—about 400,000 Vietnamese and 90,000 Cambodians—are often extremely impoverished: 36 percent of Vietnamese immigrants lived in poverty in 1980.[207]

The high proportion of Asian Americans who are self-employed is often cited as evidence to support the model-minority image. For instance, over half a million Koreans immigrated to the United States between 1961 and 1986. One in eight Koreans in the United States was self-employed or an unpaid family worker in 1980, a rate 50 percent higher than that among whites. Koreans have gained great visibility in small retail businesses, especially in produce markets. In fact, this overrepresentation in small retail firms reflects discrimination against Koreans in the labor market—rather than true success—as it did for the Chinese and Japanese before them. Most of the Koreans heading small businesses have been unable to put their high levels of education and training to full use in the United States because of employment discrimination and language and accreditation barriers. Furthermore, their success extracts a high toll in self-exploitation, with entire families working from six in the morning to midnight. A 1972 survey of minority-

Table 7-4

Relative Concentrations of Women in Selected
White-Male-Dominated Occupations, 1980

	Chinese American	Japanese American	Filipina American	European American
Executive, Administrative, & Managerial	100	80	61	76
Engineering	44	15	18	11
Health Diagnosing	127	30	322	25

NOTE: European American does not include Latinas.
SOURCES: 1980 Census, see Appendix A.

owned businesses found that more than half of Asian businesses had no paid employees. Their gross receipts per year averaged from $8,000 to $14,000, compared to a median family income for all Asian Americans of $11,116.[208]

Asian Americans have achieved their relative economic success via high rates of labor force participation, high numbers of workers in the family, and high levels of education. In 1980, a full 80 percent of Asian American families had two workers, compared to 68 percent for non-Latina/o whites. Asian American women had higher labor force participation rates than white non-Latina women for almost every ethnic and age category. Over one-third of Asian American women with incomes were full-time, full-year workers, compared to 29 percent of non-Latina white women. As a result, even though Chinese and Filipino men have lower median earnings for full-time work than white men, Chinese and Filipina/o families have higher mean and median incomes than whites. When we look at Asian American income *per person*, rather than income per family, we find that it is actually 10 percent lower than that of non-Latina/o whites. In addition, their higher family incomes generally do not translate into higher standards of living since so many Asian Americans are concentrated in high-cost urban areas.[209]

Even though Asian Americans have been typed a model minority, labor market discrimination persists. In one study, equivalent resumes were sent out to employers, with one group identified as Filipina/o and the other as white; the whites received requests for interviews five times more often than the Filipinas/os.[210] Asian Americans have filed discrimination suits against a number of employers, including United Airlines, Pacific Telephone, Pacific Gas and Electric, and the San Francisco Police Department.[211] And, as shown earlier, Asian Americans receive lower pay and lower-status jobs than whites with equivalent educations.

Asian American groups charge that top colleges and universities are now discriminating against Asian American applicants. Margaret Chin and David Ho found that Asian acceptance rates for Harvard and Brown have fallen since 1980 and are lower than those of any other group, while the advocacy group Chinese for Affirmative Action noted that Asian Americans admitted to the major California universities averaged higher grade-point averages than whites. In the face of growing evidence of discrimination, the U.S. Department of Education is investigating Harvard and the University of California at Los Angeles to see if they have established illegal quotas to limit the number of Asian Americans admitted.[212]

Finally, the model-minority myth, combined with the increasing economic power of Japan, may actually be responsible for intensified anti-Asian violence. The Justice Department found that anti-Asian incidents increased by 62 percent between 1984 and 1985. Anti-Asian incidents rose from 15 percent to 50 percent of all racial incidents in Los Angeles between 1985 and 1986, and from 2 percent to 29 percent of Boston's incidents between 1981 and 1986. As with anti-Asian violence in the past, economic self-interest in the face of Asian competition is one of the central motives. For instance, both Lee Iacocca and Roger Smith, the chief executive officers of Chrysler and General Motors, have used racial slurs against Asians to urge consumers to buy domestic cars. These statements from top management may be contributing to racism among workers. In 1982, an unemployed white auto worker, Ronald Ebens, and his stepson, Michael Nitz, beat Vincent Chin, a Chinese American draftsman, to death with a baseball bat. Nitz claimed he mistook Chin for a Japanese worker, pleaded guilty to manslaughter, and did not spend even a day in jail.[213] On the Texas Gulf coast, white fishermen have organized Ku Klux Klan rallies and threatened mob violence against 500 Vietnamese fishermen. One said on television, "I think they ought to be put on a reservation somewhere or some of them put in a compound to teach our laws and our ways, the way we live, our courtesy as a people."[214] Anti-Asian attacks also come from other minority groups: Asian American shopkeepers faced Black boycotts in New York City and fire-bombings in Washington, D.C.

Asian Americans are often depicted as foreigners who should "go home." Whether a recent immigrant or fourth-generation American, people of Asian heritage are subjected to xenophobia: "It's very sinister... You're not even a second-class citizen, you're a foreigner," says Doris Koo, executive director of Asian Americans for Equality.[215]

Anti-Asian prejudice has caused Asian Americans to organize across their ethnic and language divisions. As attorney Alan S. Yee observed, "We find that, from the outside, we're all perceived as the same, and, despite an image as 'model minorities,' we see the search for the scapegoat still there." [216]

Wars in Asia, War Brides, and the Sexploitation of Asian American Women

Asian American women have faced a special kind of exploitation. The long history of U.S. involvement in wars in Asia—World War II in Japan and the Philippines, the Korean War, and the Vietnam War (which included Laos and Cambodia)—and the presence of U.S. bases in those countries have brought generations of U.S. servicemen into contact with Asian women, mostly as prostitutes or tea-house girls. As a result, Amerasian children abound in Korea, the Philippines, and Vietnam, and many are ostracized by their local communities. As a further result of this contact, 200,000 Japanese, Korean, Vietnamese, Thai, and Filipina women have married white U.S. servicemen and moved to the United States. Here their lives are made difficult by social isolation on military bases, lack of familiarity with U.S. culture, and language problems, including poor communication with their spouses. Many husbands, far from assisting their wives' efforts to adapt, become disenchanted or abusive. Lacking information on their legal rights, wives have been divorced, lost child custody and financial support, and have even been deported. [217]

The war bride problem has been compounded by the recent growth of a mail-order bride industry, which supplies Asian women to U.S. and European men. Unlike the long-distance arranged marriages or wife-sales of the past, which matched men with women of the same racial-ethnic background, the mail-order marriage business matches Asian women with predominantly non-Asian men, and relies on the presumed difference of Asian women from U.S. women. One survey of the men involved found that they:

> ...see the women's liberation movement as the cause of their problems. They start with certain negative stereotypes of American women as aggressive, selfish, not family oriented. Then they add positive stereotypes of Asian women—family centered, undemanding, untouched by women's liberation. [218]

Many of these men remember Asian women from their experiences in Asia as servicemen.

The women involved in the mail-order bride industry—mostly extremely poor English-speaking Filipinas seeking economic security—respond to newspaper advertisements by over 100 agencies that offer prospective husbands in the United States and in Europe. The agencies compile catalogues with women's pictures, descriptions, and addresses, which they sell for about $150. An estimated 2,000 to 3,000 U.S. men find wives in this way each year. Grace Lyu-Vockhausen, an Asian American feminist activist and member of the New York City Commission on the Status of Women, describes these operations: "I consider this an international sex ring. The men who apply, basically they're losers. They cannot make it in this country so they go out and look for women who can be their total slaves." [219] Many mail-order brides have complained to Lyu-Vockhausen of beatings by their husbands, but fear deportation if they ask for help. Siriporn Skrobanek, a founder of the Women's Information Center in Bangkok, Thailand, views these marriages as:

> ...another form of economic exploitation of the periphery by the center, one which is so intensive that women in the peripheral countries have to sell their labor and sexuality to men on a commercial marriage market. [220]

Asian women are also commonly featured in tourist campaigns and in pornography. These forms of sexploitation, magnified by media stereotypes, undermine all Asian women in the United States. As one woman told Connie Chan, a Chinese American psychologist:

> I wanted to hide whenever a man told me I had beautiful almond-shaped eyes, or that I was such a petite little Asian doll...I felt more like an object, like someone else's idea of an Asian woman, than like a worthwhile person on my own. [221]

The sexual stereotypes of Asian women affect Asian American women in the economic and legal arenas. As Asian American feminist Germaine Wong pointed out at a conference on the educational and occupational needs of Asian American women, male employers or co-workers expect Asian women to be "...good, faithful, uncomplaining, totally compliant, self-effacing, gracious servants who will do anything and everything to please, entertain, and make them feel comfortable and carefree..." [222] These stereotypes reinforce Asian women's concentration in office work, and make it more difficult for them to advance in a variety of fields. Assuming Asian American women to be particularly pleasing and unaggressive, employers deny them raises and claim they lack the leadership qualities needed for executive jobs. Stereotypes have also led to sexual harassment by police. Asian American women reporting such incidents often do not receive justice from the courts because of the "prostitute stereotype." [223]

Asian American Feminists Respond

White society's racism, Asian patriarchal practices, and the special sexploitation of Asian women have led increasing numbers of Asian American women to become active in Asian groups organizing for justice, including women's groups and lesbian and gay organizations. As Chan argues:

> As women living in this country, we are all too familiar with the oppression and sexual violence directed towards all women. As Asian women, like many other women of color, we exist with the added burden of dehumanizing sexual stereotypes and racial/sexual exploitation...As women, we must begin to examine and confront the racist and sexist attitudes which allow *any* woman to be advertised in our magazines and newspapers as a "mail-order bride." In addition, we have to begin—all of us, whether Asian, Asian-American, women of color, or white women—to recognize that such a racist and sexist system dehumanizes and objectifies each of us.[224]

There are many impediments to Asian American feminist organizing. Activists face hostility from many Asian American men who claim they are destroying community solidarity and racism from white women who lack knowledge of the history or present status of Asian American women. Organizing is also impeded by the vast differences among Asian women, including ethnicity, language, class, and sexuality, and by many women's needs to concentrate their energies on economic survival.

Nevertheless, Asian American women have founded Asian women's studies courses and study groups, writers' groups, such as Pacific Asian American Women's Writers West, and regional feminist organizations like the National Organization of Pan Asian Women, the National Network of Asian and Pacific Women, and Asian American Women United. Asian lesbians have formed nationwide political groups such as Asian/Pacific Lesbian Network and created a slide show of Asian lesbian history in India, China, and Japan. Asian feminists have also joined in coalitions with other feminists of color, moving beyond historical differences and antagonisms.[225]

One central focus of Asian American feminist concern and struggle has been the issue of battering. While domestic violence is as prevalent in the Asian community as in the country in general, it remains hidden under the model-minority myth and by victims' extreme reluctance to speak out and seek help.[226] Nilda Rimonte, Filipina founder of the Center for the Pacific-Asian Family and of the first shelter for Pacific Asians in the United States, finds that Asian women are especially vulnerable to battering when they are employed and traditional sex roles are upset or even reversed. Among recent immigrants without knowledge of English, battered-women's counselor and social worker Tina Shum found:

> ...the woman will get a job much more easily, because she will be willing to work in a sewing factory, or sell dim sum in a restaurant or be a dishwasher. So she becomes the breadwinner. Since the man is used to being head of the household, he can become frustrated and beat his wife.[227]

The traditionally closed and hierarchical nature of the Asian family and a strong stigma against divorce exacerbate Asian American women's vulnerability to battering. Mail-order brides, who are on temporary visas for the first two years of their marriages, are particularly exposed; there were 3,449 such women in 1987. Organizers have established shelters for Asian American battered women in Los Angeles, San Francisco, and New York.[228]

Asian American feminists reject the patriarchal aspects of their cultures, yet they value their ethnic identities and histories. They remember the painful struggles their foremothers and forefathers waged in order to survive in a hostile United States. In her "Letter to Ma," self-proclaimed "Yellow Feminist" Merle Woo chides her mother for teaching her self-contempt because of her race, her sex, and her sexuality; at the same time, Woo writes:

> Do you realize, Ma, that I could never have reacted the way I have if you had not provided for me the opportunity to be free of the binds that have held you down, and to be in the process of self-affirmation? Because of your life...I saw myself as having worth; now I begin to love myself more, see our potential, and fight for just that kind of social change that will affirm me, my race, my sex, my heritage. And while I affirm myself, Ma, I affirm you...We have such a proud heritage, such a courageous tradition. I want to tell everyone about that, all the particulars that are left out in the schools. And the full awareness of being a woman makes me want to sing. And I do sing with other Asian Americans and women, Ma, anyone who will sing with me.[229]

CHAPTER 8

YO MISMA FUI MI RUTA[1]

(I Was My Own Path)

Puerto Rican Women

Río Grande de Loíza! Río grande. Llanto grande.
El más grande de todos nuestros llantos isleños,
si no fuera más grande el que de mí se sale
por los ojos del alma para mi esclavo pueblo.

Río Grande de Loíza! Great river. Great tear.
The greatest of all our island tears,
but for the tears that flow out of me
through the eyes of my soul for my enslaved people.

—Julia de Burgos, "Río Grande de Loíza"[2]

Puerto Rico is a small island in the Caribbean Sea—between the Dominican Republic and the Virgin Islands—whose lush tropical vegetation and beautiful beaches lead its inhabitants to call it *Isla del Encanto* (Island of Enchantment) and *Perla del Caribe* (Pearl of the Caribbean). Puerto Ricans have lived under colonial domination for five centuries, first by Spain and then by the United States. The fertile lands of the island were exploited by both colonial powers, and its indigenous inhabitants were enslaved and exterminated. Today, three million Puerto Ricans remain on the island, impoverished by their legacy of colonialism, while two million live in the United States. The economic history of Puerto Rican women has been buffeted by external political and economic forces. Still, in the words of their poet Julia de Burgos, they have pursued their own paths, struggling to maintain a distinct Puerto Rican women's identity in the face of colonialism, repression and poverty.[3]

Puerto Rico, Puerto Pobre (Rich Port, Poor Port)

Before the arrival of the Spanish *conquistadors,* Puerto Rico was populated by 50,000 to 70,000 Taino Indians, whose horticultural societies resembled those of many North American Indian peoples. Taino society was matrilineal—family name was passed down through the mother—and goddesses, particularly Guabancex, the mother goddess, were as important as gods. Women had access to the highest social positions, and when the Spaniards arrived on the island, they found that many of the Taino chiefs were women, including Anacaona, Higuanama, Guayerbas, and a mother and daughter, Yayo and Catalina, in the Caguas region.[4]

The Spanish colonizers quickly destroyed the Taino people and their sexual egalitarianism. Christopher Columbus arrived in Borikén, as the Tainos called the island, in 1493. By 1510, 300 Spanish colonists, whom the Tainos had welcomed as guests, had begun the merciless process of taking Taino lands and forcing the natives to mine for gold and other riches. Superior firearms allowed the Spaniards to crush the Taino rebellions, and the native population was virtually extinct by the 1550s.[5]

Spaniards came to Puerto Rico in search of wealth; indeed, they first called the island *Isla de San Juan Bautista* (Island of Saint John the Baptist) but later changed its name to *Puerto Rico* (Rich Port). As the Taino labor force dwindled, the Spaniards began importing African slaves to mine the gold. By 1530, the island's population was made up of 369 whites, 1,148 Indians, and 1,523 African slaves (of whom 355 were female), and most of the gold was depleted. Many Spaniards left for richer pickings in Peru and Mexico, while those who remained turned to agriculture. Slaveholders who owned large amounts of land set up sugar plantations and refineries, while poorer whites began subsistence farming. To encourage further migration, Spain declared Puerto Rico a refuge for emigrating slaves who, if they accepted Catholicism and promised loyalty to the Crown, were admitted as free persons. Another boost to white immigration came when Spain, recognizing the strategic importance of the island, built a military garrison in San Juan in 1582. Nevertheless, the island stagnated economically throughout the sixteenth and seventeenth centuries as Spain's neglect of the colony, along with its costly monopoly on trade with the island, restricted development and encouraged contraband trading.[6]

There were few Spanish women among the early colonists, and sexual exploitation of indigenous and African women was widespread. The Spanish crown allowed intermarriage with Indian women if they converted to Christianity, but such marriages were rare. Some men recognized the children born to them through informal unions, thereby preventing them from falling into slavery. Otherwise, when these women and their children were deserted, they formed single-mother families, and the children inherited the slave status of their mothers. A mixed-race population soon formed on the island, some free and some enslaved.[7]

The Spanish government made many attempts to induce women to emigrate, including an order that ships leaving for the island had to include at least 10 percent women, a law that colonists had to take their wives with them, and a plan to send white Christian slave women to Puerto Rico as future brides. Marriage was further encouraged by the assignment of special lands, Indian slaves, and administrative posts to those who were married. At the same time, the Spanish Crown opposed lifting its ban on the migration of Moors and Jews to the Americas, even though this migration would have eased the sex imbalance (apparently, many Moors and Jews emigrated illegally in spite of the ban). Between 1509 and 1538, about 10 percent of the immigrants to the West Indies from Spain were women; of these, 39 percent were single, independent adults and 24 percent were daughters who travelled with their fathers.[8]

In the eighteenth and nineteenth centuries, Puerto Rico's population and economy grew rapidly. From 45,000 in 1765, the population had grown to 155,000 in 1801, 44 percent of whom were Black, Indian, or of mixed racial backgrounds. Slave rebellions in Puerto Rico—along with the news in 1801 that Haiti's slaves and *mestizas/os* had successfully declared independence from France and abolished slavery—raised Spanish concern over the racial composition of the island. Fearful of a similar revolt in Puerto Rico, the colonial government promulgated the *Cédula de Gracias* (Decree of Free Entry) to encourage European immigration under the principle, *tenemos que mejorar la raza* (we have to improve [whiten] the race). Under the decree, uncultivated land was made available to new white immigrants, who came to Puerto Rico for a wide variety of reasons. Many whites, such as Mallorcans, Catalonians, Corsicans, and Chuetas (Jews who had been forced to convert to Christianity in Spain), came to the island to flee oppression. Over two-thirds of the women who immigrated between 1800 and 1830 were political exiles and widows who received a pension or other aid from the military. Spanish soldiers made up nearly half of the total nineteenth-century immigration. By 1860, the population had grown to over 583,000, and by 1899, it was almost 1 million. However, in spite of Spain's efforts, Puerto Rico remained racially diverse: in 1865, 49 percent of the population was classified as "colored."[9]

In the nineteenth century, new commercial policies allowing trade with nations other than Spain helped fuel economic development, and production of coffee, sugar, and tobacco for export grew. By 1899, these crops occupied 41 percent, 15 percent, and 1 percent of the arable land, respectively; the production of other edible foods for subsistence or for sale in the domestic market occupied less than one-third of the land. Coffee *haciendas* worked by sharecroppers or tenant farmers grew up alongside slave plantations and small family farms.[10]

Throughout the nineteenth century, large landowners used their political and economic power to take lands from smaller landowners and squatters. To serve their interests, an 1838 law created a class of *jornaleras/os* (day-laborers). The law mandated that a person not "in possession of a property that will provide the means for subsistence" had to "be engaged at the services of someone that can take care of his needs." *Jornaleras/os* had to carry *la libreta*, written proof of their employment, or be arrested. By the end of the nineteenth century, land ownership was very concentrated: the richest 5 percent of all landowners owned 50 percent of the land, while the poorest 57 percent of landowners cultivated only 10 percent.[11]

Women's Lives and Work Under Spanish Colonialism

In this developing export economy, a woman's work varied greatly according to her race and class. Women slaves were forced to do backbreaking field work as well as domestic and reproductive labor; slavery was not abolished until 1873, when 32,000 slaves were freed (at that time, they made up 5 percent of the total population). Women on small family or tenant farms raised livestock and engaged in production of food and other goods for family needs. However, under a strict sexual division of labor, peasant women rarely worked on cash crops except during harvest time. Women day laborers also seldom worked in cash agriculture. Instead, they were forced into employment as domestic servants, cooks, seamstresses, or laundresses. As Puerto Rican economist Marcia Rivera points out, their work in these occupations "served to strengthen the social hegemony of one class over another, and...maintained women in a subordinate position, subject to constant economic, social, and sexual exploitation."[12]

In addition, all women were subject to Spanish law, which gave men virtually absolute power over their wives and daughters. As Puerto Rican sociologist Edna Acosta-Belén explains, colonial Puerto Rico was:

> ...a patriarchal, paternalistic, and military-oriented society in which the subordination of women to men was almost absolute. Women of all classes were conditioned to be obedient daughters, faithful wives, and devoted mothers. Their inferior status was reinforced by juridical inequality. Laws concerning the family, the administration of community property in marriage, authority over the children, and some labor practices limited the rights of women.[13]

Spanish-designed family and labor laws in Puerto Rico were not revised to eliminate sex discrimination until 1976.[14]

Few women received formal education in nineteenth-century Puerto Rico. Illiteracy was rampant among the peasantry, and in 1899, half of the population had less than one year of schooling. Only one-half of one percent of the population had more than a primary education, and men were six times as likely as women to be in this elite group. However, as in the United States at that time, the elite class supported education for their women as preparation for motherhood, and some elite women even worked to extend education to women of all classes. Celestina Cordero founded one of the first schools for girls in the 1820s, and Belén Zequeira, who in 1886 founded the *Asociación de Damas para la Instrucción de la Mujer* (the Ladies' Association for Women's Instruction), advocated for poor women's right to education. Because there were so few educated Puerto Rican women, the development of a movement for women's rights was hampered in this period, despite growing feminism in other American countries. Nevertheless, feminist activity was evidenced by the publication by Ana Roque of the first women's magazine, *La Mujer* (The Woman), beginning in 1893.[15]

Upper-class, educated women were also active in the late nineteenth-century separatist movement for independence from Spain. Mariana Bracetti and Eduviges Beauchamp embroidered Puerto Rican flags that flew over the town of Lares during the famous *Grito de Lares* (Cry of Lares), when the separatist movement briefly took over the town on September 23, 1868 and declared Puerto Rico's independence from Spain. Bracetti was jailed for her involvement. Lola Rodríguez de Tío, a dedicated separatist and well-known writer, wrote the words to "*La Borinqueña*," a song that urged Puerto Ricans to take up arms against Spanish rule. In 1897, the Puerto Rican separatist movement won autonomy from Spain. As the Spanish empire rapidly declined around the world, it appeared that full independence would soon be won.[16]

Exit Spain; Enter the United States

However, as in the case of the Philippines, the United States planned to prevent such independence. The U.S. government had long been eyeing Puerto Rico as the location for a Caribbean military base and, in 1898, U.S. troops invaded Puerto Rico and quickly took control. General Nelson Miles, who had played a central role in the U.S. wars against American Indians, led the attack. In his first speech to the Puerto Rican people, Miles promised:

> ... not to make war upon the people of a country that for centuries has been oppressed but, on the contrary, to bring you protection, not only to yourselves, but to your property, to promote your

prosperity, and to bestow upon you the immunities and blessings of the liberal institutions of our government and to give to all within the control of its military and naval forces the advantages and blessings of enlightened civilization.[17]

What was actually a new colonial government was outlined in the Foraker Act of 1900. The United States would appoint Puerto Rico's governor and the members of its upper legislative chamber, while voters (male Puerto Ricans who passed the literacy requirement) would elect the lower chamber. Both chambers had to approve any Puerto Rican law, which both the governor and the U.S. Congress could then veto. The Jones Act of 1917 unilaterally "awarded" Puerto Ricans U.S. citizenship. However, Puerto Ricans had neither representatives in the U.S. government nor the right to vote for the U.S. president, although they were subject to the U.S. military draft.[18]

Profiting from Colonialism, 1900-1930

While U.S. designs on Puerto Rico were at first military, U.S. banks and investors soon found ways to profit from Puerto Rico's colonial status. Between 1900 and 1930, U.S. absentee investment totalled $120 million. Puerto Rican historian Manuel Maldonado-Denis points out that, "The first four decades of imperialist domination in Puerto Rico made a period during which inch by inch our country gradually fell into the hands of U.S. industrial and financial capitalists."[19] By 1930, four U.S.-based corporations nearly monopolized production in each of four distinct areas: 60 percent of sugar production, 80 percent of tobacco, 60 percent of public services and banks, and 100 percent of maritime lines.[20]

In the first decades of the twentieth century, the Puerto Rican economy was reorganized to complement—and become dependent upon—the U.S. economy and to generate high profits for U.S. capital. Agricultural production was shifted further away from food for internal consumption to "after-dinner crops" for export, such as sugar, tobacco, and coffee, although the latter declined rapidly. U.S. capitalists also developed the tobacco-processing and needlework industries. Already a major market for Puerto Rican products in the late 1800s, by the mid-1920s the United States was buying 95 percent of Puerto Rico's exports. By the same period, colonial trade policies had forced Puerto Rico to purchase 90 percent of its imports from the United States.[21]

These changes spelled the decline of independent family farming, sharecropping, and tenant farming, and the growth of a landless rural labor force. By 1930, 80 percent of the those living in rural areas did not own land (73 percent of Puerto Rico's population was still rural). The swelling rural proletariat found seasonal employment in sugar and tobacco production, working during the harvests but barely surviving in between. Agricultural employment grew by only about 65,000 between 1899 and 1930, while the labor force grew by almost 200,000. As a result, many landless peasants were forced to migrate to urban areas to work in manufacturing; factory jobs grew by a factor of four during this period.[22]

From Home to Factory: Changes in Women's Employment Patterns in Puerto Rico, 1900-1930

Although independent agricultural production was in the process of disappearing, most men still remained employed in agriculture.[23] In 1899, 73 percent of employed men worked in agriculture, and in 1930, 67 percent. Men monopolized paid agricultural work. Only 9 percent of men had moved into manufacturing employment by 1930.[24]

On the other hand, women's employment was affected more dramatically by the colonial economic transformation. Most important, a growing number of women were drawn into the paid labor force. Forced out of subsistence production, families squeezed by men's low wages and high unemployment sent women to work, and the share of women seeking paid work grew rapidly, from 14 percent in 1899 to 23 percent in 1930. The number of women employed more than doubled in this period, and women grew to comprise one-quarter of the total labor force.[25]

The kinds of work women performed also changed rapidly in the first third of the twentieth century, as shown in Table 8-1. The share of employed women found in domestic service fell from 78 percent in 1899 to 28 percent in 1930, as they moved into better jobs in agriculture and in manufacturing. The number of women employed as agricultural laborers grew six-fold between 1899 and 1910 alone, and then almost doubled between 1910 and 1920. However, in the 1920s, women began leaving farm labor for other work, and by 1930, less than 10 percent of all women worked in agriculture.

At the same time, the availability of women's cheap labor drew U.S. manufacturers to the island, and the availability of factory work in turn drew poor Puerto Rican women to urban areas. The share of employed women working in manufacturing skyrocketed from 15 percent in 1899 to over 52 percent in 1930—compared, for example, to 38 percent of American Indian women and 21 percent of white women in the United States. Indeed, by 1930, women workers, who constituted only 25 percent of the total labor force, made up over two-thirds of the manufacturing workforce in Puerto Rico.[26]

Women's manufacturing employment centered in the tobacco, cigar, and garment industries. Cigar-making was strictly sex-typed, with women "stemming" and classifying the tobacco leaves by hand while men rolled the

Table 8-1

Occupational Distribution of Island Puerto Rican Women Workers,
1899-1980 (in Percent)

	1899	1930	1960	1970	1980
Agriculture	3.9	9.5	1.6	0.6	0.3
Manufacturing	14.6	52.4	31.3	30.3	22.0
Private Household Service	78.4	27.5	13.7	4.9	1.4
Service (not Private Household)	n.a.	1.3	12.2	13.7	14.8
Sales	1.2	0.9	4.8	5.4	7.6
Clerical	1.2	2.3	16.9	23.1	26.9
Professional & Technical	0.7	4.5	15.5	18.5	21.1
Managerial, Administrative, & Official	n.a.	1.6	3.9	3.5	6.0

NOTES: Totals do not always sum to 100 because of rounding. Manufacturing includes craft and transportation workers; agriculture includes mining, fishing, and forestry; managerial, administrative, & official includes some self-employment, and excludes farm managers. For 1899, workers in the Census category "Trade and Transportation" were evenly divided between Manufacturing, Sales, and Clerical; Private Household Service includes other service workers. For a full listing of occupational categories included, see Appendix B. For a discussion of comparability problems between Census years, see Appendix D.
SOURCES: See Appendix A.

cigars. The numbers of women employed at this work grew from 1,340 in 1909 to 9,290 in 1930, and throughout the entire period, women workers outnumbered men. Needlework, an almost exclusively female job, also experienced even more rapid growth. Beginning in the late 1910s, U.S. producers sent material to Puerto Rico to be embroidered, returning it to the United States for sale. U.S.-owned and -organized, the industry subcontracted out its Puerto Rican work to *talleristas*, Puerto Rican agents, usually women. The *talleristas* often further subcontracted the work out to other agent-supervisors, each agent receiving a profit from the workers' labor. Seventy-five percent of the work was actually done in the workers' homes, while the rest took place in factories. By 1930, the industry employed almost one-third of all women workers. A 1934 report by the U.S. Department of Labor revealed horrific working conditions:

> [W]omen worked extremely long hours, days and evenings... Hourly earnings in needlework were extremely low: for 31.4 percent of the women they were less than 1 cent, for 31.1 percent they

were 1 and under 2 cents, and for 31.4 percent they were 2 and under 4 cents.[27]

The Rise of Women's Labor Organizing in Puerto Rico

The rapid rise of a wage-earning class which suffered low wages and poor working conditions created the impetus for a strong workers' movement on the island. Women found themselves especially oppressed, earning only one-third to one-quarter of the already low wages earned by their male counterparts. Many women became actively involved in union struggles to better their conditions, and in this process, developed feminist consciousness in themselves and in their male co-workers. Rivera argues that this equal participation of women and men in factory work fostered egalitarian ideas among workers:

> Hand in hand with their male counterparts, women workers rejected views of feminine fragility, moral superiority, and passivity that were attributed to women by other social classes. Relative equality between the sexes was thus achieved in the process of proletarianization.[28]

Women workers were active in mixed-sex organizations which took up women's causes and in autonomous women's groups. Beginning in the early 1900s, wage-earning women began to organize women's associations within trade unions, including town-wide unions of working women in Puerto de Tierra, Guayama, and Mayaguez, a domestic workers' union in Ponce, a coffee pickers' union in Arecibo, and a tobacco strippers' union at the big factory of La Colectiva. Women were also among the creators of the *Federación Libre de Trabajadores* (Free Labor Federation or FLT), formed in 1899, which represented almost all Puerto Rican organized workers in the early twentieth century. The FLT held the First Congress of Women Workers of Puerto Rico in 1919. At the Congress, women formed a national federation of local feminist chapters and a Women's Organization Committee, and committed themselves to fight for universal suffrage and better working conditions for women, including a minimum wage.[29] During this period, the workers' movement was connected to a political movement, the Socialist Party, founded in 1916. The socialists took up the demand of universal suffrage—for men and women, literate and illiterate—and required all their committees to be at least one-third female. One of the Party's most militant members, Juana Colón of Comerío, worked as an ironer and washer-woman, and later as a tobacco worker. Colón organized tobacco strippers and was known by her co-workers as "Joan of Arc of Comerío."[30]

One of the most striking examples of this combination of feminism and working-class activism was Luisa Capetillo. Capetillo was a socialist, a feminist, and a writer. She was a major force behind the FLT's adoption of feminist demands such as women's suffrage, and a noted organizer of sugar plantation workers and of one of the first craft unions of the FLT. The first Puerto Rican woman to wear slacks in public, Capetillo challenged sexist social conventions by having children outside marriage. She also wrote three books, was a reporter for a workers' paper, *Unión Obrera*, and edited the women's journal, *La Mujer*. In 1911, she wrote to her sisters:

> Oh you woman! who is capable and willing to spread the seed of justice; do not hesitate, do not fret, do not run away, go forward! And for the class benefit of the future generations place the first stone for the building of social equality in a serene but firm way, with all the right that belongs to you, without looking down...[31]

However, class differences prevented activist women workers and socialists from aligning with the parallel movement for women's rights organized by educated, professional women.

Professional Puerto Rican Women

Because of the U.S. takeover of the Puerto Rican land and economy, Puerto Rico lacked a sizable capitalist class. However, in the first third of the twentieth century, Puerto Rico had an active middle class made up of small farmers, professionals, small businesspeople, government employees, and teachers in public schools and universities. Moreover, the number of educated women was growing. As small- and medium-size landowners lost their land and moved to the cities, many of their daughters pursued education and professional work, both as a means to self-fulfillment and economic survival. At the same time, colonial administrators were expanding the educational system and making it coeducational. At the University of Puerto Rico, set up in 1903 on the model of the North American Teacher's College, almost three-quarters of the graduates between 1903 and 1924 were women. With the transplantation of the U.S. educational system, the teaching profession became a women's job, switching from 70 percent men in 1899 to 75 percent women in 1930. By 1930, almost 5 percent of employed Puerto Rican women worked in the professions, compared to less than 1 percent in 1899. In 1940, the vast majority of professional women were employed in feminine professions as teachers, nurses, social workers, and librarians. However, a handful were employed in male-dominated professions: there were 4 women engineers, 14 lawyers, 80 pharmacists, and 26 doctors.[32]

Many of these educated, professional women were women's rights activists. In 1909, for instance, teachers demanded eligibility for appointment to local school boards. In 1917, educated women formed the island's first feminist organization, *La Liga Femenina Puertorriqueña* (the Puerto Rican Feminine League). In 1925, they began *La Asociación Puertorriqueña de Mujeres Sufragistas* (the Puerto Rican Association of Woman Suffragists). One of its leaders, Mercedes Solá, wrote in a 1922 essay on feminism:

> Without education it is impossible for feminism to triumph, since this sustains ability and right, and the former cannot be obtained without an efficient preparation...The economic base is also indispensable since a woman cannot conquer her emancipation without first obtaining the economic independence that will relieve her from the tutelage of man.[33]

Working-class feminists did not participate in the suffrage movement, believing with reason that it would only win suffrage for literate (at that time, privileged) women, thus reinforcing the power of the wealthy over the poor and working classes. Indeed, when suffragists won women the vote in 1929, literacy requirements were kept in place. However, universal suffrage for literate and illiterate men and women was approved by the legislature in 1936. The suffrage movement was also split off from the movement seeking to win Puerto Rican independence from the United States because male *independentistas* argued against feminist measures, claiming that they had been imposed by the U.S. colonizers and that they detracted from the more urgent anti-colonial struggle.[34]

Early Migration to the United States, 1900-1930

Puerto Ricans were drawn to the United States in the first three decades of the twentieth century by a variety of factors. High unemployment, particularly seasonal agricultural unemployment, pushed many Puerto Ricans to seek work in the United States. This push was combined with the pull of labor demand from the United States. During World War I, as we have seen in pervious chapters, the U.S. experienced a severe labor shortage. In addition, the Immigration Acts of 1921, 1924, and 1929 increasingly restricted the supply of European workers to the East Coast, just as the Chinese Exclusion Act and the Gentlemen's Agreement had previously restricted Asian immigration to Hawaii and the western United States.[35] None of these immigration restrictions, however, applied to Puerto Ricans, who had been made U.S. citizens by the Jones Act of 1917. As a result, East Coast U.S. employers and Hawaiian planters actively recruited Puerto Rican semiskilled and unskilled workers. In addition, the compulsory military service mandated by the Jones Act acquainted Puerto Rican servicemen with the United States. As a result of all of these factors, 71,000 Puerto Ricans migrated to the United States between 1909 and 1940—draining the island of about one-seventh of its labor force.[36]

Once an individual gained a foothold in the United States, other family members followed, and a Puerto Rican *colonia* (neighborhood) was formed. The biggest *colonias* were in New York City, which was home to 62 percent of the U.S. Puerto Rican population in 1920 and 81 percent by 1940. There were more men than women among early Puerto Rican migrants (114 males to 100 females in 1925), and many women migrated alone to join extended family members in the States. From the story of Elisa Baeza, we gather that at least some young women saw migration as a way to free themselves from heavy family responsibilities as well as from poverty:

> We were eleven, six females and five males. My father always provided for us selling fruits and vegetables at the *Puente de Balboa*. But we were poor and as the oldest female I was like a second mother. The burden of caring for the younger children was always on me. In 1930, I was invited to go to New York to live with my cousin. I went and I stayed. I was seventeen years old at the time.[37]

While language discrimination was a problem for many Puerto Rican migrants (some had learned English in their colonial schools), being "Spanish" exempted some Puerto Ricans from the extreme racism that was leveled at African Americans. Nevertheless, non-white Puerto Ricans met a level of discrimination not experienced by European immigrants. As one Puerto Rican woman explained, "If you looked Irish or German, it didn't matter how limited your English was. Most jobs were on assembly lines and it didn't take much talking to learn the procedure."[38]

The race discrimination which migrants faced in the United States came as a shock. In the color-conscious United States, Puerto Ricans were viewed as inferior both ethnically and racially if they could not pass as white. In Puerto Rico, in contrast, racism involved (and still does) differentiation across a wide range of racial types, including *blancos* (whites), *indios* (Indians), *morenos* (browns), *trigueños* (dark-skinned and curly-haired people), and *negros* (blacks). Social class and hair type as well as facial features contributed to the racial classification. Furthermore, in Puerto Rico, there was much less racial segregation and much more intermarriage than in the United States, so, in the words of Puerto Rican social scientist Clara Rodriguez, "the world of most Puerto Rican children [is] one that is inhabited by people of many colors…"[39]

Employers hired Puerto Ricans for the low-wage jobs previously held by newly arrived European immigrants: garment manufacturing, light factory work, hotel and restaurant jobs, cigar-making, domestic service, and laundry work. About 25 percent of New York Puertorriqueñas worked outside their homes in the 1920s: about 40 percent as domestic workers and 40 percent in manufacturing, most in garment- and cigar-making. But unlike in Puerto

Rico, there is little evidence of union activity among U.S. Puerto Rican workers during this period, although Luisa Capetillo is known to have visited the United States. This invisibility may have been due to small numbers and to the racism of the U.S. labor movement.[40]

As in Puerto Rico, the majority of Puerto Rican women in the *colonias* worked as homemakers. Many of these women also performed skilled but very low-paid work in their homes. Large numbers took in piecework, such as sewing or embroidering and making lampshades, hats, artificial flowers, and jewelry. Others provided child care to other women for pay. As Puerto Rican social scientist Virginia Sanchez Korrol noted:

> ...a grass-roots system of day-care was born from the merger of working mothers, who could ill afford to lose job security or union benefits, and women who remained at home for any number of reasons. Working Puerto Rican mothers left their children in the care of friends or relatives; the arrangement basically consisted of bringing the child, food and additional clothing to the mother-substitute and collecting [the child] after work.[41]

Taking in boarders and lodgers was also common; in 1925, 24 percent of the Puerto Ricans living in Spanish Harlem were lodgers, often staying with extended family members or hometown acquaintances. Besides funneling Puerto Rican earnings to working homemakers, lodging strengthened community ties and helped small *colonias* preserve their culture and traditions.[42]

As on the island, the U.S. Puerto Rican community also included some highly educated, middle-class women; indeed, professionals were over-represented among migrants. Some educated immigrant women were active feminists, such as Doña Josefina Silva de Cintron, who led the *Unión de Mujeres Americanas* (Union of American Women) and the League of Spanish-Speaking Democrats. Doña Josefina also started a journal, *Artes y Letras*, which published the work of a gifted Puerto Rican poet, Julia de Burgos, a feminist and *independentista* who lived in New York.[43]

When the Depression arrived in the 1930s, Puerto Ricans in the *colonias* were hard hit. Large numbers of workers were laid off and had to take any jobs they could find as dishwashers, countermen and -women, laundry workers, or janitors. Unable to find work, about one-fifth of the Puerto Ricans who had been living in the United States returned to Puerto Rico between 1930 and 1934. But conditions there were no better.[44]

Island Puerto Ricans During the Depression

If economic conditions had been difficult for most Puerto Ricans from 1900 to 1930, the situation was even more dire during the Depression of the 1930s. Between 1930 and 1940, employment in Puerto Rico grew by a sluggish 2 percent, while the population grew by 25 percent. All areas of production other than needlework were cut back. Estimates of unemployment ranged from 37 percent to 65 percent of the labor force, not counting seasonal unemployment. Coffee production was hardest hit, with 80 percent of the workers regularly employed in its production put out of work. Unemployment was also extremely high among tobacco workers. People sought part-time work or *chiripas* (odd jobs) to survive, and growing numbers of families lived on women's low and declining earnings in domestic service and garment work. The economic plight of the islanders was so appalling that President Roosevelt felt compelled to extend some New Deal programs to Puerto Rico.[45]

Workers looked to the labor movement for a source of assistance and resistance. In Mayaguez, the center of the needlework industry, workers went on strike on August 30, 1933. Employers called in the police, who killed two people (a woman and a three-year-old girl) and wounded 70 others, mostly women. The courage and militancy of these women (the police said women had stoned both the police and the factory building) inspired others to organize. By 1934, the FLT had organized nine unions of home garment workers, and more than 75 percent of all garment workers employed in factories or working at home were represented by a union.[46]

Unemployed workers also organized during the Depression period. Women formed the Unemployed Women Workers Association and they made up one-third of the crowd of 6,000 attending a November 1934 demonstration to demand, "We don't want relief, we want work." The *Unión de Trabajadores de la Aguja* (Needleworkers' Union) also fought for the application of the Fair Labor Standards Act, which included a minimum wage provision, to Puerto Rico. In these struggles, the Needleworkers' Union went even further than the national labor union leadership, since in 1933 the FLT and the Socialist Party had joined a winning political coalition with the conservative Union Republican party, and had sided with big business against the minimum wage.[47]

As European American author John Gunther described it in his 1941 best-selling book, *Inside Latin America*, Puerto Rico had become the "poorhouse of the Caribbean."[48] Forty-two years after General Miles had promised the islanders "to promote your prosperity," Puerto Rico's infant mortality rate was one of the highest in the world, while its average income per worker was one of the lowest, less than 40 cents per day. Capitalists extracted high sugar and garment profits from the islands, while thousands of workers were unemployed. Earning less than subsistence wages, garment workers were being evicted from their houses because they could not afford the rent. Disillusioned with the promises of U.S. control, growing numbers joined a revolutionary movement for political independence, under the leadership of Pedro Albizu Campos and his Nationalist Party.[49]

Puerto Rican women remember the years before World War II as particularly difficult. In a recent interview, Mayor Ofelia Torres de Meléndez described the town of Orocovis in this period: "In 1941...men and women would bathe in the creeks. There was no water system. People would sell water for two cents a big can. We had no hospitals—no roads, bridges, running water."[50] Survival was particularly difficult for single mothers. As one woman whose mother lived through those times explained:

> At that time women who had a problem, who had left their husbands, the majority became prostitutes, right? Because they had no choice. If they were very young, they didn't want them working in families [as domestic servants] because they fell in love with the husband. And since they couldn't find work, those women went to sin because they didn't have any schooling.[51]

The 'Populares,' Fomento, and Operation Bootstrap: Colonial Economic Development

In the face of Puerto Rico's economic crisis of the 1930s and the growing independence movement, the U.S. government brought a new development plan to Puerto Rico through its 1941 appointee, Governor Tugwell. The plan called for developing Puerto Rico's economic infrastructure in order to attract more U.S. industry. A government agency established in 1942, the Puerto Rican Development Corporation (called *Fomento* in Puerto Rico), created public corporations to provide basic services—electricity, water, roads, and sewage—financing these activities with taxes on Puerto Rican rum sales to the United States. The peasants were to be won over to this plan (and out of the independence movement) by promises of land and by an agriculture extension service to provide training, seeds, and other assistance.[52]

In this planning, U.S. colonial administrators collaborated with a burgeoning Puerto Rican political movement, the *Partido Popular Democrático* (Popular Democratic Party, PPD), led by charismatic Luis Muñoz Marín. The party mobilized small landowners and the displaced peasantry: its symbol was a peasant with a straw hat and its motto promised "Bread, Land, and Freedom." On a wave of popular support for change, the PPD won the 1940 and 1944 elections and succeeded in making Muñoz Marín the island's first popularly elected governor.[53]

However, by 1947, the program for independent Puerto Rican economic development had been transformed into "Operation Bootstrap," a new invitation to U.S. capital to "develop" the island. European American economist Richard Weisskopf described how the strategy of integrated agricultural development and state-owned factories was replaced in the 1950s by:

> ...a return to the familiar colonial plantation model of the nine-teenth and early twentieth centuries, in which the foreigner owns and operates the factory while the local elite oversees the workers and overlooks the foreigner. The true genius of Puerto Rico in the 1950s and 1960s was to extend this model from agriculture into industry in the face of all the conventional wisdoms of the times...All during this process, the old elites have retained their position in Puerto Rico. The political dynasties that served the Spanish in the nineteenth century as autonomists or annexationists ...have survived to serve the Americans in the twentieth century as commonwealthers or statehooders...[54]

The peasants were sold out as land reform was abandoned and public corporations were dismantled. New U.S. capital was attracted to the island by 10 to 25 years of tax exemptions, low wages (27 percent of the U.S. wage level), rent and building subsidies, and government-insured political stability. More capital flowed into the island when the Cuban revolution repelled U.S. tourists in 1959. Even more attractive to capital was the decline of the Puerto Rican labor movement under a combination of pressures, including internal divisions in the unions, a rise in the number of marginal and unemployed workers, the incorporation of the Socialist Party into the PPD, the 1947 application of the Taft-Hartley Act (which forbade solidarity strikes) to Puerto Rico, and the arrival of pro-business U.S. labor organizers.[55]

Plans for political independence were also dropped by some Puerto Rican leaders. Muñoz Marín, who at first had sought independence for the island, opted instead for making Puerto Rico a United States "Common-wealth," an entity with some independent power over its own affairs, but still under the power of the U.S. government. Disenchanted *independentistas* broke away from the PPD in 1946 and founded the *Partido Independentista Puertorriqueño* (Puerto Rican Independence Party, or PIP). Women's polit-ical participation spanned across the party spectrum, including the more militant left, where Albizu Campos and the Nationalists continued their armed opposition to all forms of U.S. colonialism. Blanca Canales was a leader in the Nationalist revolt in 1950, and Lolita Lebrón was part of a small group of Nationalists who attacked the U.S. House of Representatives in 1954; both were imprisoned.[56]

Under Operation Bootstrap, the Puerto Rican economy was dramati-cally transformed. Between 1940 and 1970, agricultural employment fell, manufacturing employment tripled, and the value of manufacturing output rose from $120 million to over $1 billion. Per capita output rose from $118 to $1,425. The number of automobiles increased 20 times and telephones 17 times. Illiteracy fell sharply and by 1970, most of the population had at least an elementary education. With better health care and sanitation, life expectancy grew from 41 years in 1930 to 72 years in 1970.[57]

Women's employment patterns shifted dramatically because of Operation Bootstrap (see Table 8-1). As more and more men were drawn into factory jobs, working women's share of manufacturing fell from 67 percent in 1930 to 49 percent in 1970. Women left domestic work in droves; the share of employed women doing domestic work fell from 28 percent to 5 percent between 1930 and 1970. The main growth sectors for women were clerical and professional: the share of women workers in clerical jobs grew from 2 to 23 percent, while professionals grew from 5 to 19 percent.[58]

But there was a seamy underside to Operation Bootstrap. Overall employment in Puerto Rico grew very little. In the 1950s, employment actually fell by 0.7 percent per year, and then grew in the 1960s by about 2.3 percent per year. The growth in manufacturing employment was unable to absorb the thousands of workers pushed out of agriculture (agricultural employment dropped by 78 percent between 1940 and 1974). As a result, vast numbers of Puerto Ricans were forced to migrate to the United States in search of work. The History Task Force of the Center for Puerto Rican Studies estimates that almost 1 million Puerto Ricans (nearly 40 percent of the 1965 population) were "siphoned out" of the Puerto Rican economy between 1950 and 1965, if the migrants' offspring are included in the count. High unemployment rates (averaging from 12 to 15 percent through the 1970s) made survival difficult for those who stayed on the island, and were reflected in a large drop in the formal labor force, defined as people either employed or actively looking for work. For Puerto Rican men, the labor force participation rate fell from 79 percent in 1940 to 55 percent in 1970; women's rate fell from 25 to 23 percent. Because men's labor force participation rate fell faster, and men's unemployment rate was higher than women's, women grew from one-quarter of all workers in 1930 to almost one-third in the 1970s.[59]

Poverty and inequality were widespread. One-fifth of the population was receiving emergency food aid in 1969. Economic inequality was extreme: the top 9 percent of Puerto Rican families received 40 percent of total family income, while the poorest 25 percent made do with only 3 percent. Ligia Vazquez de Rodriguez summed up Puerto Rico's economic woes in 1971:

> In sum, 5.4 percent of the total population has the richness of the country, 45 percent has malnutrition and for every working person, there are 4.5 persons depending upon him, who are unemployed. Thirteen percent of the population is unemployed, which includes one of every four persons between the ages of 18 and 24 who are

actively seeking work. Many more are underemployed or do not continue to look for a job after having lost all hope of finding one.[60]

If migration was one solution to the large numbers of Puerto Ricans rendered "surplus" by Operation Bootstrap, the other was reducing population growth. The colonial government put a very aggressive sterilization program into effect in the 1960s and 1970s, sending a small army of health workers around Puerto Rico to tout the benefits of *la operación* (sterilization). The government's high-pressure techniques included telling women that the sterilization operation was easily reversible (it isn't). The techniques succeeded, partly because they coincided with women's desires to take control of their reproduction. By 1948, an estimated 7 percent of women over 15 had been sterilized; by 1954, the share had risen to 17 percent of those over 20; and by the mid-1960s, a full third of Puerto Rican women were sterilized. U.S. pharmaceutical companies also tested birth-control pills on Puerto Rican women during the 1950s. The 1956 tests on 132 women resulted in three deaths, none of which were investigated.[61]

The colonial invasion of women's bodies was matched by a military invasion of the country. In the 1960s, the United States expanded its military bases in Puerto Rico to occupy 13 percent of Puerto Rican territory. Counting the military, the CIA, the FBI, and the local police force, there was one policeperson for every 28 residents in 1970. If all else failed, the threat of force would keep the impoverished Puerto Rican population under control.[62]

Puerto Rican Migrants to the United States and the U.S. Puerto Rican Community, World War II Through 1970

After World War II, Puerto Ricans were again pushed off the island by high unemployment rates and pulled into the United States, where the economy was booming and there was a shortage of low-wage labor. Puerto Ricans who travelled to the United States in the post-World War II period reported that the wages in their first U.S. job averaged twice as much as they had received at their last job in Puerto Rico. After rapid migration in the 1950s, migration slowed slightly but persisted. By 1970, one-third of all Puerto Ricans were living in the United States.[63]

U.S. growers recruited Puerto Rican men in large numbers to solve the World War II labor shortage. Puerto Ricans were desirable workers because they were known as excellent farmers and would accept low wages in their desperate economic straits. As a result, beginning in 1948, formal contracts for migrant farm workers were negotiated between growers and the Commonwealth of Puerto Rico. Although the contract was an agreement between the grower, the Commonwealth, and the farmworker, farmworkers had no say in these negotiations. Contracts did not provide the workers with any basic protections such as overtime pay or grievance procedures, nor did they promise adequate food, housing, or health care. Many migrants were sugar workers, seasonally unemployed in Puerto Rico during the peak of the growing season in the United States. Almost all were married men who left their families on the island. In 1948, approximately 5,000 came on contract to work in 14 states; by 1973, about 14,000 were under contract and another 60,000 were working without a formal employment contract. They worked "sugar beets in Michigan, tobacco in Connecticut, garden crops in New Jersey, potatoes in Long Island, and a range of other crops from Massachusetts to Illinois." [64]

While many workers returned to Puerto Rico at the end of the season, others stayed in the United States, sent for their wives and families, and established new Puerto Rican *colonias*. One such wife, Doña Sucha, told of her arrival in Waltham, Massachusetts in 1958:

> ...my husband's cousin who worked on a tomato farm in Lexington got a job for my husband in the same place. My husband decided to take the opportunity since at that time the working situation in Puerto Rico was bad. Ten months after my husband was established he sent for me and we moved to Waltham...Later my husband, searching for something better, began working in a metal factory...after 1960 when many of the neighbors and their families from the town where we lived in Orocovis came... I had approximately 100 persons living off and on with us. I remember opening the door at 11:00 P.M. and at 2:00 A.M. in the morning to people who were arriving, with their suitcases, from Puerto Rico. [65]

The racism Puerto Rican migrants faced within the United States was exacerbated by employers' actions. Typically, two-thirds of recruited farmworkers remained in the area after the harvest was over and the growers had pocketed their profits. Anglo taxpayers in the communities in which these now unemployed farmworkers lived were left with the burden of providing them with jobs or subsidies, while the growers, exempted from unemployment insurance laws, escaped all responsibility. [66]

During the 1950s and 1960s, Puerto Rican migrants to urban areas continued to be drawn into low-wage jobs in the service sector, taking on work as waiters, kitchen helpers, or hospital workers, and into low-wage light manufacturing jobs, especially in the garment industry. Rodriguez argues that without the low-wage labor of Puerto Rican women, the New York garment industry would never have stayed the "garment capital of the world" during this period. Single Puerto Rican women were also recruited as domestics by agencies in New York, Chicago, and Florida. As a result of their need for income and the presence of plentiful (if low-wage) job

Table 8-2

Occupational Distribution of U.S. Puerto Rican Women Workers,
1960-1980

	1960	1970	1980
Agriculture	0.3	0.3	0.4
Manufacturing	69.3	43.2	29.1
Private Household Service	1.2	1.0	0.7
Service (not Private Household)	7.3	13.5	14.4
Sales	2.8	3.9	8.0
Clerical	13.9	29.7	31.9
Professional & Technical	4.0	7.1	10.9
Managerial, Administrative, & Official	1.2	1.5	4.6

NOTES: Totals do not always sum to 100 because of rounding. Manufacturing includes craft and transportation workers; agriculture includes mining, fishing, and forestry; managerial, administrative, & official includes some self-employment, and excludes farm managers. For a full listing of occupational categories included, see Appendix B. For a discussion of comparability problems between Census years, see Appendix D.
SOURCES: See Appendix A.

opportunities, the labor force participation rate for U.S. Puerto Rican women in 1950 was 39 percent, compared to 28 percent for Anglo women.[67]

Over the next 20 years, however, the number of jobs in garment and other light manufacturing work declined sharply, particularly in New York City, where over half of Puerto Ricans lived. This decline, as shown by Puerto Rican analysts Rosemary Santana Cooney and Alice Colón, was the major cause of a sharp drop in Puerto Rican women's labor force participation rates—to 36 percent in 1960 and 32 percent in 1970—at a time when rates were climbing for all other groups of women.[68]

Table 8-2 shows the occupational distribution of employed Puerto Rican women in the United States between 1960 and 1980. Between 1960 and 1970, the share in manufacturing jobs dropped by over one-third; employment in professional, service, and clerical jobs grew, but these sectors were unable to absorb all the displaced factory workers. Most striking was the increase in the share of workers in clerical employment, which more than doubled to comprise almost 30 percent of U.S. Puerto Rican women workers in 1970. Relative to island Puerto Rican women, a larger share of U.S.-based women workers were employed in manufacturing and clerical and a smaller share (less than half that on the island) in managerial and professional work.

The 1960s and early-1970s were also a time of political ferment for U.S. Puerto Ricans. By this time, the urban Puerto Rican community included both recent migrants and a substantial second generation of U.S.-born Puerto Ricans. The latter, argues activist Pablo Guzmán, were radicalized by growing up in the *barrio* amidst high poverty rates, job discrimination, and low pay. Between 1969 and 1973, they launched a series of radical movements for power and self-determination that paralleled the Black- and Red-Power movements, in groups including the Young Lords, the Puerto Rican Socialist Party, *El Comité* (The Committee), and the Puerto Rican Students' Union. Puerto Rican participation was also crucial in the formation and expansion of Local 1199, a militant union representing mainly Black and Puerto Rican hospital workers that became national in 1969.[69]

The Decline of the Formal Labor Force in Puerto Rico after 1970

The early-1970s were a time of recession in the United States and of depression in Puerto Rico, where the recession combined with several long-term economic trends to generate devastatingly high unemployment. Agricultural employment continued to decline precipitously from 10 percent of total employment in 1970 to 5 percent in 1984. Puerto Rican manufacturing wages, which had averaged half of U.S. wages in 1970, rose relative to those in the United States, particularly when U.S. minimum wage laws were applied to Puerto Rico in the mid-1970s. This contributed to a third trend: slow growth in manufacturing jobs, both because of higher wages and because of a related shift out of labor-intensive industries into capital-intensive industries such as petrochemicals. While there was some new investment, particularly in pharmaceuticals, electronics, and scientific instruments, non-agricultural employment grew at an annual rate of only 1 percent per year between 1970 and 1984. High unemployment in the United States, particularly in urban manufacturing, restricted the migration "safety valve": annual net emigration in the 1970s slowed to 5,000 from a level of 17,000 in the 1960s. In some years, such as 1971-72 and 1975-76, more Puerto Ricans returned to the island than left. However, the Puerto Rican economy had so deteriorated by the early-1980s that over 30,000 Puerto Ricans left the island yearly between 1981 and 1983.[70]

Very slow job growth, along with a growing population, created a sharp rise in the numbers of unemployed workers and a decline in the share of the total population which was employed, as shown in Table 8-3. Between 1970 and 1985, the number of Puerto Ricans over 16 years of age grew by 653,000, while the number employed grew only by 63,000. The overall unemployment rate almost doubled to 21 percent. The percentage of the

Table 8-3

Labor Force Participation, Unemployment, and
Employment-to-Population Ratios in Puerto Rico,
by Gender, 1970-1985

	Labor Force Participation Rate		Unemploy- ment Rate		Employment-to- Population Ratio			Women's Share of Total Employment
	Men	Women	Men	Women	Men	Women	M-W	
1970-1	71	28	12	10	63	25	38	31
1975-6	64	27	21	15	51	23	28	34
1980-1	60	28	21	13	48	24	24	36
1984-5	58	28	25	17	44	23	21	38

NOTES: The employment-to-population ratio is the number employed divided by the total population over 16. M-W in table heads means men's minus women's.
SOURCE: Estado Libre Asociado de Puerto Rico, Departamento del Trabajo y Recursos Humanos, "Empleo y Desempleo en Puerto Rico," Informe Especial Numero E-47, Tables 17 and 18.

total population over 16 which was employed fell from 43 percent in 1970-71 to only 33 percent in 1984-85. The situation was so bad that, by 1983, over one half of all families were without wage earners.[71]

These economic changes affected men and women differently, as shown in Table 8-3. Employment opportunities decreased most for men because of their concentration in agricultural employment and because manufacturers preferred women over men for their lower wages. The total number of men employed actually *fell* between 1970 and 1985, and in the latter year, only 44 percent of adult men were employed. On the other hand, women's total employment grew by 67,000 during this period. Women's unemployment rates, although high, were substantially lower than men's, and their employment-to-population ratio declined by only two percentage points. As a result, women's share of total employment increased from 31 to 38 percent between 1970 and 1985.[72] The situation would have been even worse had it not been for job growth in the public sector. In 1978, 39 percent of employed Puerto Ricans worked for the Commonwealth (37 percent) or the federal government (2 percent)—compared, for example, to 17 percent of all workers in the United States.[73]

Survival Strategies on the Island: The Informal Sector and Food Stamps

Declining employment opportunities and participation rates in the formal labor force have forced Puerto Ricans to seek other means to survive. Growing numbers of jobless islanders support themselves in what is called "the informal sector" and over half receive federal assistance to purchase food.

Over two-thirds of the Puerto Rican adult population on the island— the 68 percent without formal jobs—now is forced to support itself through informal economic survival activities. These *chiripas* include subsistence production, bartering, occupying land, illegal activities such as crime or drug dealing, and producing goods and services for sale to others. All these activities are unreported to the government, are unregulated, and hence are untaxed—as well as difficult to study. However, one study revealed an extraordinary variety of *chiripas* through which women earn income: teaching art classes, taking in boarders, doing child care, aiding others with childbirth, domestic work, dressmaking and alteration, embroidery, flower arranging, food preparation, making and selling jewelry, tutoring, typing, and teaching piano. Of the women employed in *chiripas,* 67 percent were heads of families, and 79 percent were without a regular full-time job in the formal sector; most worked in their homes. Men's *chiripas* include fishing, fruit and vegetable vending, house construction and repair, carpentry, painting, masonry, plumbing, trucking, gardening, and car-repair work. Puerto Rico's large informal sector helps corporate profits because it reduces the cost of living for workers, who can purchase goods and services cheaply from the informal sector. In addition, the informal sector provides a pool of unorganized workers from which firms can hire temporarily, and thus escape paying Social Security taxes or fringe benefits. This pool of unemployed or informally employed workers also makes union organizing virtually impossible, contributing to the declining unionization rate.[74]

A second result of the decline of formal employment opportunities in Puerto Rico has been growing dependency on federal welfare programs for survival, in particular, on food stamps. Food stamps were introduced in 1975 in the midst of skyrocketing unemployment and poverty, when more than 60 percent of the population was living in poverty. Soon, food stamps became a means of survival for the majority of Puerto Ricans. By 1980, a shocking 58 percent of the population had qualified to receive them. The food stamp program has cost U.S. taxpayers $1 billion per year (although had there been no program, more Puerto Ricans might have migrated to U.S. cities and increased welfare costs there). The food stamp program has also been extremely costly to the Puerto Rican people. It places them in a situation of dependency and financial insecurity (one-fifth of families were cut from the program between 1982 and 1984), reduces their sense of economic power and independence, substantiates to some degree a belief that their country needs the United States and hence needs to remain a colony, and forces their participation in the informal sector for survival.[75]

In his 1985 book, *Factories and Food Stamps*, European American economist Richard Weisskopf suggested an alternative plan for U.S. assistance that would promote Puerto Rican development rather than dependency. U.S. government funds, he argued, should be used to promote Puerto Rican agricultural self-sufficiency by re-employing the half of Puerto Ricans who still live in rural areas on small farms, to help develop an agricultural export sector, and to encourage Puerto Rican industry to use local inputs and sell some of its products locally. Weisskopf predicted that the same number of dollars, used in this way, could raise Puerto Ricans out of unemployment, poverty, and dependency on the United States.

Weisskopf was unable to convince the U.S. Senate Committee on Agriculture to take his plan seriously. Indeed, his plan flies in the face of U.S. corporate interests: the billions of dollars taxpayers spend to provide food stamps actually subsidize U.S. agribusiness and other corporations. Food stamps are spent on U.S. food exports (Puerto Rico was the United States's seventh largest market in 1978), and help subsidize the low-wage labor which keeps U.S. investments in Puerto Rico profitable. In this artificial economy, Puerto Rico imported $50 billion of goods and exported $30 billion between 1970 and 1983, most to and from the United States, receiving $10 billion in new capital investment and about the same amount in transfers (mostly food stamps) from the U.S. government. Investors in Puerto Rico earned a whopping $22.6 billion in profits, according to Weisskopf's calculations, while the Puerto Rican people and U.S. taxpayers footed the bill.[76]

Back in the United States: Unemployment, Low Wages, and Poverty

If the Puerto Rican economy was deteriorating in the 1970s and 1980s, Puerto Ricans who had come to the United States seeking economic security were not doing much better. In 1970, there were approximately 1.4 million Puerto Ricans living in the United States. This number had grown to over 2 million in 1980—about 40 percent of the entire Puerto Rican population— and immigration has sped up since then. Moving back and forth to the United States in search of work has become an important strategy for economic survival for many Puerto Ricans. In 1980, more than half of the migrants to the United States had previously spent time there. Among 1982-83 migrants, 60 percent came to the United States in search of work, while 58 percent of return migrants to the island were doing the same. While most Puerto Rican women in the United States were born in Puerto Rico (in 1976, an estimated 80 percent), 59 percent had been in the United States for 12 or more years.[77]

However, coming to the United States in the 1970s did not bring Puerto Ricans economic security. The recession of 1973-75 combined with longer-term trends to create high unemployment, to lower labor force participation rates, and to keep Puerto Ricans at the bottom of the U.S. racial-class hierarchy. By 1980, the unemployment rate for Puerto Ricans, 11.7 percent, was more than double that of whites. Over one-third of Puerto Rican families lived below the poverty level, 8.5 percentage points higher than the next poorest racial-ethnic group, African Americans, and over five times the non-Latina/o white poverty rate. Per capita income was also the lowest of all major racial-ethnic groups, at only $3,905 in 1980, less than one-half that of non-Hispanic whites. As in Puerto Rico, high percentages received public assistance income for survival: almost 33 percent, compared to 23.5 percent among African Americans and 5.4 percent among non-Latina/o whites.[78]

Education has not provided Puerto Ricans with the opportunity to climb the job market ladder that it has for some groups. Most Puerto Ricans are concentrated in urban ghettos where they are served by poor quality schools. To make things worse, although most young Puerto Ricans learn only Spanish at home, there is little or no bilingual education for them at school. As Luis Fuentes, a former school superintendent of a New York City school, whose students were 73 percent Puerto Rican, 15 percent African American, and 8 percent Chinese, said of his district:

> … eighty-five percent of these youngsters by the time they reach the eighth grade are functional illiterates—three to four years behind grade level in reading. There are those who call these statistics a sign of failure; but if 85 percent of the products of any industry shared a basic characteristic, we would assume that it was the intention of the industry to mark its products with that characteristic….The system is 85 percent *successful*. Illiteracy is its product.[79]

With such poor education, high school drop-out rates are an incredibly high 80 percent. The lack of education is particularly problematic at a time of declining availability of jobs for those with eight or fewer years of schooling. However, some U.S. Puerto Ricans have been able to obtain, either in the United States or on the island, the schooling required for executive, administrative, and managerial occupations: 6 percent of em-

ployed men and 5 percent of employed women worked in these occupations
in 1980. Nevertheless, for Puerto Ricans with education, discrimination
practically erases the benefits: in 1978, the average Puerto Rican college
graduate earned what a non-Puerto Rican high school graduate earned.[80]

The Rise of Female-Headed Households Among U.S. Puerto Ricans

While the proportion of Puerto Rican families maintained by women
has been growing in Puerto Rico (from 16 to 19 percent between 1970 and
1980), rates are much higher and growing faster in the United States, where
35 percent of all Puerto Rican families were female-headed in 1980, more
than double the proportion in 1960. Although some researchers have hy-
pothesized that this high proportion is due to the migration of large numbers
of single-mother families to the United States in order to obtain welfare
benefits, only 6 percent of Puerto Rican families headed by a woman in the
United States were migrants. Some of the reasons for the increasing prevalence of female-headed families include the growing tendency for such
women to live on their own instead of with relatives, and a shortage of Puerto
Rican men in New York (where there were 84 Puerto Rican men for 100
women in 1970).[81]

The economic situation of Puerto Rican single-mother families is
precarious, and has been deteriorating *vis-à-vis* other types of families.
Two-thirds of these households lived in poverty in 1980; three-quarters of
those with children under 18 were poor. Median incomes for Puerto Rican
single-mother families have fallen sharply relative to Puerto Rican husband-
wife families (from 67 percent of their median income in 1960 to only 32
percent in 1980) and relative to non-Latina, white, single-mother families
(from 70 percent of their median income in 1960 to only 43 percent in 1980).[82]

One reason for the worsening economic situation of Puerto Rican
single mothers is a drop in their labor force participation rates. These declined
rapidly between 1960 and 1970, from 53 percent to only 28 percent. Cooney
and Colón argue that low wages and unemployment combined with welfare
programs to create this decline:

> We have already referred to the deteriorating economic opportu-
> nities for Puerto Rican women with low education. These data
> suggest that this decline in job opportunities affected the participa-
> tion of Puerto Rican female family heads more than Puerto Rican
> wives. Female family heads with children have an alternative to
> low-paying jobs that wives with children do not have—welfare.[83]

In addition, single mothers must combine the roles of breadwinner and home giver. This makes labor force participation significantly more difficult than for wives, who can share these responsibilities with their husbands.

Puerto Rican Women Today

Today's Puerto Rican community is split between the island and the United States. Migration back and forth continues, although there is a growing population of second- and third-generation U.S. Puerto Ricans. Three-fifths of Puerto Ricans live on the island, while the remainder live in the United States.

On the island, women's labor force participation rates, while low, are rising (from 23 percent in 1970 to 28 percent in 1985), and women's employment patterns have continued to shift, as shown in Table 8-1. The proportion of employed women who hold manufacturing jobs fell between 1970 and 1980; declines in garment industry employment (from 40,300 in 1973 to 33,900 in 1980), as firms sought cheaper labor elsewhere in the Caribbean or in Asia, were not offset by new jobs in areas such as pharmaceuticals. The proportion of women working in clerical jobs continued to grow, as did the share in managerial and official jobs. Women comprised more than half of the workers in the government sector on the island; a full 43 percent of all employed women worked for the government in 1980.[84]

The female labor force in Puerto Rico is becoming increasingly skilled. In 1980, 18 percent of women over 25 had graduated from college; of women in the labor force, almost half had some college education. While the number of employed women increased by only 24 percent between 1970 and 1980, the number of women doubled in the male-dominated occupations of lawyers and judges, engineers, social and physical scientists, doctors and dentists, managers and administrators, and craft workers.[85]

Overall, however, sex-typing of jobs persists in the Puerto Rican labor market. In 1980, almost one-fifth of women with college degrees were employed as factory operatives, sales persons, office workers, or service workers. Women were overrepresented at least two-fold in the traditionally feminine jobs of nursing, teaching, and private household service, and among health technologists, secretaries, and typists. On the other hand, women had far less than half their labor market share of many white masculine jobs, including engineer, doctor, sales supervisor and proprietor, broker, truck driver, protective service, farming, and construction. Not surprisingly, women's earnings also remained much lower than men's. In 1980, the earnings of women professionals were 63 percent of those of men professionals; for managers, 74 percent; for sales workers, 78 percent; and for service workers, 62 percent.[86]

Feminist organizing has undergone a revival in Puerto Rico, beginning in the early-1970s. Women have organized a government commission for women's affairs, activist groups such as *Feministas en Marcha* (Feminists on the Move) and women's studies programs at the University of Puerto Rico and the Inter-American University. Feminists have placed the issues of rape, spouse abuse, sexual harassment, and sex discrimination in employment in the public eye. Their efforts won the passage, in 1988, of a bill outlawing sexual harassment, and, in 1989, of a sweeping law against domestic violence, including funds for education and violence prevention as well as stricter punishment for offenders. At the same time, feminist researchers have been studying and exposing Puerto Rico's form of sexism, "machismo," and its relationship to U.S. colonialism.[87]

Working-class women are also active in organizing efforts. The *Organización Puertorriqueña de la Mujer Trabajadora* (Puerto Rican Organization of Women Workers) has organized conferences and workshops for working women and publishes a newsletter, "Women on the March." A group of women called Committee to Rescue Our Health has organized in Mayaguez against chemical leaks and other health risks at the Mayaguez Industrial Park, which employs over 4,000 workers, 98 percent of them women. Nurses were key to the successful 1985 campaign to unionize the Pediatric Hospital.[88]

For Puerto Rican women in the United States, the occupational distribution has also been changing, although earnings and incomes remain low and poverty rates are high. We have seen how the decline of garment work depressed Puerto Rican women's labor force participation rates in United States during the 1950s and 1960s (although they remained higher than on the island). Women adjusted to the structural shift in job opportunities by moving out of manufacturing work and into service, sales, and clerical work, as shown in Table 8-2; the share employed in manufacturing fell by more than half between 1960 and 1980, while clerical and service employment more than doubled. Nonetheless, the proportion of employed Puerto Rican women working in manufacturing remained higher than that of women in any other racial-ethnic group.[89]

With these adjustments, U.S. Puerto Rican women's labor force participation rate rose again in 1980 to 40 percent, but remained lower than for any other group other than island Puerto Rican women. High unemployment rates continue to be a major factor discouraging labor force participation; in 1980, U.S. Puerto Rican women's unemployment rates were 13 percent, higher than for any other group of U.S. women. Ruth Zambrana and Marsha Hurst argue that work in manufacturing has also depressed labor force participation rates because of its effects on health. They found that, among

Puerto Rican women who had not worked for at least a year, the main reason given for not being employed was "poor health, illness, or disability."[90] In sum, structural unemployment and poor job opportunities, exacerbated by low educational attainment, are still the major factors that discourage Puerto Rican women from participating in the labor force.[91]

There has been some progress of U.S. Puerto Rican women into higher-paid, higher-status jobs. The share employed in managerial and professional work rose from 5 to 16 percent between 1960 and 1980, when there were over 1,000 Puerto Rican women engineers or doctors in the United States. However, poor educational opportunities continue to hamper advancement. Only 5 percent of U.S. Puerto Ricans over the age of 25 had four or more years of college (compared to 18 percent of island Puerto Ricans), and only 39 percent were high school graduates, levels lower than any other U.S. racial-ethnic group other than Chicanas/os. This lack of education, compounded by the effects of discrimination, accounts for the fact that a much smaller share of U.S. Puerto Rican women (16 percent) are in managerial and professional jobs than island Puerto Rican women (27 percent). Selective migration also reinforces this result, since Puerto Rican professional and managerial women are less likely to migrate to the United States than women further down the occupational hierarchy. Most white-collar jobs for U.S. Puerto Rican women are clerical; almost one-third are employed in this sector.[92]

Figure 8-1 summarizes the job distribution of Puerto Rican women workers across labor market sectors in 1980. On the island and on the continental United States, Puerto Rican women workers are more likely to be found in the secondary sector than in the primary sector, facing a distribution which is similar to that of Anglo women. However, U.S. Puerto Rican women in the primary sector are far less likely than European American women or island Puerto Rican women to hold jobs in the prestigious upper tier of the primary sector, and are more concentrated in the upper tier of the secondary sector.

In the United States, local Puerto Rican feminist groups, such as Boston's *Comite de Mujeres Puertorriqueñas* (Committee of Puerto Rican Women) and Connecticut's *Mujeres Latinoamericanas de New Haven* (Latin American Women of New Haven, or MULANEH), as well as the National Conference of Puerto Rican Women, have organized around a broad variety of issues, from educational and employment discrimination to Puerto Rico's political status and support of the island's political prisoners. While criticizing the sexist behavior of Puerto Rican men, many of these women are, at the same time, working through mixed organizations to better the social and economic position of Puerto Ricans in the United States and on the island

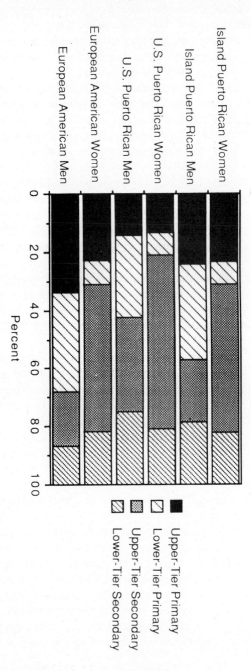

Figure 8-1: The Distribution of Island Puerto Rican, U.S. Puerto Rican, and European American Workers across Labor Market Segments, by Gender, 1980

NOTES: See Table 10-5 for a listing of the occupations in each labor market segment. See Table 10-6 for the actual percentages employed in each segment.

SOURCE: 1980 Census; see Appendix A.

and, increasingly, these organizations are integrating feminist issues into their platforms.

One major area of feminist concern and activism has been sterilization. As in Puerto Rico, U.S. Puerto Rican women have fallen victim to high-pressure sterilization programs. MULANEH found in 1979 that 44 percent of the Puerto Rican women in New Haven, Connecticut had been sterilized; a study in Hartford found a rate of over 51 percent. New York *puertorriqueñas*, organized in the Committee to End Sterilization Abuse (CESA, which means "stop" in Spanish), argued that sterilization is a form of genocide, and forced public health officials to more fully inform patients about the procedure, give them time to make up their minds, and require that they sign consent forms.[93]

Yo misma fui mi ruta (I was my own path), declared Julia de Burgos in the early-1900s. Puerto Ricans have been buffeted by strong external forces, from four centuries of Spanish colonialism to almost a century of U.S. control. Their hard work and low living standards have enriched many U.S. investors, while eventually bringing many Puerto Ricans a modicum of economic well-being, in the form of good schools, roads, and rising wages. However, as long as Puerto Rico remains a source of cheap labor, the possibility for wage increases is limited; as wages rise, firms move their plants away from Puerto Rico to countries where they can pay workers even less. The result of this dependent economic development has been high unemployment and poverty rates, low wages, and food stamps. Unemployment has fueled continual migration to the United States, but even there Puerto Rican women have faced job loss, low wages, and discrimination. Yes, Puerto Rican women have been their own paths, and these have, for the most part, been paths of economic hardship, paths which have sent them to the cold streets of New York City and back to their tropical island, paths which have come up against both Anglo racism and Puerto Rican sexism. Yet *puertorriqueñas* maintain a distinctive Puerto Rican spirit which informs their struggle for survival and self-determination.

Part III: Transforming Women's Works

Chapter 9

THE GROWTH OF WAGE WORK

The four centuries of U.S. economic history we have studied have been a period of dynamic economic growth. Not only have the population, production of goods and services, and standard of living increased greatly, but the ways in which people work and fill their needs have been transformed. This rapid process of quantitative and qualitative economic change and growth has both built on and in turn influenced the gender, racial-ethnic, and class hierarchies of the pre-industrial, colonial economy. The types of work people perform and the distribution of work among people have changed radically, and all these changes have been shaped by racial-ethnic and gender processes.

From the colonial economy through the second half of the nineteenth century, women and men participated in a variety of non-capitalist labor systems. By the middle of the nineteenth century, wage labor in capitalist enterprises became more prominent. However, people of different racial-ethnic groups and genders did not enter wage labor evenly; furthermore, to this day, women of all racial-ethnic groups are far more likely to perform unpaid household work than men. In the next two chapters we explore, in very broad strokes, the ways in which capitalist economic development, race-ethnicity, and gender have affected the organization and distribution of work. In this chapter we focus on the growing predominance of wage labor among women of all racial-ethnic groups and on the changing distribution of paid and unpaid work between the genders. Then, in Chapter 10, we look at the transformation of women's wage work over time, examining the ways in which the racial-ethnic and gender hierarchy in the labor market has been both reproduced and challenged.

The Diversity of Women's Works in the Pre-Capitalist Period

In the pre-capitalist period, women participated in a variety of labor systems, as illustrated in Figure 9-1. From colonial times through the nineteenth century, most American Indians engaged in self-sufficient production, although nations varied enormously in the ways that they provided for their material needs. Nations organized work in many different ways, some of which were sexually egalitarian. They interacted to some degree with the emerging market system, trading with one another and with white settlers, but few performed wage labor. Much of their energy was consumed by the struggle for survival against the invading Europeans.

In this period, most free whites participated in a "family economy," in which husbands, wives, and children worked together. Families provided for many of their needs through their own labors, producing much of their own food, housing and furniture, clothing, and health care. However, even in the earliest colonial times, there was some production for the market. Settlers in the Northeast sold provisions to newcomers; family farmers produced cash crops or sold surplus butter and eggs; craftsworkers and artisans manufactured guns, silver, and furniture; and merchants sold imported products, from cloth to spices.

While these European American families were free in the sense of not being enslaved or indentured, the social relations within these families were far from egalitarian. The husband/father was the accepted household head, empowered to command his wife and children and to represent their interests in the larger society. Daughters were commonly forced into arranged marriages in which they lost their property rights, while children could be bound out to work for other families if their parents wished.

During the pre-capitalist period, production for the market was hampered by a labor shortage. While white families had access to the labor of their members, there was little labor available for hire on the market. Native Americans resisted wage labor for whites, and most free whites could find land (taken from Native Americans) to farm for themselves. As a result, those whites with wealth or large landholdings who wished to employ others developed systems of labor—indentured servitude, slavery, and contract labor—into which they imported workers from Europe, Africa, and Asia, respectively. These labor systems were less free than either family production or wage labor: slaves were literally owned by their masters, indentured servants were bound to their masters for years, and contract laborers could not quit during the term of their contracts.

A somewhat similar combination of labor systems existed in colonial Mexico and Puerto Rico. In Mexico, Spanish colonizers employed Native Americans and *mestizas/os* under the labor systems of *encomienda*, *repartimiento*, and the *hacienda*. Some family farm production also existed. In Spain's Puerto Rican colony, Spanish-owned plantations and mines utilizing African and indigenous slaves co-existed with small family farms, while the *libreta* system forced the free but landless into wage labor for the

Figure 9-1: From Non-Capitalist To Capitalist Labor Systems

FAMILY SYSTEM[1]
Owners/Workers: household heads, mostly adult males
Workers: wives, children, apprentices, indentured servants

(European American, free African American, and some Puerto Rican Chicanas/os, and Asian families)

PLANTATION SYSTEM
Owners/Non-workers: large landowners, mostly men and their families (European American)[2]

Workers: indentured servants (European American)[3], slaves (African American), contract laborers (Asian, Puerto Rican)

HACIENDA SYSTEM
Owners/Non-workers: large landowners, mostly men, and their families (Spanish origin)
Workers: peon families (mestiza/o, American Indian, Chicana/o)

TRIBAL SYSTEMS
(Different American Indian nations)

CAPITALIST SYSTEM[4]
Owners: capitalists, mostly men (mostly European American)

Workers: wage laborers in primary, secondary, and informal sectors (all racial – ethnic groups), and unpaid reproductive workers (women of all racial – ethnic groups)

[1] Family-owned farms with a few slaves, and sharecroppers and tenant farmers, exhibited characteristics of both the family system and the plantation system.

[2] In some rare instances, people of color had slaves, such as some American Indians in the "Five Civilized Tribes" and some free African Americans.

[3] In early colonial times, before the slave system was established, African Americans also worked as indentured servants.

[4] Vestiges of the previous labor systems survive alongside the capitalist system, such as family businesses and farms and tribal systems, while some agricultural employers subject their workers to plantation-like conditions. New forms of non-family self-employment also coexist with capitalism.

landed. Relations within families, constructed according to Spanish custom and law, were male-dominated.

This diversity of systems of labor meant that a woman's work was generally more similar to that of men of her racial-ethnic group and class position, who were employed within the same system of labor, than it was to that of women in other systems and classes. Most American Indian women engaged in subsistence production, with few ties to the market. Mexican women worked with their husbands and children on family farms, or as peons on the *hacienda*. Most European American women worked with their families in farming or small businesses, although many began their lives in the United States as indentured servants. African American women were almost all enslaved, and most worked in the fields alongside African American men. Asian women worked with Asian men as contract laborers in agriculture, in family businesses or farms, or as indentured or enslaved prostitutes. However, life among the upper classes had some similarities across racial-ethnic groups: wives and daughters of the wealthy pursued leisure and supervised large staffs of servants to maintain and display their husbands' and fathers' social status. In addition to these kinds of labor, women in all racial-ethnic groups bore the major responsibility for the reproductive work of rearing children, cooking, and cleaning for their families. However, as we have seen, the nature of their reproductive work also depended upon the system of labor under which they and their families worked. Immigration restrictions, the reservation system, and forced labor systems produced enormous differences in the conditions of women's reproductive work. Furthermore, childbearing and childrearing served different economic functions within these different systems: in chattel slavery, it increased the wealth of the master, while in the family economy, it expanded the family's workforce. Finally, wealthy women assigned most of their reproductive work to propertyless women who worked for them under one of the forced labor systems.

The rise of capitalism drew people out of pre-capitalist labor systems and into wage work unevenly, depending upon gender, race-ethnicity, marital status, and class. In this chapter, we examine two aspects of this transition. First, we compare the movement out of non-wage labor forms into wage labor in the nineteenth and twentieth centuries across racial-ethnic groups. Then, we look across racial-ethnic groups and classes at the ways in which families participating in the wage labor system allocated responsibility for paid and unpaid work between the sexes.

The Uneven Movement of Racial-Ethnic Groups into Wage Labor

As capitalism overtook the family economy and the plantation system, wage labor increasingly replaced both independent forms of labor, especially family businesses and farms, and less free forms such as slavery and peonage. This process is illustrated in Figure 9-1. In 1780, approximately 64 percent of the non-native population lived in families engaged in self-employment, 20 percent were slaves, and only 16 percent were wage workers or indentured servants. By 1890, there were twice as many people working for wages or salaries as there were self-employed; by 1970, there were nine times as many people working for wages or salaries as there were self-employed.[1] However, this transition to wage labor was both very drawn out and very uneven. There have even been some reversals of the process in the post-World War II period, as African Americans and Puerto Ricans have been increasingly marginalized from the wage labor force and pushed into the informal and underground economies.

Among whites, the rise of wage labor involved both the proletarianization (loss of property and movement into working for capitalists) of large numbers of independent family producers, and the elimination of indentured servitude, which occurred for whites by the beginning of the nineteenth century. While homesteading of western lands continued through the early twentieth century, family farms began to decline as land was exhausted, as large wealthy farmers wiped out their smaller competitors, or simply when better standards of living could be had in the urban, wage-labor sector. Indeed, one of the earliest groups of factory workers, the textile mill workers of the 1820s and 1830s, were drawn from the daughters of failing small farmers in the Northeast. European American men who had made their livings as independent craft producers were increasingly unable to compete with factory production, and were driven into the wage labor force. European immigrants in the second half of the nineteenth century—most often peasants displaced from the land or fleeing persecution in their countries of origin—were increasingly channelled into factories and domestic service for wages when they arrived in the United States.

For most African Americans, the movement into wage labor entailed moving up from the unfree labor form of slavery through the intermediary stages of sharecropping and tenant farming, which afforded a mixture of self-employment and unfree, even semi-feudal conditions. When slavery ended in 1863, it was at first replaced by a contract labor system. This quickly gave way to sharecropping and tenant farming, organized as family production but controlled by white landowners through the mechanisms of debt-peonage and white political and legal dominance. Concentrated in the South,

Blacks were barred from most wage labor other than domestic service for whites; the latter accounted for over 40 percent of the gainful employment of Black women in 1900. However, many Blacks were able to escape economic entrapment in the South by migrating to the industrial cities of the North when wartime labor shortages allowed Blacks to break into factory and office work in large numbers. However, deindustrialization in the 1970s and 1980s has drained urban Black ghettos of employment opportunities, pushing many Blacks into the underground economy.

For Asians, the movement into non-contract wage labor was also slower than for whites. Beginning in the 1850s, Asians labored under contract in Hawaii and in the United States, on plantations, railroads, farms, and in brothels. Although they comprised a significant portion of the early California wage labor force, their movement into wage labor was slowed by the organized hostility of white workers. Asians were driven out of many areas and jobs and confined to service, migrant, and seasonal work. Some Asians responded by setting up family farms and other small businesses. Not until the labor shortage of World War II did Chinese and Filipinas/os break into a wider range of occupations; at the same time, the internment of the ethnic Japanese transformed them from family farmers to urban wage workers. However, family businesses have remained a refuge for the wave of new Asian immigrants in the post-World War II period.

For Native Americans, the destruction of tribal life was the first step in the movement towards wage labor. The policies which contributed to this destruction included the placement of children in boarding schools, the allotment program of the late-1800s, and the Urban Relocation Program of the 1950s and 1960s. As tribal life disintegrated, many American Indians became property owners, producing for the market on small farms and ranches, but this land was increasingly lost to white settlers and to agricultural, mining, and railroad companies. As a result, some American Indians entered the urban labor force, while others remained on reservations, surviving through a combination of subsistence and wage labor.

The movement of Chicanas/os into the wage labor force began in the second half of the nineteenth century and coincided with the takeover of Mexican lands by Anglos. While the timing was different in different parts of the Southwest, the process was similar. The *ricos* intermarried with Anglos or lost their lands. The *pobres,* small landholders and peons, were driven into the wage labor force, where they were confined to menial and low-paid jobs such as domestic service, garment work, and migrant farm work.

In Puerto Rico, slavery was abolished in 1873, and family farm production declined rapidly after the U.S. takeover of the island in 1898, creating a landless agricultural wage labor force (mostly men) and an urban workforce (disproportionately women). By 1930, women made up two-thirds of manufacturing workers. High unemployment rates on the island led Puerto Ricans to migrate to the United States in search of work, some as agricultural contract labor, others as factory and sweatshop workers. In the post-World War II period, persistent and growing unemployment has forced island families into the informal sector; many depend for survival upon food stamps provided by the U.S. government.

While the movement into wage labor has occurred differently for the various racial-ethnic groups, once families became involved in wage labor they created similar sexual divisions of labor. In the remainder of this chap·ər, we examine the changes in the sexual divisions of labor within families under capitalism, dividing the capitalist period into two historical stages. In the first stage, lasting from approximately 1830 to 1930, men and a significant share of single women concentrated on wage work, while most married women focused on unpaid, reproductive work. In the second stage, from 1930 to the present, the majority of married women moved into wage work but retained responsibility for unpaid reproductive work.

Breadwinners and Working Girls: The Sexual Division of Labor in the Family Under Capitalism, 1830-1930

As families began to participate in capitalist economic relations, the labor which they had performed producing goods and services for the market as slaves, peons, or workers in a family business was replaced by wage labor for capitalist firms. In contrast, the family's reproductive work—childbearing, childrearing, feeding, clothing, and caring for family members—stayed within the sphere of the family, and became more separate and distinct from market-oriented work. While most wage work took place in factories and offices, reproductive work took place in the home. This separation of location was accompanied by a differentiation of working conditions. Wage labor was paid, reproductive labor was not (except indirectly, through the pooling of income within the family). And while the wage laborer worked under the direction of a "boss," reproductive labor was done independently, if ultimately under the authority of the household head.

Although the relationship between productive and reproductive labor was changing in this way, the sexual division of labor between the two did not change—if anything, it became more extreme. As before, mothers in all racial-ethnic groups continued to bear the main responsibility for reproductive work. The new development under capitalism was that mothers were largely excluded from market-oriented work as the latter became wage labor. Thus, wage labor developed as the province of husbands, and to a lesser extent, of sons and daughters.

Part of the explanation for this new sexual division of labor was the shared social view that females, as the sex biologically able to bear children, were also automatically more qualified for other reproductive tasks. Married women's exclusion from wage labor "naturally" followed, since most wage work took place outside the home and was difficult to combine with child care. However, racial-ethnic and class processes also played important roles in constructing and differentiating the sexual divisions of labor within families.

Among upper- and middle-class European Americans, the nineteenth-century cult of domesticity developed and formalized a division of labor in which husbands were property owners and professionals while wives were homemakers and mothers. The ideology of domesticity elevated the status of these women in the home as nurturers of children and civilizers of men; wives stayed in the home to enjoy leisure, aided by servants, or entered the public and political sphere to participate in volunteer social homemaking activities. The lives of wealthy African American, Mexican American, and Asian American women appear to have followed a similar domestic ideal of womanhood.

At the same time, some highly educated single women interpreted the cult of domesticity as a call to enter the women's professions of teaching, social work, and nursing. For many, these vocations were desirable precursors to full-time homemaking, while for others, they served as lifelong alternatives to homemaking. Some women, particularly women of color, saw these vocations as part and parcel of a commitment to the liberation of the poor and oppressed. Even if they quit their professions upon marriage, many followed active careers as volunteer social homemakers in the late nineteenth and early twentieth centuries, dedicated to helping their poorer sisters.

For the poor and working-class majority of the population, married men also tended to take on greater responsibility for wage work during this period, while women performed the main share of unpaid household work. For these women, however, the work involved was very different from that undertaken by the wives of capitalists and highly paid professionals. The vast majority of poor and working-class wives subscribed to the domestic ideal in the sense that they did not take up wage work outside the home. But domesticity had a very different meaning for women without class privilege, who did not stay at home to cultivate their minds or contemplate lofty notions of motherhood. In urban areas, household work in crowded tenements without running water or electricity and, of course, without servants, was arduous and time consuming.[2] In rural areas, these problems were compounded by isolation from neighbors and stores. Furthermore, most of the paid jobs available to poor and working-class women were low-paid, and

Table 9-1

Gainful Employment Rates, by Gender and
Racial-Ethnic Group, 1920

	Women	Men	Men/Women
American Indian	11.5	58.4	5.1
European American	19.5	77.9	4.0
African American	38.9	81.1	2.1
Japanese American	25.9	87.8	3.4
Chinese American	12.5	87.0	7.0
Filipina/o American	11.6	96.5	8.3
Island Puerto Rican	18.9	72.0	3.8

NOTES: Rates are for persons 10 years of age and older. Data on Puerto Ricans in the
United States and Chicanas/os are not available for 1920. European Americans and African Americans include Latinas/os and mixed American Indians classified as whites
and Blacks, respectively. The American Indian data are probably underestimated
since the 1920 Census undercounted the native population, particularly those of
mixed heritage (see Fifteenth Census of the United States, 1930, *The Indian Population of the United States and Alaska*, 199-200). Data for Filipina/o Americans only include those living in Hawaii; data for Japanese and Chinese Americans include both
Hawaii and the continental United States.
SOURCES: See Appendix A.

many were hazardous factory jobs or servile domestic jobs. Since most paid
work was located outside the home, mothers in the workforce were forced
to leave their children unattended unless a neighbor or family member could
be found to look after them.

Hence, among the poor and working classes, the majority of married
women of all racial-ethnic groups focused their efforts on reproductive work,
which included saving money and doing odd jobs for pay in their own
homes. One researcher estimated that in poor urban households in the 1840s
and 1850s, the money a homemaker saved her family by scavenging, bargain
shopping, caring for her own children, doing her own housecleaning, and
taking in boarders or performing odd jobs was more than double what she
could have earned in the formal, paid labor force.[3] Freed Black women
especially sought to avoid wage work, since domesticity allowed them to
escape the racial and sexual exploitation of a white master or mistress and
enabled them to devote time and energy to their own children. However,
when mothers lost their husband/providers through separation, divorce, or
widowhood, most were forced into gainful employment to support their
families; for rural women, this also often involved migration to the cities.

Putting their sons and daughters to work enabled many working-class

Table 9-2

Women's Gainful Employment Rates by Marital Status and Domesticity
Rates, by Racial-Ethnic Group, 1920

	Gainful Employment Rate		Domesticity Rate
	Married	Other	
American Indian	8.9	19.8	1.2
European American	6.5	45.0	5.9
African American	32.5	58.8	0.8
Asian American	18.5	38.7	1.1
Island Puerto Rican	13.1	32.2	1.5

NOTES: Rates are for persons 15 years of age and older; Asian data include only those
in the continental United States, and also include Hawaiians, Koreans, and Asian Indians. Otherwise, Notes to Table 9-1 apply. We define the domesticity rate as non-married women's gainful employment rate minus married women's gainful employment
rate, divided by the gainful employment rate of married women. Other includes single, widowed, and divorced women.
SOURCES: See Appendix A.

or poor farm families to make ends meet while the wife concentrated on
unpaid, reproductive labor. If a daughter's earnings or energies were needed
to support her parents, she delayed marriage; in addition, young men and
women normally postponed marriage until they could survive on the man's
earnings alone.[4]

In this way, participation in wage labor versus unpaid, reproductive
work was affected by gender and marital status as well as by race-ethnicity.
Table 9-1 shows gainful employment rates for 1920, which approximate the
share of the population engaged in wage labor. (The data do not correspond
exactly to these categories since they also count people who were self-employed and at least some of those who worked without pay in family
businesses or farms.) Rates varied greatly across racial-ethnic groups, but in
each group, men were at least twice as likely as women to be gainfully
employed. The share of women engaged in work for pay ranged from 12
percent among American Indians to a high of 39 percent among African
Americans. The disparity between men's and women's workforce participation was highest among Filipinas/os and Chinese.

Table 9-2 shows how marital status affected the participation of women
in paid work in 1920 across racial-ethnic groups. In each racial-ethnic group,
non-married women were far more likely to work for pay than married
women, but rates varied greatly across groups. Non-married Black women
were the most likely to participate in paid work. The vast majority of white

married women stayed out of paid work, with only 7 percent gainfully employed at any one time. A substantial share of married women of color, especially African Americans, worked for pay, but in all groups the share was less than one-third.

Table 9-2 also illustrates the extent to which a group was able to subscribe to the domestic ideal, measured by the "domesticity rate." We define the domesticity rate as the difference between non-married and married women's labor force participation rates divided by married women's labor force participation rates. In 1920, domesticity rates ranged from a high of five among whites to a low of one among Blacks.

The cultural prescription against married women's labor force participation was often institutionalized by employers in the form of a "marriage bar." Many employers had implicit or explicit policies of firing single women when they married and/or of refusing to hire married women. Marriage bars, which began in the late 1800s, were especially prevalent in teaching and clerical work, and continued in force through the 1940s.[5]

The Economic Costs of Domesticity

This uneven participation of men and women in wage labor and unpaid work in the late nineteenth and early twentieth centuries had many important repercussions. In 1900, men made up 82 percent of those gainfully employed, and, therefore, wage work came to be viewed as a predominantly masculine activity. Men (especially educated white men) were able to monopolize primary labor market jobs. Wage work became the central arena in which most white men not only earned their families' keep, but also competed for economic advancement. Even among extremely wealthy whites, the practice of working for one's living came to be associated with successful manhood. Men of color also entered wage labor in high proportions. Still, all but a tiny class-privileged and still-segregated elite were kept out of the best jobs and were unable to earn family wages—making them less than "men," according to the dominant ideology.

During this first phase of capitalist development, sexual divisions of labor within all racial-ethnic groups generally gave men economic power over women. Men earned more income than women of their racial-ethnic and class background, both because they participated in the labor force for longer periods and because their jobs paid more than women's jobs (as we discuss more below). Since white men controlled the highest-paid jobs, most white men could survive financially without women, while most white women remained financially dependent upon their husbands or fathers. Women of color earned such low wages that survival was nearly impossible without access to a male wage earner or to an extended family network.

Unpaid reproductive work in the home—shopping, meal preparation, cleaning, and child care—was clearly typed as women's work. Since society increasingly measured worth in terms of dollars, women's unpaid work, so vital to individual and social survival, came to be seen as less valuable than wage work.

The specialization of men in paid and women in unpaid work had a variety of other negative implications for women. It proved disastrous for unwed mothers, deserted wives, and widows, to whom the sexual division of labor still assigned primary responsibility for child care, but who lacked the income to support their families. This allocation also meant that many women, especially those with children, were financially trapped in unhappy, even violent, marriages. Furthermore, since unpaid work had come to be seen as women's work, men were reluctant to share women's burden of housework and child care, even when women entered wage work.

The fact that most women worked for pay only up until marriage or after divorce or widowhood affected the sex-typing of jobs as well as the wages women received. Women were less likely than men to invest in specialized job skills or to fight to move up the job hierarchy, as most planned to leave the labor force upon marriage. Employers slotted women into dead-end jobs which required few job-specific skills, and paid women less than they did men with comparable skills and responsibility.[6] In addition, since most educated upper- and middle-class women avoided labor force participation, the share of women workers with low educational attainment and few skills was higher than the share of men workers.

At the same time, the predominance of single, widowed and divorced women in the labor force created an association between women's wage work and failure in the domestic sphere. Women who preferred to remain in the paid labor force and did not marry were seen as unattractive or unfeminine. The connection between non-marriage and wage work for women was exemplified in the use of the expression "spinster"—a woman who spins thread for pay—to mean an unmarriageable woman.

A woman's labor force participation also reflected on her husband or father. Since poor families were more likely than wealthier families to send their wives and daughters into the workforce in the nineteenth and early twentieth centuries, a woman who worked for pay signaled a husband's or father's failure to provide adequately for his family. Married women's labor force participation thus acquired a social stigma. For husbands and sons, in contrast, labor force participation was fast becoming an essential sign of manhood. These moral judgments reinforced families' practices of assigning wage work to men and unpaid work to women.

White women's more limited job aspirations and their greater commit-

Table 9-3

Women's Labor Force Participation Rates by Marital Status and
Domesticity Rates, by Racial-Ethnic Group, 1920 and 1980

| | Labor Force Participation Rate | | | | Domesticity Rate | |
| | 1920 | | 1980 | | | |
	Married	*Other*	*Married*	*Other*	*1920*	*1980*
American Indian	8.9	19.8	47.9	47.6	1.2	0.0
Chicana	n.a.	n.a.	46.1	52.6	n.a.	0.1
European American	6.5	45.0	48.1	51.1	5.9	0.1
African American	32.5	58.8	60.5	49.4	0.8	-0.2
Chinese American	18.5	38.7	60.8	55.0	1.1	-0.1
Japanese American	18.5	38.7	56.1	62.3	1.1	0.1
Filipina American	18.5	38.7	70.6	64.5	1.1	-0.1
U.S. Puerto Rican	n.a.	n.a.	44.8	36.6	n.a.	-0.2
Island Puerto Rican	13.1	32.2	29.2	28.9	1.5	0.0

NOTES: 1920 data measure gainful employment rates; 1980 data measure labor force participation rates. Rates for 1920 are for ages 15 and over; for 1980, 16 and over. American Indian includes Eskimo and Aleut in 1980. Asian American data for 1920 were not borken down; they are for the continental United States only and also include Hawaiians, Koreans, and Asian Indians. For 1920, European Americans and African Americans include Latinas classifed as white or Black, respectively.
SOURCES: See Appendix A.

ment to the domestic ideal spilled over to further limit the economic opportunities of women of color. To the extent that white women claimed the best jobs in the labor force hierarchy, and often worked to exclude women of color from these jobs, white women's jobs came to define the maximum opportunities for women of any color. Most women of color were consigned to the lowest-paid, least desirable jobs, and were barred from advancement up the labor market hierarchy. In terms of lost job opportunities and wages, this was particularly costly to those women, disproportionately African American, who worked continuously throughout their lifetimes.

The Decline of Domesticity, 1920-1980

In the course of the twentieth century, women's domesticity has declined as major economic trends have drawn more and more married women into the paid labor force. Both the willingness of women to take on wage work and employers' need for women workers have increased. The decline of the domestic ideal has been most pronounced among middle-class, white, married women.

Capitalist production bore fruit for consumers in the first half of the twentieth century as firms seeking profits produced new goods and services that eased the burden of household work. New appliances, processed foods, and utilities such as electricity and running water directly reduced the work involved in many homemaking tasks.[7] In addition, service-producing firms such as restaurants, child-care centers, hospitals, and convalescent homes made available for sale services that had previously been provided by homemakers.

As family well-being became more and more dependent upon store-bought goods and services, women's unpaid work in the home shifted from producing at home to consuming in the marketplace. The strategy of economizing through home-made substitutes became less and less feasible, as many of the new commodities simply could not be produced in the home. While at first most new goods and services were only affordable by the upper class, rising real wages soon made them accessible to working-class families. Thus, needs grew along with income as higher standards of living transformed items like electricity and vacuum cleaners from luxuries into necessities. Even as men's real incomes increased, families' needs for income expanded even faster, and married women increasingly sought jobs to earn the income required to fill these needs.[8]

For an elite of white, college-educated women, an additional factor underlay the growing labor force participation of wives. Having acquired higher education in order to become better mothers, and having experienced the fulfillment of a career such as teaching or social work up until marriage, many educated white women found full-time homemaking a frustrating and unfulfilling activity. As the twentieth century progressed, more and more of these career women kept their jobs after they married or reentered the labor force once their children were of school age. The decreasing availability of domestic servants (which we discuss in detail in Chapter 10) also contributed to this process by reducing the attractiveness of full-time homemaking to these class-privileged women.[9]

As more women sought paid work, other factors contributed to a growth in the demand for their labor. Firms hired women to perform the market-equivalents of women's household work, such as preparing and serving food, cleaning floors, and caring for children and for the sick and elderly. Furthermore, with the increasing complexity and bureaucracy of the modern corporation, firms needed more and more clerical workers, a job typed as white women's since the late 1800s. Office work offered an abundance of relatively well-paid jobs, first to white women, and later to women of color. Finally, during the two World Wars, married as well as single women were exhorted to "serve their country" by entering paid work.

These interacting changes in the supply of and demand for labor brought increases in women's labor force participation rates for all racial-eth-

Table 9-4

Labor Force Participation Rates, by Gender and Race-Ethnicity,
1920 and 1980

	1920			1980		
	Women	Men	M/W	Women	Men	M/W
American Indian	11.5	58.4	5.1	47.7	69.2	1.5
Chicana/o	n.a.	n.a.	n.a.	49.0	79.7	1.6
European American	19.5	77.9	4.0	49.4	76.0	1.5
African American	38.9	81.1	2.1	53.3	66.7	1.3
Japanese American	25.9	87.8	3.4	58.5	79.3	1.4
Chinese American	12.5	87.0	7.0	58.3	74.3	1.3
Filipina/o American	11.6	96.5	8.3	68.1	77.6	1.1
Island Puerto Rican	18.9	72.0	3.8	29.1	54.4	1.9
U.S. Puerto Rican	n.a.	n.a.	n.a.	40.1	71.4	1.8
Total U.S.	21.1	78.2	3.7	49.9	75.1	1.5

NOTES: 1920 data measure gainful employment rates; 1980 data measure labor force participation rates. Rates for 1920 are for ages 10 and over; for 1980, 16 and over. American Indian includes Eskimo and Aleut in 1980. For Japanese Americans and Chinese Americans, 1920 data include both the United States and Hawaii, but for Filipinas/os, the 1920 data refer only to Hawaii. For 1920, European Americans and African Americans include Latinas/os classifed as white or Black, respectively. Total U.S. does not include island Puerto Rican.
SOURCES: See Appendix A.

nic groups and classes during the twentieth century, as shown in Figure 9-2.[10] Starting in the mid-1970s, this process was accelerated by a decline in husbands' real wages, as the world economy entered a prolonged period of stagnation and inflation. In response, many wives took jobs to maintain their families' standards of living.

Married women experienced the most pronounced and widespread changes (across racial-ethnic groups) in labor force participation rates, as shown in Table 9-3. White married women, the least likely to be in the labor force at the beginning of the century, were the most affected by these trends: their labor force participation rate rose from 7 percent in 1920 to 48 percent in 1980. Still, increases were significant for married women in other racial-ethnic groups between 1920 and 1980: rates quintupled for married American Indian women, tripled for Asian women, doubled for island Puerto Rican women, and almost doubled for African American women.[11] Participation rates of non-married women rose much less dramatically than those of wives, for whites, American Indians, and Japanese Americans, and actually fell for African Americans and island Puerto Ricans.[12]

As married women's labor force participation rates grew closer to those

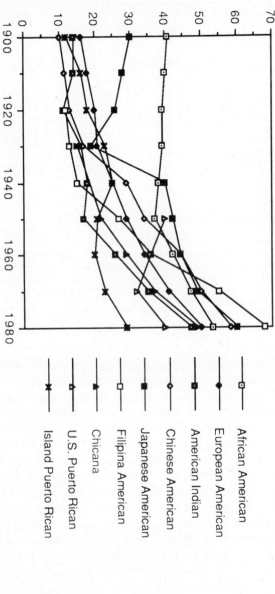

Figure 9-2: Women's Labor Force Participation Rates, by Racial-Ethnic Group, 1900-1980

NOTE: For detail on the definitions of the variables for the different years, and for the labor force participation rates themselves, see Appendix C.

SOURCE: See Appendix A.

of non-married women, the domesticity rate fell dramatically for all racial-ethnic groups (see Table 9-3). In 1980, no domesticity rates were significantly different from zero, and all domesticity rates were lower than the lowest domesticity rate in 1920, that for African American women.

These changes have narrowed the gap between men's and women's participation rates, as shown in Table 9-4. Between 1920 and 1986, the difference between men's and women's labor force participation rates fell from 57 to 25 percentage points. As a result, women's share of the workforce grew from 18 percent in 1900 to 45 percent by 1988.[13] Across all racial-ethnic groups, paid work became less and less a predominantly masculine activity. By 1980, gender differences between women's and men's labor force participation rates were greatest for Puerto Ricans, Chicanas/os, and whites, and least among Blacks and Asians.

The Sexual Division of Labor at Home and at Work: Persistence and Change

Despite the narrowing gap between men's and women's labor force participation rates, domesticity has persisted for all groups, if in a somewhat weaker form. Men are still more likely than women to work for pay and to work full time. At the same time, women still bear most of the responsibility for unpaid household work. Many men refuse to take on their fair share of household work because they view it as "women's work." In addition, some women have been unwilling to give up this work, which they see as an important aspect of their gender identity. As a result of these factors, women still shoulder the burden of most parenting work and structure their labor force participation around it.[14]

Thus, as married women have taken on more and more paid work in the post-war period while retaining the responsibility for unpaid, reproductive work, they have increasingly borne the burden of the "double day." Unfortunately, we have been unable to locate any studies which compare the distribution of household work across racial-ethnic groups. At the aggregate level, however, there appear to be clear trends. As shown in Table 9-5, in the 1960s, employed wives worked longer hours than wives who were full-time homemakers, averaging nearly two hours more work per day than non-employed wives. Employed wives also averaged one and one-half more hours of work each day than their husbands.

The imbalance was somewhat corrected in the 1970s, not by an increase in husband's household work, but by a decrease in the household work performed by employed wives (from an average of 4.6 hours in the 1960s to 3.1 hours in the 1970s). This decrease, also experienced by many non-employed wives, was largely due to fewer hours spent in child care:

Table 9-5

Time Spent per Day on Unpaid and Paid Work,
by Women and Men, 1960s and 1970s

	WIVES			
	Nonemployed		Employed	
	1960s	1970s	1960s	1970s
Unpaid Work	7.6-8.6	4.6-6.8	4.0-5.3	2.3-4.0
Work for Pay	0.0-0.6	0.1-1.9	4.8-5.3	5.0-6.5
Total Work	7.6-8.6	6.5-6.8	9.3-10.1	7.9-9.3

	HUSBANDS			
	Nonemployed Wives		Employed Wives	
	1960s	1970s	1960s	1970s
Unpaid Work	1.0-1.6	0.6-1.8	1.1-1.6	0.6-1.9
Work for Pay	7.5-7.8	7.0-7.7	6.3-6.9	6.9-7.1
Total Work	8.4-8.5	8.3-8.9	7.9-8.0	7.7-8.8

SOURCE: Francine D. Blau and Marianne A. Ferber, *The Economics of Women, Men, and Work* (Englewood Cliffs, NJ: Prentice-Hall, 1986), 126. These are range estimates which Blau and Ferber compiled from a number of studies.

women had fewer children (the birth rate fell by one-third between 1960 and 1980) and increasingly turned to some form of day care.[15] Under the pressure of the double day, women have organized to force the government and employers to recognize the value of their childrearing work, demanding the right to paid parental leaves, sick days for children's illnesses, reduced work weeks, and affordable day care.[16]

While the overall increase in women's participation in wage work relative to men has put increasing pressure on women's time and squeezed parenting, it has also had many positive effects. First, women's relationships to their jobs have changed. Women are more likely to be in the labor force for a larger portion of their lives, whether or not they are married; a woman's expected worklife (years in the labor force) in 1979-80 was 29 years.[17] As school-aged women plan ahead for more years of paid labor, many more have focused on gaining and developing skills that will help them attain jobs offering higher wages and better working conditions. And more have organized against discriminatory barriers for access to such jobs.

Furthermore, the increased labor force participation of women has spurred women's struggles to improve wages and working conditions and to attack head-on the multiple forms of discrimination they face in the labor force, from sexual harassment to racism. More women are participating in unionization drives to improve their wages and working conditions. Whereas ten years ago, women made up 25 percent of membership in unions and employee associations, today their share is 41 percent.[18] African American women, for instance, have been in the forefront of many union battles, particularly in the public sector. Within unions, as well as through political pressure on state legislatures, women workers have spearheaded a drive to be paid equally when their work is of "comparable worth" to that of men.[19]

Greater labor force participation has also created new opportunities for women of color, who have been able to progress up the job hierarchy a step behind white middle- and upper-class women. For example, we have seen how the expansion of clerical jobs and the increasing availability of white women workers in the first half of the twentieth century stereotyped these jobs as appropriate for white women, and brought about a vast increase in white women's clerical employment. Clerical jobs employed one-quarter of white women workers in 1930, and one-third by 1960. By World War II, women of color had begun to gain access to these jobs. Between 1970 and 1980, increasing numbers of white women moved up and out of clerical jobs, and the share of white women in clerical work fell from 37 to 32 percent. As a result, Black women were able to increase their representation in clerical work, which employed one-fourth of Black women in 1980, up from one-fifth in 1970.[20]

Even though the labor force experiences of women across racial-ethnic groups have been converging in these ways, many differences remain which result in different strategies and demands. For instance, hospital workers who are women of color have generally sought to increase their wages and improve working conditions through unionization, while registered nurses, predominantly white women, are divided on the merits of unionization compared to professional associations. On the other hand, there are instances in which demands and agendas have been changed to become more inclusive of the experiences of different women workers. For example, pressure from women of color has led white advocates of comparable worth to incorporate a demand for pay equity between whites and people of color into their agendas.

The net effect of women's shift into work for pay has been an increase in their financial independence from men, particularly when the effect of government welfare programs is added to the increased presence of wage income. While women's earnings and incomes remain low, a much greater share of women had direct access to income in 1980 than in 1960 (rather than only receiving income through a father or husband). However, women's

Table 9-6

Women's Median Incomes, by Racial-Ethnic Group, 1980

	Median Income	As Percent of Men of Same Racial-Ethnic Group	As Percent of European American Women
American Indian	$4,247	53	79
Chicana	4,556	51	85
European American	5,378	41	100
African American	4,676	60	87
Chinese American	6,064	56	113
Japanese American	7,410	49	138
Filipina American	8,253	77	153
Island Puerto Rican	2,775	64	52
U.S. Puerto Rican	4,473	52	83

NOTE: American Indian includes Eskimo and Aleut peoples.
SOURCES: See Appendix A.

access to income still varied greatly across race, as did women's incomes relative to those of men in their racial-ethnic group (see Table 9-6). For all racial-ethnic groups except U.S. Puerto Ricans and Chinese Americans, the gap between women's and men's median incomes narrowed between 1960 and 1980, giving women more financial power within marriage.[21] However, much of this increase came about because women were working longer hours in the paid labor force. The hourly earnings of full-time women workers as a share of men's remained fairly constant between 1960 and 1980, and increased only slightly (by about three percentage points) between 1980 and 1985.[22]

Women on Their Own

Increasing participation in wage work has not necessarily produced greater economic security for women, since their financial responsibilities have increased along with their income. Over the past 30 years, growing numbers of women have set up their own households and raised families without a male partner. Paid work is both a cause and an effect of this increasing tendency to live on their own: women who have their own incomes are less likely to remain in unsatisfactory relationships, and women who find themselves alone are more likely to seek paid work.

Married-couple family households, which comprised 74 percent of all households in 1960, had declined to only 56 percent of all households by 1989, and only 27 percent of all households conformed to the traditional nuclear family model (a married couple with children under 18).[23] For some women this was a choice, facilitated by greater economic independence and increasing social acceptance. For others, especially African American women, this was also the result of a shortage of men caused primarily by high death and incarceration rates. Whatever the reason, over the past 30 years, the share of households maintained by a woman (including families, unrelated individuals living together, and people living alone) has grown rapidly, from 18 percent in 1960 to 28 percent in 1990.[24]

There is great diversity within this growing category of woman-maintained households. Many women live alone, in nontraditional households such as lesbian couples, or with friends or roommates. Among them are many younger women who recently have left their parents' homes. The number of women living alone or with non-relatives more than doubled between 1960 and 1988 to over 17 million, to comprise 18 percent of all women.[25]

It is also increasingly common for women to parent without a husband. In 1988, 55 percent of all African American children, 28 percent of Latina/o children, and 20 percent of white children lived with their mothers only. Now that both spouses are often employed, the choice to end an unhappy marriage is more easily made by husband and wife alike, and the divorce rate has risen more than five-fold between 1910 and 1986, from 0.9 to 4.9; it is now estimated that 40 percent of new marriages may end in divorce.[26] The rising divorce rate, by raising an individual woman's expectation of divorce, also tends to cause women to choose to increase their education, job-training, and labor force participation.

Divorce is not the only cause of female-headed families. Growing numbers of women—unable to find desirable marriage partners, uninterested in marriage, unable to afford to parent in a couple without federal aid, or living as lesbians—are choosing to raise children on their own, without marrying. This trend is most pronounced among African American women: in 1988, 2.9 percent of European American and 28.2 percent of African American families with children were headed by single, never-married women.[27]

The rise of female-headed families (leaving aside households which women head but in which they live without relatives) has been uneven across racial-ethnic groups, but substantial for each, as shown in Figure 9-3. Between 1960 and 1980, the share of families which was female-headed increased in all racial-ethnic groups. African Americans, American Indians, and island Puerto Ricans began with higher shares of female-headed families, and African Americans and U.S. Puerto Ricans ended with the highest shares, 37 and 35 percent, respectively.

However, women's ability to support themselves and their children

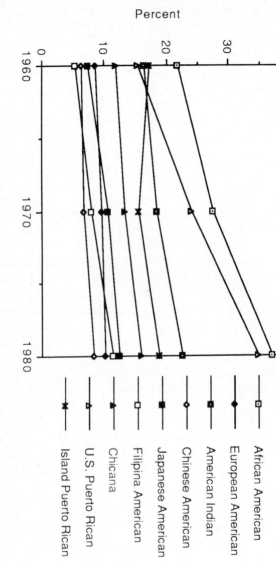

Figure 9-3: Female-Headed Families as Share of All Families,
by Racial-Ethnic Group, 1960-1980

NOTE: For 1960 and 1970, African American and European American include Latinas classified as
Black or white; American Indian includes Eskimo and Aleut peoples in 1980.
SOURCES: See Appendix A.

Table 9-7

Poverty Rates of Female-Headed Families, by Racial-Ethnic Group, 1970 and 1980

	1970	1980	Change (1980-1970)
American Indian	55.7 %	46.3 %	-9.4
Chicana	50.6	44.3	-6.3
European American	25.7	21.0	-4.7
African American	53.1	46.2	-6.9
Japanese American	24.7	14.5	-10.2
Chinese American	20.3	22.3	+2.0
Filipina American	39.6	20.4	-19.2
U.S. Puerto Rican	57.5	66.8	+9.3
Island Puerto Rican	73.7	71.1	-2.6

NOTE: American Indian includes Eskimo and Aleut peoples; European American and African American include Latinas in 1970.
SOURCES: See Appendix A.

varies greatly according to class and race. In 1986, there were almost 25 million female householders (no husband present). A small minority of these were doing quite well economically, especially the never-married and divorced women. Among never-married women heading households, 14 percent had incomes of over $35,000 yearly, and 38 percent had incomes greater than $20,000 yearly. For divorced women heading households, these percentages were 13 and 41, respectively; for widows, 8.2 percent and 22.6 percent. Of those women heading family households, most with children present, 13 percent had incomes above $35,000, and 35 percent had incomes above $20,000. There were, of course, substantial racial differences in access to income. Median incomes for Black and Latina women living alone were only about two-thirds those of white women; those for Black and Latina single mothers were less than 60 percent of the white level.[28]

Not surprisingly, most single-mother families have lower incomes and higher poverty rates than husband-wife families. In 1987, 34 percent of female-headed families were poor, and 41 percent were below 125 percent of the poverty level; poverty rates by racial-ethnic group vary widely, as shown in Table 9-7.[29] Continued gender- and racial-ethnic stereotyping of jobs, which we discuss in more detail in Chapter 10, make it very difficult for most women to support a family. Single mothers with little education, especially those who face racial-ethnic discrimination, find it virtually impossible to avoid poverty through labor force participation. Child support is inadequate, especially for women of color, as illustrated in Table 9-8: half or fewer of mothers with children from absent fathers were awarded any, and

Table 9-8

Child Support by Racial-Ethnic Group, 1987			
	Percent Awarded	Percent Received	Mean Amount Received
European American	69	77	$2,950
African American	36	73	1,503
Latina	42	76	2,628

NOTES: Data not available for Asians or American Indians. Percent awarded is the share of all women with children from absent fathers who were awarded child support divided by total number of women with children from absent fathers. Percent received is the share of all women due child support in 1987 who actually received any payments.
SOURCE: Current Population Reports, *Child Support and Alimony: 1987*, Special Studies, Series P-23, No. 167.

the average amount received was less than $3,000. Many single mothers rely on Aid to Families with Dependent Children (AFDC). While in no state do AFDC benefits support families above the poverty level, AFDC does offer a single mother an opportunity to receive free medical care, and is sometimes a better alternative than a low-wage job providing no health benefits. When single mothers organize to increase AFDC benefits, they raise the issues of the social worth of nurturing work and the right of all members of society, adults and children, to the basic necessities of life.

The increasing movement of women into work for pay in the course of the twentieth century has had both positive and negative consequences for women, with these consequences largely dependent upon their class, marital status, and racial-ethnic group. While women have become more economically independent, more equal within marriage, and more able to live on their own, the labor market has exposed them to discrimination, sexual harassment, and the double day. At the same time that women have become more financially independent, their financial responsibilities have increased. Women's economic well-being in the future will depend in large measure on the extent of their progress in the paid labor force. It is to this that we now turn. In the next chapter we examine in detail the historical transformation of women's work for pay and the mechanisms through which the job market has reproduced gender, racial-ethnic and class inequality.

Chapter 10

THE TRANSFORMATION OF WOMEN'S WAGE WORK

Over the last two centuries, the paid work performed by women has changed dramatically. This chapter focuses on the transformation of women's occupations over the course of the twentieth century and on the changes in the racial-ethnic, gender, and class hierarchies within paid work.

The transformation of women's jobs must be viewed within the larger framework of the growth of the U.S. economy. Through a combination of immigration and childbearing, the total U.S. population grew more than seven-fold between 1870 and 1980, from almost 40 million to over 225 million. This population growth helped fuel the rapidly industrializing economy, as the labor force grew from 13 to 98 million.[1] Productivity increases in agriculture, combined with growing employment opportunities in the manufacturing and service sectors, meant that the labor force increasingly shifted from the former to the latter. Totally new jobs were created, such as automobile worker and word processor, while others, such as buggy maker and livery-stable keeper, disappeared. Meanwhile, as a growing share of women entered the paid labor force, the workforce became less of a white male preserve. In 1900, white men made up 72 percent of all workers, but by 1980, their share had fallen to less than 50 percent. (See Table 10-1.)

How has the growing participation of white women and people of color in the paid labor force affected racial-ethnic and gender hierarchies? While this movement into paid work brought white women, women of color, and men of color into the same economic arena as white men, as free workers exchanging their labor time for a wage, it did not bring these groups into equality. Even though by 1980 they constituted a minority relative to other groups, white men have continued to monopolize most highly paid and powerful jobs.

As white women and people of color entered the labor market from other labor systems, they found themselves engaged in a struggle for earnings and power in which they were at a disadvantage. Employers commonly used them as a low-wage labor force, often as replacements for or strikebreakers

Table 10-1

Racial-Ethnic and Gender Composition of the Labor Force,
1900 and 1980

	1900		1980	
	Number	*Percent of Labor Force*	*Number*	*Percent of Labor Force*
Total	29,285,922	100.0	97,639,355	100.0
White men	21,041,792	71.8	46,916,660	48.1
Men of color	2,914,323	10.0	9,088,030	9.3
White women	3,992,797	13.6	33,875,824	34.7
Women of color	1,337,010	4.6	7,758,841	7.9
White people	25,034,589	85.5	80,792,484	82.7
People of color	4,251,333	14.5	16,846,871	17.3
Men	23,956,115	81.8	56,004,690	57.4
Women	5,329,807	18.2	41,634,665	42.6

NOTES: 1900 data is gainfully employed persons; 1980 is persons in the labor force.
In 1900, whites and people of color include Latinas/os, as racially classified; in 1980,
all Latinas/os are counted as people of color. Island Puerto Ricans are not included in
these calculations. See Appendix D.
SOURCE: See Appendix A.

against existing workers. The threatened workers, usually white and/or male,
fought to defend their jobs by attacking these less powerful workers. In other
instances, when people of color had established a foothold in areas not
directly competing with whites, whites reacted with attempts to exclude
them, such as the "Great Driving Out" of Chinese in the 1870s, Irish
immigrants' displacement of free Black servants and construction workers in
the mid-1800s, and southern whites' post-bellum attacks on Black
craftsworkers and tenant farmers. Whites and men also used their power to
maintain their privileged access to education and training, further solidifying
their claim on elite jobs.

The operation of gender, class, and racial-ethnic power in the labor
market has had two main consequences. First, disempowered groups have
been concentrated in jobs with lower pay, less job security, and more difficult
and dangerous working conditions. Second, workplaces have been places
of extreme segregation, in which workers have worked in jobs only with
members of their same racial-ethnic, gender, and class group, even though
the particular racial-ethnic group and gender assigned to a job may have

varied across firms and regions.

Within this context, oppressed groups have had to fight, individually and collectively, for economic survival. They have battled for higher wages for their jobs and for access to better jobs, struggling to advance within an inherently unequal structure. In the 1960s and 1970s, for example, the civil rights movement of African Americans, the Chicano student and Red Power movements, and the white feminist movement all incorporated demands for the elimination of discrimination in hiring, promotion, and access to education and training. Struggles to acquire education have been central to both individual and group efforts to break through labor market barriers, and white women and people of color with income and educational privilege have been the first to advance in the hierarchy.

Macroeconomic Changes and the Sex-Race-Typing of Jobs

Macroeconomic cycles—changes in the level of economic activity as a whole—have played an important role in racial-ethnic and gender struggles over jobs. While the U.S. economy has expanded dramatically over the past four centuries, growth has not been stable or smooth, since, like all capitalist economies, the United States experiences cycles of economic activity. During the twentieth century, the U.S. economy has experienced over 15 recessions and two periods of economic crisis. Recessions are short downturns in the economy when unemployment rises and remains at a high level for between one and three years. Longer-term downturns are called depressions or, equivalently, crises of profitability; during a crisis, the profitability of capitalist firms falls. After a recession, the economy recovers, economic growth and production resume, and unemployment falls. A crisis, on the other hand, forces a restructuring of key economic and political institutions before profitability can be restored. After the crisis of the Great Depression, for instance, the U.S. government assumed a more extensive role in regulating employment, banking, and social welfare. The increased spending of World War II also helped the economy emerge from the crisis. The post-war period was a time of nearly unprecedented economic growth, which continued until a new period of crisis set in during the 1970s. Since then, wages have failed to grow and unemployment has remained at high levels.[2]

Those who lose their jobs during downturns function as a cyclical "reserve army of the unemployed." Members of this reserve army are available to be drawn into the labor force during periods of expansion, but can be readily expelled when they are no longer needed. Those who are not in the wage labor force actively looking for work, but who can be drawn into it during economic upturns, constitute a latent reserve army. Because members of the reserve army can be called upon whenever wages threaten to rise, their existence protects the profits of capitalist employers.

White women and people of color have been disproportionately represented in both parts of the reserve army. Their weak political and economic status has meant that they have had more difficulty than white men protecting themselves from expulsion during economic downturns. Further, married women working as full-time homemakers have been an important part of the latent reserve army, drawn into the labor force, for example, during the two World Wars, and expelled at peace time. Finally, foreign workers, most of them of color and male, have been an important part of the reserve army—for example, Mexican workers brought into the U.S. economy by the Bracero Program, and Asians and Puerto Ricans who travelled to the U.S. and Hawaii on contracts as agricultural workers.[3] One recent example from the 1970s was the importation of Filipina workers. Hospitals recruited Filipina nurses under a program which required them to return home after two years.

Thus, job loss during recessions and depressions has not affected all workers, or all occupations, equally. For instance, during the Great Depression, employers fired their domestic servants to save money; since immigrant women and women of color, especially Black women, were disproportionately employed in domestic service, they were hardest hit. Also during that era, falling cotton prices and the collapse of credit pushed many tenant farmer families, again disproportionately Black, off the land.[4] Many employers adopted or strengthened bars against the employment of married women.[5] In contrast, when the recession of the early-1980s decimated the midwestern steel and automobile industries, men, especially men of color, were disproportionately affected. However, in the context of the post-World War II era—characterized by greater labor force participation of married women and the end of the marriage bar—wives increasingly entered the labor force to take up the slack. Indeed, British economist Jane Humphries found that women's employment has been less affected by economic downswings since World War II than it was in the first part of the twentieth century.[6]

Often the process of job loss has been institutionalized in labor market practices that protect those workers with the most seniority. In general, the last hired have been the first laid off. During the twentieth century, white women and people of color have gradually gained entrance to occupations from which they previously had been excluded. Since they are thus more likely to be the "last hired" in these jobs than are white men, white women and people of color are more likely to be the "first fired" during an economic downturn.

Furthermore, in severe downturns, as people have lost their jobs, they have searched for work further down the occupational hierarchy, pushing out those beneath them. Often this has meant taking the jobs of a subordinate race or class—although, thus far, job displacement rarely appears to have crossed gender lines. That is, white men have displaced men of color, and white women have displaced women of color. For example, during the 1930s, white women who lost their jobs took the jobs of women of color in domestic service and sales.[7] Already at the bottom of the job hierarchy, Black women had few choices other than to apply for government relief.

Job displacement during periods of high unemployment sometimes has taken on an organized, political form. Heightened competition for scarce jobs has tended to inflame racism and nativism, and, indeed, whites have often blamed people of color for a rise in unemployment. As we saw in Chapter 4, during the 1930s hundreds of thousands of Mexicans—including many with U.S. citizenship—were deported to Mexico. During the early 1980s, when unemployment in the auto and steel industries was at historically high levels, white auto workers and automobile executives alike began blaming the Japanese, and anti-Asian violence rose dramatically. In a somewhat similar vein, during the Great Depression, men attempted to pass laws curbing the employment of married women, claiming that men, as heads of households, were more deserving of the scarce jobs.

At the same time, however, widespread economic distress has sometimes led to organizing efforts that cross racial and gender lines. The unions affiliated with the Congress of Industrial Organizations brought white and Black workers together during the Great Depression, and in the 1980s, Jesse Jackson's presidential campaign forged a coalition which included white family farmers, low-wage Black service workers, Mexican farmworkers, and unemployed auto and steel workers of all races.

If recessions and depressions have tended to be especially hard on white women and people of color, have periods of rapid growth boosted their fortunes? As we saw in Part II, employers have often made exceptions to their racist and sexist hiring policies during times of rapid employment growth and scarce labor. And, since discrimination has kept oppressed peoples from being employed at levels consistent with their education and training, they represent a reserve of workers who can be drawn out of lower-paid jobs during economic upturns. During wars, military service has taken many men from their usual jobs, and created additional jobs in war industries. Employers' needs for labor, combined with efforts by white women and people of color, sometimes have overruled prejudice by bosses and workers alike. During the Civil War, many women went into teaching, previously a male-dominated profession, to replace men who had been drawn into combat. World War I was a watershed for the employment of Black men and women and white married women. World War II facilitated the entry of Chinese and Filipina/o Americans into white-collar jobs, broke down more barriers against Black employment in industrial and clerical work, and drew more white married women into paid work. While returning servicemen pushed out some of these new workers, these groups had gained many footholds which they were able to maintain in the postwar period. These historical patterns suggest the centrality of a full employment policy— the guarantee of paid work for all who seek it—to an agenda for economic justice in the 1990s.

The expansion of employment opportunities during periods of economic growth has not been automatic. Instead, economic growth has provided an opportunity which can be captured by organized political pressure. Without the union organizing of the 1930s and the marches and demonstrations organized by A. Philip Randolph and other Black leaders, Blacks might not have gained a greater share of World War II industry jobs. However, the combination of political pressure and economic growth made possible great economic gains. Similarly, during the late-1960s and early-1970s, the economy expanded rapidly and civil rights organizing by Blacks and other people of color—sometimes in coalition with whites—ensured that a greater share of the new jobs would go to people of color. When expansions end, however, those who were able to find better jobs can, again, be fired, forced into jobs further down the job ladder or thrown into the reserve army in spite their best efforts to protect themselves.

In summary, these cyclical changes in employment have uneven effects on the distribution of employment and unemployment among racial-ethnic groups and genders. Long-term, or secular, changes in the U.S. economy have also transformed women's paid work. These secular changes include the movement of paid work out of the home and the rise of non-household service employment, the decline of agriculture, the metamorphosis of manufacturing jobs, and the growth of professional employment. It is to these changes that we now turn.

The Growth and Decline of Women's Paid Domestic Work

Along with agricultural work, domestic service was one of the first major occupations for women in all racial-ethnic groups. Although early domestic work was unpaid, performed by indentured servants, slaves, or apprentices, the job gradually came to be compensated in wages (although a substantial proportion of live-in servants still receive their pay in the form of room and board). Over the course of the twentieth century, employment in domestic service declined dramatically, moving much of women's paid employment out of the home sphere. At the same time, much of the work once assigned to women domestic servants is now performed by women employed by profit-motivated firms.

In Part II, we showed that homemaking was an arduous task from early colonial times through much of the nineteenth century, involving not simply child care and housework, but also the production of many household goods. Families of means employed others to do most of this work, and very wealthy families had large staffs of servants of both sexes, from maids and butlers to coachmen and cooks. In 1870, over half of all wage-earning women were found in domestic service, either as servants, laundresses, or as self-employed boarding and lodging housekeepers. Of all domestic servants, 89 percent were women.[8]

Regional differences in the racial-ethnic nature of the employer-servant relationship produced distinct differences in women's work experiences. In the South, Southwest, and West, domestic service usually involved a woman of color laboring for a white woman or family, and thus the work both reflected and reinforced racial domination. As slavery took hold in the South, domestic service there became a Black occupation. African American intellectual W.E.B. Du Bois noted, "Blacks...became associated with servitude generally...wherever Blacks served, domestic service was labeled 'nigger's work.' "[9] After the Civil War, domestic service continued to be seen as an occupation dominated by Black women. In the Southwest and West, domestic service was also racially typed and devalued, and Mexicans, American Indians and Asians predominated. On the West Coast, Asian men were often employed in domestic service since there was a shortage of women of all racial-ethnic groups.

Live-in servants in the North and Midwest generally enjoyed better treatment than those in the South and the West, particularly from the Revolution to about 1850, since servants and employers usually belonged to the same racial-ethnic group. During that period, most northern and midwestern servants were U.S.-born whites who worked under relatively egalitarian conditions—indeed, they often were referred to as "help," not servants. The North's egalitarian view of domestic help began to change in the mid-nineteenth century as U.S.-born servants were replaced by immigrants, especially Irish women. The combination of ethnic, religious and class difference opened up a vast social distance between white, U.S.-born employers and their immigrant servants. However, this process took decades: as late as 1900, there were still twice as many U.S.-born white women employed as private household workers as there were foreign-born, white women.[10]

During the nineteenth century domestic service coincided with and promoted the cult of domesticity. Domestic servants were essential to wealthy women's aspirations towards ideal womanhood. Servants freed the homemaker from the drudgery of housework so that she could attend to the "higher" functions of homemaking: mothering, socializing, and for some, the volunteer work that was a form of social homemaking. At the same time, a large pool of women willing to work as domestic servants for low wages was guaranteed by the lack of other jobs for poor, racially subordinated, and immigrant women. As shown in Table 10-2, over 40 percent of African American and European immigrant women were in domestic service, compared to only 25 percent of U.S.-born white women. A substantial share of African American and Asian American men were also so employed, but only 1 percent of European American men performed domestic work.

Through the early twentieth century, most domestic servants lived in their employers' homes. Single women were far more likely to live in than married women, since living in provided a roof over their heads. Most worked for married, middle- and upper-class white homemakers in what was seen as helpful training for the servants' futures as homemakers. Hence domestic service often involved a generational relationship (as well as a racial-ethnic one) in which an older, married woman used her husband's income to pay a younger, single woman—and where the servant's pay was then often transferred to her parents.

However, taking on another woman's domestic work did not always involve living in the employer's home. Married women servants, who were disproportionately Black, preferred day work to live-in service whenever they could obtain it. Large numbers of married Black women took in laundry in their own homes in order to escape the direct supervision of a white mistress. On the West Coast, the Chinese, especially men, did laundry work. Caring for other women's children—the precursor of today's day-care centers—was another form of domestic service which could be performed in one's own home. In urban areas, taking in boarders and lodgers provided yet another path to escape from domestic service in another woman's home, allowing married women and their daughters to contribute cash income to their families through cooking, cleaning, and laundering for their clients; this was especially common in immigrant communities. Boarding services were also in high demand by adult men in communities where women were scarce, such as Asian plantation workers in Hawaii. Unlike domestic service, boarding and lodging appears rarely to have involved racial inequality. Boarding and lodging was, instead, an exchange between persons of the same class and racial-ethnic group who were of different ages and phases in their working lives.

Although domestic service was the single most important occupation for women in 1900, its significance declined dramatically in the course of the twentieth century. Between 1900 and 1980, although the population tripled

Table 10-2

Private Household Workers, by Gender and Race-Ethnicity, 1900			
	Number	As Percent of All Private Household Workers	As Share of Group's Total Employment
TOTAL	2,107,977	100	–
European American women (U.S. born)	784,617	37	25
African American women	573,022	27	44
European American women (foreign born)	406,654	19	46
African American men	123,469	6	5
European American men (U.S. born)	103,743	5	1
European American men (foreign born)	68,069	3	1
Chinese American men	40,163	2	38
Japanese American men	4,490	<1	7
American Indian women	1,996	<1	3
Japanese American women	1,260	<1	29
Chinese American women	296	<1	36

NOTES: African Americans and European Americans include Latinas/os as racially classified. Data refer to continental United States, Hawaii, and other territories, but do not include Puerto Rico. See Appendix B for occupations included.
SOURCE: 1900 Census, see Appendix A.

and per capita output more than quadrupled, the total number of private household workers fell from about two million to one-half million. The share of women employed in private household service fell from 35 percent to 1 percent.[11]

Both supply and demand factors contributed to the decline in women's paid domestic work. Many family needs formerly filled by women's domestic work—such as health care, child care and education, and meal preparation—are now serviced by hospitals, convalescent homes, medical and health professionals, schools, day-care centers, and hotels and restaurants, lowering the economy's overall demand for domestic workers. In addition, new commodities that reduce the amount of physical work necessary to fill family

Table 10-3

Share of Employed Women Working in Private Household Service, by
Racial-Ethnic Group, 1900-1980

	1900	1930	1960	1980
African American	43.5	53.5	39.3	5.0
European American	29.8	12.0	4.4	0.8
American Indian	13.4	22.5	16.8	1.4
Chinese American	35.6	12.1	1.7	0.8
Japanese American	28.6	29.9	8.2	1.4
Filipina American	n.a.	34.4	3.7	0.9
Chicana	n.a.	33.1	11.5	2.4
U.S. Puerto Rican	n.a.	n.a.	1.2	0.7
Island Puerto Rican	78.4	27.5	13.7	1.4

NOTES: See Appendix B for a listing of occupations included in this category, and Appendix D for a discussion of comparability issues. Asian American data include Hawaii for all years; 1980 data for American Indians include Eskimo and Aleut peoples; for 1900-1960, African American and European American include Latinas.
SOURCES: See Appendix A.

needs have become available and affordable: hot and cold running water; electricity and telephones; durable goods such as refrigerators, washing machines, and vacuum cleaners; and processed foods. All these changes have reduced the need for domestic servants, laundresses, and women who take in boarders and lodgers. At the same time, the growing availability of other jobs for women—many of them in the service sector, as well as in manufacturing and clerical work—has decreased the supply of women available for domestic work, and consequently increased the wages of domestic servants.

The movement out of domestic service has, however, been uneven across racial-ethnic groups, as shown in Table 10-3. African American women have remained the most likely to work as domestic servants. Since the overwhelming majority of the families employing domestics have been white, the majority of African American women's wage work entailed housework, childcare, and laundry for white women and their families, through the first third of the twentieth century. This direct, personal, and continuing experience of racial subordination has been central to the lives of contemporary Black women's mothers and grandmothers.[12] On the other extreme, white and Asian American women were able to leave domestic service most rapidly. By 1980, no more than one in twenty women worked in domestic service in any racial-ethnic group; the share for Blacks and Chicanas, however, remained much greater than for whites.

Table 10-4

Share of Employed Women Working in Service Occupations
(Other than Private Household Service),
by Racial-Ethnic Group, 1900-1980

	1900	1930	1960	1980
African American	7.9	7.5	23.0	24.2
European American	3.8	8.1	13.2	15.3
American Indian	12.1	2.9	25.8	23.9
Chinese American	8.7	8.8	9.2	13.0
Japanese American	3.8	10.1	12.9	15.8
Filipina American	n.a.	4.1	16.6	15.8
Chicana	n.a.	3.8	16.5	20.4
U.S. Puerto Rican	n.a.	n.a.	7.3	14.4
Island Puerto Rican	n.a.	1.3	12.2	14.8

NOTES: See Appendix B for a listing of occupations included in this category, and Appendix D for a discussion of comparability issues across Census years. Asian American data include Hawaii for all years; 1980 data for American Indians include Eskimo and Aleut peoples; for 1900-1960, African American and European American include Latinas.
SOURCES: See Appendix A.

Thus women left employment in the homes of other women for jobs in new settings, such as factories, offices, schools, nursing homes, and restaurants. In this process, they exchanged the direct supervision of a mistress or master for a more complicated and bureaucratic hierarchy of supervision. In some cases, this meant that supervision became less personal, and it often meant that the supervisor was no longer another woman.

The New Service Work

As we have seen, domestic service declined partially because women's traditional work of caring for the personal needs of others was taken over by firms. Whereas in the past domestic servants were hired by individual employers and worked in their households, today this work is increasingly organized by capitalist entrepreneurs in search of profits. Domestic work is now performed by day-care center workers, cooks and waitresses in restaurants, nurses and aides in hospitals, and commercial laundry workers. While the form and usually the location of service work changed in this process, today's personal service workers—like the domestic servants before them—are still confined to the bottom of the labor market hierarchy.

Employment in service occupations grew rapidly between 1900 and 1980, from about 2 to 12 million workers. Today, service occupations outside the private household include food preparation and service (waiters and waitresses, cooks, counter workers, and kitchen workers), health service (dental assistants, nurses aides, orderlies, and attendants), cleaning and building service (maids, janitors, and elevator operators), personal service (barbers, hairdressers, guides, and child-care workers), and protective service (police officers, firefighters, and guards).

The expansion of service occupations in the twentieth century drew in large numbers of women workers. Service occupations employed 16 percent of women workers in 1980, compared to less than 3 percent in 1900. As shown in Table 10-4, the rate of entrance of women into these new service jobs varied across racial-ethnic groups. African American and American Indian women were overrepresented in 1980, just as they were in domestic service work.

Women are overconcentrated in service jobs other than protective service: although they make up less than half of the workforce, women are two-thirds of these service workers. Many service jobs involve traditionally female tasks such as cooking, cleaning, and caring for the sick, the aged, and the very young. However, service work is not simply or only a women's job. First, there are racial-ethnic hierarchies within female-dominated service jobs. For instance, white and Asian women are about 50 percent more likely than other women to be supervisors. Black women are three times as likely as white and Asian American women to be janitors and cleaners, while American Indian and Latina women are about twice as likely.[13] Racial-ethnic typing is even more severe when we look within a region or within a place of work. In many northeastern and midwestern cities, all of the nurses aides and cleaning-service workers are women of color; in most restaurants, waitresses are all from the same racial-ethnic group.

Second, just as men of color were significantly represented in domestic service jobs during the nineteenth and early twentieth centuries, so also a significant share are employed in non-protective service work today. Indeed, certain service jobs are dominated by poor or immigrant white men and men of color, such as janitors, bellhops, and elevator operators.

Another exception to women's dominance in service work occurs in the elite service jobs known as protective service, consisting predominantly of police officers and firefighters (see Table 10-5). Protective service was monopolized by white men for decades. In 1900, white men accounted for only 72 percent of the labor force, but made up 97 percent of all policemen, firemen, and watchmen. Men of color, in contrast, were seriously underrepresented and women's shares were insignificant. Over the course of the century, struggles by white women and people of color, especially in the 1960s and 1970s, have brought them a somewhat greater share of these jobs. By 1980, men of color's share had grown from 3 percent to almost 12 percent,

Table 10-5

The Distribution of Protective Service Jobs, 1900 and 1980					
	1900			1980	
(1) Share of Protective Service Jobs	(2) Share of Labor Force	(3) Relative Concentration [(1)/(2)] x100	(4) Share of Protective Service Jobs	(5) Share of Labor Force	(6) Relative Concentration [(4)/(5)] x100
White Men	97	72	135	84	48	175
White Women	<1	14	<7	3	35	9
Men of Color	3	10	30	12	9	133
Women of Color	<1	5	<2	1	8	13

NOTES: For 1900, "Watchmen, policemen, firemen, etc."; for 1980, "Police and fire-fighters." In 1900, both whites and people of color included Latinas/os, as racially classified. In 1980, all Latinas/os are counted as people of color. Island Puerto Ricans are not included in these calculations.
SOURCES: See Appendix A.

while their share of all jobs had decreased from 10 to 9 percent. Women of all racial-ethnic groups other than Chinese Americans have also increased their relative concentrations in protective service, with American Indian, Black, and Puerto Rican women making the greatest gains. Despite these inroads, white men are still overrepresented.[14]

Were women's working conditions improved by moving out of domestic service into new service jobs? Certainly, most women have seen these jobs as an improvement over live-in domestic service, involving as they do more limited hours and the ability to live in one's own home and with one's children. Furthermore, earnings are higher, on the average: with median earnings of $10,816 for full-time, full-year workers in 1988, service occupations offered better pay than private household and agriculture (at $7,228 and $10,452, respectively). However, service workers' earnings are considerably less than those of manufacturing, sales, or clerical workers. Forty-five percent of women's service jobs are part-time (compared to about one-quarter of all women's jobs), and 45 percent of service jobs involve work on weekends.[15] New unionizing efforts among hospital, hotel, and janitorial workers promise to bring the new service workers some measure of justice and dignity on the job.

Out of the Fields

Through 1870, the majority of workers in the United States worked in agriculture. However, agriculture meant very different things to different people: for some, self-employment and a chance at earning wealth; for others, slavery, extreme exploitation as a migrant or plantation worker, or the perpetual debt of sharecropping or tenant farming.

The types and conditions of agricultural work depended in large measure on race-ethnicity, which to a large extent determined access to land. European immigrants, especially before the late-1800s, were able to homestead on lands stolen from Native Americans; thus, they were most likely to be self-employed farmers or ranchers. However, an elite of white farmers and ranchers held large parcels of land, squeezing smaller farmers; in the South, many poor whites were forced into tenant farming and sharecropping. During slavery, most African Americans worked in agriculture. Once freed, most were kept by Jim Crow racist practices from acquiring land of their own, and continued to labor for whites as sharecroppers or tenant farmers. The colonization of the Mexican Southwest stripped land from the indigenous peoples and concentrated ownership among a wealthy few. The remaining American Indians and Mexicans were reduced to the status of landless peasants or subsistence farmers. After the U.S. takeover, Anglos acquired most of the Mexican lands, leaving Chicanas/os to work as tenant farmers, sharecroppers, or migrant workers. American Indians, forced onto smaller, less fertile land areas, tried to continue the self-sufficient farming and ranching in which most had been occupied before the European invasion. Island Puerto Ricans also suffered from the concentration of lands in the hands of a few, with many small family farmers driven gradually into agricultural wage labor for wealthy farmers. Chinese, Japanese, and Filipina/o peoples were brought to the United States and Hawaii as plantation laborers and migrant workers, and prohibited by law from acquiring land in the United States. Nonetheless, some were able to escape from this landless status, and entered into family farming and gardening.

The degree to which women participated in agricultural work varied greatly among these groups, depending both upon the overall importance of agricultural work for the racial-ethnic group as a whole and on the share of the work allocated to women. Census data on women's agricultural employment are somewhat unreliable since they probably undercount women's participation; nevertheless, they may be useful for comparative purposes.

As we can see from the first column of Table 10-6, in 1900 over half of all American Indian, African American, island Puerto Rican, and Japanese American workers were employed in agriculture, compared to only one-third

Table 10-6

	Share of Group Employed in Agriculture	Women as Share of Group's Agricultural Workers	Share of Women Workers Employed in Agriculture
	Women in Agriculture, by Racial-Ethnic Group, 1900		
European American	33	5	10
African American	54	27	44
American Indian	61	17	47
Chinese American	24	<1	7
Japanese American	63	6	58
Island Puerto Rican	63	1	4

NOTES: Data not available for Filipinas/os, Chicanas/os, or U.S. Puerto Ricans. African American and European American include Latinas/os, as racially classified. Data includes Hawaii. Agricultural employment includes some unpaid family workers; see Appendix B for occupations included.
SOURCES: 1900 Census, see Appendix A.

of all whites, and less than one-fourth of Chinese Americans. This is due to a number of different reasons, including the rural nature of American Indian life, the importation of African and Asian workers to the United States specifically to perform agricultural work, the Great Driving Out of Chinese people in the late-1800s, and the exclusion of people of color, especially Blacks, from non-agricultural employment. In general, however, a higher share of people of color remained in agriculture in 1900 than that of whites.

The share of agricultural work done by women within each racial-ethnic group was also higher among women of color in 1900 (except among Asians, whose population was still mostly male), as shown in the second column of Table 10-6. Among American Indians, this stemmed from a cultural tradition involving women in farming. African American women's participation can be traced both to African traditions and to slaveowners' practice of employing women in the fields. Among Puerto Ricans, farming was traditionally men's work. On the other hand, these data may understate the share of agricultural work performed by European American and Puerto Rican women, especially on family farms, where women usually contributed to cash crop production through harvesting, dairying, gardening, and cooking and cleaning for hired hands.

In the course of the twentieth century, agricultural productivity increased greatly as a result of labor-saving technological changes, especially mechanization. As a result, agricultural employment fell from over 10 million

Table 10-7

Share of Employed Women Working in Agriculture, by Racial-Ethnic Group, 1900-1980				
	1900	1930	1960	1980
African American	44.2	24.7	3.7	0.5
European American	9.8	4.1	1.5	1.0
American Indian	47.2	26.1	10.5	1.2
Chinese American	7.3	2.5	0.7	0.3
Japanese American	58.1	22.9	6.7	1.3
Filipina American	n.a.	27.5	4.3	1.2
Chicana	n.a.	21.2	4.3	2.9
U.S. Puerto Rican	n.a.	n.a.	0.3	0.4
Island Puerto Rican	3.9	9.5	1.6	0.3

NOTES: See Appendix B for a listing of occupations included in this category, and Appendix D for a discussion of comparability issues across Census years. Asian American data include Hawaii for all years; 1980 data for American Indians include Eskimo and Aleut peoples; for 1900-1960, African American and European American include Latinas.
SOURCES: See Appendix A.

to less than 3 million, and vast numbers of people left rural areas for the cities. In 1900, agriculture employed more than one in three workers; in 1980, the share had fallen to fewer than one in 30. Table 10-7 shows the changing shares of women workers employed in agriculture from 1900 through 1980. Through the first third of the twentieth century, substantial shares of American Indian, African American, Chicana, Filipina American, and Japanese American women continued to work in agriculture; however, by 1980, no more than 3 percent of women was so employed in any racial-ethnic group.

For those women who remain in agricultural wage labor, disproportionately Chicanas, conditions have barely improved since the early twentieth century. Wages continue to be extremely low, with the presence of substantial numbers of undocumented workers allowing super-exploitation by growers and foremen. The recent employers' offensive against unions in the 1980s has also taken its toll on farmworker organizing.

Women family farmers have also suffered reversals in the last decade. As farm indebtedness and bankruptcy soar, huge corporate firms increasingly dominate the agricultural landscape, absorbing family farms and turning farm owners into farm managers and tenants. Black farm ownership has fallen disproportionately, and farm women of all racial-ethnic groups have taken on a triple day: work on the farm, a second job in town, and continued responsibility for child care and other family work.[16] Despite this punishing schedule, women throughout the Midwest and South have organized to fight foreclosures, lobby for aid to farmers, and develop farmer cooperatives.

Table 10-8

Share of Employed Women Working in Manufacturing,
by Racial-Ethnic Group, 1900-1980

	1900	1930	1960	1980
African American	2.6	8.4	15.5	18.4
European American	32.6	21.2	18.5	12.6
American Indian	24.9	37.6	18.1	17.0
Chinese American	41.1	20.8	24.0	20.8
Japanese American	7.7	12.2	19.0	12.5
Filipina American	n.a.	15.3	17.4	13.8
Chicana	n.a.	24.7	29.1	26.0
U.S. Puerto Rican	n.a.	n.a.	69.3	29.1
Island Puerto Rican	14.6	52.4	31.3	22.0

NOTES: See Appendix B for a listing of occupations included in this category, and Appendix D for a discussion of comparability issues across Census years. Asian American data include Hawaii for all years; 1980 data for American Indians include Eskimo and Aleut peoples; for 1900-1960, African American and European American include Latinas.
SOURCES: See Appendix A.

Many of these groups draw on the old populist traditions described in Chapter 5, exhorting farmers to raise "less corn and more hell."[17]

Manufacturing Inequality

As capitalism developed in the United States, labor shifted out of agriculture and domestic service into manufacturing. Manufacturing itself gradually changed from predominantly skilled craft and artisan work to unskilled and semi-skilled factory work.

By 1900, manufacturing made up approximately one-fourth of total employment. There was great variation in the proportions of women and men workers of the different racial-ethnic groups who were employed in manufacturing occupations. Among women, more than one-fourth of European American, American Indian, and Chinese American women held manufacturing jobs, while for Japanese American, island Puerto Rican, and African American women, the share in manufacturing was much lower, as shown in Table 10-8. Among men, only European Americans held more than their labor market share of manufacturing jobs; men of color remained relatively concentrated in agriculture. Thus, in 1900, manufacturing jobs still represented a white preserve from which most men and women of color were excluded.

Particular manufacturing occupations were typed by gender and/or by race-ethnicity. For example, skilled garment making—performed by dress-

makers, seamstresses, shirt, collar and cuff makers, tailors and tailoresses—
was a job undertaken by women of all racial-ethnic groups, often in their
own homes. Women made up 78 percent of these workers in 1900, and only
African American women had less than their labor market share. European
American women had five times their share (with immigrant women more
likely to be so employed than U.S.-born), American Indian women four
times, and Japanese American and Chinese American at least twice.[18] Needlework jobs were also important for Puerto Rican and Chicana women.

In contrast, in 1900, textile mill operatives were almost exclusively
white, and about half men and half women. White men held less than their
labor market share of these jobs (since they could find more lucrative jobs),
while white women held more than three times their labor market share.
Within the mills, jobs were typed according to sex and ethnicity. European
immigrants, especially Irish, Italian, English, and Welsh, had relative concentrations in mill jobs higher than did U.S.-born whites. On the other hand, no
group of men or women of color had achieved more than one-twentieth of
their labor market share of textile mill jobs, which paid considerably more
than the agricultural and domestic service jobs into which they were
crowded.

A third set of jobs was monopolized by white males: traditional,
masculine crafts, such as carpentry, masonry, plumbing, blacksmithing,
cabinet-making, and machine-making (machinists). In all these jobs, European American men maintained a near monopoly. We saw in Chapter 6 how
many slave men, trained in these crafts, were prevented by white men from
practicing their trades by white men after Emancipation. However, this
exclusion worked unevenly: in 1900, African American men held about their
labor market share of masonry and plastering jobs, a little less than half their
share of carpentry and blacksmithing, and only about one-tenth their share
of plumbing and machinist jobs. No other group of men held even half its
labor market share, although Chinese American, Japanese American, and
American Indian men had a significant part of their shares in carpentry and
blacksmithing. Women of all racial-ethnic groups were the most excluded
from the crafts, with none receiving more than six percent of their labor
market share.[19] Exclusion was costly since the crafts were generally much
higher-paid than other manufacturing jobs.

Between 1900 and 1980, as the economy grew and changed, the
number of manufacturing jobs quadrupled and manufacturing's share of total
employment increased. Women's manufacturing employment also quadrupled, but women's total employment grew even faster, so the share of women
in manufacturing fell. However, the decline in women's manufacturing
employment was very uneven across racial-ethnic groups. Only among

white women was there a smooth decline, as white women found better-paid jobs as sales, clerical, and professional and managerial workers. Not until the mid-twentieth century did Black women gain entry to manufacturing, as a result of organizing, war-time labor shortages, and white women's exodus. Very high percentages of Puerto Rican women have been employed in manufacturing, both in Puerto Rico and in the United States, at rates which have fluctuated widely with the movement of firms in and out of Puerto Rico or New York.

If we look at the overall pattern, an interesting change is clear. In 1900, when manufacturing represented a relatively good job, white women's share was greater than that of most women of color. In contrast, in 1980, most women of color, other than Japanese Americans, had higher participation in manufacturing than white women. This signifies not a reversal of the racial-ethnic hierarchy, but the movement of white women into higher-paid, higher-status jobs such as clerical and professional work.

Since 1970, overall U.S. employment in manufacturing (excluding construction) has fallen in absolute terms as a result of a combination of factors, including productivity increases, the transfer of plants abroad, and competition from foreign producers. The decline has taken a disproportionate toll on women of color, for many of whom unionized manufacturing jobs offered steady income. New immigrant women, speaking Spanish or other languages, are particularly affected by the loss of manufacturing jobs, since white-collar work demands English-language proficiency.

With factory jobs in decline, employers have increasingly relied on two forms of manufacturing work common in the nineteenth and early twentieth century, sweatshops and industrial homework. Now, as then, these jobs employ a disproportionate number of immigrant women. As we saw in Chapter 7, many Southeast Asian refugee women, undocumented Mexican immigrant women, and recent Chinese immigrant women are finding employment in the newly resurgent sweatshops. Industrial homework—manufacturing work contracted out to workers in their own homes—has also been on the rise. For employers, homework offers freedom from unionization, government regulations, and overhead costs. Women, on the other hand, turn to homework in the hopes of combining work and family, or because no other work is available. Under the Reagan administration, regulations prohibiting homework were dismantled. As a result, capitalists are opting to locate more work in workers' homes and have expanded the range of manufacturing jobs contracted out to homeworkers, including electronic component assembly as well as the traditional garment work.[20]

Today, as in the past, women of different racial-ethnic groups are unevenly represented in different manufacturing jobs. Garment work—both

Table 10-9

Share of Employed Women Working in Clerical Occupations,
by Racial-Ethnic Group, 1900-1980

	1900	1930	1960	1980
African American	0.1	0.6	8.0	25.8
European American	6.9	25.3	34.5	32.3
American Indian	0.1	3.3	14.2	27.4
Chinese American	0.5	11.7	32.1	24.7
Japanese American	0.1	3.7	30.5	31.6
Filipina American	n.a.	1.6	24.3	28.2
Chicana	n.a.	2.8	21.8	26.2
U.S. Puerto Rican	n.a.	n.a.	13.9	31.9
Island Puerto Rican	1.2	2.3	16.9	26.9

NOTES: See Appendix B for a listing of occupations included in this category, and Appendix D for a discussion of comparability issues across Census years. Asian American data include Hawaii for all years; 1980 data for American Indians include Eskimo and Aleut peoples; for 1900-1960, African American and European American include Latinas.
SOURCES: See Appendix A.

by dressmakers and by sewing machine operators—continues to be female-dominated. However, Black women are no longer excluded and now hold more than twice their labor market share of these jobs; Asian American women and Latinas each have five to six times their labor market share, while white women have twice theirs.

On the other hand, as a result of the anti-discrimination struggles of the past twenty years, women and people of color are gaining entrance into craft occupations. The most significant improvement has been for men of color. For example, in the three white male crafts we looked at in 1900, plumbing, carpentry, and machine-making, Black, American Indian, and Latino men all now have more than their labor market share, as do white men. On the other hand, women of all racial-ethnic groups have no more than one-third of their labor market share; these crafts, then, shifted from white-male-dominated to male-dominated. Women of color are doing better than white women in the crafts: Chicana, Japanese American, Puerto Rican, Filipina, and American Indian women have the highest proportion of their labor market shares in craft work, ranging from 31 to 24 percent respectively, with white women at 17 percent of their labor market share. Since craft work offers relatively high-paying and secure employment to people who cannot afford higher education, it is not surprising that women of color, who have less access to education, choose this route to economic security.

The Rise of Office Work

One of the most important occupational changes for women in the twentieth century has been the growth of clerical work. Women's clerical employment grew from 320,000 in 1900 to over 2 million in 1930 and 12 million in 1980.[21] Clerical work provides an interesting example of the transformation and reproduction of gender and racial-ethnic hierarchies. In the nineteenth century, a clerk was typically an educated white man who worked in an office as training for managerial work. When the typewriter was introduced, young European American middle-class women were hired to operate the machine and the job was feminized: the clerical worker's career path to management was eliminated, and clerical workers found themselves low-level assistants to male managers, treated as office wives.

The feminization of the office, as this process is called by European American sociologist Margery Davies, was at first a European American phenomenon. As we saw in Chapter 5, white immigrant women other than the English were kept out of offices, and women of color's access to clerical occupations was severely restricted through World War II. In 1900, as shown in Table 10-9, only white women were significantly employed in clerical work. U.S. women of color were almost totally excluded from this new, relatively high-status job. Indeed, the relative concentration of white *men* among stenographers and typists (about one-third of their labor market share) was eight times higher than that of Black women.[22]

Clerical employment grew by over 1.5 million jobs between 1900 and 1930. Most of these new jobs were taken by European American women, although women of color made small gains. Black women continued to face the greatest obstacles. However, as clerical jobs continued to multiply in the post-World War II era, racial barriers eventually broke down as a result of both the persistence of women of color and the economy's burgeoning demand for workers. Education and urbanization have also provided opportunities for women of color to gain access to clerical work. As a result of all these changes, the differences between women of different racial-ethnic groups were greatly reduced: in 1980, from one-fourth to one-third of each group's employed women worked as clericals. Since women's clerical jobs pay substantially more than their jobs in services, manufacturing, and sales ($15,860 in 1988, compared to $10,816, $12,376, and $13,728, respectively) and since many women prefer office working conditions to those in the factory or in service work, this is a genuine step forward for women of color.[23]

While clerical work is no longer reserved for white women, racial-ethnic and gender segregation persist. For instance, in 1980, 31 percent of white women were secretaries, compared to 18 percent of African American women. In contrast, women of color were more likely to be typists, data entry keyers, and file clerks—all occupations that were lower in pay and status than those dominated by white women. Furthermore, automation threatens to displace many lower-skilled clerical jobs, and it is likely that women of color, whose hold on clerical work is more tenuous, will be more affected by a retrenchment in this sector than white women. While women of color were concentrated in lower-level clerical jobs, the men in clerical work were concentrated in supervisory work, where they made up 41 percent of all workers, compared to only 2 percent of secretaries, stenographers, typists, and receptionists.[24]

As we saw in Part II, union organizing among clerical workers is succeeding in raising wages, much of it using the strategy of comparable worth, which demands equal pay for jobs of comparable skill, responsibility, and working conditions regardless of the gender of the worker or the sex-typing of the job. Some of today's women office workers have also successfully fought to remove from their job descriptions such "wifely" tasks as preparing the office coffee and shopping for their bosses' anniversary gifts. However, many clerical workers continue to perform these tasks, receiving little recognition and low wages in return. Worse, office workers, like all women workers, continue to experience sexual harassment by male supervisors and co-workers.

Career Women: Women in Professional Jobs

Professional jobs offer women high wages and status. Like other jobs, they have been typed by gender and race-ethnicity, with white men at the top, although white women and people of color have made progress recently into some jobs which once were dominated by white males.

In 1900, over one-tenth of European American women were employed in professional jobs, compared to less than one in 50 workers among women of color. European American women were largely confined to a small set of professional jobs, including teaching, library science, and social work, all jobs which extended and professionalized woman's nurturing and caring roles. Indeed, educated white women played a major role in the fight to develop and feminize these professions, which they saw as outgrowths of social homemaking.

Before the Civil War, most teachers were white men; during the war white women were hired to replace them, and they remained after the war, arguing that teaching was, after all, a form of mothering. For Black women, teaching played a special role as a means to elevate and emancipate their people.[25] In 1900, white women had five times their labor market share of elementary and secondary school teaching jobs. The only other group of men or women to have at least their labor market share was Native American women. Next came Black women with 78 percent of their labor market share, Chinese American women with 64 percent, and white men with 33 percent. Just as schools were racially segregated, so teachers of color were assigned to teach children of their own racial-ethnic group; however, given the underrepresentation of men and women of color in teaching, white women also commonly taught students of color.

By 1900, women, mostly but not entirely white, had begun to professionalize nursing, elevating it from a form of domestic service to a skilled job which required professional education. As a broad occupational category, it was women's work; women of color had three times their labor market share of these jobs, and white women over five times, while men of color and white men each had less than one-tenth their labor market share. Within nursing, however, as within teaching, jobs were racially typed according to clientele, and access to nursing schools was limited for women of color.[26]

Other professions—medicine, law, and engineering, among others—became the province of white men. These jobs typically offered higher pay than white women's professions, called for more formal training, and involved control over rather than service of others. Indeed, they often required assistance by women, as nurses, receptionists, or legal secretaries. In 1900, no group other than white men held even half its labor market share of these elite professions, although a few individuals had gained admittance. Chinese American men, American Indian men, and white women had made the most progress in medicine; American Indian men, Black men, and white women in law.[27] Women of color were almost totally excluded. The greatest relative concentration for women of color in white men's professions was that of Black women in law, at one-twentieth their labor market share; in most of the white men's professions, no Chinese American, Japanese American, or American Indian women were even recorded in 1900.[28]

Over the course of the twentieth century, professional and technical employment has increased 12 times, and the share of these jobs in total employment has risen from one-tenth to over one-quarter. Although men continue to make up the majority of these workers, women's share of professional and technical jobs rose from 34 to 48 percent between 1900 and 1980.

Central to women's entrance into professional jobs have been their successful struggles for access to higher education, which constituted an important part of African American, Chinese American, and Japanese American economic history, as well as that of white women. Not surprisingly, the share of women in professional and technical occupations by racial-ethnic group is highly correlated with the share of college graduates.[29] Because educational opportunity has such an important effect on labor market

Table 10-10

Share of Employed Women Working in Professional and Technical
Occupations, by Racial-Ethnic Group, 1900-1980

	1900	1930	1960	1980
African American	1.2	3.4	7.8	15.2
European American	10.2	16.2	14.6	18.0
American Indian	1.9	4.6	9.1	14.5
Chinese American	1.4	22.0	17.9	20.4
Japanese American	0.3	6.6	12.3	17.8
Filipina American	n.a.	6.0	26.4	27.1
Chicana	n.a.	2.7	5.9	8.4
U.S. Puerto Rican	n.a.	n.a.	4.0	10.9
Island Puerto Rican	0.7	4.5	15.5	21.1

NOTES: See Appendix B for a listing of occupations included in this category, and Appendix D for a discussion of comparability issues across Census years. Asian American data include Hawaii for all years; 1980 data for American Indians include Eskimo and Aleut peoples; for 1900-1960, African American and European American include Latinas.
SOURCES: See Appendix A.

opportunities for women, lower educational attainment is also related to lower labor force participation rates, and may be both a cause and a result of Chicana's and U.S. Puerto Rican women's relatively low labor force participation rates.[30]

While women's representation in professional work increased for all racial-ethnic groups between 1900 and 1980, levels and rates of growth differ (see Table 10-10). The share in the professions increased most dramatically for women of color, who had nearly been excluded from such jobs in 1900. By 1980, Chinese American, Filipina American, and island Puerto Rican women were more likely to hold professional and technical jobs than European American women. However, in 1980, African American, Native American, Chicana, and U.S. Puerto Rican women were still less likely to hold professional and technical jobs than European American women had been in 1930.

Much of the growth in women's professional employment occurred in jobs that have historically been dominated by women: pre-kindergarten, kindergarten, and elementary school teacher, nurse, librarian, dietician, and social worker. In 1980, these professions (each of which was at least 75 percent female) employed 56 percent of women professionals.[31] In 1980, for example, women made up 96 percent of all registered nurses and 75 percent of all elementary school teachers. The racial-ethnic composition of the professions also changed, as the near-monopoly of white women was

Table 10-11

Definition of Labor Market Segments, 1980

UPPER-TIER PRIMARY:
-managerial and professional specialty occupations, except health
          assessment and treating
-supervisors and proprietors, sales occupations
-sales representatives, commodities, and finance
-farm operators and managers

LOWER-TIER PRIMARY:
-health assessment and treating
-technologists and technicians, except health
-protective service
-precision production, craft, and repair
-transportation occupations
-material moving equipment operators

UPPER-TIER SECONDARY:
-health technologists and technicians
-other sales
-administrative support occupations, including clerical
-machine operators and tenders
-fabricators, assemblers, inspectors

LOWER-TIER SECONDARY:
-private household occupations
-service occupations, except protective and household
-handlers, equipment cleaners, helpers, and laborers
-farming, forestry, and fishing, except farm operators and managers

challenged. Between 1900 and 1980, white women's relative concentration in elementary and secondary teaching fell from 525 to 175, while that of Black, American Indian, and Japanese women rose to nearly the same level as that of white women. On the other hand, Chicana, U.S. Puerto Rican, Chinese, and Filipina women continued to be underrepresented in teaching; still, each of these groups held over half their labor market share of teaching jobs, and more than any racial-ethnic group of men. Nursing has continued to be dominated by women; in 1980, women in all racial-ethnic groups, except Chicanas, held more than their labor market share, and Filipina nurses had more than seven times their labor market share.[32]

By 1980, white men continued to make up the large majority of lawyers, engineers, and physicians; indeed, between 1900 and 1980, white men's share of all jobs fell much more rapidly than their share of white men's professions, increasing their relative concentrations. However, all excluded groups (and especially Asian American women and men) have made significant progress, increasing both their share of these jobs and their relative concentrations between 1900 and 1980 in almost all cases.[33] Among engi-

Table 10-12

Distribution of Workers Across Labor Market Segments,
by Racial-Ethnic Group and Gender, 1980

	Upper-Tier Primary	Lower-Tier Primary	Total Primary	Upper-Tier Secondary	Lower-Tier Secondary	Total Secondary
WOMEN						
American Indian	18	8	26	45	28	73
Chicana	11	7	18	52	30	82
European American	23	8	31	51	18	69
African American	15	7	22	46	32	78
Japanese American	23	9	32	48	20	68
Chinese American	24	10	34	51	15	66
Filipina American	15	19	34	46	19	65
Island Puerto Rican	24	8	32	51	18	69
U.S. Puerto Rican	13	8	21	60	19	79
MEN						
American Indian	19	39	58	19	23	42
Chicano	12	33	45	24	31	55
European American	34	34	68	19	13	32
African American	14	32	46	26	28	54
Japanese American	41	25	66	16	17	33
Chinese American	43	17	60	16	25	41
Filipino American	24	25	49	26	24	50
Island Puerto Rican	24	33	57	22	21	43
U.S. Puerto Rican	14	28	42	33	25	58

NOTES: For a list of occupations included in each labor market segment, see Table 10-11. Numbers may not add to 100 as a result of rounding. American Indian includes Eskimo and Aleut peoples.
SOURCES: See Appendix A.

neers, American Asian men surpassed white men in terms of relative concentration; among physicians, both Asian American men and women had higher relative concentrations than white men—seven and three times their labor market share, respectively. However, these professions continue to be male-dominated: with the exception of Asian American women in medicine, white men and men of color's relative shares surpassed those of white women and women of color. Finally, racial-ethnic and gender hierarchies persist within each profession (and, indeed, within all occupations), in the form of different job assignments, different treatment, and unequal pay for equal work. For example, in 1980, among those working full-time, full-year as engineers, architects, or surveyors, white men earned more than twice as much as American Indian women.[34]

The Persistence of Racial-Ethnic, Gender, and Class Hierarchies in the Labor Market

This survey of occupations reveals a mixed picture: racial-ethnic and gender hierarchies have been reproduced and maintained at the same time as they have broken down. Asian Americans have surpassed European Americans according to many average indicators, and small shares of previously marginalized groups have broken into the elite jobs from which they were once excluded. Yet, men still earn much more than women, on average, as do whites compared to non-Asian people of color.

One summary measure of the labor market experience of different racial-ethnic and gender groups is their distribution across labor market segments. Again, the 1980 Census provides the most recent data broken down by detailed racial-ethnic group. Table 10-11 describes the jobs in each segment, Table 10-12 shows the 1980 shares of each group in each segment, and Figure 10-1 expresses these data in a bar graph.

Shares of workers in the top occupations—upper-tier primary jobs— varied greatly by group, from a high of 43 percent of all Chinese American men to a low of only 11 percent of Chicanas. The shares in upper-tier primary jobs were almost identical—at 23 or 24 percent—among Chinese American, European American, island Puerto Rican, and Japanese American women. These shares exceeded those of both male and female American Indians, U.S. Puerto Ricans, African Americans, and Chicanas/os. Among most of these latter groups, men's share of upper-tier primary jobs was close to or less than women's—not because women's share was unusually high, but because men's was unusually low. White men still held the majority of these elite jobs (61 percent); added to white women's 31 percent share, this created a near monopoly for whites, who held 92 percent of the total.[35] Even though Japanese American and Chinese American men and women were doing as well or better than whites in this segment of the occupational hierarchy, they constituted such a small part of the labor force that whites maintained their numerical dominance in the primary sector.

Men predominated in the lower tier of the primary sector, which includes traditional male jobs such as craft work, truck driving, and protective service, as well as feminine jobs such as nursing. Approximately 30 percent of men of all racial-ethnic groups were found in this tier, which represents a blue-collar, working-class route to high salaries and job stability. The shares of women workers in these jobs, however, were 10 percent or less for all groups except Filipinas, who had very high numbers in nursing.

Jobs in the upper tier of the secondary labor market include traditionally feminine clerical jobs, as well as sales clerks, health technologists and technicians, and some manufacturing jobs (including machine operators or

Table 10-13

Median Incomes of Full-Time, Full-Year Workers,
by Gender and Race-Ethnicity, 1980

	Women	Men	W/M	W/EAM
European American	$10,564	$18,157	58 %	58 %
African American	9,589	12,677	76	53
Chicana/o	8,616	12,623	68	47
U.S. Puerto Rican	9,390	12,108	78	52
Island Puerto Rican	6,452	7,218	89	36
American Indian	9,350	14,034	67	51
Japanese American	11,916	20,262	59	66
Chinese American	11,891	17,945	66	65
Filipina/o American	12,007	15,101	80	66

NOTES: EAM equals European American men. American Indian includes Eskimo and
Aleut peoples.
SOURCES: See Appendix A.

tenders, fabricators, assemblers, and inspectors). These jobs employed over
44 percent of women in each racial-ethnic group, with fairly small variations
among the groups. Men's shares were considerably lower.

Non-Asian men and women of color were more likely than other
groups to be employed in the lower tier of the secondary sector of the labor
market, which includes service workers, laborers, farm workers, and private
household workers. Roughly 30 percent of women of color held jobs in this
sector, compared to less than 20 percent of white women. Almost one-third
of Chicanos, and approximately one-quarter of Black, Chinese American,
Filipino American, and U.S. Puerto Rican men were confined to this sector;
not surprisingly, white men had the lowest share.

In the contemporary economy, race-ethnicity is less directly linked to
economic status than it was in earlier centuries, or even during the first half
of the twentieth century—just as gender is less linked to unpaid work and
economic dependence on men. There is now considerable labor force
hierarchy *within* each racial-ethnic group and *among* women. At least 11
percent of women and of men in each racial-ethnic group were in the top
tier of the labor market; at least 13 percent of women and of men in each
racial-ethnic group—including European American men—fell in the bottom
tier. For those white women and people of color who have made it to the
top tier of the primary labor market, race and gender oppression no longer
cause low incomes. Indeed, those with top credentials may actually find

themselves especially sought after, as employers attempt to create the impression that they are not sexist or racist.

Unfortunately the successes of some white women and people of color—as executives of corporations, legislators, or doctors—have led many to conclude that gender and race no longer play a significant role in generating economic inequality.[36] However, even these privileged persons continue to experience gender and racial-ethnic discrimination. This discrimination at the top of the labor market is sometimes referred to as "hitting the glass ceiling," an invisible barrier halting their progress into the highest reaches of executive status.[37]

More important, the attenuation of the links between race-ethnicity, gender, and labor market status has been relatively slight. The very fact that so few who are not white men have made it to the top illustrates the pervasiveness of gender and race oppression. For those confined to the secondary sphere, gender, racial-ethnic, and class oppression are inseparable and ubiquitous. Most women still work in female-dominated jobs which pay less than men's jobs requiring comparable levels of education and responsibility. Blacks, Chicanas/os, and U.S. Puerto Ricans continue to be segregated into ghettos with inferior schooling and few employment opportunities other than the corner McDonald's, the local hospital or convalescent home, or the underground economy.

One way to quantify the persistence of racial-ethnic and gender hierarchies is to look at earnings and income inequality. Table 10-13 presents median incomes for 1980. Unfortunately, earnings data are not available in detailed racial-ethnic categories; the best data available are median incomes of full-time, full-year workers (which do closely approximate earnings).[38] The striking progress of Asian Americans, who now surpass whites in many income categories, is evident.

Women workers' incomes ranged from 58 percent to 89 percent of men's, according to racial-ethnic group. The male-female gap is the largest for European American and Japanese American women because the men in these groups earn such high incomes. Racial-ethnic differences in median incomes for full-time, full-year workers were also substantial in 1980: island Puerto Rican men's median incomes stood at only 36 percent of Japanese American men's. When race, ethnicity, and gender are combined, the full import of the labor market hierarchy on workers' incomes is clear: the highest median income (Japanese American men) was over three times the lowest (island Puerto Rican women).

Even these data underestimate the full extent of gender and racial-ethnic inequality in incomes because they ignore the role of part-time work and unemployment. In each racial-ethnic group, fewer women worked full-time

Table 10-14

Unemployment Rates, by Race-Ethnicity and Gender, 1980		
	Women	Men
American Indian	11.9 %	14.1 %
European American	5.6	5.8
African American	11.3	12.3
Chicana/o	9.9	8.7
Chinese American	4.1	3.2
Japanese American	3.3	2.7
Filipina/o American	4.6	5.1
U.S. Puerto Rican	12.7	11.1
Island Puerto Rican	16.4	14.4
Highest/Lowest	5.0	4.5

NOTE: American Indian includes Eskimo and Aleut peoples.
SOURCES: See Appendix A.

than did men, largely as a result of women's continuing responsibility for unpaid work. Comparing median incomes of all women and men with incomes (not just full-time, full-year workers), we find that the incomes of island Puerto Rican women stood at a meager one-fifth that of white men and Japanese American men.[39] Unemployment rates also varied substantially across groups, as shown in Table 10-14, and were highest for those racial-ethnic groups on the bottom of the income hierarchy. Unemployment rates for Chicanas/os, African Americans, American Indians, and Puerto Ricans all ranged from one and one-half to over five times higher than those for Asian American and white men and women.

Together, lower earnings and higher unemployment rates created shocking differences in per capita income and poverty rates across racial-ethnic groups in 1980, as shown in Table 10-15. Among American Indians, African Americans, Chicanas/os, and both U.S. and island Puerto Ricans, incomes per person were less than three-fifths those of European Americans. Poverty rates varied widely, from a low of 6.5 percent to a high of 62 percent; for non-Asian people of color, the share which lived in poverty was from two and one-half to seven times higher than that for whites. At least 6 percent of each racial-ethnic group, and one-quarter or more of non-Asian people of

Table 10-15

Per Capita Income and Poverty Rates,
by Racial-Ethnic Group, 1980

	Per Capita Income	Poverty Rates
Japanese American	$9,068	6.5 %
European American	7,942	8.9
Chinese American	7,476	13.5
Filipina/o American	6,915	7.1
American Indian	4,618	27.6
African American	4,556	29.8
Chicana/o	4,231	23.3
U.S. Puerto Rican	3,905	36.3
Island Puerto Rican	2,126	62.4

NOTE: American Indian includes Eskimo and Aleut peoples.
SOURCE: See Appendix A.

color, live in poverty. Since these data represent the share in poverty at one time, a much larger share experiences poverty at some time in their lives.

No Individual Solutions

Increasingly, as men and women of different racial-ethnic groups have been incorporated into paid work, the struggle for economic survival has become a struggle for advancement in the labor market. Unfortunately, the capitalist economy is a pyramid: only a small percentage can be highly paid managers and professionals, while most workers are consigned to lower-level white- or blue-collar positions. Even when whole communities have pulled together to advance the opportunities of individuals—such as with the civil rights and white women's movements—economic inequality has not been eliminated. Indeed, as mentioned above, the presence of some white women and some men and women of color in elite jobs can lead to complacency in the face of the racial-ethnic, gender and class oppression experienced by most white women and people of color.

Thus, individual efforts to scale the labor market pyramid will not eliminate economic injustice as long as the hierarchy persists. Instead, collective struggles must begin to challenge the labor market hierarchy itself, as well as the other social institutions which reproduce inequality. This will require radical structural changes across the economy, the polity and the family. In what follows, we do not provide a full agenda for economic justice, but rather suggest some of the key changes which must take place to address the racial-ethnic, gender, and class hierarchy in the economy.

Secondary sector jobs can be restructured to provide dignity and meaning: for instance, child-care and kitchen workers should be paid more and allowed more opportunities to manage and control their own working conditions. Recent initiatives by service sector workers—such as the Justice for Janitors campaign based in Atlanta, which seeks to raise wages and benefits for office cleaners—have helped to improve the wages and working conditions of some of the lowest paying jobs. Similarly, office workers are organizing to demand better earnings and treatment on the job. Many unions have taken on comparable worth campaigns, which reevaluate the pay scale for fairness, and advocate solidarity wage agreements which provide higher percentage pay raises to the lowest-paid workers. These campaigns call into question the historical bases of pay hierarchies and can lead workers to question the justice and even the necessity of any wage inequality.[39] To the extent that such campaigns represent the interests of all workers—and hence confront racial-ethnic and gender as well as class oppression—they can offer real progress towards economic justice.

Furthermore, new forms of economic democracy, including worker ownership of enterprises, can transform a hierarchical economy into a participatory community. Worker ownership can be a mechanism for breaking down the firm's internal class structure and allowing for new forms of worker management and democracy.[40] But democracy in the workplace is not enough. Democracy must be extended to the entire economy through planning mechanisms that give communities the power to determine, for example, what jobs will be located in their midst and what technologies will be adopted. These changes must be accompanied by movements toward democracy in the polity, such as greater voter participation, elimination of the power of the corporate media, and public financing of electoral campaigns.

The historical record suggests that struggles against the labor market hierarchy will be most effective in the context of a national commitment to full employment and adequate minimum wages, so that all who want to work can find a living-wage job. Full employment not only strengthens the bargaining power of workers vis-à-vis capital, but the guarantee of a job is a basic human right, which guarantees incorporation into and participation in social life.

The labor market hierarchy cannot be eliminated unless we also end the concentration of wealth in the hands of a few, with policies such as redistributive inheritance and wealth taxes. As part of such a redistributive

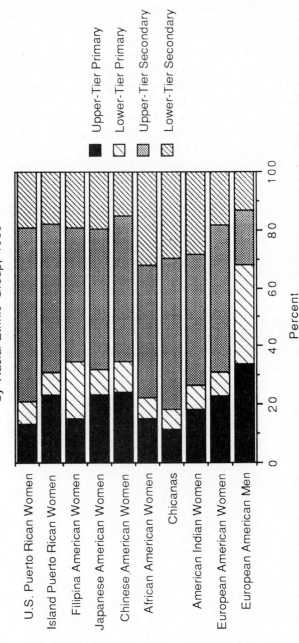

Figure 10-1: The Distribution of Women Workers across Labor Market Segments, by Racial-Ethnic Group, 1980

NOTES: American Indian includes Eskimo and Aleut peoples. See Table 10-5 for a listing of the occupations in each labor market segment. See Table 10-6 for the actual percentages employed in each segment.
SOURCES: 1980 Census; see Appendix A.

effort, it would be just to pay reparations to the racial-ethnic groups whose lands and wealth were stolen over the course of U.S. economic history. The legislation enabling reparations payments to Japanese Americans is one example—albeit too little and too late—of such repayment.

Finally, changes in the economics of the family, and in the relationship between family and work life, are necessary. Given the power that accompanies money in a capitalist economy, a sexual division of labor which assigns the major share of unpaid work in the home to women (and the higher-paid jobs to men) reproduces inequality. Not only does it disempower married women, especially mothers, but it impoverishes single mothers, assigning them both responsibility for children and jobs which cannot support those children. Paid parental leaves that can be shared between parents, as in Sweden, are one route to encouraging a more equal sharing of household work, especially if the total amount of leave increases when both parents participate. Changes in the labor market—including a more equal pay structure for women and men in which all receive higher wages, a shorter work week, and full employment—would also encourage more symmetrical marriages, allow a better balance between family and work for both men and women, and make parenting a less difficult and impoverishing activity for single parents. Additional policies which would address inequality inside the home and in the labor market include affordable and safe birth control and abortion (along with sex education), affordable child and dependent care, national health care, and high quality education for all.

The twentieth century has been a time of significant movement in the direction of greater economic justice, particularly during the 1960s and 1970s. However, our progress has been countered by a strong reaction from the wealthy and powerful, who wish to leave the economy to the "invisible hand" of the market, with its legacy of race, class, and gender oppression. If we are to defend past gains, and move further towards economic justice, we must "seek beyond history" for a truly inclusive movement for economic justice.[41]

Chapter 11

SEEKING BEYOND HISTORY

"We seek beyond history for a new and more possible meeting."[1]

—Audre Lorde

It is difficult to find concluding words for a project as broad, complex, and wide-ranging as this one. Here we sum up some of the basic themes and insights of the book, and offer some thoughts about how activists can build on the histories we have examined.

Women's Works: Essential and Diverse

The simplest lesson of this book is that women—of all racial-ethnic groups, ages, classes, and sexual preferences—have been essential to the development and reproduction of the U.S. economy. Few of the women we have encountered spent their lives in leisure; most worked from dawn to far past dusk to care for themselves and their families. In the colonial and nineteenth-century economies, women's household work was indispensable to the direct provisioning of their families' needs. Women also contributed to production of goods and services for sale to others through their labor in family businesses and through paid work performed in the home. The labor of enslaved African American women in the fields and homes of white Southerners was essential to the southern economy and to early U.S. economic growth. And women comprised a critical part of the growing wage-labor force: young girls produced the first factory-made cloth in the early textile mills, domestic servants helped care for and reproduce generations of children, women have taught youngsters in elementary and secondary schools, and clerical workers continue to be at the core of the communication and accounting network of the modern economy. Finally, women have given birth to and raised new workers, without financial compensation and with little social recognition.

Second, and equally evident, is the diversity of women's works not simply across history, but during any one period. While some women labored virtually around the clock, others lived in different degrees of leisure.

Some women worked without pay, while others were paid, and pay levels ranged widely. Many women directly served other women as domestic servants. We cannot identify a shared *work* in which all women participated, for any period. What women have shared has been differentiation from and, in most cases, economic and political subordination to, the men of their racial-ethnic group and class.

Stages in Women's Works

We have identified three broad stages in the organization and differentiation of women's works across the sweep of U.S. economic history. These stages do not correspond precisely to distinct periods, as they overlap in time. In the first stage, spanning the colonial era and the nineteenth century, a variety of labor systems existed, within which class positions were closely tied to race-ethnicity; women's works were vastly and qualitatively different across racial-ethnic groups as well as classes. In the second stage, which characterizes the late nineteenth century and the first half of the twentieth, wage labor in the capitalist mode of production gained dominance, and the economic positions of women became more qualitatively similar across racial-ethnic groups; married women concentrated their efforts on unpaid work in their homes, while husbands, sons, and daughters participated in wage work which was strictly gender-race-ethnicity typed. In the third stage, beginning after World War II, married women increasingly participated in paid labor, and rigid gender and racial-ethnic differences in the job hierarchy began to break down. We discuss each of these stages briefly here.

Up through the early twentieth century, the U.S. economy included different labor systems that segregated racial-ethnic groups into qualitatively different kinds of work; these different types of work were attached to different legal and political statuses. American Indians worked within tribal economies, fighting a losing war against destruction and displacement by the European invaders. Colonial European immigrants mostly lived and worked in family-owned businesses and farms, some as indentured servants, while Europeans who immigrated after the mid-1800s were increasingly channeled into factories and mines. Africans were brought into the South to work as slaves for propertied whites, while Asians were imported as contract laborers for railroads and plantations and prevented by law from owning land. The Mexicans of the Southwest, working within the racial hierarchy of the *hacienda* and family-farm economy, were politically subordinated and displaced from their lands by Anglos. Puerto Rico and the Philippines were colonized by the U.S. military at the end of the nineteenth century, bringing their economies into the sphere of U.S. domination. In summary, women participated in the U.S. economy in vastly different ways according to their racial-ethnic group and class position.

Within each racial-ethnic and class group, sexual divisions of labor underlay and organized marriage and reproduction. However, the form taken by these divisions of labor were affected and often destabilized by the process of white domination. For example, Asian women were prevented from joining their husbands, creating a split-household family; enslaved Africans were commonly sold away from spouses and children; and Native American children were taken from their families to be raised in Protestant boarding schools. In this way, the family was a site not simply of gender oppression, but also of racial-ethnic domination. Simply surviving as a family required struggle, and it constituted a form of resistance to racial and class domination.

In the second stage of women's works, which began in the late nineteenth century, wage labor for capital became the dominant economic activity. Slavery and indentured servitude were abolished, contract labor declined, and self-sufficient production and self-employment dwindled. People of all racial-ethnic groups were funneled into wage-labor capitalist relationships at uneven rates and into a hierarchy of positions. Whites claimed the highest-paid, highest-status jobs, and white supremacy was strengthened by residential, school, and labor force segregation and by anti-miscegenation laws. Men entered the labor force to a greater degree than women, single women more than married women, and women of color (especially Black) more than white; men's wages were higher than women's. This sexual division of paid labor, along with the assignment of unpaid household work to women, perpetuated male supremacy.

The joint and simultaneous processes of white and male domination maintained a rigid gender and racial-ethnic typing of work inside and outside the home in spite of the dramatic transformation in the content of work during this stage. Up through World War II, paid jobs were strictly race-sex typed—many on a national level, others by region or workplace. White men were able to monopolize the top managerial, administrative, and professional jobs, while white women monopolized the feminine professions and clerical work. People of color remained overly concentrated in the pre-industrial sectors of agriculture and domestic work. Although professional schools, associations, and craft unions continued to erect barriers to the entrance of white women and people of color into white masculine jobs, some gained admission by virtue of wealth and class privilege—or dogged perseverance. Others bypassed the segregated institutions and educated themselves. Those few people of color or white women who established themselves in elite jobs such as the professions rarely worked alongside white men. In sum, racial-ethnic and gender processes essentially ascribed individuals to jobs which were simultaneously segregated by race-ethnicity and by gender.

In the post-World War II period, this racial-ethnic and gender segregation has partially broken down. Married women, especially white, middle-class, married women, have rapidly entered the paid labor force. Feminist and civil rights struggles have challenged the legal and ethical basis for gender and racial-ethnic segregation. Anti-miscegenation laws, racial segregation in housing and schools, and discriminatory practices in schools and workplaces have all formally been overturned. Yet, while a privileged minority of white women and people of color now has access to top positions, gender and racial-ethnic segregation and inequality live on in the labor market, in housing and schools, and in the political system. Furthermore, women continue to perform the bulk of unpaid work in the home.

Directions for Future Research

There is a great need for more research about the interconnections among race-ethnicity, gender, and class. We relied heavily on national Census Bureau data, but further research is needed to explore the variations in race-gender typing of work across regions and companies. Informal and underground economies comprise a growing part of the work experiences of many racial-ethnic groups, especially Blacks and Puerto Ricans; detailed studies of women's role in the informal economy of many Third World countries are underway, but little is known about women's participation in the informal economies of the United States. We were unable to locate any detailed studies of racial-ethnic or class differences in the division of household labor between the sexes, and we suspect that study of these differences would yield important insights into the dynamics of racial-ethnic, class, and gender processes. The nature and extent of class differences within racial-ethnic groups are starting to command more attention from social scientists; we hope that the focus will include the interaction between these differences and gender processes. The work and family arrangements of lesbians remain invisible in most analyses, and we hope that more studies will soon become available in that area. Finally, since the 1990 Census will make available more up-to-date information on detailed racial-ethnic groups, future research can assess the impact of the conservative policies of the 1980s on racial-ethnic and gender inequality.

Liberatory Knowledge, Liberatory Practice

In Chapter 1, we spoke of our commitment, as political activists, to economic and social justice, and of our view of this book as "liberatory knowledge." What can one take from this book in terms of direction and political inspiration? What can we say about women's activism?

First, there is much to be done. Economic injustice, endemic in our system since its inception, continues. However, in the face of such continual injustice, we can take heart in the constancy of social change. Many people think of the economy as unchangeable, as though economic activity lay outside the realm of human control. But the economy is a set of shared social practices, ideas, and institutions that are created, maintained, and reproduced by people; it has changed rapidly through history and will be further transformed in the future. The direction of such change is at least partially up to us. Hierarchies and injustices can and have been eliminated. Slavery no longer exists; white women and people of color have undermined the justifications for sex and race discrimination and segregation; the union movement has won increasing recognition of workers' rights. At the same time, change can be for the worse as well as for the better. Affirmative Action policies, workers' rights, and the right to abortion—which many took for granted in the 1970s—were severely undermined in the 1980s, and may be lost in the 1990s. Progress towards economic justice is not inevitable; it is won by people through their work, individually and collectively, to better the economic practices and institutions they have inherited from the past. Very simply, what we do with our lives in the present will make history.

The previous chapters have described the many arenas in which women have struggled for economic justice. In the realm of the family and reproduction, women have organized against battering by their husbands and fathers, for their rights to sex education and reproductive freedom, and for their right to love other women. Trade union women have pushed for better wages and working conditions and women's organizations have sought to overturn the sex and race discrimination which has barred entry into better jobs. Women have played an important role in national liberation and civil rights movements.

Women take into all of these movements for economic justice multi-faceted identities that are constructed by interconnected racial-ethnic, class, and gender processes. Many bring multiple experiences of oppression into their struggles, and their movements simultaneously combat their many oppressions. For example, Chicana cannery workers in Watsonville confronted class, race, and gender hierarchies, as did welfare mothers in the NWRO. Similarly, the Asian feminists fighting sexploitation and the mail-order bride market confront a complex web of gender, racial-ethnic, and class oppression.

At the same time, women's efforts to address injustice may be undermined if their political work is also informed by privilege. In a context of simultaneous privilege and oppression, organizing out of self-interest often attacks one form of oppression while strengthening another, and can heighten antagonisms among women. For example, throughout the nineteenth and early twentieth centuries, white workers attempting to protect their jobs from low-wage competition advocated the expulsion of Asian and Chicana/o workers. This racist and nativist sentiment served to further divide workers of different racial-ethnic groups, preventing the formation of multiracial coalitions that might have provided the entire working class with greater political and economic power. Similarly, white suffragists pursued the vote for "all women," but in the process sacrificed the voting rights of people of color and the possibilities for political transformation that might have followed universal enfranchisement.

In Chapter 1, we set forth the goal of liberatory knowledge for this project, defining it as knowledge of one's position in the complex hierarchy of domination and subordination in which we live.[2] Liberatory knowledge reveals that no woman's experience is generic, and that there is no generic experience of racial-ethnic, class or gender oppression. Furthermore, liberatory knowledge demands awareness of our privileges as well as of the different forms of oppression which we and others experience.

Hence, liberatory knowledge can incite us to eradicate all forms of oppression, even when this involves attacking our own privileges. Liberatory knowledge can lead a man to commit himself to feminist struggle against gender divisions and male domination; a wealthy woman to spend her life and resources fighting against economic injustice; and a white woman to work to transform racist institutions and practices. In other words, liberatory knowledge leads us to a more inclusive understanding of "self-interest," one that goes beyond individual income and status in the economic hierarchy to embrace the well-being of the entire social community.

Many political movements, especially movements which have organized in the name of a generic group such as "all workers" or "all women," have attempted to suppress or ignore differences within the group in the interests of a larger unity. But differences—whether based on gender, race-ethnicity, class, sexual preference, or other characteristics—cannot be split off or put aside like the pop beads we discussed in Chapter 2. When a movement attempts to ignore such differences, the interests of a privileged sub-group, such as male workers or white women, tend to prevail. For example, the "women's movement" of the 1970s was dominated by upper-middle-class, white, heterosexual women. These women posited a generic "women's interest," which they equated to their own limited experience of oppression as women. Thus, the "women's movement" failed to understand the distinct needs of working-class women, women of color, and lesbians.

Liberatory knowledge can help transcend these problems, which have plagued movements for economic justice. Indeed, because movements bring together people with diverse experiences of oppression, political activism is often an important locus for the production of liberatory knowledge. Pressure from white women and workers of color, for example, has forced the trade union movement to recognize that these workers are additionally exploited; to address their exploitation, many unions have taken up the demand of comparable worth.

The women's movement has also been a site of liberatory knowledge and practice as women have learned about each other's experiences of oppression. In the movement, many middle-class women have encountered working-class and impoverished women and learned about class exploitation; white women have encountered women of color and learned about racial oppression; women of color have encountered one another and learned about the different forms of racial oppression they have experienced; and heterosexual women have encountered lesbians and learned about homophobia. Out of such learning, different parts of the women's movement have developed agendas that are more representative of women's diverse needs. For example, white women first took the lead in defining reproductive freedom as women's right to sex education, birth control, and abortion, ignoring sterilization abuse, the major reproductive freedom issue for many women of color. In response to pressure from women of color, feminists united to form the Coalition for Abortion Rights and Against Sterilization Abuse (CARASA) and the Reproductive Rights National Network (R2N2), each with platforms that eventually redefined reproductive freedom to include the right to have children along with the right not to have children. Thus, women were united in an alliance that acknowledged their differences rather than denied them.

We agree with bell hooks' analysis of the appropriate direction for feminist organizing:

> We do not need to share common oppression to fight equally to end oppression...We can be sisters united by shared interests and beliefs, united in our appreciation for diversity, united in our struggle to end sexist oppression.[3]

And, we would add, this recognition of difference has to go even further. Feminists need to acknowledge that much struggle against sexist oppression has taken place and continues to be waged outside the women's movement, in civil rights, workers', and gay movements. Further, as we have argued, gender oppression cannot meaningfully be split off from other kinds of oppression. While each of us must choose the arenas in which we struggle, given the limits of our time and energies, we must at the same time seek awareness of the ways in which all forms of oppression operate in that arena.

Only through such awareness can we construct a political practice that is truly liberatory.

In this book, we have tried to acquaint you with the extraordinary array of women's histories, ranging from oppression to privilege. Can we use the liberatory knowledge of these different histories to create liberatory practice, and in so doing, take control of our joint destinies? In the words of Audre Lorde, can we "seek beyond history for a new and more possible meeting"?

> We have chosen each other
> and the edge of each other's battles
> the war is the same
>
> if we lose
> someday women's blood will congeal
> upon a dead planet
> if we win
> there is no telling
> we seek beyond history
> for a new and more possible meeting.[4]

NOTES

Preface and Acknowledgments

1. Andrea Timberlake, Lynn Weber Cannon, Rebecca F. Guy, and Elizabeth Higginbotham, eds., *Women of Color and Southern Women: A Bibliography of Social Science Research, 1975 to 1988* (Memphis: Center for Research on Women, Memphis State University, 1988).

Chapter 1

1. Some of the economics journals which publish work in radical political economics are *The Review of Radical Political Economics, The Cambridge Journal of Economics, Rethinking Marxism,* and *Social Concept; Dollars & Sense* and *Monthly Review* are monthly radical economics publications.

2. Some of the ovular works here have been Bonnie Thornton Dill, "The Dialectics of Black Womanhood," *Signs* 4 (Spring 1979): 543-55; Cherríe Moraga and Gloria Anzaldúa, eds., *This Bridge Called My Back: Writings by Radical Women of Color* (Watertown, MA: Persephone Press, 1981); Gloria Joseph and Jill Lewis, *Common Differences: Conflicts in Black and White Feminist Perspectives* (New York: Doubleday Anchor, 1981); Gloria T. Hull, Patricia Bell Scott, and Barbara Smith, eds., *All the Women Are White, All the Blacks Are Men, But Some of Us Are Brave: Black Women's Studies* (Old Westbury, NY: Feminist Press, 1982); and Bell Hooks, *Feminist Theory: From Margin to Center* (Boston: South End Press, 1984). The Memphis State University Center for Research on Women (Memphis, TN 38152) has published excellent papers on race-ethnicity and women, including an extremely helpful bibliography, *Women of Color and Southern Women: A Bibliography of Social Science Research, 1975 to 1988,* ed. Andrea Timberlake, Lynn Weber Cannon, Rebecca F. Guy, and Elizabeth Higginbotham.

3. See Linda Nicholson, *Gender and History: The Limits of Social Theory in the Age of the Family* (New York: Columbia University Press, 1986), and Julie Matthaei, "Marxist-Feminist Contributions to Radical Economics," in *Radical Economics,* ed. Susan Feiner and Bruce Roberts (Norwell, MA: Kluwer-Nijhoff, forthcoming).

4. There is an important feminist literature on this topic; see, for example, Sandra Harding, ed., *Feminism and Methodology* (Bloomington, IN: Indiana University Press, 1987), which includes Nancy Hartsock's essay, "The Feminist Standpoint: Developing the Ground for a Specifically Feminist Historical Materialism"; Nancy Fraser, *Unruly Practices: Power, Discourse, and Gender in Contemporary Social Theory* (Minneapolis: University of Minnesota Press, 1989); and Gayatri Chakravorty Spivak, *In Other Worlds: Essays in Cultural Politics* (New York: Methuen, 1987). In economics, see especially the work of Arjo Klamer, for example, "Economics as Discourse," in *The Popperian Legacy in Economics,* ed. Neil de Marchi, (Cambridge: Cambridge University Press, 1988), 259-78, and the journals *Social Concept* and *Rethinking Marxism.*

5. Quote from Richard Levins, Harvard School of Public Health, "Science, Anti-Science, and the Future of Both," Paper presented at *Marxism Now* Conference, University of Massachusetts, Amherst, 2 December 1989. The origins of this stance lie in liberation theology and in works such as Paulo Freire, *Pedagogy of the Oppressed* (New York: Continuum, 1982). See also Sandra Harding, "The Instability of the Analytical Categories of Feminist Theory," in *Sex and Scientific Inquiry,* ed. Sandra Harding and Jean F. O'Barr (Chicago: University of Chicago Press, 1987), 283-302.

6. Sandra Harding, "Is Marxism Enough? Feminist Approaches to Science," Paper presented at *Marxism Now* Conference.

7. Ibid.

8. For example, in the early twentieth century, gainful employment rates rather than labor

force participation rates were gathered; in different Census years, enumerators were given different instructions as to whether or not to count unpaid work in the home as employment. For occupations, categories must of necessity shift as jobs change; nursing, for example, was once a form of domestic service. Sometimes the problems can be surmounted by creating new job categories and aggregating jobs, but in some years the Census does not provide enough occupational detail for re-categorization. See Appendix A for a complete listing of the different Census Bureau sources used in this book, and Appendix D for a short discussion of the comparability problem.

9. "Minority Populations Grow at Faster Rate: 1980-88," *CENSUS and You: Monthly News from the U.S. Bureau of the Census* 25 (April 1990): 8. Data were not broken down by detailed racial-ethnic group, nor were non-Latina/o whites separated out in these 1988 data. We calculated from these numbers that the population of color (including Latinas/os) was 23.7 percent of the total population in 1988 by assuming that Latinas/os had reported their race as white.

10. An earlier book that also compares women's work across racial-ethnic groups, and that served as a model for this study, is Elizabeth McTaggart Almquist's excellent volume, *Minorities, Gender, and Work* (Lexington, MA: D.C. Heath, 1979). Almquist treats separately and comparatively American Indian, African American, Mexican American, Puerto Rican, Chinese American, Japanese American, and Filipina American (but not European American) women.

Chapter 2

1. See, for example, Michael Omi and Howard Winant, *Racial Formation in the United States: From the 1960s to the 1980s* (New York: Routledge & Kegan Paul, 1986); E. San Juan, "Problems in One Marxist Project of Theorizing Race," in *Rethinking Marxism* 2 (Summer 1989): 58-80; Elizabeth V. Spelman, *Inessential Woman: Problems of Exclusion in Feminist Thought* (Boston: Beacon Press, 1988); Julie Matthaei, "Marxist Contributions to Radical Economics," in *Radical Economics*, ed. Susan Feiner and Bruce Roberts (Norwell, MA: Kluwer-Nijhoff, forthcoming).

2. On Agassiz, a Swiss immigrant to the United States who headed Harvard University's Department of Comparative Biology, see Steven Jay Gould, *The Mismeasure of Man* (New York: W.W. Norton and Company, 1981), 42-51. On Gobineau, see Omi and Winant, 59.

3. A dual systems approach to class and gender oppression is presented and debated in Lydia Sargent, ed., *Women and Revolution* (Boston: South End Press, 1981). For a tri-systems approach covering race, gender, and class, see Ann Ferguson, "On Conceiving Motherhood and Sexuality: A Feminist Materialist Approach," in *Mothering: Essays in Feminist Theory*, ed. Joyce Treblicot (Totowa, NJ: Rowman and Allanheld, 1983).

4. Spelman, 136.

5. See Claude Levi-Strauss, "The Family," in *The Family in Transition*, ed. Arlene Skolnick and Jerome Skolnick (Boston: Little Brown, 1971); Michelle Zimbalist Rosaldo, "Women, Culture, and Society: A Theoretical Overview," in *Woman, Culture, and Society*, ed. Michelle Rosaldo and Louise Lamphere (Stanford: Stanford University Press, 1974). More recent anthropological work has questioned and refined the Rosaldo/Lamphere hypothesis of the universality of male dominance.

6. For example, the U.S. government only recognized men as "treaty chiefs" of American Indian nations in spite of the fact that many nations had women chiefs.

7. This practice was most pronounced among the Spanish conquistadors against indigenous women in Puerto Rico and Mexico and among southern slave owners against their slaves. See Chs. 4 and 8.

8. See Herbert Gutman, *The Black Family in Slavery and Freedom, 1750-1925* (New York: Pantheon Books, 1976).

9. See, for example, Omi and Winant; John Hodges et al., *The Cultural Bases of Racism and Group Oppression* (Berkeley: Two Riders Press, 1975); Oliver C. Cox, *Class, Caste & Race: A Study in Social Dynamics* (New York: Monthly Review Press, 1959); and Michael Banton and Jonathan Harwood, *The Race Concept* (New York: Praeger, 1975), Ch. 1.

10. See Gould, 323, for a discussion of contemporary scientific understandings of racial

differences.

11. Omi and Winant, 58.

12. Cox, Part 3, especially Ch. 16.

13. Harold Baron, "Racial Domination in Advanced Capitalism: A Theory of Nationalism and Divisions in the Labor Market," in *Labor Market Segmentation,* ed. Richard Edwards, Michael Reich, and David Gordon (Lexington, MA: D.C. Heath and Company, 1975).

14. U.S. Bureau of the Census, *Statistical Abstract of the United States: 1990* (Washington, DC: GPO, 1990), 386.

15. This represents an increase for the top 0.5 percent, from 25.4 percent of total wealth 20 years ago; 20 years ago, the poorest 90 percent of all households had 34.9 percent of all wealth, 6.7 percentage points more than they have presently. There has been a controversy over these numbers; after these data, collected by the Federal Reserve Board, were publicized by the Joint Economic Committee of Congress, the Federal Reserve claimed that a mistake had been made in the original survey, and that actually there had been no increase in the share of wealth held by the top 0.5 percent. See "Scandal at the Fed? Doctoring the Numbers on Wealth Concentration," *Dollars & Sense,* No. 125 (April 1987): 10.

16. For good discussions of this process, see David Gordon, Richard Edwards, Michael Reich, eds., *Segmented Work, Divided Workers: The Historical Transformation of Labor in the United States* (New York: Cambridge University Press, 1982); and Eric Wright, "Class Boundaries and Contradictory Class Locations," in *Classes, Power, and Conflict,* ed. Anthony Giddens (Berkeley: University of California Press, 1982), 112-29.

17. Marxist-feminists did attempt to analyze this work as "domestic labor" in a theoretical debate in the 1970s; for a review of this debate, see Wally Seccombe, "Reflections on the Domestic Labor Debate and Prospects for Marxist-Feminist Synthesis," in *The Politics of Diversity,* ed. Roberta Hamilton and Michele Barrett (Canada: Book Center Inc., 1986). Some claim that the household is part of a different mode of production which coexists with capitalism; see Harriet Fraad, Stephen Resnick, and Richard Wolff, "For Every Knight in Shining Armor, There's a Castle Waiting to Be Cleaned: A Marxist-Feminist Analysis of the Household," *Rethinking Marxism* 2 (Winter 1989): 10-69; and the comments by Julie Matthaei, Zillah Eisenstein, Kim Lane Scheppele, Nancy Folbre, Heidi Hartmann, and Stephanie Coontz in the same issue.

18. See Edna Bonacich, "Advanced Capitalism and Black/White Race Relations in the United States: A Split Labor Market Interpretation," *American Sociological Review* 41 (February 1976): 34-51.

19. Audre Lorde, "The Uses of Anger," *Women's Studies Quarterly* 9 (Fall 1981): 7.

Chapter 3

1. We use the terms American Indian and Native American interchangeably here following current practice. We also use the term "nation" in place of the more familiar term "tribe" to call attention to Native Americans' status as sovereign peoples.

2. Quoted in Jane B. Katz, ed., *I Am the Fire of Time: The Voices of Native American Women* (New York: E.P. Dutton, 1977), vii.

3. Algonquian was spoken by nations including the Algonquin, Blackfoot, Cheyenne, Micmac, Penobscot, and Shawnee; Shoshonean by the Comanche, Hopi, Shonone, and Ute; Caddoan by Arikara, Caddo, and Pawnee; Iroquoian by the Cherokee, Mohawk, and Seneca; Muskogean by the Chickasaw, Choctaw, and Creek; Siouan by the Crow, Dakota, Sioux, and Winnebago; Athabascan by the Apache and Navajo; and Sahaptin-Chinook by the Chinook, Modoc, and Nez Percé. See Angie Debo, *A History of the Indians of the United States* (Norman, OK: University of Oklahoma Press, 1970), 8-9; and Judith Levey and Agnes Greenhall, eds., *The Concise Columbia Encyclopedia* (New York: Columbia University Press, 1983), s.v., "American Indian Languages," 25.

4. Edwin R. Embree, *Indians of the Americas* (New York: Collier Books, 1970), 113-7; *Concise Columbia Encyclopedia,* s.v., "North American Indians," 609-10.

5. Debo, 8-18.

6. Priscilla K. Buffalohead, "Farmers, Warriors, Traders: A Fresh Look at Ojibway Women,"

Minnesota History 48 (Summer 1983): 236.

7. See Bruce Johansen and Roberto Maestas, *Wasi'chu: The Continuing Indian Wars* (New York: Monthly Review Press, 1979), 331; and James Axtell, *The Indian Peoples of Eastern America: A Documentary History of the Sexes* (New York: Oxford University Press, 1981), 150-51.

8. Quoted in Charles Hamilton, ed., *Cry of the Thunderbird: The American Indian's Own Story* (Norman, OK: University of Oklahoma Press, 1972), 215.

9. Carolyn Neithammer, *Daughters of the Earth: The Lives and Legends of American Indian Women* (New York: MacMillan, 1977), 176-83.

10. Axtell, 103-39.

11. Quoted in Axtell, 138.

12. Alice Kehoe, "The Shackles of Tradition," in *The Hidden Half: Studies of Plains Indian Women*, ed. Patricia Albers and Beatrice Medicine (Lanham, MD: University Press of America, 1983), 69.

13. Mary Jane Schneider, "Women's Work: An Examination of Women's Roles in Plains Indian Arts and Crafts," in Albers and Medicine, 103, 107.

14. Buffalohead, 236-8; Axtell, 142.

15. See Janet Spector, "Male/Female Task Differentiation Among the Hidatsa: Toward the Development of an Archeological Approach to the Study of Gender," 77-99; Patricia C. Albers and Beatrice Medicine, "The Role of Sioux Women in the Production of Ceremonial Objects: The Case of the Star Quilt," 123-40; and Schneider, 101-21. All three in Albers and Medicine.

16. Maryann Oshana, "Native American Women in Westerns: Reality and Myth," *Frontiers: A Journal of Women's Studies* 6 (Fall 1981): 46.

17. Ibid.

18. Quoted in Dexter Fisher, ed., *The Third Woman: Minority Women Writers of the United States* (Boston: Houghton Mifflin, 1980), 11.

19. Beatrice Medicine, "'Warrior Women'—Sex Role Alternatives for Plains Indian Women," in Albers and Medicine, 270, 274; Oshana, 46-47.

20. Neithammer, 174.

21. Ibid., 173-97.

22. Fisher, 10; Paula Gunn Allen, *The Sacred Hoop: Recovering the Feminine in American Indian Traditions* (Boston: Beacon Press, 1986), 13.

23. For an account of cross-gender practices, see Evelyn Blackwood, "Sexuality and Gender in Certain Native American Tribes: The Case of Cross-Gender Females," *Signs: Journal of Women, Culture, and Society* 10 (Autumn 1984): 27-42; see also Neithammer, 229-32.

24. Walter Williams, *The Spirit and the Flesh: Sexual Diversity in American Indian Culture* (Boston: Beacon Press, 1986), 245-46. Ann Boerner, a student of Julie Matthaei, discovered this aspect of Woman Chief's life when working on an analysis of a more popular account by a prominent historical fiction writer, Benjamin Capp, *Woman Chief* (New York: Ace Books, 1979). Boerner was suspicious of Capp's depiction of Woman Chief's love life (which he portrayed as heterosexual), and indeed found that he had fabricated it.

25. Laura Waterman Wittstock, "Native American Women, Twilight of a Long Maidenhood," in *Comparative Perspectives of Third World Women: The Impact of Race, Sex, and Class*, ed. Beverly Lindsay (New York: Praeger Publishers, 1980), 212; Diane Rothenberg, "The Mothers of the Nation: Seneca Resistance to Quaker Intervention," in *Women and Colonization: Anthropological Perspectives*, ed. Mona Etienne and Eleanor Leacock (New York: Praeger Publishers, 1980), 63-80.

26. Axtell, xvi.

27. Robert T. Coulter and Steven M. Tullberg, "Indian Land Rights," in *The Aggressions of Civilization: Federal Indian Policy Since the 1880s*, ed. Sandra Cadwalader and Vine Deloria, Jr. (Philadelphia: Temple University Press, 1984), 209.

28. Robert Steven Grumet, "Sunksquaws, Shamans, and Tradeswomen: Middle Atlantic Coastal Algonkian Women During the 17th and 18th Centuries," in Etienne and Leacock, 50-51.

29. Debo, 21-34; Axtell, xvi.

30. Quoted in Hamilton, 133.

31. Quoted in Debo, 40.

32. Quoted in Eleanor Leacock, "Montagnais Women and the Jesuit Program for Colonization," in Etienne and Leacock, 30.

33. Ibid.

34. Debo, 50.

35. James Clifford, *The Predicament of Culture: Twentieth-Century Ethnography, Literature, and Art* (Cambridge: Harvard University Press, 1988), 277-346.

36. Roy W. Meyer, *History of the Santee Sioux: United States Indian Policy on Trial* (Lincoln: University of Nebraska Press, 1967), 72; Debo, 82-84.

37. Quoted in Debo, 91.

38. Ibid., 97-98.

39. James E. Officer, "The American Indian and Federal Policy," in *The American Indian in Urban Society*, ed. Jack O. Waddell and O. Michael Watson (Boston: Little, Brown and Company, 1971), 17; quoted in Debo, 104.

40. Debo, 101-4.

41. Ibid., 106.

42. Ibid., 109.

43. Ibid., 112; Neithammer, 107.

44. Debo, 111.

45. Rosemary Agonito and Joseph Agonito, "Resurrecting History's Forgotten Women: A Case Study from the Cheyenne Indians," *Frontiers: A Journal of Women's Studies* 6 (Fall 1981): 8-9.

46. See Debo, 181-2. In 1875, Congress extended the Homestead Act to American Indians, in a precursor to the later allotment policy. However, few American Indians homesteaded, and the effect of the Act was to transfer the majority of their lands to white settlers and companies. For a discussion of the Homestead Act and its relationship to allotment, see Officer, 32.

47. Debo, 236-38; Fisher, 7-9.

48. Debo, 133, 235.

49. Officer, 28-30.

50. Quoted in Debo, 238.

51. Quoted in Wittstock, 219.

52. Officer, 35-36; and Joseph Jorgensen, "A Century of Political Economic Effects on American Indian Society, 1880-1980," *The Journal of Ethnic Studies* 6 (Fall 1978): 13-14; see also Bea Medicine, "The Interaction of Culture and Sex Roles in the Schools," in U.S. Department of Education, Office of Educational Research and Improvement, National Institute of Education, *Conference on the Educational and Occupational Needs of American Indian Women, October 1976* (Washington, DC: GPO, 1980), 149-51.

53. Medicine, "Culture and Sex Roles in the Schools," 149.

54. Quoted in Hamilton, 246.

55. Alan L. Sorkin, *The Urban American Indian* (Lexington, MA: Lexington Books, 1978), 1.

56. For an historical account of corporate-Indian relations, see H. Craig Miner, *The Corporation and the Indian: Tribal Sovereignty and Industrial Civilization in Indian Territory, 1865-1907* (Columbia: University of Missouri Press, 1976); Debo, 251 ff.

57. Officer, 34; Gary D. Sandefur, "Federal Policy toward Minorities: 1787-1980," *Focus* 10 (Summer 1987): 22.

58. Debo, 251-52; quoted in Debo, 261.

59. Debo, 34, 252; Officer, 32-40.

60. Debo, Ch. 18; Roxanne Dunbar Ortiz, "Land and Nationhood: The American Indian Struggle for Self-Determination and Survival," *Socialist Review* 63-64 (May-August 1982): 113; Laurence M. Hauptman, "The Indian Reorganization Act," in Cadwalader and Deloria, Jr., 143.

61. Debo, 283.

62. See Appendix A; while enumerators did count unpaid family workers in cash agriculture as gainfully employed, the Census undercounted such workers as well as those engaged in non-market production.

63. Edward T. James, ed., *Notable American Women 1607-1950* (Cambridge: Harvard University Press, 1971), s.v. "Gertrude Simmons Bonnin," Mary E. Young, 198-200; Debo, 288.

64. Debo, 284.

65. Ibid., 290-94.

66. David M. Strausfield, "Reformers in Conflict: The Pueblo Dance Controversy," in Cadwalader and Deloria, Jr., 38; Ortiz, 113, 116.

67. Sorkin, 3.

68. Debo, 308-9; Sorkin, 3.

69. Ortiz, 116.

70. Sorkin, 13-5; as Sorkin points out, some statistics may overstate this gap, since reservation Indians receive free medical care from the U.S. Public Health Service and can live rent-free on tribal or allotted land.

71. Population growth during the decade may have been somewhat overestimated as a result of an increasing tendency for American Indians to identify themselves as such to Census takers. Jojo Hunt, "American Indian Women: Their Relationship to the Federal Government," 304-5; and Rosemary Wood, "Health Problems Facing American Indian Women," 179-80. Both in U.S. Department of Education, Office of Educational Research and Improvement, National Institute of Education, *Conference on the Educational and Occupational Needs of American Indian Women, October 1976* (Washington, DC: GPO, 1980).

72. See Appendix A.

73. Wittstock, 217.

74. Sorkin, 97-99; Susan Braudy, " 'We Will Remember' Survival School," *Ms.* (July 1976): 77-120.

75. Ortiz, 112; *Ohoyo—A Bulletin for American Indian-Alaska Native Women* (July 1981).

76. Sandefur, 24.

77. Ortiz, 111; Johansen and Maestas, 97 ff.; conversation with Ward Churchill, January 1991.

78. Ortiz, 107.

79. *Ohoyo* (July 1981 and July 1982); Wilcomb E. Washburn, "Indian Policy Since the 1880s," in Cadwalader and Deloria, Jr., 49; Peter Matthiessen, *Indian Country* (New York: Viking Press, 1984), 192-99.

80. Ismaelillo and Robin Wright, eds., *Native Peoples in Struggle: Cases from the Fourth Russell Tribunal and Other International Forums* (Bombay, NY: Anthropology Resource Center and E.R.I.N. Publications, 1982), 134; Seventh Generation Fund, Annual Report 1986-87, 9-10; *Akwesasne Notes* 19 (Fall 1987).

81. Matthiessen, *Indian Country*, 119-26.

82. *Ohoyo* (October 1983), 3; Wittstock, 212.

83. Quoted in Peter Matthiessen, *In the Spirit of Crazy Horse* (New York: Viking Press, 1983), 417.

84. Janet Larson, "And Then There Were None," *Christian Century* 94 (26 January 1977): 61-63; cited in Robin Jarrell, "Women and Children First: The Forced Sterilization of Native American Women," Unpublished student paper, Wellesley College, December 1988.

85. Johansen and Maestas, 72, 74; Gail Marks-Jarvis, "The Fate of the Indian," *National Catholic Reporter*, 27 May 1977, 4.

86. Evelyn Lance Blanchard, "Organizing American Indian Women," in U.S. Department of Education, Office of Educational Research and Improvement, National Institute of Education, *Conference on the Educational and Occupational Needs of American Indian Women, October 1976* (Washington, DC: GPO, 1980), 125-26.

87. *Ohoyo* (July 1981): 9; *Ohoyo* (Summer 1982).

88. Quoted in Joan M. Jensen, *With These Hands: Women Working on the Land* (Old Westbury, NY: Feminist Press, 1981), 232.

89. Elizabeth Almquist, *Minorities, Gender, and Work* (Lexington, MA: Lexington Books, 1979), 41-43; Sorkin, 34-35.

90. U.S. Congress, Senate Committee on Labor and Human Resources, Subcommittee on Employment and Productivity, *Guaranteed Job Opportunity Act: Hearing on S. 777*, 100th Cong., 1st sess., 23 March 1987 and 3 April 1987, 23; 1980 Census, see Appendix A.

91. U.S. Department of the Interior, Bureau of Indian Affairs, *American Indians Today: Answers to Your Questions* (Washington, DC: GPO, 1988), 4; U.S. Department of the Interior,

Bureau of Indian Affairs, *Indian Service Population and Labor Force Estimates* (Washington, DC: GPO, January 1989); Debo, 343.

92. U.S. Senate, *Guaranteed Job Opportunity Act,* 26; U.S. Congress, House Select Committee on Children, Youth, and Families, *Native American Children, Youth, and Families: Hearing,* 99th Cong., 2d sess., 7 January 1986, 96.

93. Cardell Jacobsen, "Internal Colonialism and Native Americans: Indian Labor in the United States from 1871 to World War II," *Social Science Quarterly* 65 (1984): 158-71; quoted in U.S. House, *Native American Children, Youth, and Families,* 82.

94. See Wood, passim; Sorkin, 47-60; 1980 Census, see Appendix A.

95. Washburn, 55.

96. 1980 Census, see Appendix A.

97. 1970 and 1980 Censuses, see Appendix A.

98. 1980 Census, see Appendix A.

99. Ibid.

100. Ibid.

101. See, for example, Paula Gunn Allen, *The Sacred Hoop* and *Spiderwoman's Granddaughters: Traditional Tales and Contemporary Writing by Native American Women* (Boston: Beacon Press, 1989); Louise Erdrich, *Love Medicine* (New York: Holt, Rinehart, and Winston, 1984) and *Tracks* (New York: Holt Rinehart, and Winston, 1989); Leslie Marmon Silko, *Ceremony* (New York: Viking Press, 1977) and *Storyteller* (New York: Seaver Books, 1981).

102. Quoted in Fisher, 14.

Chapter 4

1. Gloria Anzaldúa, *Borderlands/La Frontera: The New Mestiza* (San Francisco: Spinsters/Aunt Lute, 1987), 202.

2. While we will discuss the displacement of American Indians here, most of our analysis of the many Indian nations indigenous to the Southwest who did not intermarry with the Spaniards is in Ch. 3.

3. The term "Chicano" was adopted by U.S. citizens of Mexican descent during the height of the Chicano movement in the 1970s to signify their identification with Mexico and, particularly, with their Indian heritage. Chicanos/as also refer to themselves as "la raza," a term which conveys both a racial identity (white, Indian, and Black) and an ethnic identity.

4. Alfredo Mirandé and Evangelina Enríquez, *La Chicana: The Mexican-American Woman* (Chicago: University of Chicago Press, 1979), 36; Judith S. Levey and Agnes Greenhall, eds., *Concise Columbia Encyclopedia* (New York: Columbia University Press, 1983), 58; Maria L. Apodaca, "The Chicana Woman: An Historical Materialist Perspective," *Latin American Perspectives* 12-13 (Winter and Spring 1977): 75-89.

5. Mirandé and Enríquez, 16-19; Apodaca, 78.

6. Mirandé and Enríquez, 246-47.

7. Martha Cotera, *Diosa y Hembra: History and Heritage of Chicanas in the U.S.* (Austin, Texas: Statehouse Printing, 1977), 20-22.

8. Ibid., 77.

9. Ibid., 36; Apodaca, 76.

10. While the literature refers to "intermarriage," it does not appear that the Spaniards legally married Indian women, although many did recognize their offspring; Mirandé and Enríquez, 38-39.

11. S. Dale McLemore and Ricardo Romo, "The Origins and Development of the Mexican American People," in *The Mexican American Experience: An Interdisciplinary Anthology,* ed. Rodolfo O. de la Garza, Frank D. Bean, Charles M. Bonjean, Ricardo Romo, and Rodolfo Alvarez (Austin: University of Texas Press, 1985), 6.

12. See, for example, the writings of Adelaida R. Del Castillo, "Malintzin Tenepal: A Preliminary Look into a New Perspective," *Encuentro femenil* 1 (1974): 58-78; and Juana Armanda Alegría, *Psicología de las mexicanas,* 2d ed. (Mexico City: Samo, 1975).

13. Mirandé and Enríquez, 38.

364 RACE, GENDER, AND WORK

14. Ibid., 39; Apodaca, 78-79.
15. Mirandé and Enríquez, 47-50; Cotera, 30.
16. Mirandé and Enríquez, 56; McLemore and Romo, 8-9.
17. Mirandé and Enríquez, 53-58; Cotera, 48-49.
18. Mirandé and Enríquez, 55-57.
19. Ibid., 55-58.
20. Cotera, 49, 52.
21. Mirandé and Enríquez, 21.
22. Ibid., 56; Cotera, 49-50.
23. Cotera, 67.
24. Ibid., 38; Mirandé and Enríquez, 51.
25. Alfredo Mirandé, *The Chicano Experience: An Alternative Perspective* (South Bend, IN: University of Notre Dame Press, 1985), 17-18.
26. Ibid., 23-27.
27. Mirandé and Enríquez, 8.
28. McLemore and Romo, 8-9.
29. Jane Dysart, "Mexican Women in San Antonio, 1830-1860: The Assimilation Process," *The Western Historical Quarterly* 7 (October 1976): 370-71.
30. McLemore and Romo, 11.
31. Mario Barrera, "The Historical Evolution of Chicano Ethnic Goals: A Bibliographic Essay," *Sage Race Relations Abstracts* 10:1 (February 1985): 2; Mirandé, *Chicano Experience*, 18; McLemore and Romo, 9.
32. Mirandé, *Chicano Experience*, 19.
33. Quoted in Mirandé, *Chicano Experience*, 21.
34. Cortina was known as the "Red Robber of the Rio Grande." Mirandé, *Chicano Experience*, 26.
35. Mirandé, *Chicano Experience*, 21; Mirandé and Enríquez, 86.
36. Cotera, 42; Mirandé and Enríquez, 204-5, 252.
37. Mirandé and Enríquez, 221.
38. Robert Daniel, *American Women in the 20th Century: The Festival of Life* (San Diego: Harcourt Brace Jovanovich, 1987), 179-80; Mirandé, *Chicano Experience*, 49; Rosalinda M. González, "Chicanas and Mexican Immigrant Families 1920-1940: Women's Subordination and Family Exploitation," in *Decades of Discontent: The Women's Movement, 1920-1940*, ed. Lois Scharf and Joan M. Jensen (Westport, CT: Greenwood Press, 1982), 59.
39. González, 68.
40. Quoted in González, 63.
41. González, 68.
42. Mirandé, *Chicano Experience*, 36; González, 68-70.
43. James Cockcroft, *Outlaws in the Promised Land: Mexican Immigrant Workers and America's Future* (New York: Grove Press, 1986), 62; 1930 Census, see Appendix A.
44. Mirandé, *Chicano Experience*, 51-52.
45. Ibid.
46. Cockcroft, 53, 61; González, 76.
47. González, 75-76.
48. Ibid., 70.
49. Vicki L. Ruiz, "'And Miles to Go...': Mexican Women and Work, 1930-1985," in *Western Women: Their Land, Their Lives*, ed. Lillian Schlissel, Vicki L. Ruiz, and Janice Monk (Albuquerque: University of New Mexico Press, 1988), 129.
50. Mirandé and Enríquez, 229-32.
51. Quoted in Philip S. Foner, *Women and the American Labor Movement: World War I to the Present* (New York: The Free Press, 1980), 266.
52. Cotera, 62.
53. Cockcroft, 68-70; Thomas Archdeacon, *Becoming American: An Ethnic History* (New York: Free Press, 1983), 179.
54. Mirandé, *Chicano Experience*, 54-55.

55. Cockcroft, 68.

56. González, 79.

57. Cockcroft, 69; Frank Bardacke, "Watsonville: A Mexican Community on Strike," in *Reshaping the US Left: Popular Struggles in the 1980s*, ed. Mike Davis and Michael Sprinker (London: Verso, 1988), 159.

58. Leobardo F. Estrada, F. Chris Garcia, Reynaldo Flores Macís, and Lionel Maldonado, "Chicanos in the United States," *Daedalus* 110 (Spring 1981): 122.

59. Ibid.

60. Ruiz, "And Miles to Go," 118.

61. Mirandé, *Chicano Experience*, 56.

62. The group received its name when 10 members of the film industry refused to cooperate with Congressional hearings aimed at identifying Communist Party members in Hollywood. See Herbert Biberman, *Salt of the Earth: The Story of a Film* (Boston: Beacon Press, 1965) for details of the making of the film, and Michael Wilson and Deborah Silverton Rosenfelt, *Salt of the Earth* (Old Westbury, NY: The Feminist Press, 1978) for the screenplay and a commentary.

63. Cotera, 100; quoted in González, 79.

64. Rudolfo Acuña, *Occupied America: A History of Chicanos* (New York: Harper and Row, 1988), 295-98.

65. 1950 and 1960 Censuses, see Appendix A.

66. Cockcroft, 86-87.

67. Ibid.

68. 1960 and 1970 Censuses, see Appendix A; Cotera, 103.

69. Cotera, 104-5.

70. Ibid., 106.

71. For an excellent description of the movement, see Juan Gómez-Quiñones, *Mexican Students Por La Raza: The Chicano Student Movement in Southern California, 1967-1977* (Santa Barbara, CA: Editorial La Causa, 1978).

72. Sylvia Gonzales, 49.

73. For instance, one Chicano argued:

> I am concerned with the direction that the Chicanas are taking in the movement. The words such as liberation, sexism, male chauvinism...plus the theme of individualism is a concept of the Anglo society: terms prevalent in the Anglo Woman's movement. The familiar has always been our strength in our culture. But it seems evident...that [you] are not concerned with the familiar, but are influenced by the Anglo woman's movement.

Quoted in Mirandé and Enríquez, 237.

74. Cotera, 109; Sara M. Evans, *Born for Liberty: A History of Women in America* (New York: The Free Press, 1989), 309-10.

75. Ellen Cantarow, Susan Gushee O'Malley, and Sharon Hatman Strom, *Moving the Mountain: Women Working for Social Change* (Old Westbury, NY: Feminist Press, 1980), 120-1.

76. Maxine Baca Zinn, "Familialism Among Chicanos: A Theoretical Review," *Humboldt Journal of Social Relations* 10 (Fall/Winter 1982/83): 228.

77. Ibid.

78. Lea Ybarra, "Empirical and Theoretical Developments in the Study of the Chicano Family," in *The State of Chicano Research on Family, Labor, and Migration: Proceedings of the First Stanford Symposium on Chicano Research and Public Policy*, ed. Armando Valdez, Albert Camarillo, and Tomás Almaguer (Stanford, CA: Stanford Center for Chicano Research, 1983), 96.

79. Acuña, 395.

80. U.S. Bureau of the Census, *Statistical Abstract of the United States: 1988* (Washington, DC: GPO, 1988), 371.

81. Differences in education, language, age, and geographical area account for 27 percent of the occupational status gap between Chicana and white women, according to a study prepared by Marta Escutia and Margarita Prieto of the National Council of La Raza, a Chicana/o advocacy group. Marta Escutia and Margarita Prieto, "Hispanics in the Workforce, Part II: Hispanic

Women," (Washington, DC: National Council of La Raza, 1986), 10; the study is for all Latinas/os, of which Chicanas/os are the majority; 1980 Census, see Appendix A; Arturo Vargas, *Literacy in the Hispanic Community* (Washington, DC: National Council of La Raza, 1988), 7-8.

82. Laurie Coyle, Gail Hershatter, and Emily Honig, "Women at Farah: An Unfinished Story," in *A Needle, A Bobbin, A Strike: Women Needleworkers in America,* ed. Joan M. Jensen and Sue Davidson (Philadelphia, PA: Temple University Press, 1984), 241.

83. Ibid.

84. Calculated from the 1980 Census, see Appendix A.

85. Ruiz, "And Miles to Go," 122; Vicki Ruiz, "Working for Wages: Mexican Women in the American Southwest, 1930-1980," Working Paper No. 19 (Tucson, AZ: Southwest Institute for Research on Women, University of Arizona, 1984), 4.

86. Vicki L. Ruiz, "By the Day or Week: Mexicana Domestic Workers in El Paso," in *To Toil the Livelong Day: America's Women at Work, 1780-1980,* ed. Carol Groneman and Mary Beth Norton (Ithaca, NY: Cornell University Press, 1987), 272; 1980 Census, *U.S. Summary,* 166; Ruiz, "Mexicana Domestic Workers," 280.

87. Ruiz, "Mexicana Domestic Workers," 280.

88. 1980 Census, see Appendix A; Ruiz, "And Miles to Go," 129-30.

89. U.S. Department of Labor, Bureau of Labor Statistics, *Employment and Earnings,* January 1989, Table 59, 225; Ruiz, "And Miles to Go," 130.

90. Ruiz, "And Miles to Go," 132-33.

91. Coyle, Hershatter, and Honig, 227-28; Acuña, 448.

92. Bardacke, 149-82.

93. Escutia and Prieto, 13-14; 1980 Census, see Appendix A.

94. Ruiz, "And Miles to Go," 121.

95. *U.S. Statistical Abstract 1988,* 10.

96. Roberto Suro, "1986 Amnesty Law Is Seen As Failing to Slow Alien Tide," *New York Times,* 18 June 1990, 16; Cockcroft, 92.

97. Suro, 16.

98. MacNeil-Lehrer News Broadcast, Public Broadcasting Corporation, 29 March 1990; quoted in Abel Valenzuela, "A Borderline Case: The Aftermath of Immigration Reform," *Dollars & Sense,* No. 146 (May 1989), 20.

99. Valenzuela, 21.

100. Acuña, 440; Valenzuela, 21.

Chapter 5

1. The vast majority of people considered "white" in the United States are of direct European descent, and in this chapter we refer to them as European American or white. Some U.S. citizens of Mexican or Puerto Rican descent are also considered white, and are also of European (mostly Spanish) descent, but we devote separate chapters to them because their economic histories are so different from that of European Americans.

2. Edith Fowke and Joe Glazer, *Songs of Work and Protest* (New York: Dover Publications, Inc., 1973), 71.

3. Edna Bonacich, "United States Capitalist Development: A Background to Asian Immigration," in *Labor Immigration Under Capitalism: Asian Workers in the United States Before World War II,* ed. Lucie Cheng and Edna Bonacich (Berkeley: University of California Press, 1984), 116.

4. U.S. Department of Justice, Immigration and Naturalization Service, *1980 Statistical Yearbook of the Immigration and Naturalization Service* (Washington, DC: GPO, 1980), Table 2.

5. Barbara Mayer Wertheimer, *We Were There: The Story of Working Women in America* (New York: Pantheon Books, 1977), 9-11; Mary Ryan, *Womanhood in America: From Colonial Times to the Present* (New York: F. Watts, 1983), 5-6.

6. Ryan, 6; Wertheimer, 9.

7. Wertheimer, 8-10; Bruce Levine et al., *Who Built America? Working People and the Nation's Economy, Politics, Culture, and Society: From Conquest and Colonization Through Reconstruction and the Great Uprising of 1877* (New York: Pantheon Books, 1989), 52.

8. Quoted in Julie Matthaei, *An Economic History of Women in America: Women's Work, the Sexual Division of Labor, and the Development of Capitalism* (New York: Schocken Books, 1982), 30.

9. Ryan, 7, 26; Joan M. Jensen, ed., *With These Hands: Women Working on the Land* (Old Westbury, NY: Feminist Press, 1982), 33; Matthaei, Ch. 1. As we show in Chs. 1, 2, and 4, the slave system deprived African Americans, women and men, of property and income. European Americans took land from American Indians and Chicanas/os as they moved West; this land and other property was then controlled by white men.

10. Ryan, 25.

11. Alice Kessler-Harris, *Out to Work: A History of Wage-Earning Women in the United States* (New York: Oxford University Press, 1982), 3; and Matthaei, Ch. 2.

12. Joan M. Jensen, "Cloth, Butter and Boarders: Women's Household Production for the Market," *Review of Radical Political Economics* 12 (Summer 1980): 14-25; Matthaei, Chs. 1 and 2.

13. Susan Estabrook Kennedy, *If All We Did Was to Weep at Home: A History of White Working-Class Women in America* (Bloomington, IN: Indiana University Press, 1979), 9.

14. Matthaei, Ch. 3.

15. Quoted in ibid., 63.

16. Ibid., 68-70.

17. Ibid., Part I.

18. Wertheimer, 67. There is a good deal of debate about which motive was more prevalent among the mill girls: see Matthaei, Ch. 7, and Thomas Dublin, *Women at Work: The Transformation of Work and Community in Lowell, Massachusetts, 1826-1860* (New York: Columbia University Press, 1979), Ch. 3.

19. See Dublin.

20. Kennedy, 44; Dublin, 113.

21. Letter printed in *Voice of Industry*, 13 March 1846, quoted in Dublin, 125.

22. "Female Department," *The Voice of Industry*, 6 March 1846, quoted in Matthaei, 232.

23. bell hooks points out this pattern among white abolitionist/feminist women later in the century in her book, *Ain't I a Woman: Black Women and Feminism* (Boston, MA: South End Press, 1981), 126.

24. Dublin, Ch. 12.

25. Matthaei, Ch. 7; 1900 Census, see Appendix A.

26. For a detailed discussion of this literature, see Nancy F. Cott, *The Bonds of Womanhood* (New Haven: Yale University Press, 1977), Ch. 2.

27. From *Ladies Magazine*, 3 May 1830; and Caleb Cushing, "The Social Condition of Woman," 1836, quoted in Cott, 74.

28. Matthaei, Ch. 6.

29. Faye E. Dudden, *Serving Women: Household Service in Nineteenth-Century America* (Middletown, CT: Wesleyan University Press, 1983), 155.

30. David Katzman, *Seven Days a Week: Women and Domestic Service in Industrializing America* (New York: Oxford University Press, 1978), 45.

31. Katzman, Ch. 2.

32. Jensen, *With These Hands*, 106; Matthaei, Ch. 6.

33. Quoted in Matthaei, 192.

34. See Jonathan Katz, *Gay American History* (New York: Thomas Y. Crowell Co., 1976), Ch. III.

35. Levine et al., 351-54.

36. Jensen, *With These Hands*, 108.

37. Black families theoretically were allowed to homestead after the Civil War abolished slavery, but lack of the funds for transportation and overt white hostility and sabotage closed this option for most. Mexican American families experienced the white movement westward as, for the most part, a process through which they were deprived of their lands; see Ch. 2. Jensen, *With These Hands*, 104-5.

38. Jensen, *With These Hands*, 102.

39. Quoted in ibid., 129-31.

40. Amy Kesselman, "Diaries and Reminiscences of Women on the Oregon Trail," quoted in *America's Working Women: A Documentary History—1600 to the Present,* ed. Rosalyn Baxandall, Linda Gordon, and Susan Reverby (New York: Random House, 1976), 69.

41. "Random Recollections of Harriet Taylor Upton," quoted in ibid., 73.

42. Mary Eleanor Wilkins Freeman, "The Revolt of 'Mother,'" in *The Revolt of Mother and Other Stories* (Old Westbury, NY: Feminist Press, 1974), 116-40.

43. Levine et al., 352; Jensen, *With These Hands,* 145.

44. Jensen, *With These Hands,* 103-4; Valerie Quinney, "Farm to Mill: the First Generation," in *Working Lives: The "Southern Exposure" History of Labor in the South,* ed. Mark S. Miller (New York: Pantheon, 1980), 5-18.

45. Quinney, 142-45.

46. Ibid., 145-46.

47. Quoted in Jensen, *With These Hands,* 155-60.

48. Ibid., 142-47.

49. Bonacich, 113.

50. Bonacich, 116; U.S. Bureau of the Census, *Statistical Abstract of the United States: 1988* (Washington, DC: GPO, 1987), 10, 16.

51. In 1924, Congress passed a law that limited the annual number of immigrants admitted to the United States. Quotas were established based on the nationalities represented in the white population as counted by the 1920 Census. Since persons of British, Irish, German, and Scandinavian descent made up three-quarters of the 1920 white population, these four countries were allowed to send three-quarters of the total immigrants to be admitted under the new quota system. See Thomas J. Archdeacon, *Becoming American: An Ethnic History* (New York: The Free Press, 1983), 173-176.

52. Katzman, 66.

53. Kennedy, 55; Cecyle S. Neidle, *America's Immigrant Women* (Boston: Twayne Publishers, 1975), 107; Katzman, 68.

54. Lynn Weiner, *From Working Girl to Working Mother: The Female Labor Force in the United States, 1820-1980* (Chapel Hill: University of North Carolina, 1985), 21.

55. Ryan, 121; Dublin, 153-56; quoted in Dublin, 156.

56. Ryan, 122.

57. Neidle, 73.

58. Interview with Florence Cohen Gross by Dana Gross Schechter, 14 November 1975, as quoted in Wertheimer, 234.

59. Kennedy, 113.

60. Ryan, 122.

61. Wertheimer, 234.

62. Katzman, 70-71; Weiner, 28.

63. Cited in Neidle, 95.

64. Ryan, 124-25.

65. Kessler-Harris, 121.

66. Dudden, 60; Katzman, 73.

67. Katzman, 80; Dudden, 61-69.

68. Katzman, Table 2-9, 67.

69. Katzman, 70.

70. Ryan, 124-25.

71. By 1852, half of the operatives in New England mills were foreign born. Kessler-Harris, 64; Robert Ernst, "Immigrant Life in New York City," in Baxandall, Gordon, and Reverby, 56.

72. Louis Levine, "The Women Garment Workers," in ibid., 102; Kessler-Harris, 124.

73. Philip S. Foner, *Women and the American Labor Movement: From World War I to the Present* (New York: Free Press, 1980), 281-82; Neidle, 133-40.

74. Neidle, 147-50.

75. Foner, 328.

76. Ibid., 325-29.

77. Neidle, 140.

78. Foner, 358-60.

79. Ibid., 309.

80. Kessler-Harris, 54, 124-27.

81. Ryan, 129.

82. Ibid., 133.

83. Jensen, *With These Hands,* 60.

84. Neidle, 100.

85. Foner, 281-82.

86. Maxine Schwartz Seller, ed., *Immigrant Women* (Philadelphia: Temple University Press, 1981), 264. See also Kennedy, 116. Kennedy argues that Jones was an anti-feminist who "saw no reason to support working-class women except by improving the wages and working conditions of their husbands," and treated women as auxiliaries to their men.

87. bell hooks, *Ain't I a Woman* (Boston: South End Press, 1981), 163.

88. Quoted in Matthaei, 179.

89. Ibid.

90. Jacqueline Jones, *Soldiers of Light and Love: Northern Teachers and Georgia Blacks, 1865-1873* (Chapel Hill: University of North Carolina Press, 1980), 30-31; quoted in Jones, 121.

91. Matthaei, 179-80, 206-8; 1900 Census, see Appendix A.

92. Susan M. Reverby, *Ordered to Care: The Dilemma of American Nursing, 1859-1945* (Cambridge: Cambridge University Press, 1987), 63.

93. Ibid.

94. Midwives were replaced by male practitioners during the seventeenth and eighteenth centuries in Europe, and early in the twentieth century in the United States. Barbara Ehrenreich and Deirdre English, *Witches, Midwives, and Nurses: A History of Women Healers* (Old Westbury, NY: Feminist Press, 1973), 20-21; and Mary Roth Walsh, *"Doctors Wanted: No Women Need Apply": Sexual Barriers in the Medical Profession 1835-1975* (New Haven: Yale University Press, 1977).

95. Quoted in Matthaei, 174.

96. Foner, 292; for more information on social homemaking, see Matthaei, Ch. 8, and Ryan, Ch. 4.

97. Ryan, 163.

98. Quoted in Elaine Partnow, ed., *The Quotable Woman: An Encyclopedia of Useful Quotations* (Garden City, New York: Anchor Books, 1978), 13.

99. Quoted in Ryan, 246.

100. Eleanor Flexner, *Century of Struggle: The Women's Rights Movement in the United States* (New York: Atheneum, 1974), 64-65.

101. Allen F. Davis, *Spearheads for Reform: The Social Settlements and the Progressive Movement 1890-1914,* (New York: Oxford University Press, 1967), 3-12, cited in Michael Katz, *In the Shadow of the Poorhouse: A Social History of Welfare in America* (New York: Basic Books, 1986), 159.

102. Quoted in Ryan, 131.

103. 1900 Census, see Appendix A; Colette Hyman, "Labor Organizing and Female Institution-Building: The Chicago Women's Trade Union League 1904-1924," in *Women, Work and Protest,* ed. Ruth Milkman (Boston: Routledge & Kegan Paul, 1985), 34-38; Neidle, 136-37; Foner, 471-76.

104. Ryan, 140.

105. Wertheimer, 241.

106. Quoted in hooks, *Ain't I a Woman,* 127.

107. Foner, 481-82; Belle Kearney, quoted in Robin Miller Jacoby, "The Women's Trade Union League," in *Class, Sex, and the Woman Worker,* ed. Milton Cantor and Bruce Laurie (Westport, CT: Greenwood Press, 1977), 203-24.

108. Bettina Aptheker, *Woman's Legacy: Essays on Race, Sex, and Class in American History* (Amherst: The University of Massachusetts Press, 1982), 63; quoted in Linda Gordon, *Woman's Body, Woman's Right: A Social History of Birth Control in America* (New York: Grossman Publishers, 1976), 281.

109. Ryan, 142-43.

110. Weiner, Table 5, 28; quoted in Matthaei, 250.

111. Foner, 4-8.

112. Ibid., 203.

113. Ibid., 214-16.

114. Quoted in Foner, 248.

115. Quoted in Matthaei, 222.

116. For a description of the rise of the modern corporation, see Alfred Dupont Chandler, *The Visible Hand: The Managerial Revolution in American Business* (Cambridge, MA: Belknap Press, 1977); for an excellent analysis of the feminization of clerical work, see Margery Davies, *A Woman's Place Is at the Typewriter: Office Work and Office Workers, 1870-1930* (Philadelphia: Temple University Press, 1982).

117. Kessler-Harris, 252; Weiner, Table 6, 89; Winifred D. Wandersee, *Women's Work and Family Values, 1920-1940* (Cambridge, MA: Harvard University Press, 1981), 91, 99; Kennedy, 172.

118. Kennedy, 172; Wandersee, 32.

119. Quoted in Wandersee, 95.

120. Jensen, *With These Hands,* 191.

121. Ibid., 189.

122. Lois Rita Helmbold, "Making Choices, Making Do: Women's Work in the Great Depression," in *Women and Work in the 80s: Perspectives from the 30s and 40s* (Berkeley: University of California, Center for the Study, Education and Advancement of Women, 1981), 19.

123. See, for example, Roger Stansfield, *The Great Depression* (New York: Harper & Row, 1982).

124. Jill Quadagno, "From Old-Age Assistance to Supplemental Security Income: The Political Economy of Relief in the South, 1935-1972," in *The Politics of Social Policy in the United States,* ed. Margaret Weir, Ann Shola Orloff, and Theda Scocpol (Princeton: Princeton University Press, 1988), 235-64.

125. Kennedy, 175; Kessler-Harris, 263.

126. Foner, 301-2; Kennedy, 177.

127. Sharon Hartman Strom, "'We're no Kitty Foyles': Organizing Office Workers for the Congress of Industrial Organizations, 1937-50," in *Women, Work and Protest,* ed. Ruth Milkman (Boston: Routledge & Kegan Paul, 1985), 212; quoted in Strom, 221.

128. Ibid., 226.

129. Kessler-Harris, 247.

130. Ibid., 276.

131. Ryan, 189; Kessler-Harris, 292.

132. Kessler-Harris, 279, 286; Susan M. Hartmann, "Women's Organizations During World War II: The Interaction of Class, Race, and Feminism," in *Woman's Being, Woman's Place: Female Identity and Vocation in American History,* ed. Mary Kelley (Boston: G.K. Hall and Co., 1979), 313-28.

133. Kessler-Harris, 286-87, 297; U.S. Census, see Appendix A.

134. Ryan, 174.

135. Ibid., 175, 202; quoted in ibid., 205.

136. U.S. Census, see Appendix A; Weiner, 89.

137. Ryan, 154.

138. Betty Friedan, *The Feminine Mystique* (New York: Norton, 1963). See also Marcia Cohen, *The Sisterhood: The True Story of the Women Who Changed the World* (New York: Simon and Schuster, 1988).

139. Ralph Smith, ed., *The Subtle Revolution: Women at Work* (Washington, DC: Urban Institute, 1979); Frances Fox Piven and Richard A. Cloward, *Poor People's Movements* (New York: Vintage Books, 1979), 251.

140. In Greek mythology, the giant Procrustes tied his victims to beds and then cut or stretched them until they fit. Women's Majority Union, "Lilith Manifesto," in *Sisterhood is Powerful: An Anthology of Writings from the Women's Liberation Movement,* ed. Robin Morgan (New York:

Random House, 1970), 528.

141. See Gloria Joseph, "The Incompatible Ménage à Trois: Marxism, Feminism, and Racism," in *Women and Revolution: A Discussion of the Unhappy Marriage of Marxism and Feminism*, ed. Lydia Sargent (Boston, MA: South End Press, 1981), 91-108; and bell hooks, *Feminist Theory from Margin to Center* (Boston, MA: South End Press, 1984), Ch. 1.

142. The feminists include radical feminists such as Shulamith Firestone, *The Dialectic of Sex* (New York: Bantam Books, 1971); lesbian separatists such as Mary Daly, *Beyond God the Father: Toward a Philosophy of Women's Liberation* (London: Women's Press, 1986, c. 1973); Andrea Dworkin, *Letters from a War Zone: Writings: 1976-1987* (London: Secker and Warburg, 1988); Catharine A. MacKinnon, *Toward a Feminist Theory of the State* (Cambridge: Harvard University Press, 1989); and socialist feminists such as Zillah R. Eisenstein, *Capitalist Patriarchy and the Case for Socialist Feminism* (New York: Monthly Review Press, 1979), and Lydia Sargent, ed., *Women and Revolution: A Discussion of the Unhappy Marriage of Marxism and Feminism* (Boston, MA: South End Press, 1981). Friedan was President of NOW when she coined this homophobic phrase. Rita Mae Brown had confronted heterosexism in NOW in 1970 as newsletter editor of NY NOW. Friedan's response was to warn that lesbians were undermining feminism's credibility and to purge Brown and others thought to be lesbians from NOW. Barry Adam, *The Rise of a Gay and Lesbian Movement* (Boston: G.K. Hall & Co., 1987), 90. See, in contrast, Adrienne Rich, "Compulsory Heterosexuality and the Lesbian Existence," *Signs* 5 (Summer 1980), and Sidney Abbott and Barbara Love, *Sappho Was a Right-On Woman* (New York: Stein and Day, 1972). Also see Alison Jaggar and Paula Rothenberg, eds., *Feminist Frameworks: Alternative Theoretical Accounts of the Relations Between Women and Men* (New York: McGraw-Hill, 1978).

143. U.S. Bureau of the Census, *Household Income and Poverty Status,* 1987, Table 40, 166; 1970 and 1980 Censuses, see Appendix A.

144. Sarah Kuhn and Barry Bluestone, "Economic Restructuring and the Female Labor Market: The Impact of Industrial Change on Women," in *Women, Households, and the Economy,* ed. Lourdes Benería and Catharine R. Stimpson (New Brunswick: Rutgers University Press, 1979), 9; U.S. Census, see Appendix A.

145. Foner, 491-92; see Teresa Amott and Julie Matthaei, "Comparable Worth, Incomparable Pay: The Issue at Yale," *Radical America* 18 (September/October 1984).

146. Foner, 562.

147. In contrast, Black wives contributed 67 percent. Heidi Hartmann, "Changes in Women's Economic and Family Roles in Post-World War II United States," in Benería and Stimpson, 33-64; Rebecca M. Blank, "Women's Paid Work, Household Income, and Household Well-Being," in *The American Woman: 1988-89: A Status Report,* ed. Susan E. Rix, for the Women's Research & Education Institute (New York: W.W. Norton & Company, 1988), 137.

148. Blau and Ferber, 128.

149. Elaine McCrate, "Trade, Merger and Employment: Economic Theory on Marriage," *Review of Radical Political Economics* (Spring 1987): 73; Barbara Ehrenreich, *The Hearts of Men: American Dreams and the Flight from Commitment* (Garden City, NY: Anchor Press/Doubleday, 1983).

150. Mary Jo Bane, "Household Composition and Poverty," in Sheldon H. Danziger and Daniel H. Weinberg, eds., *Fighting Poverty: What Works and What Doesn't* (Cambridge: Harvard University Press, 1986), 227.; U.S. Bureau of the Census, Current Population Reports, Series P-23, No. 162, "Studies in Marriage and the Family," (Washington, DC: GPO, 1989), 14; *Statistical Abstract 1988,* 358; U.S. Bureau of the Census, Current Population Reports, Series P-60, No. 166, *Household Income and Poverty Status in the United States: 1988 (Advance Data from the March 1989 Current Population Survey)* (Washington, DC: GPO, 1989), 142.

Chapter 6

1. We use the terms African American and Black interchangeably to refer to Americans with some African heritage. This includes those who came to the United States directly as indentured servants or slaves and their ancestors, as well as immigrants with African ancestry from the

English and French-speaking Caribbean. Puerto Ricans, a large proportion of whom have African heritage, are treated in Chapter 8; many Cuban Americans also have African heritage, but are considered Latina/o or Hispanic rather than African American. These conceptions have changed, and will continue to change, since they reflect socially defined categories rather than fixed biological realities.

2. From *Jonestown & Other Madness: Poetry by Pat Parker* (Ithaca, NY: Firebrand Books, 1985), 74-75.

3. See Eric Williams, *Capitalism and Slavery* (Chapel Hill: University of North Carolina Press, 1944).

4. Marianna Davis, *Contributions of Black Women to America* (Columbia, SC: Kenday Press, 1982), 2-3; *Say Brother: The Search for the Blackamoor, Part II,* produced by Say Brother Productions, Boston, MA.

5. Paula Giddings, *When and Where I Enter: The Impact of Black Women on Race and Sex in America* (New York: Bantam, 1984), 37.

6. Giddings, 38; Thomas Sowell, *The Economics and Politics of Race: An International Perspective* (New York: William Morrow, 1983), 122.

7. Vincent Harding, *There Is a River: The Black Struggle for Freedom in America* (New York: Vintage, 1983), 33.

8. Sowell, 121; Giddings, 35; Winthrop Jordan, *White Over Black: American Attitudes Toward the Negro, 1550-1812* (Chapel Hill: University of North Carolina Press, 1979), 154.

9. Sowell, 120; Christie Farnham, "Sapphire? Dominance in the Slave Family," in *"To Toil the Livelong Day": America's Women at Work, 1780-1980,* ed. Carol Groneman and Mary Beth Norton (Ithaca, NY: Cornell University Press, 1987), 70-71.

10. Igor Kopytoff and Suzanne Miers, "African 'Slavery' as an Institution of Marginality," in *Slavery in Africa: Historical and Anthropological Perspectives,* ed. Igor Kopytoff and Suzanne Miers (Madison: University of Wisconsin Press, 1977), 3-14. Of course, the fact that Africans also had a form of slavery does not justify European American profiteering from the slave trade or the establishment of slavery in the Americas.

11. Alexander Flaconbridge, *An Account of the Slave Trade on the Coast of Africa* (London: J. Phillips, 1788), 29; Sowell, 120; U.S. Bureau of the Census, Current Population Reports, Series P-23, No. 80, *The Social and Economic Status of the Black Population in the United States: An Historical View, 1790-1978* (Washington, DC: GPO, 1979), 9, 12, 13.

12. The South Atlantic region was comprised of Delaware, Maryland, District of Columbia, Virginia, North Carolina, South Carolina, Georgia, and Florida; *Black Population,* 9, 12, 13; Julie A. Matthaei, *An Economic History of Women in America: Women's Work, the Sexual Division of Labor, and the Development of Capitalism* (New York: Schocken Books, 1982), 80.

13. Matthaei, 88-94.

14. Quoted in Jacqueline Jones, *Labor of Love, Labor of Sorrow: Black Women, Work, and the Family from Slavery to the Present* (New York: Basic Books, 1985), 21.

15. Marianna Davis, 9; Jones, 20-21; Gerda Lerner, ed., *Black Women in White America: A Documentary History* (New York: Vintage Books, 1973), 12-75; quoted in Dorothy Sterling, *We Are Your Sisters: Black Women in the Nineteenth Century* (New York: W.W. Norton & Company, 1984), 56.

16. Marianna Davis, 9-11; Giddings, 39-40.

17. Matthaei, Ch. 4; Jones, Ch. 1; Sterling, 13-17.

18. Quoted in Jones, 16.

19. Ibid., 16; quoted in ibid., 17.

20. Quoted in ibid., 18.

21. Matthaei, 91.

22. Quoted in Sterling, 38.

23. Farnham, 78-80; Angela Davis, "Reflections on the Black Woman's Role in the Community of Slaves," *Black Scholar* 3 (December 1971): 2-16.

24. Quoted in Sterling, 25.

25. Sterling, 59.

26. bell hooks, *Ain't I a Woman: Black Women and Feminism* (Boston: South End Press,

1981), 27; quoted in Sterling, 27.

27. Jones, 26; Sterling, 29-31.

28. Matthaei, 85.

29. Jones, 35.

30. Quoted in Sterling, 58-59.

31. Ibid., 59.

32. Some scholars also relate the weakness of the father-child tie relative to the mother-child tie to African roots; in Africa, in the practice of polygyny, men were peripheral to the mother-child groups. See Joyce Ladner, "Racism and Tradition: Black Womanhood in Historical Perspective," in *The Black Woman Cross-Culturally,* ed. Filomina C. Steady (Cambridge, MA: Schenkman, 1981), 285; Deborah Gray White, *Ar'n't I a Woman? Female Slaves in the Plantation South* (New York: W.W. Norton, 1985), 119-23, 159. As Christie Farnham notes, single white women in the nineteenth century faced a shortage of potential husbands (men were migrating to the frontier) but were prevented from raising families alone by strong social stigmatization. Farnham, 81-83.

33. *Black Population,* 11; Marianna Davis, 36-39.

34. Marianna Davis, 12; Sowell, *Economics and Politics,* 121.

35. George Blackburn and Sherman Ricards, "The Mother-Headed Family Among Free Negroes in Charleston, South Carolina, 1850-1860," *Phylon* 42 (March 1981): 13.

36. Leon Litwack, *North of Slavery: The Negro in the Free States, 1790-1860* (Chicago: University of Chicago Press, 1961), 157-65; a Pennsylvania law of 1725, quoted in Sharon Harley, "Northern Black Female Workers: Jacksonian Era," in *The Afro-American Woman: Struggles and Images,* ed. Sharon Harley and Rosalyn Terborg-Penn (Port Washington, NY: Kennikat Press, 1978), 10.

37. Harley, 154.

38. Blackburn and Ricards, 23; Lorenzo Greene and Carter Woodson, *The Negro Wage Earner* (New York: AMS Press, 1930), quoted in Harley, 10.

39. Eileen Boris, "Black Women and Paid Labor in the Home: Industrial Homework in Chicago in the 1920s," in *Homework: Historical and Contemporary Perspectives on Paid Labor at Home,* ed. Eileen Boris and Cynthia R. Daniels (Chicago: University of Illinois Press, 1989), 33-39; Susan Lebsock, "Free Black Women and the Question of Matriarchy: Petersburg, Virginia, 1784-1820," *Feminist Studies* 8 (Summer 1982): 277, in *Sex and Class in Women's History,* ed. Judith L. Newton, Mary Ryan, and Judith Walkowitz (Boston: Routledge & Kegan Paul, 1983), 146-66.

40. Linda Perkins, "Black Women and Racial 'Uplift' Prior to Emancipation," in *The Black Woman Cross-Culturally,* ed. Filomina C. Steady (Cambridge, MA: Schenkman, 1981), 318-19; Giddings, 72.

41. Litwack, 169-84; Blackburn and Ricards, 25; quoted in Litwack, 184-85.

42. Litwack, 169-84.

43. Blackburn and Ricards, 23-24; Lebsock, 277-82.

44. Lebsock, 277, 285-87; Blackburn and Ricards, 16, 21.

45. Quoted in Bert James Loewenberg and Ruth Bogin, eds., *Black Women in Nineteenth-Century American Life: Their Words, Their Thoughts, Their Feelings* (University Park, PA: Pennsylvania State University Press, 1976), 188.

46. Perkins, 323, 328, 330; Loewenberg and Bogin, 234-35.

47. Loewenberg and Bogin, 322.

48. Perkins, 321-22; quoted in Giddings, 60.

49. Quoted in Marianna Davis, 53-55.

50. We will discuss this more later; for early discrimination within the women's movement, see Rosalyn Terborg-Penn, "Discrimination Against Afro-American Women in the Woman's Movement, 1830-1920," in *The Afro American Woman,* ed. Harley and Terborg-Penn, 17-27.

51. Perkins, 319-23; Marianna Davis, 43-46.

52. Perkins, 320-22; Marianna Davis, 18.

53. Mary Elizabeth Carnegie, *The Path We Tread: Blacks in Nursing, 1854-1984* (Philadelphia: J.B. Lippincott, 1986), 5-11; Jones, 49.

54. Quoted in Perkins, 324.

55. Ibid., 323-31.

56. Perkins, 324-30.

57. Jones; Manning Marable, *Blackwater: Historical Studies in Race, Class Consciousness, and Revolution* (Dayton, OH: Black Praxis Press, 1981), 53-55, 59-60; *Black Population*, 81; Sowell, 128.

58. Quoted in Marianna Davis, 70-72.

59. Quoted in Giddings, 72.

60. W.E.B. Du Bois, *Black Reconstruction: An Essay Toward a History of the Part which Black Folk Played in the Attempt to Reconstruct Democracy in America, 1860-1880* (New York: Harcourt, Brace and Co., 1935), 701.

61. Gerald David Jaynes, *Branches Without Roots: Genesis of the Black Working Class in the American South, 1862-1882* (New York: Oxford University Press, 1986), Ch. 13; William Harris, "Work and the Family in Black Atlanta," *Journal of Social History* 9 (March 1976): 321; William Harris, *The Harder We Run: Black Workers Since the Civil War* (New York: Oxford University Press, 1982), 40-46. White men formed the Jockey Club to deny licenses to Black jockeys, who had earlier monopolized the dangerous occupation, thereby transforming the occupation into a white monopoly; Jaynes, 267, 275.

62. Jaynes, 256; Harris, *Harder We Run*, 43; Philip S. Foner, *Organized Labor and the Black Worker, 1619-1973* (New York: Praeger Publishers, 1974), 34.

63. Marianna Davis, 78; as African American author Pauline Hopkins wrote in 1900:

> Lynching was instituted to crush the manhood of the enfranchised black. Rape is the crime which appeals most strongly to the heart of the home life... *The men who created the mulatto race, who recruit its ranks year after year by the very means which they invoked lynch law to suppress,* bewailing the sorrows of violated womanhood!
>
> No; it is not rape. If the Negro votes, he is shot; if he marries a white woman, he is shot...or lynched—he is a pariah whom the National Government cannot defend. But if he defends himself and his home, then is heard the tread of marching feet as the Federal troops move southward to quell a "race riot."

Quoted in Hazel Carby, "On the Threshold of Woman's Era: Lynching, Empire, and Sexuality in Black Feminist Theory," in *"Race," Writing, and Difference,* ed. Henry Louis Gates, Jr. (Chicago: University of Chicago Press, 1986), 314; Jaynes, 256.

64. Jaynes, 256.

65. Jaynes, 253-57; *Black Population*, 72.

66. U.S. Bureau of Census, *Statistics of Women at Work*, 1907, cited in Lynn Weiner, *From Working Girl to Working Mother: The Female Labor Force in the United States, 1820-1980* (Chapel Hill, NC: University of North Carolina Press, 1985), 84; the rate for women over 65 is for southern women in 1900. See Janice L. Reiff, Michael R. Dahlin, and Daniel S. Smith, "Rural Push and Urban Pull: Work and Family Experiences of Older Black Women in Southern Cities, 1880-1900," *Journal of Social History* 16 (1983): 40.

67. Giddings, 75.

68. 1900 Census, see Appendix A.

69. *Black Population*, 13, 15.

70. *Black Population*, 13-14, 73, 81; Marable, 53-55; Reiff, Dahlin, and Smith, 41.

71. Marable, 55; Jaynes, Ch. 9.

72. Jaynes, 229; Jones, 59-60; quoted in Jaynes, 231-32.

73. See Jaynes, 187-90, for a detailed discussion of this transition.

74. Jones, 65.

75. Quoted in Giddings, 71.

76. Jones, 62-64; Reiff, Dahlin, and Smith, 41.

77. Jones, 82-83; Harris, *Harder We Run*, 9-13.

78. *Black Population*, 72; Jones, 128.

79. Quoted by Elizabeth Clark-Lewis, "This Work Had a End: African-American Domestic Workers in Washington, D.C., 1910-1940," in Groneman and Norton, 199-200.

80. Reiff, Dahlin, and Smith, 41.

81. Jones, 128; quoted in Jones, 129.

82. Jones, 132-33.

83. Quoted in Hooks, 57.

84. Ibid., 55.

85. Ibid., 60-62.

86. Philip S. Foner, *Women and the American Labor Movement: From Colonial Times to the Eve of World War I* (New York: Free Press, 1979), 188; Harris, *Harder We Run* 26-28.

87. Quoted in Giddings, 81.

88. Lerner, 119.

89. Jones, Ch. 4; Lerner, 119, 132; Giddings, 76.

90. Marianna Davis, 78-82.

91. Giddings, 83, 92.

92. Ibid., 17-20, 83, 89-98; and Marianna Davis, 78-82, 96.

93. Marianna Davis, 11, 90; Rosalyn Terborg-Penn, "Survival Strategies Among African-American Workers," in *Women, Work, and Protest: A Century of U.S. Women's Labor History*, ed. Ruth Milkman (Boston: Routledge and Kegan Paul, 1985), 142-43, 148-50.

94. Terborg-Penn, "Discrimination in the Woman's Movement, 1830-1920," 21.

95. Ibid.

96. Harris, *Harder We Run*, 58-59.

97. Ibid.

98. *Black Population*, 15; quoted in Jones, 160.

99. *Black Population*, 13.

100. Jones, 161; Harris, *Harder We Run*, 55; Marianna Davis, 107-8.

101. 1920 Census, see Appendix A.

102. Quoted in Debra Lynn Newman, "Black Women Workers in the Twentieth Century," *Sage*, III (Spring 1986): 10.

103. Quoted in Harris, *Harder We Run*, 65.

104. Jones, 168, 178-81. Jones provides an excellent picture of the blatant and subtle workings of race discrimination in this period, 160-82.

105. 1930 Census, see Appendix A; Jones, 181; quoted in Jones, 179.

106. 1930 Census, see Appendix A; *Black Population*, 72; Jones, 167-68, 177.

107. Boris, 37; 1910 and 1920 Censuses, see Appendix A.

108. Calculated from the 1910 and 1930 Censuses, see Appendix A. The *Black Population* study found a greater increase, from 42 percent to 63 percent, 72; Clark-Lewis, 197.

109. Jacqueline Jones, interview by Julie Matthaei, August 1989, Wellesley, MA; Clark-Lewis, 202-6.

110. Harris, *Harder We Run*, 63; Marianna Davis, 108.

111. Jones, 181.

112. Thomas Sowell, *Ethnic America: A History* (New York: Basic Books, 1981), 216-19; Terborg-Penn, "Survival Strategies," 150; Terborg-Penn's foremother, Delia Bierman Terborg, was one such West Indian immigrant woman who worked in needlework. Among the West Indian immigrants and their descendants are many who rose to prominence, including Marcus Garvey, Shirley Chisholm, Malcolm X, Sidney Poitier, Harry Belafonte, and Black feminist scholars and writers Barbara Christian, Audre Lorde, and Rosalyn Terborg-Penn.

113. Rosalyn Terborg-Penn, "Discontented Black Feminists: Prelude and Postscript to the Passage of the Nineteenth Amendment," in *Decades of Discontent: The Women's Movement, 1920-1940*, ed. Lois Scharf and Joan M. Jensen (Westport, CT: Greenwood Press, 1983), 269-70.

114. Jones, 181-82; quoted in Jones, 185.

115. Harris, *Harder We Run*, 104.

116. Jones, 199.

117. Lerner, 229-31. These slave markets are described somewhat differently by Harris, who says they took place on subway stations in Harlem. *Harder We Run*, 107; Jones, 199; Jacqueline Jones, interview; 1930 Census, see Appendix A.

118. Harris, *Harder We Run*, 106; quoted in Jones, 197.

119. Harris, *Harder We Run*, 110; Foner, *Labor and the Black Worker*, 216; Jones, 212.

120. Quoted in Dolores Janiewski, "Seeking 'a New Day and a New Way': Black Women and Unions in the Southern Tobacco Industry," in Groneman and Norton, 175.

121. Harris, *Harder We Run,* 107; Lerner, 232; Marianna Davis, 114-15.

122. Quoted in Leah Wise and Sue Thrasher, "The Southern Tenant Farmers' Union," in *Working Lives: The "Southern Exposure" History of Labor in the South,* ed. Marc S. Miller (New York: Pantheon, 1980), 120-22, 128-29, 132.

123. Harris, *Harder We Run,* 98-101.

124. Alice Kessler-Harris, *Out to Work: A History of Wage-Earning Women in the United States* (New York: Oxford University Press, 1982), 279; Newman, 13; Harris, *Harder We Run,* 112-18.

125. *Black Population,* 15; Harris, *Harder We Run,* 122; Kessler-Harris, 279; Jones, 253.

126. David Roediger, "'Labor in White Skin': Race and Working-class History," in *Reshaping the US Left: Popular Struggles in the 1980s,* ed. Mike Davis and Michael Sprinker (London: Verso, 1988), 297.

127. Jones, 240.

128. Quoted in Ibid., 234.

129. *Black Population,* 36, 75, 81.

130. Quoted in Foner, *Labor and the Black Worker,* 302-3.

131. During the 1950s about 300,000 went West. *Black Population,* 15.

132. *Eyes on the Prize,* produced by Blackside Productions, available from PBS Video. See also Jack M. Bloom, *Class, Race, and the Civil Rights Movement* (Bloomington: Indiana University Press, 1987) 89-95, 134-39.

133. Jones, 280.

134. Giddings, 261-62; Jones, 278-79.

135. Jones, 282-88.

136. Jones, 310-15; see also Stokely Carmichael and Charles V. Hamilton, *Black Power: The Politics of Liberation in America* (New York: Random House, 1967), and John H. Bracey, Jr., August Meier, and Elliott Rudwick, eds., *Black Nationalism in America* (Indianapolis, IN: Bobbs Merrill, 1970).

137. Sullivan also created the "Sullivan Principles," which rate South African corporations' treatment of Blacks, and urged colleges and governments to divest their stock in U.S. companies whose South African subsidiaries received low ratings. In 1987, Sullivan repudiated these principles as not bringing change quickly enough, and called for total divestment. James B. Stewart, "Building a Cooperative Economy: Lessons From the Black Experience," *Review of Social Economy* 42 (December 1984): 360-68.

138. Frances Fox Piven and Richard A. Cloward, *Poor People's Movements: Why They Succeed, How They Fail* (New York: Vintage, 1979), 272-73.

139. Foner, *Labor and the Black Worker,* 394; Lerner, 234-38.

140. Piven and Cloward, 271-72.

141. Alice Walker, *In Search of Our Mothers' Gardens* (San Diego, CA: Harcourt Brace Jovanovich, 1983); Combahee River Collective, "A Black Feminist Statement," in *Home Girls: A Black Feminist Anthology,* ed. Barbara Smith (New York: Kitchen Table Women of Color Press, 1983), 272.

142. Michelle Wallace, *Black Macho and the Myth of the Superwoman* (New York: Warner Books, 1980); Ntozake Shange, *For Colored Girls Who Have Considered Suicide When the Rainbow Was Enuf* (New York: Collier Books, 1977); Alice Walker, *The Color Purple* (New York: Harcourt Brace Jovanovich, 1982); Barbara Smith, ed., *Home Girls: A Black Feminist Anthology* (New York: Kitchen Table Women of Color Press, 1983); Gloria Joseph, *Common Differences: Conflicts in Black and White Feminist Perspectives* (Boston: South End Press, 1981); bell hooks, *Feminist Theory: From Margin to Center* (Boston: South End Press, 1984).

143. Teresa Amott, "Black Women and AFDC: Making Necessity Out of Entitlement," in *Women and the Welfare State,* ed. Linda Gordon (Madison: University of Wisconsin Press, 1990), 288-89; Piven and Cloward, 335-37.

144. Linda Gordon, "What Does Welfare Regulate?" *Social Research* 55 (Winter 1988); Johnnie Tillmon, "Welfare Is a Women's Issue," *Liberation News Service* no. 415, (26 February 1972), reprinted in *America's Working Women: A Documentary History—1600 to the Present,* ed. Rosalyn Baxandall, Linda Gordon, and Susan Reverby (New York: Vintage, 1976), 355-58.

145. 1980 Census, see Appendix A; *Black Population,* 31, 49.

146. 1950, 1970, 1980 Censuses, see Appendix A; *Black Population*, 47.

147. Michael Reich, "Black-White Income Differences," in *The Imperiled Economy, Book II, Through the Safety Net*, ed. Robert Cherry, et al. (New York: Union for Radical Political Economics, 1988), 117.

148. Michael Podgursky and Paul Swaim, "The Duration of Joblessness Following Plant Shutdowns and Jobs Displacement," Paper presented to the Eastern Economic Association, 6 March 1987.

149. William Julius Wilson, *The Truly Disadvantaged: The Inner City, The Underclass, and Public Policy* (Chicago: University of Chicago Press, 1987); *Black Population*, 74; Troy Duster, "Social Implications of the 'New' Black Urban Underclass," *The Black Scholar* 19 (May/June 1988): 4; calculated from 1980 Census, see Appendix A.

150. National Urban League, *State of Black America 1988*, 144; U.S. Bureau of the Census, *Statistical Abstract of the United States: 1988* (Washington, DC: GPO, 1988), 381.

151. U.S. Bureau of the Census, *Statistical Abstract of the United States 1990* (Washington, DC: GPO, 1990), 397.

152. See Appendix A; U.S. Department of Labor, *Employment and Earnings*, January 1989, Table 39.

153. Wilson, *The Truly Disadvantaged*, 43; William Julius Wilson and Kathryn M. Neckerman, "Poverty and Family Structure," in *Fighting Poverty: What Works and What Doesn't*, ed. Sheldon H. Danziger and Daniel H. Weinberg (Cambridge: Harvard University Press, 1986), 246; U.S. Department of Labor, *Employment and Earnings* (January 1989), Tables 3, 39.

154. Center on Budget and Policy Priorities, *Still Far From the Dream: Recent Developments in Black Income, Employment and Poverty*, (Washington, DC: GPO, October 1988); *Statistical Abstract: 1988*, 433, 435.

155. For an interesting analysis of the underclass concept, see Christopher Jencks, "What is the underclass—and is it growing?" in *Focus* 12 (Spring and Summer 1989): 14-36.

156. Wilson, *The Truly Disadvantaged*; Douglas S. Massey and Mitchell L. Eggers, "The Ecology of Inequality: Minorities and the Concentration of Poverty, 1970-1990," *American Journal of Sociology* 95 (March 1990): 1153-88.

157. Julianne Malveaux, "Race, Class, and Black Poverty," *Black Scholar* 19 (May/June 1988): 18-19.

158. U.S. Bureau of the Census, Current Population Reports, Series P-20, No. 437, *Household and Family Characteristics: March 1988* (Washington, DC: GPO, 1989), 4-6; Wilson and Neckerman, 235; U.S. Bureau of the Census, *Statistical Abstract of the United States, 1989* (Washington, DC: GPO, 1989), 46.

159. However, the birth rate for Black unwed mothers fell by 11 percent between 1970 and 1987, while the rate for white unwed mothers rose by 77 percent. *Statistical Abstract of the United States: 1990*, 67. For a historical discussion of Black single mothers, see Rose Brewer, "Black Women in Poverty: Some Comments on Female-Headed Families," *Signs* 13 (Winter 1988): 337.

160. In 1986, for example, 41.9 percent of Black men did not survive to the age of 65, compared to only 25.2 percent of white men, 25.1 percent of Black women, and 14.3 percent of white women. *Statistical Abstract of the United States: 1989*, 72, 173, 182, 183; *Statistical Abstract of the United States, 1990*, 85.

161. *Statistical Abstract of the United States 1990*, 43; Teresa Amott, "The 'Feminization of Poverty,' 1970 to the Present: The Influence of Race, Class and Gender," *Socialist Politics* (April-May 1985): passim; *Black Population*, 15.

162. *Statistical Abstract of the United States 1988*, 50; U.S. Bureau of the Census, Current Population Reports, Series P-60, No. 166, *Money Income and Poverty Status in the United States: 1988 (Advance Data from the March 1989 Current Population Survey)* (Washington, DC: 1989).

163. Mary Jo Bane, "Household Composition and Poverty," in *Fighting Poverty*, ed. Sheldon H. Danziger and Daniel H. Weinberg (Cambridge: Harvard Press, 1986), 227; *Focus*, Summer 1987.

164. Franklin Frazier, *The Negro Family in the United States* (Chicago: University of Chicago Press, 1939); U.S. Department of Labor, Office of Policy Planning and Research, *The Negro*

Family: The Case for National Action, by Daniel Moynihan (Washington, DC: GPO, 1965); Lebsock, 273.

165. Charles Murray, *Losing Ground: American Social Policy 1950-1980* (New York: Basic Books, 1984); Amott, "Black Women."

166. For further information, contact the National Welfare Rights Union, 29 McLean, Highland Park, MI 48203; Julianne Malveaux, "The Political Economy of Black Women," in *The Year Left 2: Toward a Rainbow Socialism,* ed. Mike Davis, Manning Marable, Fred Pfeil, and Michael Sprinker (London: Verso, 1987); *Money Income and Poverty Status in the United States: 1988,* 33-34.

167. Barbara Omolade, "It's a Family Affair: The Real Lives of Black Single Mothers," *Village Voice* (15 July 1986).

168. For more information on the Sisterhood of Black Single Mothers, write to the organization at 1360 Fulton Street, Suite 423, Brooklyn, NY 11216.

169. Bette Woody, *Black Women in the New Services Economy: Help or Hindrance in Economic Self-Sufficiency?* Wellesley College Center for Research on Women, Working Paper No. 196, 1989, 20; Elizabeth Higginbotham, "Employment for Professional Black Women in the Twentieth Century," in *Ingredients for Women's Employment Policy,* ed. Christine Bose and Glenna Spitze (Albany: State University of New York Press, 1987), 84-86.

170. *Statistical Abstract of the United States: 1990,* 133.

171. Randy Albelda, "'Nice Work If You Can Get It': Segmentation of White and Black Women Workers in the Post-War Period," *Review of Radical Political Economics* 17 (Fall 1985): 73; *Money Income and Poverty Status in the United States: 1988,* 47-48; U.S. Department of Labor, Bureau of Labor Statistics, *Employment and Earnings,* January 1989, 76; Rhonda Williams, *Beyond Human Capital: Black Women, Work, and Wages,* Wellesley College Center for Research on Women, Working Paper No. 183, 1988, 6-7, 35; U.S. Bureau of the Census, Current Population Reports, Series P-60, No. 162, *Money Income of Households, Families, and Persons in the United States: 1987,* 104-5; data on share of families that were female-headed in 1987 is from U.S. House of Representatives, Select Committee on Children, Youth, and Families, "Barriers and Opportunities for America's Young Black Men," Fact Sheet, July 1989.

172. Williams, 40.

173. 1980 Census, see Appendix A; U.S. House, "Barriers and Opportunities." According to the House study, over 21 percent of Blacks are persistently poor, compared with less than 3 percent of whites.

Chapter 7

1. Kitty Tsui, "Chinatown Talking Story," *Making Waves: An Anthology of Writings By and About Asian American Women,* ed. Asian Women United of California (Boston: Beacon Press, 1989), 132.

2. "Minority Populations Grow at Faster Rate: 1980-88," *Census and You: Monthly News From the U.S. Bureau of the Census* 25 (April 1990): 8. Nineteen eighty five was the latest year for which we could find numbers of Asians by detailed racial-ethnic group, in Jayjia Hsia, *Asian Americans in Higher Education and at Work* (Hillsdale, NJ: Lawrence Erbaum Associates, 1988), 10; 1980 Census, see Appendix A.

3. This creates some difficulties in characterizing Asians in the United States as Asians or Asian Americans. Generally, we use the term Asian to describe immigrants and Asian American to describe second and higher generations.

4. Edna Bonacich, "U.S. Capitalist Development: A Background to Asian Immigration," in *Labor Immigration Under Capitalism: Asian Workers in the United States Before World War II,* ed. Lucie Cheng and Edna Bonacich (Berkeley: University of California Press, 1984), 116.

5. Evelyn Nakano Glenn, *Issei, Nisei, War Bride: Three Generations of Japanese American Women in Domestic Service* (Philadelphia: Temple University Press, 1986), 10-11; Bonacich, "U.S. Capitalist Development," 173-78.

6. Quoted in Roberto V. Vallangça, *Pinoy: The First Wave (1898-1941)* (San Francisco: Strawberry Hill Press, 1977), 113.

7. Megumi Dick Osumi, "Asians and California's Anti-Miscegenation Laws," in *Asian and Pacific American Experiences: Women's Perspectives,* ed. Nobuya Tsuchida (Minneapolis: Asian/Pacific American Learning Resource Center and General College, University of Minnesota, 1982), 1; Edna Bonacich, "Asian Labor in the Development of California and Hawaii," in Cheng and Bonacich, 175.

8. Glenn, *Issei, Nisei,* 11.

9. Stanford Lyman, "Strangers in the City: the Chinese in the Urban Frontier," in *Roots: An Asian American Reader,* ed. Amy Tachiki, Eddie Wong, and Franklin Odo with Buck Wong (Los Angeles: Asian American Studies Center, University of California, 1971), 162; Peter Kwong, *The New Chinatown* (New York: The Noonday Press, 1987), 16-18.

10. Kwong, 17-19.

11. Ibid., 10-11; June Mei, "Socioeconomic Origins of Emigration: Guangdong to California, 1850-1882," in Cheng and Bonacich, 219-20.

12. Paul C.P. Siu, *The Chinese Laundryman: A Study of Social Isolation* (New York and London: New York University Press, 1987), 44-45; Glenn, *Issei, Nisei,* 23-24; Bonacich, "Asian Labor," 165-66; John Liu, "Race, Ethnicity, and the Sugar Plantation System: Asian Labor in Hawaii, 1850-1900," in Cheng and Bonacich, 190, 220.

13. Edna Bonacich, "Some Basic Facts: Patterns of Asian Immigration and Exclusion," in Cheng and Bonacich, 65; Alexander Saxton, *The Indispensable Enemy: Labor and the Anti-Chinese Movement* (Berkeley: University of California Press, 1971), 7; Lyman, 162-65; Glenn, *Issei, Nisei,* 24.

14. Quoted in Siu, 49.

15. Siu, 48; June Mei, "Socioeconomic Developments Among the Chinese in San Francisco, 1848-1906," in Cheng and Bonacich, 376; Glenn, *Issei, Nisei,* 17.

16. Bonacich, "Asian Labor"; Glenn, *Issei, Nisei,* Ch. 1; Mei, "Socioeconomic Developments," 381.

17. One exception was the Wobblies (the radical left International Workers of the World). See Philip S. Foner, *Women and the American Labor Movement: From Colonial Times to the Eve of World War I* (New York: Free Press, 1979), 392; Joyce L. Kornbluh, ed., *Rebel Voices: An I.W.W. Anthology* (Ann Arbor: University of Michigan Press, 1964).

18. Mei, "Socioeconomic Developments," 385-86, lists guilds of tailors of men's clothing, makers of women's clothing, makers of work clothes, shoemakers, and cigar makers as the main trade guilds.

19. Lyman, 164-65; Siu, 47-49; Sucheng Chan, "The Chinese in California Agriculture, 1860-1900," in *The Chinese American Experience: Papers from the Second National Conference on Chinese American Studies (1980),* ed. Genny Lim (San Francisco: Chinese Historical Society of America and Chinese Culture Foundation, 1984), 68-77; Judy Yung, *Chinese Women of America: A Pictorial History* (Seattle and London: University of Washington Press, 1986), 15.

20. Mei, "Socioeconomic Developments," 366-67.

21. See, for example, Sucheng Chan, 70.

22. Mei, "Socioeconomic Developments," 388, 390-91; Lucie Cheng Hirata, "Chinese Immigrant Women in Nineteenth-Century California," in Tsuchida, 48-49.

23. Mei, "Socioeconomic Developments," 384-85; Diane Mei Lin Mark and Ginger Chih, *A Place Called Chinese America* (Organization of Chinese Americans, Inc., 1982), 54-56; Roger Daniels, *Asian America: Chinese and Japanese in the United States Since 1850* (Seattle: University of Washington Press, 1988), 81-83.

24. Bonacich, "Some Basic Facts," 65; Liu, 195.

25. Bonacich, "Some Basic Facts," 65; Liu, 195; Yung, 10, 11, 36.

26. Yung, 36-37.

27. Ibid.

28. Liu, 190.

29. Ibid., 197-203; quoted in ibid., 203.

30. Yung, 14; Lucie Cheng, "Free, Indentured, Enslaved: Chinese Prostitutes in Nineteenth-Century America," in Cheng and Bonacich, 405; Lyman, 169. However, in Hawaii, where women's immigration was encouraged and there was intermarriage with Hawaiians, there were

more families, and the sex ratio was a bit lower, about 12 men to one woman; Yung, 36-37.

31. Evelyn Nakano Glenn, "Split Household, Small Producer and Dual Wage Earner: An Analysis of Chinese-American Family Strategies," *Journal of Marriage and the Family* (February 1983): 35-46.

32. Mark and Chih, 62; Lyman, 169-70; Victor Nee and Herbert Y. Wong, "Asian American Socioeconomic Achievement: The Strength of the Family Bond," *Sociological Perspectives* 28 (July 1985): 289; Siu, 165-66.

33. Mei, "Socioeconomic Origins," 238-41; Glenn, *Issei, Nisei,* 24; Cheng, 405.

34. Yung, 10; Siu, 164.

35. Cheng, 404-7.

36. Yung, 14-15.

37. Cheng, 408.

38. Ibid., 405, 407, 411; Yung, 13.

39. Cheng, 407, 411.

40. Ibid., 407-15.

41. Mark and Chih, 62; Yung, 18; Cheng, 411.

42. Hirata, 44; Cheng, 419, 424; Yung, 18-23.

43. Mei, "Socioeconomic Origins," and "Socioeconomic Developments"; Mark and Chih, 54-56; Roger Daniels, *The Politics of Prejudice: The Anti-Japanese Movement in California and the Struggle for Japanese Exclusion* (New York: Atheneum, 1969), 81-83.

44. Yung, 20. One Chinatown leader responded to attacks on Chinese prostitution: "Yes, yes, Chinese prostitution is bad. What do you think of German, French, Spanish and American prostitution? Do you think them good?" Quoted in Yung, 23.

45. Yung, 19, 24, 28-30; Hirata, 46-50.

46. Lyman, 164-65; quoted in Lyman, 165.

47. Glenn, *Issei, Nisei,* 25.

48. Quoted in Lyman, 173.

49. Lyman, 174; Siu, 50.

50. Lyman, 174-75.

51. Siu, 209-10; Mark and Chih, 36, 41, 43.

52. Calculated from Tables 2.1 and 2.5 in Bonacich, "Some Basic Facts," 62, 65. Numbers include Hawaii.

53. Lyman, 170; Yung, 83. According to Lyman, "Racial intermarriage has been illegal in thirty-nine states. In fourteen of these states the law specifically prohibited marriage between Chinese or 'Mongolians' and whites. California's anti-miscegenation statute was originally enacted in 1872 to prohibit marriage between [whites and] Negroes or mulattoes; in 1906 it was amended to prohibit marriages between whites and 'Mongolians.'" Lyman, 185, note 131. California anti-miscegenation laws were revoked in 1948.

54. Yung, 27. According to Yung, New York City allowed Chinese men to marry Irish women; Kwong, 14; Lyman, 170.

55. Glenn, "Split Household," 38; Yung, 42-44; *Carved in Silence,* produced and directed by Felicia Lowe, available from Crosscurrent Media, c/o NAATA, 346 9th St., San Francisco, CA 94103.

56. Glenn, "Split Household," 38; quoted in Siu, 165-67.

57. See Sucheng Chan, 76-79. A few managed to purchase land in spite of the alien land laws, such as Chin Shin, who purchased over 3,000 acres between 1893 and 1899.

58. Lyman, 174; Kwong, 130; Glenn, "Split Household," 39-40; Mei, "Socioeconomic Developments," 396; Mark and Chih, 92; Yung, 47.

59. Glenn, "Split Household," 39-41; Yung, 44.

60. Yung, 44.

61. Ibid., 30, 48, 50.

62. Mark and Chih, 72; Yung, 61; Dean Lan, "Chinatown Sweatshops," in *Counterpoint: Perspectives on Asian America,* ed. Emma Gee (Los Angeles: Asian American Studies Center, University of California, 1976), 347-58; H. Mark Lai, "A Historical Survey of the Chinese Left in America," in Gee, 67-69.

63. Yung, 53.

64. Quoted in ibid., 49; earlier material is from ibid., 49, 53.

65. 1900 and 1930 Censuses, see Appendix A; ibid., 48-57.

66. Yung, 66-67; *Mariner,* 26 June 1943, quoted in Yung, 67.

67. Kwong, 20.

68. See Appendix A.

69. Yung, 67; Siu, 202-3.

70. However, it was not until 1952 that Chinese American women could send for their husbands and children. Mark and Chih, 97-99.

71. Yung, 80-81.

72. Kwong, 20, 59; Cheng, 404.

73. Kwong, 22.

74. Ibid., 59.

75. Kwong, 59-60; Yung, 86.

76. Kwong, 60-61.

77. Ibid., 60.

78. Ibid., 22, 50.

79. Glenn, "Split Household," 42; Kwong, 26-27.

80. Glenn, "Split Household," 41-42; the study referred to is Chalsa Loo and Paul Ong, "Slaying Demons with a Sewing Needle: Feminist Issues for Chinatown's Women," *Berkeley Journal of Sociology* XXVII (1982): 77-88; quoted in Yung, 81. Dong Zem Ping's life was documented in the 1982 film, *Sewing Woman,* by Arthur Dong.

81. Loo and Ong.

82. Loo and Ong; Glenn, "Split Household," 41-42.

83. Loo and Ong, 83-85; Diane Yen-Mei Wong with Dennis Hayashi, "Behind Unmarked Doors: Developments in the Garment Industry," in *Making Waves,* 164.

84. Kwong, 79-80; Diane Yen-Mei Wong, "Asian/Pacific American Women: Legal Issues," in U.S. Commission on Civil Rights, *Civil Rights Issues of Asian and Pacific Americans: Myths and Realities* (Washington, DC: GPO, 1980), 140-44, 147-48. Others applaud Chinese garment industry sub-contractors for their paternalistic concern and flexibility *vis-à-vis* their employees; see, for example, Bernard Wong, "The Role of Ethnicity in Enclave Enterprises: A Study of the Chinese Garment Factories in New York City," *Human Organization* 46 (1987): 120-30.

85. Suzanne Lee, Chinese Progressive Association, telephone interview by Betsy Wright, Boston, Massachusetts, 11 September 1987; Wong with Hayashi, 164; Terri Oshiro, "Boston's Chinatown: A Working Community," in *City Issues—The Newsletter of the Episcopal City Mission* (Boston, MA), Spring 1987.

86. Chinatown Education Project, "An Experience in Community Work," in Gee, 230-33; Elaine Chan, "It's Time," telephone interview by Betsy Wright, 15 September 1987; quoted in Nancy Diao, "From Homemaker to Housing Advocate: An Interview with Mrs. Chang Jok Lee," in *Making Waves,* 383.

87. Kwong, 70-74; David Ho and Margaret Chin "Admissions Impossible," *Bridge: Asian American Perspectives* 8 (Summer 1983): 21; Yung, 123; 1980 Census, see Appendix A.

88. Ho and Chin, 7, found that while Asian applications have sky-rocketed since the 1970s, admissions rates for Asians are now falling, and are the lowest of any racial-ethnic group; Kwong, 74.

89. Yung, 123.

90. 1980 Census; see Appendix A.

91. Robert S. Mariano, "Impact of Census Issues on Asian/Pacific Americans," in U.S. Commission on Civil Rights, *Civil Rights Issues of Asian and Pacific Americans: Myths and Realities* (Washington, DC: GPO, 1980), 85; Betty Lee Sung, *A Survey of Chinese-American Manpower and Employment* (New York: Praeger Publishers, 1976), 94; U.S. Commission on Civil Rights, *Social Indicators of Equality for Minorities and Women* (Washington, DC: GPO, 1978), 24.

92. 1980 Census, see Appendix A; Mariano, 86; Dr. Nack Young An, "Political Implications of the 1980 Census for Asian Americans" in U.S. Commission on Civil Rights, *Civil Rights Issues of Asian and Pacific Americans: Myths and Realities* (Washington, DC: GPO, 1980), 92.

93. Masako Murakami Osako, "The Effects of Asian-American Kinship Systems on Women's Educational and Occupational Attainment," in U.S. Department of Education, Office of Educational Research and Improvement, National Institute of Education, *Conference on the Educational and Occupational Needs of Asian-Pacific-American Women, August 24 and 25, 1976* (Washington, DC: GPO, October 1980), 225; Yung, 89; Osako, 226-27.

94. Roger Daniels, *Asian America: Chinese and Japanese in the United States Since 1950* (Seattle: University of Washington Press, 1988), 155.

95. Alan Takeo Moriyama, "The Causes of Emigration: The Background of Japanese Emigration to Hawaii, 1885-1894," in Cheng and Bonacich, 248-76.

96. Alan Takeo Moriyama, *Imingaisha: Japanese Emigration Companies and Hawaii 1894-1908* (Honolulu: University of Hawaii Press, 1985), 11-12.

97. Alan Takeo Moriyama, "The 1909 and 1920 Strikes of Japanese Sugar Plantation Workers in Hawaii," in Gee, 171-72, 177.

98. Bonacich, "Some Basic Facts," 62; Evelyn Nakano Glenn, "The Dialectics of Wage Work: Japanese American Women and Domestic Service, 1905-1940," in Cheng and Bonacich, 470-71; Yuji Ichioka, *The Issei: The World of the First Generation Japanese Immigrants, 1885-1924* (New York: Free Press, 1988), 72; see Appendix A.

99. Quoted in Ichioka, *Issei,* 83.

100. Ibid., 73-74.

101. Moriyama, "Causes of Emigration," 268-70.

102. Glenn, "Dialectics of Wage Work"; Nee and Wong, 292; Yukiko Hanawa, *The Several Worlds of Issei Women* (Ph.D. diss., Department of Asian Studies, California State University, 1982), 13.

103. See Appendix A.

104. All the material on prostitutes in the following paragraphs comes from Yuji Ichioka, "Ameyuki-san: Japanese Prostitutes in Nineteenth-Century America," *Amerasia* 4 (1977): 1-21.

105. Ichioka, *Issei,* 37.

106. Quoted in ibid., 39.

107. Ibid., 86.

108. Hanawa, 51; Glenn, "Dialectics of Wage Work"; Moriyama, "Causes of Emigration," 268-70.

109. Yuji Ichioka, "Amerika Nadeshiko: Japanese Immigrant Women in the United States," *Pacific Historical Review* 48 (1980): 343.

110. Ibid., 345.

111. Quoted in Emma Gee, "Issei Women," in Gee, 11.

112. Glenn, *Issei, Nisei,* 47.

113. Ibid., 47-48.

114. Gail M. Nomura, "Tsugiki, a Grafting: A History of a Japanese Pioneer Woman in Washington State," *Women's Studies* 14 (1987): 15-37.

115. See Appendix A.

116. Quoted in Glenn, *Issei, Nisei,* 146.

117. Ibid., 149.

118. Nee and Wong, 294.

119. Ichioka, *Issei,* 150-52; Yuji Ichioka, "Japanese Immigrant Response to the 1920 California Alien Land Law," in *Agricultural History* 58 (April 1984): 169; Daniels, *Asian America,* 144.

120. Ichioka, "Japanese Immigrant Response," 159-62.

121. Quoted in ibid., 169.

122. Ibid., 170-76.

123. Jerrold Haruo Takahashi, *Changing Responses to Racial Subordination: An Exploratory Study of Japanese American Political Styles* (Ph.D. diss., Graduate Division of the University of California, 1980), 64.

124. Ichioka, "Japanese Immigrant Response," 176.

125. Daniels, *Asian America,* 165.

126. Ichioka, *Issei,* 173, 175.

127. Glenn, *Issei, Nisei,* 39.

128. Roger Daniels, "Japanese America, 1930-1941: An Ethnic Community in the Great Depression," *Journal of the West* 24 (October 1985): 35, 36, 39.

129. Takahashi, 66; Daniels, "Japanese America," 39.

130. Glenn, *Issei, Nisei,* 33; Daniels, *Asian America,* 173.

131. Glenn, *Issei, Nisei,* 33; Daniels, *Asian America,* 174, 178.

132. Glenn, "Dialectics of Wage Work," 478-79.

133. Daniels, *Asian America,* 47.

134. Valerie Matsumoto, "Japanese American Women During World War II," *Frontiers* 8 (1984): 7.

135. John Tateishi, *And Justice for All: An Oral History of the Japanese American Detention Camps* (New York: Random House, 1984), xvii.

136. Matsumoto, 9.

137. Daniels, *Asian America,* 280.

138. Nomura, 25.

139. Ibid.

140. Julie's father, a teenager in Michigan at the time, was cared for by two of these internees, Kyoshi and Horuko Katamoto; Matsumoto, passim.

141. Quoted in Matsumoto, 10.

142. Daniels, *Asian America,* 252-54, 285; *The Color of Honor: The Japanese American Soldier in WWII,* produced and directed by Loni Ding, available from Crosscurrent Media, c/o NAATA, 346 9th St., San Francisco, CA 94103.

143. *The Color of Honor;* Daniels, *Asian America,* 292.

144. Daniels, 291.

145. Ibid., 294.

146. Takahashi, 222, 227.

147. Glenn, *Issei, Nisei,* 36; Akemi Kikumura and Harry H.L. Kitano, "Interracial Marriage: A Picture of the Japanese Americans," in Tsuchida, 201.

148. Canta Pian, "Immigration of Asian Women and the Status of Recent Asian Women Immigrants," in U.S. Department of Education, Office of Educational Research and Improvement, National Institute of Education, *Conference on the Educational and Occupational Needs of Asian-Pacific-American Women, August 24 and 25, 1976* (Washington, DC: GPO, October 1980), 185; Daniels, *Asian America,* 283-84; U.S. Bureau of the Census, *Statistical Abstract of the United States: 1988* (Washington, DC: GPO, 1988), 10; figure for overall Japanese population in the United States is from Hsia, 10; Glenn, *Issei, Nisei,* 36.

149. Quoted in Daniels, *Asian America,* 331.

150. During the debate on the bill in Congress, California Congressman Daniel Lundgren raised the specter of other reparations as an argument against payments: "Should the Chinese be paid back for their underpaid role in helping the railroads open the American West? Should people of German ancestry be compensated for being denied rights in World War I? Should we return to Black Americans the plantations on which their families worked for over 200 years?" Quoted in Daniels, *Asian America,* 340-41.

151. 1980 U.S. Census, see Appendix A.

152. Mariano, 85; Nee and Wong; Deborah Woo, "The Socioeconomic Status of Asian American Women in the Labor Force," *Sociological Perspectives* 26 (July 1985): 311.

153. Used to describe those from the Philippines, Filipina refers, as per the Spanish usage, to females; Filipino to males. Others write and pronounce these Pilipina and Pilipino.

154. H. Brett Melendy, *Asians in America: Filipinos, Koreans, and East Indians* (Boston: Twayne Publishers, 1977), 20-21, 29.

155. Tricia Knoll, *Becoming Americans: Asian Sojourners, Immigrants, and Refugees in the Western United States* (Portland, Oregon: Coast to Coast Books, 1982), 87; Miriam Sharma, "The Philippines: A Case of Migration to Hawaii, 1906-1946," in Cheng and Bonacich, 341-42; Delia D. Aguilar, "Women in the Political Economy of the Philippines," *Alternatives* XII (1987): 512.

156. Aguilar, 512; Renato Constantino, *A History of the Philippines: From the Spanish Colonization to the Second World War* (New York: Monthly Review Press, 1975), Chs. XI-XIII; see also, Violet Rabaya, "Filipino Immigration: the Creation of a New Social Problem," in Tachiki,

Wong, and Odo with Buck Wong, 188-89.

157. Sharma, 341-45; Melendy, *Asians in America*, 24. For information on the school system, see Knoll, 102; Antonio J.A. Pido, *The Pilipinos in America: Macro/Micro Dimensions of Immigration and Integration* (New York: Center for Migration Studies, 1986), 72.

158. Sharma, 607.

159. Melendy, *Asians in American*, 37; Sharma, 586, 582.

160. Sharma, 583.

161. Sharma, 583-85, 601; Vallangça, 37. Vallangça says that marriages with other Asians were common, but Sharma disagrees.

162. Sharma, 589; interviewed in Vallangça, 99-101.

163. H. Brett Melendy, "Filipinos in the United States," in Gee, 427, quoting a farmer in 1927.

164. Sharma, 587.

165. Ibid., 595-602.

166. Ibid., 585, 591.

167. Ibid., 585, 591-93; 1930 Census, see Appendix A.

168. Vallangça, 66, 96-97; Roberto Vallangça writes of escaping many such attacks, "because I looked more Chinese or Japanese than Filipino."

169. Melendy, *Asians in America*, 62; Manuel Buaken, 1940, quoted in Knoll, 102. See also Vallangça, 72-73.

170. 1980 Census, see Appendix A; Vallangça, 99-101.

171. Knoll, 90.

172. Rabaya, 189-90; Melendy, *Asians in America*, 32-33; Vallangça, 8, 27-29, 62-63, 96-97, 113. Roberto Vallangça worked from 1927 to 1945 as a houseboy, in agriculture, and in the navy, before finally getting his degree in chiropractic school at the age of 38.

173. Melendy, *Asians in America*, 43.

174. 1930 Census, see Appendix A.

175. Vallangça, 22-25, 115.

176. Pido, 67-68.

177. Ibid., 24, 68.

178. Rabaya, 194.

179. Frank Cordova, *Filipinos: Forgotten Asian Americans: 1763-circa 1963* (Dubuque, IA: Kendall/Hunt Pub. Co., 1983).

180. 1980 Census, see Appendix A; Melendy, *Asians in America*, 63.

181. Vallangça, 12-14, 109-110; 1930 Census, see Appendix A.

182. 1930 Census, see Appendix A.

183. Donald F. Duff and Ransom J. Arthur, "Between Two Worlds: Filipinos in the U.S. Navy," in *Asian Americans: Psychological Perspectives*, ed. Stanley Sue and Nathaniel Wagner (Palo Alto: Science & Behavior Books, 1973), 203; Rabaya, 190.

184. Rabaya, 191; Sharma, 583.

185. In contrast, Japanese and Chinese women expected to lose their parental family ties upon marriage, when they joined their husbands' parents' households; for them, migration with or to join their husbands meant being freed from service to their mothers-in-law.

186. Nobuya Tsuchida and Gail Thoen, "Interview with Belén Andrada," in Tsuchida, 151; Vallangça, 37-38; Ronald Takaki, *Strangers from a Different Shore: A History of Asian Americans* (Boston: Little, Brown and Company, 1989), 330; Pido, 69.

187. 1920 Census, see Appendix A; see Robert N. Anderson with Richard Coller and Rebecca F. Pestano, *Filipinos in Rural Hawaii* (Honolulu: University of Hawaii Press, 1984).

188. Sharma, 585; Pido, 70; Vallangça, 25-26; Melendy, *Asians in America*, Ch. IV. "They were drawn into this lifestyle out of necessity and against their wills. Eventually they, like their countrymen laboring on the Hawaiian plantations, grew accustomed to the freedoms of their uncertain lifestyle, a life without roots or responsibilities, a life that severed their ties to their families in the Philippines. This was the lifestyle of the majority of Pinoy pioneers, a life molded not by laziness or any unwillingness to better themselves, but by the social and economic conditions in America."

189. Quoted in Melendy, *Asians in America*, 67.

190. Sharma, 602-4; Vallangça, 12-14.

191. Anacleto Gorospe, interview in Vallangça, 83; Melendy, *Asians in America,* 50-51.

192. Bill Ong Hing, "An Overview of Federal Immigration Policies and Their Effects on Asian and Pacific Americans," in U.S. Commission on Civil Rights, *Civil Rights Issues of Asian and Pacific Americans: Myths and Realities* (Washington, DC: GPO, 1980), 295-96; Elaine Kim, *With Silk Wings* (San Francisco: Asian Women United, 1983), 127.

193. Quoted in Kim, 128; Pido, 80.

194. Takaki, 432; 1980 Census, see Appendix A.

195. Robert N. Anderson et al., 143-45.

196. Maria Fe Caces, "Immigrant Recruitment into the Labor Force: Social Networks Among Filipinos in Hawaii," *Amerasia* 13 (1986-87): 28-31.

197. Takaki, 432-34.

198. Belén Andrada, "Occupational Profiles of Filipino Women in Minnesota," in Tsuchida, 140-41; Pido, 76-77; Knoll, 108.

199. 1980 Census, see Appendix A, U.S. Summary, 157, and authors' calculations.

200. Amado Cabezas, Larry Hajime Shinagawa, and Gary Kawaguchi, "New Inquiries into the Socioeconomic Status of Pilipino Americans in California," *Amerasia* 13 (1986-87): 12; Dr. Anthony Kahng, "Employment Discrimination and Strategies: From Benevolence to Legal Struggle," in U.S. Commission on Civil Rights, *Civil Rights Issues,* 539; Dorothy L. Cordova, "Immigration Issues-Policy, Impact, and Strategies," in U.S. Commission on Civil Rights, *Civil Rights Issues,* 262. Cordova is director of the Demonstration Project for Asian Americans in Seattle, WA.

201. Takaki, 435-36.

202. By Filipina/o American, we mean Filipinas/os residing in the United States; 1980 Census, see Appendix A.

203. Caces, 26-27; Gordon F. De Jong, Brenda Davis Root, and Ricardo G. Abad, "Family Reunification and Philippine Migration to the United States: The Immigrants' Perspective," *International Migration Review* 20 (Fall 1986): 608-9; Rebecca Villones, "Women in the Silicon Valley," in *Making Waves,* 172-6; Aurora Fernandez, "Pilipino Immigrants," *East Wind* (Fall/Winter 1982): 35.

204. Tania Azores, "Educational Attainment and Upward Mobility: Prospects for Filipino Americans," *Amerasia* 13 (1986-87): 40-42.

205. William Peterson, "Success Story, Japanese American Style," *New York Times Magazine,* 6 January 1966, as cited in Daniels, *Asian America,* 317-20.

206. Asian enrollment figures for Berkeley from *Newsweek on Campus,* April 1984, 4; Harvard from *Newsweek,* 6 December 1982, 39; 1980 Census, see Appendix A.

207. 1980 Census, see Appendix A. The service worker category excludes protective service occupations.

208. *Statistical Abstract 1988,* 10; 1980 Census, see Appendix A; "Presentation of Joseph Chung, Professor of Economics, Illinois Institute of Technology, Chicago, Illinois," and "Presentation of Amado Cabezas, Director, Human Services Research, ASIAN, Inc., San Francisco, California," in U.S. Commission on Civil Rights, *Civil Rights Issues;* 1972 median family income from *Statistical Abstract 1988,* 427.

209. Deborah Woo, 308-11, 318; 1980 Census, see Appendix A.

210. "Presentation of Setsuko Matsunaga Nishi, Professor, Department of Sociology, Brooklyn College, and the Graduate Center, City University of New York," in U.S. Commission on Civil Rights, *Civil Rights Issues,* 399.

211. Cabezas, Shinagawa, and Kawaguchi, 390.

212. Ho and Chin, 7-8; Irvin Molotsky, "Harvard and U.C.L.A. Face Inquiries on Quotas," *New York Times,* 20 November 1988. See also Julie Johnson, "Asian-Americans Press Fight For Wider Top-College Door," *New York Times,* 9 September 1989. The article suggests that under pressure from Asian Americans, acceptance rates are rising, but that Asian American applicants may be more qualified than their white counterparts.

213. Jan Wong, "Asia Bashing: Bias Against Orientals Increases with Rivalry of Nations' Economies," *The Wall Street Journal,* 28 November 1986; Daniels, *Asian America,* 341-43. This

incident was dramatized in a film by Christine Choy and Renee Tajima, *Who Killed Vincent Chin?* The film was nominated for an Oscar. David A. Kaplan, "Film About a Fatal Beating Examines a Community," *The New York Times,* 16 July 1989, H. 27.

214. Knoll, 196.

215. Jan Wong, 1, 12.

216. Quoted in Daniels, *Asian America,* 344.

217. Knoll, 130-31, on Korean American children; Bok-Lim C. Kim, "Military Wives/Emerging Roles of Asian Immigrant Women," in U.S. Commission on Civil Rights, *Civil Rights Issues,* 114, 149-52.

218. Lisa Belkin, "The Mail-Order Marriage Business," *New York Times Magazine,* 11 May 1986, 51. Other information in this section, if not otherwise noted, is from this article.

219. Ibid., 52.

220. Siriporn Skrobanek, "In Pursuit of an Illusion: Thai Women in Europe," *Southeast Asia Chronicle, Special Issue: Beyond Stereotypes: Asian Women in Development* 96 (January 1985): 10.

221. Connie S. Chan, "Asian-American Women: Psychological Responses to Sexual Exploitation and Cultural Stereotypes," *Women and Therapy* 6 (Winter 1987): 37.

222. Germaine Wong, "Impediments to Asian-Pacific-American Women Organizing," in U.S. Department of Education, Office of Educational Research and Improvement, National Institute of Education, *Conference on the Educational and Occupational Needs of Asian-Pacific-American Women, August 24 and 25, 1976* (Washington, DC: GPO, October 1980), 93.

223. Diane Wong, "Legal Issues," 142, 146.

224. Connie S. Chan, "Asian Women: We're Not for Sale," *Progress: The Newsletter of Women for Economic Justice* (Boston, MA) 6 (Fall 1985).

225. Esther Ngan-Ling Chow, "The Development of Feminist Consciousness Among Asian American Women," *Gender & Society* 1 (September 1987): 284-99; Merle Woo, 142-45. See also Esther Ngan-Ling Chow, "The Feminist Movement: Where Are All the Asian American Women?" in *Making Waves,* 362-77; Karin Aguilar-San Juan, "Challenging Asian Stereotypes," *Gay Community News,* 3-9 July 1988, 15.

226. Recently, attention was drawn to such abuse when two Asian women, one in Hawaii and one in Boston, were murdered by their husbands; correspondence with Connie Chan, August 1989.

227. Nilda Rimonte, "Domestic Violence among Pacific Asians," in *Making Waves,* 327-37; David Rubien, "For Asians in U.S., Hidden Strife," *New York Times,* 11 January 1989, C10.

228. Rubien, C10; Rimonte, 328-30.

229. Merle Woo, 142.

Chapter 8

1. Title of poem by Julia de Burgos, Puerto Rican poet; translates literally to, "I was my own path." For text of poem, see Julia de Burgos, *Antología Poética* (San Juan, Puerto Rico: Editorial Coquí, 1979), 37-38.

2. Ibid., 27.

3. By the United States, we refer to the states of the United States and its national government; although Puerto Rico is technically part of the United States it has colonial status and is not represented in the United States government as are the 50 states. We will therefore describe Puerto Rican migration as from the island of Puerto Rico to the United States. We do not use the common expression, "the mainland," for that term incorrectly views the continental United States as a central or main location for Puerto Ricans, a political and economic viewpoint against which many progressive Puerto Ricans are fighting.

4. Manuel Maldonado-Denis, *Puerto Rico: A Socio-Historic Interpretation,* trans. Elena Vialo (New York: Vintage Books, 1972), 14; Edna Acosta-Belén, "Puerto Rican Women in Culture, History, and Society," in *The Puerto Rican Woman: Perspectives on Culture, History, and Society,* ed. Edna Acosta-Belén (New York: Praeger Press, 2nd ed., 1986), 2.

5. Maldonado-Denis, 14-15.

6. Maldonado-Denis, 17-19; Julio Morales, *Puerto Rican Poverty and Migration: We Just Had to Try Elsewhere* (New York: Praeger Press, 1986), 23, 68-71.

7. Acosta-Belén, 2; Professor Lorie Roses, interview by Julie Matthaei, Wellesley, MA, 17 August 1989; in 1673, the city of San Juan had, for example, 820 whites, 667 slaves, and 304 free mulattos. See Maldonado-Denis, 18.

8. Rosa Santiago-Marazzi, "La Imigración de Mujeres Españolas a Puerto Rico en el Período Colonial Español," *Homines* 10 (1986-1987): 155-57.

9. Perfil Demográfico, Universidad de Puerto Rico, Programa Graduado de Demografía, *Perfil Demográfico de la Población de Puerto Rico, 1980,* (Universidad de Puerto Rico: 1985) Table 1, 1; Santiago-Marazzi, 160, estimates the actual population in 1801 at 200,000; Jose Luis González, *El País de Cuatro Pisos* (Rio Piedras, Puerto Rico: Ediciones Huracán, 1980); Morales, 69; Santiago-Marazzi, 161-64, points out that it is not known how many of these soldiers became permanent residents of Puerto Rico; Maldonado-Denis, 45.

10. Maldonado-Denis, 75;

11. Marcia Rivera, "The Development of Capitalism in Puerto Rico and the Incorporation of Women into the Labor Force," in Acosta-Belén, 31-32; Alfredo Lopez, *Doña Licha's Island* (Boston: South End Press, 1987), 17-18; Maldonado-Denis, 43-45, note 27; History Task Force, City University of New York, Centro de Estudios Puertorriqueños, *Labor Migration under Capitalism: The Puerto Rican Experience* (New York: Monthly Review Press, 1979), 72.

12. Morales, 23; History Task Force, 82; Rivera, 31-33.

13. Acosta-Belén, 3.

14. Ibid.

15. Calculated from Isabel Picó, "The History of Women's Struggle for Equality in Puerto Rico," in Acosta-Belén, 47 and Perfil Demográfico, Table 1, 1; Perfil Demográfico, Table 18, 30; Acosta-Belén, 5-7; Picó, 47.

16. Acosta-Belén, 6; Puerto Rico gained a degree of self-government, including "universal suffrage, representation in the high court, power to ratify commercial treaties and to set tariffs, provisions guaranteeing the consulting of the colony in all those matters in which it was affected by legislation, and other rights." Maldonado-Denis, 48.

17. Raymond Carr, *Puerto Rico: A Colonial Experiment* (New York: Vintage Books, 1984), 25; quoted in Morales, 28-29.

18. Morales, 29; Barry Levine and Ralph Clem, "Imperial Development: The Cases of American Puerto Rico and Soviet Georgia," in *Comparative Studies in Sociology,* vol. 1, ed. Richard Tomasson (Greenwich, CT: JAI Press, 1978), 324.

19. Maldonado-Denis, 72.

20. Ibid., 74.

21. Levine and Clem, 331; Virginia Sanchez Korrol, *From Colonia to Community: The History of Puerto Ricans in New York City, 1917-1984* (Westport, CT: Greenwood Press, 1983), 25.

22. Maldonado-Denis, 73, 80; calculated from U.S. Census data, as presented in Picó, 48-49 and History Task Force, 107.

23. It is unclear whether men's participation in paid work rose or fell during this period. Men's labor force participation rate rose rapidly from 60 percent to 81 percent; Picó, 48. However, according to Census data on gainful employment, the percent of men gainfully employed fell from 83 percent of those over 10 in 1899 to 69.5 percent in 1930 (as reported in History Task Force, 107). Gainful employment should be less than the labor force participation rate because of unemployment; if 83 percent were gainfully employed in 1899, at least this percentage should have been in the labor force.

24. Calculated from U.S. Census data, as presented in Picó, 48-49 and History Task Force, 107.

25. Picó, 48; U.S. women did not experience a similar growth in labor force participation during this period; their rates were 20.0 in 1900, and 23.6 in 1930. Julie A. Matthaei, *An Economic History of Women in America: Women's Work, the Sexual Division of Labor, and the Development of Capitalism* (New York: Schocken Books, 1982), 142.

26. Calculated from U.S. Census data, as described in Appendix A; History Task Force, 107.

27. Rivera, 34; Picó, 48; Blanca Silvestrini-Pacheco, "Women as Workers: The Experience of Puerto Rican Women in the 1930s," in *Women Cross-Culturally: Change and Challenge,* ed.

Ruby Rohrlich-Leavitt (The Hague: Mouton, 1975), 66; Carol Manning's U.S. Department of Labor report, quoted in Rivera, 35.

28. Rivera, 37.

29. Picó, 52; Silvestrini-Pacheco, 61; Norma Valle Ferrer, "Feminism and Its Influence on Women's Organizations in Puerto Rico," in Acosta-Belén, 77-78.

30. Picó, 54; Silvestrini-Pacheco, 63; Acosta-Belén, 9.

31. Ferrer, 78; quoted in Acosta-Belén, 9; Picó, 53.

32. Maldonado-Denis, 80; Picó, 49-50, 58, note 16; Luz del Alba Acevedo, "Política de Industrialización y Cambios en el Empleo Femenino en Puerto Rico: 1947-1982," *Homines* 10 (1986-1987): 59; the number of teachers does not include university teachers.

33. Acosta-Belén, 7-8.

34. Picó, 54-55; Acosta-Belén, 8.

35. In 1921, the number of aliens allowed from a foreign country was restricted to 3 percent of the number born in that country who were residing in the United States in 1910; the 1924 act lowered the percentage to 2 percent and set back the date to 1890. In 1929 the total annual quota on immigration was cut to 150,000; Korrol, 31. The cut-off of Asian immigration probably had less effect, as it was a West Coast phenomenon.

36. Korrol, 29-31; migrants as percentage of labor force calculated from Korrol's numbers and History Task Force, 107.

37. Korrol, 28; History Task Force, 192; quoted in Korrol, 43.

38. Virginia Sanchez Korrol, "Survival of Puerto Rican Women in New York Before World War II," in *The Puerto Rican Struggle: Essays on Survival in the U.S.*, ed. Clara E. Rodriguez, Virginia S. Korrol, and Jose O. Alers (Maplewood, NJ: Waterfront Press, 1980), 55; Korrol, *From Colonia to Community*, 39.

39. Clara E. Rodriguez, "Puerto Ricans: Between Black and White," in Rodriguez, Korrol, and Alers, 20-23.

40. Korrol, "Survival of Puerto Rican Women," 55; Virginia Sanchez Korrol, "Between Two Worlds: Educated Puerto Rican Migrant Women," *Caribbean Review* 12 (Summer 1983): 27.

41. Korrol, "Survival of Puerto Rican Women," 51.

42. Ibid., 49-55.

43. Korrol, "Between Two Worlds," 28.

44. Korrol, *From Colonia to Community*, 31-32.

45. Rivera, 40; History Task Force, 112, 115; Silvestrini-Pacheco, 64; Korrol, *From Colonia to Community*, 27; Maldonado-Denis, 81.

46. Silvestrini-Pacheco, 67-68.

47. Ibid., 67-70.

48. Quoted in Morales, 30.

49. Morales, 30; Silvestrini-Pacheco, 69; Maldonado-Denis, 81-82.

50. Quoted in Morales, 141.

51. Quoted in Helen I. Safa, "Class Consciousness Among Working Class Women in Latin America: Puerto Rico," in *Sex and Class in Latin America: Women's Perspectives on Politics, Economics, and the Family in the Third World*, ed. June Nash and Helen I. Safa (New York: J.F. Bergin Publishers, 1980), 73.

52. Morales, 33; Richard Weisskopf, *Factories and Food Stamps: The Puerto Rican Model of Development* (Baltimore: Johns Hopkins University Press, 1985), 119.

53. Acosta-Belén, 10; History Task Force, 117.

54. Weisskopf, 120-21.

55. Weisskopf, 120-121; Morales, 33; Acevedo, 44; Acosta-Belén, 41; Silvestrini-Pacheco, 72; Rivera, 40-42; Safa, 82. By 1970, only 13 percent of the Puerto Rican labor force was unionized. Rivera, 43.

56. Acosta-Belén, 11-12.

57. Margarita Ostolaza, "Política Sexual y Socialización Política de la Mujer Puertorriqueña en la Conso lación del Bloque Histórico Colonial de Puerto Rico," Ph. D. diss., Facultad de Ciencias Políticas y Sociales, Universidad Nacional Autonoma de Mexico, 1987, 137. Published as a book by Ediciones Huracán, Rio Piedras, Puerto Rico, 1989; Morales, 33; Helen I. Safa, "Female

Employment and the Social Reproduction of the Puerto Rican Working Class," in Acosta-Belén, 91; History Task Force, 186; Levine and Clem, 331; Perfil Demográfico, 30, 43. By 1970, the median years of schooling completed stood at 6.9.

58. First percentage calculated from U.S. Census data, as presented in Picó, 48-49 and History Task Force, 107, second taken from Safa, "Class Consciousness," 72; Acevedo, 57.

59. Acevedo, 47-48 and History Task Force, 128, 190; Morales, 77; Picó, 48; calculated from U.S. Census data, as presented in Picó, 48-49 and History Task Force, 107, and from Acevedo, 48.

60. Morales, 34-35; quoted in Morales, 34-35.

61. Ostolaza, 165, 182-83; Barbara Seaman and Gideon Seaman, *Women and the Crisis in Sex Hormones* (New York: Bantam Books, 1978), 82-83.

62. Morales, 34.

63. Korrol, *From Colonia to Community,* 36-38; Morales, 135.

64. History Task Force, 243-44, and Morales, 136-37.

65. Morales, 86; quoted in Morales, 91-92.

66. History Task Force, 242.

67. Clara E. Rodriguez, "Economic Survival in New York City," in Rodriguez, Korrol, and Alers, 40-41; Ostolaza, 183; Rosemary S. Cooney and Alice Colón, "Work and Family: The Recent Struggle of Puerto Rican Females," in Rodriguez, Korrol, and Alers, 60.

68. Cooney and Colón, 60, 63.

69. Pablo "Yoruba" Guzmán, "Puerto Rican Barrio Politics in the United States," in Rodriguez, Korrol, and Alers, 121-28.

70. Departamento del Trabajo y Recursos Humanos de Puerto Rico, *Resúmen del Estado de Empleo de la Población Civil No Institucional de 16 años o más,* (Negociado de Estadísticas del Trabajo, División de Estadísticas de Grupo Trabajador), Table 1; History Task Force, 191; Carlos E. Santiago and Erik Thorbecke, "A Multisectoral Framework for the Analysis of Labor Mobility and Development in LDCs: An Application to Postwar Puerto Rico," *Economic Development and Cultural Change* 37 (October 1988): 137-38; a higher cost of living in Puerto Rico also contributed to the wage increases. Rivera, 42; Santiago and Thorbecke, 135; Morales, 135. Net immigration was 23,648 and 36,201, respectively, in these years.

71. Departamento del Trabajo y Recursos Humanos, de Puerto Rico, *Empleo y Desempleo en Puerto Rico, Promedio Años Fiscales 1984-1985 y 1983-1984; Informe Especial Numero E-47,* (Negociado de Estadísticas del Trabajo, División de Estadísticas de Grupo Trabajador), Tables 17 and 18, 16-17; Junta de Planificación de Puerto Rico, Area de Planificación Económica y Social, *Boletín Social 1984* (Santurce: Junta de Planificación, October 1984), 135.

72. When Helen Safa surveyed rural garment workers, 90 percent said it was easier for women to find jobs than men. As a result of the decline in agriculture since 1950, 60 percent had husbands or siblings who had migrated to the United States. Safa, "Female Employment," 98-99; for source, see Table 8-3.

73. Frank Bonilla, "A Wealth of Poor: Puerto Ricans in the New Economic Order," *Daedalus* 110 (Spring 1981): 149-50.

74. Janice Petrovich and Sandra Laureano, "Towards an Analysis of Puerto Rican Women and the Informal Economy," *Homines* 10 (1986-1987): 70-80.

75. Weisskopf, 72; Perfil Demográfico, 35.

76. Bonilla, 146; Weisskopf, Ch. 17, and 58.

77. Junta de Planificación de Puerto Rico, *Características de la Población Migrante de Puerto Rico* (San Juan: La Junta, October 1984), 13; Vilma Ortiz, "Changes in the Characteristics of Puerto Rican Migrants from 1955-1980," *International Migration Review* 20 (Fall 1986): 617; Christine E. Bose, "Puerto Rican Women in the United States: An Overview," in Acosta-Belén, 148-49.

78. See Appendix A.

79. Luis Fuentes, "The Struggle for Local Political Control," in Rodriguez, Korrol, and Alers, 113-34.

80. Maria González, Victoria L. Barrera, Peter Guarnaccia, and Stephen L. Schensul, "'La Operación': An Analysis of Sterilization in a Puerto Rican Community in Connecticut," in *Work, Family, and Health: Latina Women in Transition,* ed. Ruth E. Zambrana (Bronx, NY: Hispanic

Research Center, Fordham University, 1982), 47; U.S. Bureau of the Census, *1980 Census, U.S. Summary,* 166; and Zambrana and Hurst, 271; 1980 Census; see Appendix A; Jose Hernández, "Social Science and the Puerto Rican Community," in Rodriguez, Korrol, and Alers, 14. His source is U.S. Civil Rights Commission, *Social Indicators of Equality for Minorities and Women,* 1978.

81. Junta de Planificación de Puerto Rico, *Indicadores Socio-Económicos de la Mujer* (San Juan: La Junta, March 1987), Table 14, A-5; U.S. Bureau of the Census, *1980 Census, U.S. Summary;* Cooney and Colón, 65-70 and Bose, 161.

82. Cooney and Colón, 68; 1980 Census, see Appendix A.

83. Cooney and Colón, 70.

84. 1970 and 1980 Censuses, see Appendix A; 1985 number comes from Departamento del Trabajo, "Empleo y Desempleo en Puerto Rico," 1; Safa, "Female Employment," 91; Alice Colón-Warren, "Puerto Rican Women in Puerto Rico and the U.S.: Employment and Underemployment," Paper presented at the Employment Policy Seminar: Puerto Ricans and Jobs, Massachusetts Institute of Technology, 1988.

85. Junta de Planificación, *Indicadores Socio-Económicos de la Mujer,* Tables 7 and 11, A-3 and A-4, Table 13, A-5.

86. Rivera, 43; Ostolaza, 159.

87. Acosta-Belén, 23, and Ferrer, 82-86; Margarita Ostolaza Bey, telephone interview by Julie Matthaei, San Juan, Puerto Rico, 22 August 1989; see, for example, Yamila Azize Vargas, ed., *La Mujer en Puerto Rico: Ensayos de Investigación* (Rio Piedras, Puerto Rico: Ediciones Huracán, 1987), Ostolaza, and Acosta-Belén.

88. *Mujeres en Marcha: Vocero Oficial, Organización Puertorriqueña de la Mujer Trabajadora,* Year 3, No. 2, December 1985; Meg Wilcox, "Puerto Rican Women Fight Health Hazards," *Sojourner: The Women's Forum,* August 1988, 19; Julia Rosa Nevarez de Jesus, "La Mujer Trabajadora Puertorriqueña y Su Lucha Diaria: 3 Entrevistas," *Pensamiento Crítico* 8 (May/June 1985): 15.

89. 1980 Census, see Appendix A.

90. Ruth E. Zambrana and Marsha Hurst, "The Interactive Effect of Health Status on Work Patterns Among Urban Puerto Rican Women," *International Journal of Health Services* 14 (1984): 271.

91. Cooney et al. did not find "traditional sex roles" to be an important factor in low labor force participation rates. The important influences were fewer and worse job opportunities and low education (as it affects job opportunities). Rosemary S. Cooney, Lloyd H. Rogler, Rosemarie Hurrell, and Vilma Ortiz, "Decision Making in Intergenerational Puerto Rican Families," *Journal of Marriage and the Family* 44 (August 1982): 399.

92. 1980 Census, *U.S. Summary,* Table 166;

93. Tirsa Quiñones of MULANEH, interview by Julie Matthaei, August 1989; González et al., "La Operación," 50; see Helen Rodríguez-Trias, "Women, Health and Law: Guidelines on Sterilization Under Attack," *Women and Health* 1 (December 1976): 30-31 and Committee for Abortion Rights and Against Sterilization Abuse, *Women Under Attack: Abortion, Sterilization Abuse, and Reproductive Freedom* (New York: CARASA, 1979).

Chapter 9

1. Calculated from Table 4-J in Michael Reich, "The Evolution of the United States Labor Force," in Richard Edwards, Michael Reich, and Thomas Weisskopf, eds., *The Capitalist System: A Radical Analysis of American Society* (Englewood Cliffs, NJ: Prentice-Hall, 1972), 175, and U.S. Bureau of the Census, *Statistical Abstract of the United States: 1988* (Washington, DC: GPO, 1988, 368.)

2. In 1910, less than 20 percent of households had electricity. Julie Matthaei, *An Economic History of Women in America: Women's Work, the Sexual Division of Labor, and the Development of Capitalism* (New York: Schocken Books, 1982), Table 10.2.

3. Jeanne Boydston, "To Earn Her Daily Bread: Housework and Antebellum Working-Class Subsistence," *Radical History Review* 35 (April 1986): 17-19.

4. Matthaei, Ch. 7.

5. For example, in 1928, 61 percent of school districts would not hire married women, and 52 percent fired single women teachers upon marriage. See Claudia Goldin, *Understanding the Gender Gap: An Economic History of American Women* (New York: Oxford University Press, 1990), 160-71. We do not know how this practice varied across the racially-segregated school system, but suspect that bars would have been more common in districts employing white women. Also, a much greater share of white women than women of color worked in clerical jobs during this period, so clerical bars would have had more effect on whites.

6. Ibid., Ch. 9.

7. At the same time, however, the hours women spent in homemaking did not fall, partly because standards for homemaking, such as cleanliness, elegance of interior decorating, and variety of meals, all increased. See Ruth Schwartz Cowan, *More Work for Mother: The Ironies of Household Technology from the Open Hearth to the Microwave* (New York: Basic Books, 1983).

8. Ibid., Ch. 10.

9. Ibid., Ch. 11.

10. Ibid., Table 10-4, shows labor force participation rates of married women by husband's income quartile for 1940, 1960 and 1977; rates rise significantly in each category, and the differences between quartiles decrease.

11. See Appendix A. Asian data are estimated from the "other non-white" category in 1920, most of which was Asian.

12. One possible explanation for the declining labor force participation of non-married African American women lies in the shrinking job opportunities available to younger African Americans of both sexes. In addition, a greater share of non-married African American women are mothers and are thus less able to enter the labor force than non-married women of other racial-ethnic groups, who are less likely to have children.

13. Matthaei, 142; U.S. Bureau of the Census, *Statistical Abstract of the United States: 1990* (Washington, DC: GPO, 1990), 386.

14. Matthaei, Ch. 13.

15. Francine D. Blau and Marianne A. Ferber, *The Economics of Women, Men, and Work* (Englewood Cliffs, NJ: Prentice-Hall, 1986), 129; *Statistical Abstract 1988*, 59.

16. For more on family policy demands, see Julie Matthaei, "Political Economy and Family Policy," in Robert Cherry et al., eds., *The Imperiled Economy, Book II: Through the Safety Net* (New York: Union for Radical Political Economics, 1988), 141-50. In this area, the United States lags far behind Western European countries.

17. *Statistical Abstract 1988*, 364. This is expected worklife at birth; for men, the expected worklife was 39 years.

18. Anne Nelson, "Women in Unions," in Sara E. Rix, ed., *The American Woman 1987-1988* (New York: W.W. Norton & Company, 1988), 232-238.

19. See Teresa Amott and Julie Matthaei, "The Promise of Comparable Worth," *Socialist Review* 88 (April-June 1988): 101-17.

20. See Appendix A and Ch. 10.

21. Calculated from Census data, see Appendix A.

22. Blau and Ferber, 171. The 1960-1980 figure is median annual earnings of full-time full-year workers, including self-employed; the increase was for median weekly earnings for full-time workers, not necessarily full-year and excluding self-employment, from 63.4 in 1980 to 66.3 in 1985.

23. The figure for white children living with their mothers also includes Latina/o children. *Statistical Abstract 1990*, 45, 48.

24. Ibid.

25. Ibid., 49.

26. Barbara Ehrenreich argues that over the course of the twentieth century men are increasingly repudiating familial responsibilities, in *The Hearts of Men: American Dreams and the Flight from Commitment* (Garden City, NY: Anchor Press/Doubleday, 1983); *Statistical Abstract 1990*, 52, 87; Blau and Ferber, 123.

27. *Statistical Abstract, 1990*, 53.

28. *Statistical Abstract 1988*, 423-24.

29. Ibid., 459.

Chapter 10

1. See Appendix A.

2. See Robert Cherry et al., eds., *The Imperiled Economy, Book I* (New York: Union of Radical Political Economics, 1988).

3. British economist Jane Humphries has argued that women constitute a latent pool of potential workers (not in the labor force) upon which capital has increasingly drawn as a low-cost substitute for male labor. Jane Humphries, "The 'Emancipation' of Women in the 1970s and 1980s: From the Latent to the Floating," *Capital & Class* 20 (Summer 1983): 11-12. Further research is needed to explore the role of women of color compared to white women in the different parts of the reserve army.

4. In 1910, Blacks made up 30 percent of the population in the South, but 44 percent of the tenant farmers (and only 6 percent of the owners). U.S. Bureau of the Census, *Current Population Reports*, Series P-23, No. 80, *The Social and Economic Status of the Black Population in the United States: An Historical View, 1790-1978* (Washington, DC: GPO, 1979), 13, 81.

5. See Claudia Goldin, *Understanding the Gender Gap: An Economic History of American Women* (New York: Oxford University Press, 1990), 162-66.

6. Jane Humphries, "Women and Recession: The Experience of American Women in Three Post WWII Recessions," in *Women and Recession*, ed. Jill Rubery (New York: Routledge and Kegan Paul, 1978), 17.

7. See Lois Rita Helmbold, "Downward Occupational Mobility During the Great Depression: Urban Black and White Working Class Women," *Labor History* 29 (Spring 1988): 135-72.

8. Julie Matthaei, *An Economic History of Women in America: Women's Work, the Sexual Division of Labor, and the Development of Capitalism* (New York: Schocken Books, 1982), 284; *1870 Census of the United States, Population and Social Statistics*, Table XXIX.

9. Quoted in Judith Rollins, *Between Women: Domestics and Their Employers* (Philadelphia: Temple University Press, 1985), 51.

10. Ibid., 50-53; 1900 Census, see Appendix A.

11. Constant dollar per capita GNP increased from $1,011 in 1900 to $3,555 in 1970, and has risen 30 percent since then. U.S. Bureau of the Census, *Historical Statistics of the United States, Colonial Time to 1970*, vol. 1 (Washington, DC: GPO, 1970); U.S. Bureau of the Census, *Statistical Abstract of the United States: 1987* (Washington, D.C.: GPO, 1987), 410; U.S. Census, 1900 and 1980, see Appendix A.

12. Bell Hooks, Presentation at New Words Bookstore, 5 March 1989, Cambridge, MA, on the occasion of the publication of *Talking Back: Talking Feminist, Talking Black* (Boston: South End Press, 1989).

13. Calculated from 1980 Census, provisional volume, U.S. Summary, Table 278.

14. Relative concentration can rise for all groups. White men's share of protective service jobs only dropped by 13 percentage points, while white men's share of all jobs dropped by 24 percentage points (as a result of women's movement into the labor force); thus, the relative concentration of white men in protective service rose. The 1980 data include police officers and firefighters.

15. 1980 Census, see Appendix A; U.S. Bureau of the Census, *Statistical Abstract of the United States: 1990* (Washington, DC: GPO, 1990), 369, 395; U.S. Department of Labor, *Employment and Earnings* (March 1989), 35.

16. Blacks fell from 14.5 percent of all farm operators in 1910 to only 3.8 percent of the total in 1969, and only 2.1 percent in 1980. *Black Population*, 81, and 1980 Census, see Appendix A.

17. One such group is the Rural Women's Leadership Development Project of Prairiefire Rural Action, which organizes an annual conference, "Harvesting Our Potential," and publishes a journal entitled "Women of the Land." Their address is 550 11th St., Des Moines, Iowa 50309.

18. The 1900 Census data presented here includes only workers within the continental United States, and hence excludes island Puerto Ricans. The numbers for Chinese women are very low, and data for Chicanas are not available.

19. Calculated from 1900 Census, see Appendix A.

20. An excellent set of essays on homework can be found in Eileen Boris and Cynthia R. Daniels, eds., *Homework: Historical and Contemporary Perspectives on Paid Labor at Home* (Urbana: University of Illinois Press, 1989).

21. See Appendix A.

22. Calculated from 1900 Census, see Appendix A.

23. *Statistical Abstract 1988,* 395.

24. U.S. Department of Labor, Women's Bureau, *Women and Office Automation: Issues for the Decade Ahead* (Washington, DC: GPO, 1985), 20-22; *Statistical Abstract, 1988,* 376-77.

25. See Matthaei, 178-82.

26. Susan Reverby, *Ordered to Care: The Dilemma of American Nursing, 1859-1945* (Cambridge: Cambridge University Press, 1987).

27. In medicine, Chinese men, American Indian men, and white women held 61, 44, and 40 percent of their labor market shares, respectively, with Black men and women at 13 and 3 percent. In law, American Indian men held 33 percent, Black men 7 percent, and white women 6 percent of their labor market shares. Calculated from 1900 Census, see Appendix A.

28. Calculated from the 1900 Census, see Appendix A; for a study of white and Black women's struggles to enter medicine, and white men's organizing to keep them out, see Gloria Moldow, *Women Doctors in Gilded-Age Washington: Race, Gender, and Professionalization* (Chicago: University of Illinois Press, 1987).

29. The shares of women with a college education are as follows: Filipina (41.2 percent), Chinese American (29.5 percent), Japanese American (19.7), island Puerto Rican (18.3), European American (13.5 percent), African American (8.3 percent), American Indian (6.4 percent), U.S. Puerto Rican (4.8 percent) and Chicana (3.7 percent). See U.S. Census, 1980, Tables 160 and 166, and Junta de Planificación de Puerto Rico, *Indicadores Socio-Económicos de la Mujer en Puerto Rico,* (San Juan: La Junta, March 1987) A-3.

30. Elizabeth Almquist, *Minorities, Gender and Work* (Lexington, MA: D.C. Heath, 1972), 149-52.

31. Francine D. Blau and Marianne A. Ferber, *The Economics of Women, Men, and Work* (Englewood Cliffs, NJ: Prentice-Hall, 1986), 159.

32. Calculated from the 1980 Census, see Appendix A; the actual job category analyzed here is "health assessment and treating."

33. Comparative data for U.S. Puerto Ricans and Chicanas/os were not available, so we do not know if their relative concentrations increased. Of those groups we were able to analyze, the only cases in which relative concentrations for lawyers, engineers, and doctors did not increase between 1900 and 1980 were white women and American Indian men for doctors. White women increased from 5 to 10 percent of all physicians and surgeons, but their share of all jobs increased much more, so their relative concentration dropped from 40 to 28; American Indian men's share of physicians and surgeons dropped slightly as their share of the labor force increased slightly. Calculated from 1900 and 1980 Censuses, see Appendix A.

34. 1980 Census, see Appendix A.

35. Calculated from 1980 Census. See Appendix A.

36. One prominent African American sociologist has argued that the true oppression experienced by impoverished Blacks is related to class rather than race. See William Julius Wilson, *The Declining Significance of Race: Blacks and Changing American Institutions* (Chicago: University of Chicago Press, 1978). For a critique of Wilson's claims that the significance of race is declining, see Satya Gabriel, "The Continuing Significance of Race: An Overdeterminist Approach to Racism," Mimeograph, Mount Holyoke College, Department of Economics, January 1990.

37. See, for example, Anne Harlan and Carol L. Weiss, "Sex Differences in Factors Affecting Managerial Career Advancement," in *Women in the Workplace,* ed. Phyllis A. Wallace (Boston: Auburn House, 1982).

38. Blau and Ferber, 173.

39. Julie Matthaei and Teresa Amott, "The Promise of Comparable Worth: A Socialist-Feminist Perspective," *Socialist Review* 88 (May-June 1988): 101-17.

40. See, for example, Martin Carnoy and Derek Shearer, *Economic Democracy: The Challenge of the 1980s* (White Plains, NY: M.E. Sharpe, 1980).

41. These are the words of Audre Lorde, in "Age, Race, Class and Sex: Women Redefining Difference," in *Sister Outsider: Essays and Speeches by Audre Lorde* (Trumansburg, NY: Crossing Press, 1984), 123.

Chapter 11

1. Audre Lorde, "Age, Race, Class and Sex: Women Redefining Difference," in Lorde, *Sister Outsider: Essays and Speeches by Audre Lorde* (Trumansburg, NY: Crossing Press, 1984), 123.

2. We are indebted to Sandra Harding for the term "liberatory knowledge." See Sandra Harding, "Is Marxism Enough? Feminist Approaches to Science," Paper presented at *Marxism Now* Conference, University of Massachusetts/Amherst, 2 December 1989.

3. Bell Hooks, *Feminist Theory: From Margin to Center* (Boston: South End Press, 1984), 65.

4. Lorde, 123.

UNITED STATES CENSUS SOURCES

A-1. Occupations

Used to calculate occupational distributions, representation across labor market segments, and relative concentrations. For definitions of major occupational categories, see Appendix B.

1870:
Sixteenth Census of the United States. 1940. Population. Comparative Occupation Statistics for the United States, 1870 to 1940. 1943. pp. 91, 104, 113, 122.

1900:
Twelfth Census of the United States. 1900. Special Reports. Occupations. Chapter III. Summary and Analysis of Results. Table 2, 10-13; Table 3, 14-15.

United States War Department. Porto Rico Census Office. *Report on the Census of Porto Rico.* 1899. pp. 40, 45, 54, 95-96.

1930:
Fifteenth Census of the United States. 1930. Population. Volume V. *General Report on Occupations.* Chapter 3. Color and Nativity of Gainful Workers. Table 4, 86-91; Table 5, 92-94; Table 6, 95-97; Table 7, 98-99. Chapter 5. Marital Condition of Occupied Women. Table 11, 291-99; Table 12, 300-307; Table 13, 308-314.

Fifteenth Census of the United States. Outlying Territories and Possessions. Hawaii. Table 8, 90. *Puerto Rico.* Table 4, 186-189.

1960:
1960 Census of Population. Subject Reports. PC(2)-1B. Table 6, 38-50. PC(2)-1C. Table 32, 101; Table 33, 104; Table 34, 108; Table 35, 111; Table 36, 114. PC(2)-1D. Table 5, 26. PC(2)-4E. Table 5, 97.

1960 Census of Population. Volume I. *Characteristics of the Population.* Part 53. *Puerto Rico.* Chapter C. General Social and Economic Characteristics. Table 52, 126.

1970:
1970 Census of Population. Subject Reports. PC(2)-1C. Table 8, 95 & 101. PC(2)-7A. Table 39, 593-608.

1970 Census of Population. Volume I. *Characteristics of the Population.* Part 53. *Puerto Rico.* Chapter 3. General Social and Economic Characteristics. Table 48, 202; Table 136, 741.

1980:
1980 Census of Population. Volume I. *Characteristics of the Population.* Part 1. *United States*

Summary. Chapter C. General Social and Economic Characteristics. Table 163, 160; Table 169, 166.

1980 Census of Population. Volume I. *Characteristics of the Population*. Part 53. *Puerto Rico*. Chapter C. General Social and Economic Characteristics. Table 51, 32.

A-2. Labor Force Participation Rates of Women and Men

See Appendix D for discussion of gainful employment versus labor force participation rates; see A-3 for labor force participation rates by marital status.

1900:

Twelfth Census of the Population. Special Reports. Occupations. Summary and Analysis of Results, lxxxiii; Table 3, 14.

Twelfth Census of the Population. Population. Vol. 1, xciv.

United States War Department. Porto Rico Census Office. *Report on the Census of Porto Rico*. 1899. p. 90.

1910 & 1920:

Fourteenth Census of the United States. 1920. Population. Volume IV. *Occupations*. Table 2, 340; Table 16, 1270. Chapter 8. Outlying Territories and Possessessions. Table 16, 1270-1; Table 29, 1286-7.

1930:

Fifteenth Census of the United States. 1930. Population. Volume V. *General Report on Occupations*. Table 1, 74.

Fifteenth Census of the United States. Outlying Territories and Possessions. Puerto Rico. Table 26, 170. *Hawaii*. Table 5, 86.

1940:

Sixteenth Census of the United States. 1940. Volume III. *The Labor Force*. Part 1. *United States Summary*. Table 23, 40.

Sixteenth Census of the United States. 1940. Special Report. Characteristics of the Non-White Population by Race. Table 7, 44.

Sixteenth Census of the United States. Population. Second Series. *Characteristics of the Population. Hawaii*. Table 8, 12.

Sixteenth Census of the United States. Puerto Rico. Population. Bulletin No. 3. *Occupations and Other Characteristics by Age*. Table 15, 43.

1950:

1950 Census of Population. Special Reports. PE-(3)A. Table 10, 58. PE-(3)B. Table 9, 27; Table 10, 32; Table 11, 37; Table 12, 42; Table 13, 47. PE-(3)C. Table 3, 16. PE-(3)D. Table 4, 30-13.

1950 Census of Population. Volume II. *Characteristics of the Population*. Part 53. *Puerto Rico*. Table 22, 53-36.

1950 Census of Population. Volume II. *Characteristics of the Population*. Part 52.Territories and Possessions. *Hawaii*. Table 45, 86.

1960:

1960 Census of Population. Subject Reports. PC(2)-1A. Table 5, 9. PC(2)-1B. Table 6, 38. PC(2)-1C. Table 32, 101; Table 33, 104; Table 34, 108; Table 35, 111; Table 36, 114. PC(2)-1D. Table 5, 26.

1960 Census of Population. Volume I. *Characteristics of the Population*. Part 53. *Puerto Rico*. Chapter C. General Social and Economic Characteristics. Table 49, 53-124.

1960 Census of Population. Volume I. *Characteristics of the Population*. Part 1. *United States Summary*. Section 1. Table 78, 1-372.

1970:

1970 Census of Population. Subject Reports. PC(2)-1B. Table 4, 30. PC(2)-1D. Table 7, 75.

PC(2)-1E. Table 6, 54. PC(2)-1F. Table 4, 27. PC(2)-1G. Table 4, 13; Table 21, 83; Table 34, 131. PC(2)-7A. Table 39, 593.

1970 Census of Population. Volume I. *Characteristics of the Population.* Part 53. *Puerto Rico.* Chapter D. Detailed Characteristics. Table 39, 189.

1970 Census of Population. Volume I. *Characteristics of the Population.* Part 1. *United States Summary.* Section 1. Table 90, 390.

1980:

1980 Census of Population. Volume I. *Characteristics of the Population.* Part 1. *United States Summary.* Chapter C. General Social and Economic Characteristics. Table 162, 159; Table 168, 165.

1980 Census of Population. Volume I. *Characteristics of the Population.* Part 53. *Puerto Rico.* Chapter C. General Social and Economic Characteristics. Table 41, 15.

A-3. Women's Labor Force Participation Rates by Marital Status

1900:

Twelfth Census of United States. 1900. Population. Volume IV. *Occupations.* Table 78.

1920:

Fourteenth Census of the United States. 1920. Population. Volume II. *General Reports and Analysis, Marital Condition.* Table 1.

Fourteenth Census of the United States. 1920. Population. Volume IV. *Occupations.* Chapter VI. Marital Conditions of Occupied Women. Tables 11-16, 708-40. Chapter VIII. Occupational Statistics for Alaska, Hawaii, and Porto Rico. Table 32, 1287.

1980:

1980 Census of Population. Volume I. *Characteristics of the Population.* Part 1. *United States Summary.* Chapter C. General Social and Economic Characteristics. Table 162, 159; Table 168, 165.

1980 Census of Population. Volume I. *Characteristics of the Population.* Part 53. *Puerto Rico.* Table 50, 31.

A-4. Women's and Men's Median Incomes, 1960-1980

1960:

1960 Census of Population. Volume I. *Characteristics of the Population.* Part 1. *United States Summary.* Chapter C. General Social and Economic Characteristics. Table 97, 228-9.

1960 Census of Population. Subject Reports. PC(2)-1B. Table 6, 38. PC(2)-1C. Table 32, 101; Table 33, 104; Table 34, 108; Table 35, 111; Table 36, 114. PC(2)-1D. Table 5, 61.

1960 Census of Population. Volume I. *Characteristics of the Population.* Part 53. *Puerto Rico.* Chapter C. General Social and Economic Characteristics. Table 47, 123; Table 60, 138.

1970:

1970 Census of Population. Special Reports. PC(2)-1B. Table 4, 30. PC(2)-1C. Table 9, 42. PC(2)-1D. Table 5, 26. PC(2)-1E. Table 6, 54. PC(2)-1F. Table 4, 27. PC(2)-1G. Table 4, 13; Table 19, 72; Table 34, 131.

1970 Census of Population. Volume I. *Characteristics of the Population.* Part 53. *Puerto Rico.* Chapter D. Detailed Characteristics. Table 153, 1096.

1970 Census of Population. Volume I. *Characteristics of Population.* Part 1. *United States Summary.* Section 2. Chapter D. Detailed Characteristics. Table 245, 36.

1980:

1980 Census of Population. Volume I. *Characteristics of the Population.* Part 1. *United States Summary.* Chapter C. General Social and Economic Characteristics. Table 162, 159; Table 164, 161; Table 168, 165; Table 170, 167.

1980 Census of Population. Volume I. *Characteristics of the Population*. Part 53. *Puerto Rico*. Chapter C. General Social and Economic Characteristics. Table 50, 31; Table 54, 35.

A-5. Female-Headed Families: As Share of All Families, and Share Living in Poverty, 1960-1980

1960:

1960 Census of Population. Subject Reports. PC(2)-1B. Table 3, 18-22; Table 5, 36. PC(2)-1C. Table 9, 9; Table 10, 12; Table 11, 16; Table 12, 19; Table 13, 22; Table 14, 25; Table 15, 26; Table 16, 27; Table 17, 28; Table 18, 29. PC(2)-1D. Table 2, 12; Table 4, 24. PC(2)-4C. Table 3, 89-90.

1960 Census of Population. Volume I. *Characteristics of the Population.* Part 53. *Puerto Rico.* Chapter C. General Social & Economic Characteristics. Table 145, 122. Chapter D. Detailed Characteristics. Table 57, 129; Table 87, 264; Table 114, 382.

1970:

1970 Census of Population. Volume I. *Characteristics of the Population.* Part 1. *United States Summary.* Section 1. pp. 1-279, 1-400. Section 2. Table 266, 1032.

1970 Census of Population. Subject Reports. PC(2)-1B. Table 9, 143. PC(2)-1C. Table 4, 32; Table 10, 121. PC(2)-1F. Table 9, 120. PC(2)-1G. Table 9, 42; Table 24, 101; Table 39, 160. PC(2)-1E. Table 4, 34; Table 9, 89.

1970 Census of Population. Volume I. *Characteristics of the Population.* Part 53. *Puerto Rico.* Chapter C. General Social and Economic Characteristics. Table 51, 206; Table 52, 208; Table 158, 119; Table 168, 198.

1980:

1980 Census of Population. Volume I. *Characteristics of the Population.* Part 1. *United States Summary.* Chapter C. General Social and Economic Characteristics. Table 100, 69; Table 161, 158; Table 164, 161; Table 165, 162; Table 167, 164; Table 170, 167; Table 171, 168.

1980 Census of Population. Volume I. *Characteristics of the Population.* Part 53. *Puerto Rico.* Chapter C. General Social and Economic Characteristics. Table 46, 25; Table 54, 35; Table 55, 36.

A-6. General Social and Economic Characteristics by Racial-Ethnic Group, 1980

1980 Census of Population. Volume I. *Characteristics of the Population.* Part 1. *United States Summary.* Chapter C. General Social and Economic Characteristics. Tables 160-171, pp. 1-157 through 1-168; Tables 232-3, pp. 1-277 and 1-280.

1980 Census of Population. Volume I. *Characteristics of the Population.* Part 53. *Puerto Rico.* Table 54, 35; Table 43, 22.

DEFINITIONS OF MAJOR OCCUPATIONAL CATEGORIES

Categorizing workers' occupations in such a way as to compare them across decades of rapid economic growth and transformation is a problematic endeavor. Not only do the kinds of work change, but also the methods by which census-takers classify workers. Early Census data on occupations were organized partially according to industry—with categories such as "Trade and Transportation," "Agriculture," and "Manufacturing and Mechanical Pursuits"—and partly occupationally, with categories of "Professional Service," and "Domestic and Personal Service." Thus, for example, in 1900, managerial and administrative categories were listed under the different industrial headings, and clerical and sales workers were a subcategory under "Trade and Transportation," which also included "packers and shippers." As the century progressed, occupational categories changed and became more occupationally based. For example, in 1980, executive, administrative, and managerial occupations were a major occupational grouping, and the "Operators, Fabricators, and Laborers" category included such workers whether they worked in factories, on railroads, or in trucking (although the 1980 Census left farm laborers under the industrial category, "Farming, Forestry, and Fishing occupations").

Given this shifting set of occupational categories, we attempted to categorize workers in a way as consistent as possible with the current categories (i.e. with the 1980 Census). We use the categories of Agriculture; Manufacturing; Private Household Service; Service (not Private Household); Sales; Clerical; Professional and Technical; and Managerial, Administrative, and Official. Agriculture, as we use it, includes all working in this field, be they managerial, family farmers, or farm workers. Manufacturing includes blue-collar workers in transportation, the crafts, and mining. Managerial, Administrative, and Official includes officials, administrators, and certain self-employed workers. When Census categories included a combination of occupations, they were listed according to the first occupation, unless otherwise specified below.

A more detailed listing of the composition of the different categories for each census year follows:

1900:

The major occupational categories listed were Agricultural Pursuits, Professional Service, Domestic and Personal Service, Trade and Transportation, and Manufacturing and Mechanical Pursuits. However, data by detailed occupation and sex, which allowed us to separate out managerial, clerical, and sales workers, were available for all groups except Chicanas and Puerto Ricans. There were no data for Chicanas; for Puerto Ricans, there was only a breakdown according to the five major occupational categories listed above. For Puerto Ricans, we divided Trade and Transportation employment equally into Clerical, Sales, and Manufacturing; and we did not estimate any Managerial or Service (not Private Household) employment.

Agriculture: Agricultural pursuits (including agricultural laborers; farmers; planters and over-seers; gardeners, florists, nurserymen; stock raisers, herders, and drovers). Under manufacturing and mechanical pursuits: fishermen and oystermen.

Manufacturing: Manufacturing and mechanical pursuits (such as carpenters and joiners; miners and quarrymen; cotton mill operatives; dressmakers, seamstresses, tailors, and tailoresses; textile mill operatives; tobacco and cigar factory operatives, but excluding fishermen and oystermen, and manufacturers and officials). Under Trade and Transportation: boatmen and sailors; draymen, hackmen, teamsters; foremen and overseers; packers and shippers; steam railroad employees; street railway employees; telegraph and telephone linemen; and other persons in trade and transportation.

Private Household Service: Under Domestic and Personal Service: housekeepers and stewards; launderers and laundresses; servants and waiters.

Service (not Private Household): Under Domestic and Personal Service: barbers and hairdressers; bartenders; janitors and sextons; laborers (not specified); nurses and midwives; soldiers, sailors, and marines; watchmen, policemen, firemen; and other persons in Domestic and Personal Service.

Sales: Under Trade and Transportation: agents; commercial travelers; hostlers; hucksters, and peddlers; porters and helpers (in stores, etc.); salesmen and saleswomen. For Puerto Ricans, estimated as one-third of Trade and Transportation.

Clerical: Under Trade and Transportation: bookkeepers and accountants; clerks and copyists; messengers and errand and office boys; stenographers and typists; telegraph and telephone operators. For Puerto Ricans, estimated as one-third of Trade and Transportation.

Professional and Technical: Professional service, except for officials (government).

Managerial, Administrative, and Official: Under Professional service: officials (government). Under Domestic and Personal Service: boarding and lodging housekeepers; hotel keepers; restaurant keepers; and saloon keepers. Under Trade and Transportation: bankers and brokers; livery stable keepers; merchants and dealers; officials of banks and companies; and undertakers. Under Manufacturing and Mechanical Pursuits: manufacturers and officials, etc.

1930:

The major occupational categories for 1930 were Agriculture; Forestry and Fishing; Extraction of Minerals; Manufacturing and Mechanical Industries; Transportation and Communication; Trade; Public Service; Professional Service; Domestic and Personal Service; and Clerical Occupations. The occupational tables by sex and race provide a great deal of detail, except for Asians living in Hawaii. However, there are some problems categorizing occupations that are described vaguely by industry (e.g. "Other pursuits in trade"). Occupations listed were somewhat different for Puerto Rico. The occupations we included under each category were as follows:

Agriculture: Agriculture (including farmers, owners and tenants; farm managers and foremen; and farm laborers, including wage workers and unpaid family workers). Forestry and fishing.

Manufacturing: Manufacturing and mechanical pursuits (including craft workers, operatives, and laborers, but not managers, officials, or manufacturers). Transportation and Communications (except owner, manager, proprietor, and official categories, and excluding express, post, radio, telegraph, and telephone, but including telegraph and telephone linemen, if separately listed). Under Trade: deliverymen, if specified. Under Domestic and Personal Service: laundry operatives. Extraction of Minerals.

Private Household Service: Under Domestic and Personal Service: charwomen and cleaners; housekeepers and stewardesses (excluding those working in hotels, restaurants, boarding houses, etc., if possible); launderers and laundresses (not in laundry); cooks and other servants (excluding in hotels, restaurants, boarding houses, etc., if possible).

Service (not Private Household): Under Domestic and Personal Service: barbers, hairdressers, and manicurists; bootblacks; forewomen and overseers; laborers and other operatives in cleaning, dying, and pressing shops; elevator tenders; housekeepers and stewards in hotels, restaurants, boarding houses, etc.; janitors and sextons; laborers in domestic and personal service; midwives and nurses (not trained); porters; cooks and other servants in hotels, restaurants, boarding houses, etc.; waiters; other pursuits. Under Professional Service: attendants and helpers, professional service. Public Service, n.e.c., excluding officials and inspectors, if possible.

Sales: Trade (including advertising agents; brokers; saleswomen; real estate agents; newsgirls; insurance agents; and other pursuits in trade, but not including bankers and bank officials; deliverymen; managers and officials; insurance companies; proprietors, managers, and officials, n.o.s.; retail dealers; undertakers; and wholesale dealers, if these are separated out.

Clerical: Clerical Occupations, including bookkeepers; cashiers; clerks (except "clerks" in stores); messenger, errand, and office boys and girls; stenographers and typists; and others, but not including accountants and auditors, if these are separated out. Under Transportation and Communications: express, post, radio, telegraph, and telephone, including operators, if these are separated out, and foremen and overseers.

Professional and Technical: Professional Service (including trained nurses and teachers among others, but not including attendants and helpers, if separated out); accountants and auditors (if listed under Clerical).

Managerial, Administrative, and Official: As listed under all major occupational categories except Agriculture, all owners, proprietors, managers, officials, inspectors, superintendents. In addition, under Manufacturing and Mechanical Industries: manfacturers. Under Trade: bankers and bank officials; retail dealers; undertakers; and wholesale dealers. Under Domestic and Personal Service: boarding and lodging house keepers; hotel keepers and managers; and restaurant, cafe, and lunch room keepers. Under Extraction of Minerals: operators, managers, and officials.

1960:

Agriculture: Farmers and farm managers; farm laborers except foremen.

Manufacturing: Craftsmen, foremen and kindred workers; operatives and kindred workers; laborers, except farm and mine.

Private Household Service: Private household workers.

Service (not Private Household): Service workers, except private household.

Sales: Sales workers.

Clerical: Clerical and kindred workers.

Professional and Technical: Professional, technical, and kindred workers.

Managerial, Administrative, and Official: Managers, officials and proprietors, except farm.

1970:

Agriculture: Farmers and farm managers; farm laborers and farm foremen.

Manufacturing: Craftsmen and kindred workers; operatives, except transport; laborers, except farm; transport and equipment operators.

Private Household Service: Private household workers.

Service (not Private Household): Service workers, except private household (including cleaning service workers; food service workers; health service workers; personal service workers; child-care workers except private household; and protective service workers).

Sales: Sales workers.

Clerical: Clerical and kindred workers (including bank tellers; cashiers; file clerks; office machine operators; receptionists; secretaries; and telephone operators).

Professional and Technical: Professional, technical, and kindred workers (including physicians; registered nurses; health technologists and technicians; religious workers; teachers; and writers, artists, and entertainers).

Managerial, Administrative, and Official: Managers and administrators, except farm.

1980:

Agriculture: Farming, forestry, and fishing occupations.

Manufacturing: Precision production, craft and repair occupations; operators, fabricators, and laborers.

Private Household Service: Private household occupations.

Service (not Private Household): Protective service occupations; service occupations, except protective and household.

Sales: Sales occupations.

Clerical: Administrative support occupations, including clerical.

Professional and Technical: Professional specialty occupations; health technologists and technicians; technologists and technicians, except health.

Managerial, Administrative, and Official: Executive, administrative, and managerial occupations.

Data for Figures 9-2 and 9-3

Labor Force Participation Rates, 1900-1980, and Share of Families Which Were Female-Headed, 1960-1980

Table C-1

Women's Labor Force Participation Rates, by Racial-Ethnic Group, 1900-1980 (Data for Figure 9-2)

	1900	1910	1920	1930	1940	1950	1960	1970	1980
American Indian	13.8	15.0	11.5	15.4	17.9	17.0	25.5	35.3	47.7
Chicana				14.8		21.9	28.8	36.4	49.0
European American	16.0	17.8	19.5	20.3	24.5	28.1	33.6	40.6	49.4
African American	40.7	39.8	38.9	38.9	37.8	37.4	42.2	47.5	53.3
Chinese American	10.4	11.5	12.5	16.3	29.0	33.7	44.2	49.5	58.3
Japanese American	30.1	28.0	25.9	19.0	38.7	41.6	44.1	49.4	58.5
Filipina American			11.6	13.0	15.1	28.0	36.2	55.2	68.1
Island Puerto Rican	13.9	16.4	18.9	22.9	25.0	21.3	20.0	22.9	29.1
U.S. Puerto Rican						38.9	36.3	31.6	40.1

NOTES: From 1900-1930, rates are gainful employment rates; from 1940 on, they are labor force participation rates; see Appendix D for further explanation. From 1900-1930, data is for age 10 and older; for 1940-60, for age 14 and older; for 1970 and 1980, for age 16 and over. Data not available for years without rates. Rate for Puerto Ricans in 1900 is from 1899 Census of Porto Rico. Rates for 1910 are interpolations from 1900 and 1920 rates; see Appendix D. For 1920, American Indian only includes pure American Indians, and hence the labor force participation rate is an underestimate; for 1980, American Indian includes Eskimo and Aleut peoples. European American and African American include Latinas classified as white or Black for all years except 1980. Rates for Asian Americans include Hawaii for all years, except that Filipina data for 1920 are for Hawaii only. Data for Chicanas for 1950 and 1960 are for whites, in five southwestern states only, with Spanish surnames or of Spanish origin, respectively.
SOURCES: See Appendix A.

Table C-2

Share of Families Which Were Female-Headed, No Husband Present,
by Racial-Ethnic Group, 1960-1980
(Data for Figure 9-3)

	1960	1970	1980
American Indian	16.4	18.4	22.5
Chicana	11.9	13.4	15.9
European American	8.1	9.0	10.6
African American	21.7	27.4	37.2
Japanese American	7.8	10.3	11.9
Chinese American	6.1	6.7	8.5
Filipina American	5.5	8.6	11.8
Island Puerto Rican	16.9	15.6	18.9
U.S. Puerto Rican	15.3	24.1	34.8

NOTES: For 1960 and 1970, European American and African American include
Latinas classified as white or Black, respectively. For 1980, American Indian includes
Eskimo and Aleut peoples. 1960 data for Chicanas are for whites of Spanish origin in
5 southwestern states, only.
SOURCES: See Appendix A.

SOME PROBLEMS OF COMPARABILITY BETWEEN CENSUS YEARS

Labor Force Participation versus Gainful Employment

Through the 1930 Census, the Census used the concept of "gainfully employed" to categorize workers, which it changed, beginning in 1940, to the concept of "persons in the labor force." The two are not strictly comparable. The Census counted as "gainfully employed" all those employed, as well as those who listed an occupation in which they "usually worked," whether or not they were working or seeking work at the time the Census was taken. Under the "labor force" definition used beginning in 1940, the Census counted as "in the labor force" those who were employed, those who were experienced but without and seeking work, and new entrants into the labor force who were seeking jobs. In general, labor force participation rates were higher than gainful employment rates since they included those seeking work who were new to the labor force.[1] Another problem with comparing labor force participation rates across the decades is the gross overcounting in 1910, due to instructions given to Census enumerators; for this reason, we use interpolations from the 1900 and 1920 data for our 1910 rates.

Ages

Gainful employment data for 1900 through 1930 count all who are age 10 and older; from 1940-1960, only those age 14 or older; in 1970 and 1980, only those 16 and older.

Racial-Ethnic Groups

For 1900, 1910, and 1920, U.S. Puerto Ricans and Chicanas/os are not enumerated. White (European American) and Black (African American) numbers include Hispanics (Chicanas/os, U.S. Puerto Ricans, etc.) for all years except 1980. In 1920, American Indians of mixed European American blood were counted as white, bringing an underestimate not only of their numbers, but probably also of their labor force participation rates and of their share of higher-paid occupations. For 1950, data for Chicanas/os were for "whites of Spanish surname" in 5 southwestern states; for 1960, they were for "whites of Spanish origin" in 5 southwestern states.

Nursing

The increasing professionalization of nursing over time led to some comparability problems. In 1900, trained nurses were not separated out from untrained; we placed the category, "Nurses and Midwives," in Service (not Private Household). In 1930, we categorized trained nurses as Professionals, and untrained as Service.[2]

Laundry Workers

While laundresses clearly can be classified under Private Household Service (although, since they are self-employed, they could also be considered Managerial), laundry operatives can be classified either as service or manufacturing workers. In 1900, laundry workers were not separated out from launderers and laundresses, and we classified them all under Private Household Service. For 1930 and after, we classified laundry operatives as manufacturing workers.

Managers, Administrators, and Proprietors

In the first half of the twentieth century, many women maintained small establishments such as boarding and lodging houses, inns, lunch and tea rooms, and shops. Their work combined aspects of management, sales, and service, which are now, for the most part, separated out into distinct occupations. We counted all of these small businesswomen under the category of Managerial, Administrative, and Official in the 1900 and 1930 Census years. The relative decline of self-employment in the course of the century diminished women's opportunities for this type of managerial work. This trend was counteracted by the growth of non-self-employed managerial jobs, and by women's increasing participation in these jobs as the century advanced.

Undercounting

In the early Census years, much of women's gainful employment took place within the family sphere, and was most certainly undercounted. The undercount was probably greatest in Agriculture (as unpaid family workers on family farms) and in boarding and lodging house keeping. In later years, production within the family declined, and this undercount became less of a problem.[3]

NOTES

1. See *Census of the United States. 1940. Population. Comparative Occupational Statistics for the United States, 1870-1940.* Part 1. Chapter III.

2. For a discussion of the professionalization of nursing, see Susan Reverby, *Ordered to Care: The Dilemma of American Nursing, 1850-1945* (New York: Cambridge University Press, 1987).

3. See, for example, Claudia Goldin, *Understanding the Gender Gap: An Economic History of American Women* (New York: Oxford University Press, 1990), 43-5.

INDEX

BLACK ROSE BOOKS

has published the following books of related interest

Finding Our Way: Rethinking Eco-Feminist Politics *by Janet Biehl*
Feminism *edited by Angela Miles and Geraldine Finn*
Women and Counter-Power *edited by Yolande Cohen*
Women and Revolution *edited by Lydia Sargent*
Aphra Behn: The English Sappho *by George Woodcock*
Louise Michel *by Edith Thomas*
Mother Was Not a Person *edited by Margaret Andersen*
Things Which Are Done in Secret *by Arlene Dixon*
Between Labor and Capital *edited by Pat Walker*
Democracy and the Work Place *by Harold B. Wilson*
The Trade Unions and the State *by Walter Johnson*
Working in Canada *edited by Walter Johnson*
Indignant Heart *by Charles Denby*

Send for our complete catalogue
BLACK ROSE BOOKS
P.O. Box 1258
Succ. Place du Parc
Montréal, Québec
H2W 2R3